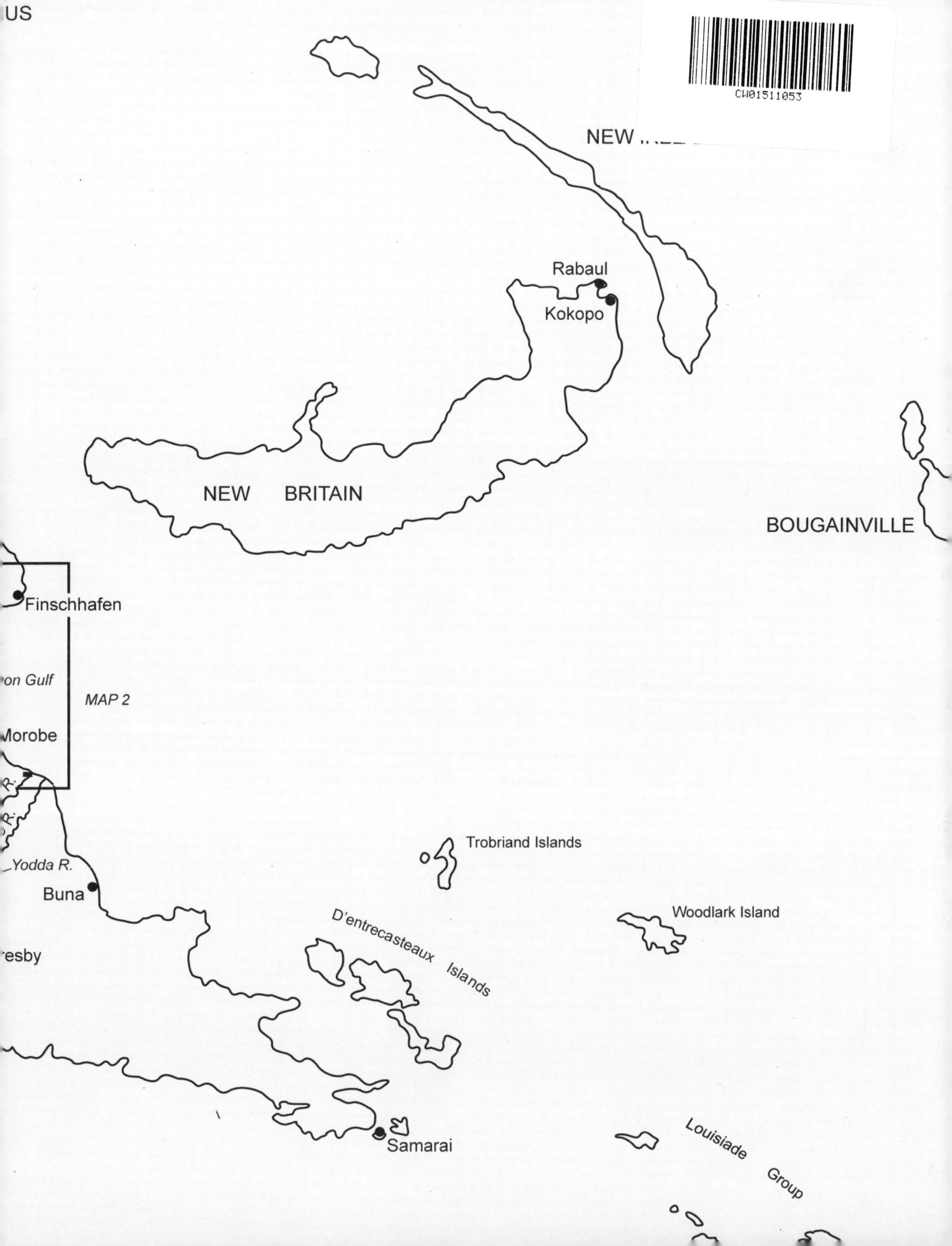

US

NEW ....

Rabaul

Kokopo

NEW BRITAIN

BOUGAINVILLE

Finschhafen

on Gulf

MAP 2

Morobe

R.

R.

Yodda R.

Buna

resby

Trobriand Islands

Woodlark Island

D'entrecasteaux Islands

Samarai

Louisiade Group

NOT A POOR MAN'S FIELD

The New Guinea Goldfields to 1942 –
An Australian Colonial History

Michael Waterhouse

HALSTEAD PRESS

The publisher and author appreciate the support of organisations which have helped make this book possible.

Additional information and photographs may be seen at

www.notapoormansfield.com

CANBERRA MMX
Published by Halstead Press
Gorman House, Ainslie Avenue
Braddon, Australian Capital Territory, 2612

and

Unit 66, 89–97 Jones Street
Ultimo, New South Wales, 2007

ISBN 9781920831837

CONTENTS

FOREWORD

THE AUSTRALIAN AND PAPUA NEW GUINEA histories are linked intimately. This reality is understood by Papua New Guineans, but less thoroughly by Australians. This fascinating, detailed, careful and authoritative story of the largest economic connection and perhaps the most intense community interaction of the first half century of Australian colonial government in Papua New Guinea will remind people in both countries of how much history they share.

For a period in the 1930s, New Guinea Goldfields and Bulolo Gold Dredging were amongst the most highly capitalised companies on the Sydney Stock Exchange. The former's initial capital raising in 1929 had been the largest ever on the exchange. Gold increased in value during the Great Depression when the value of almost all other commodities fell. Australians responded to opportunity and to the poverty of the alternatives to expand gold mining in many places in their own country, and also in the adjacent Australian Mandated Territory of New Guinea and colony of Papua, and the nearby British colony of Fiji.

The opportunity in the Wau and Bulolo Valleys was immense. But so was the challenge. To convert the alluvial gold in the creek and river beds into economic value required a feat of integrated technical and financial innovation and human leadership that had no near comparator in the first half century of the Australian Federation.

There was an important story at Wau and Bulolo before the development of large-scale mining by companies. The island of New Guinea and some of the surrounding islands were formed by folding of the earth's crust as the Australian continent drifted north and crashed into the tectonic plates that formed the geological platform of Asia. The seismic and volcanic instability caused these islands to be endowed with the world's richest deposits per square kilometre (amongst places of substantial size) of the metal that had caught the imagination of humans from and before the origins of civilisation.

Australia had been transformed by rushes to find and to extract gold in the second half of the nineteenth and early twentieth centuries. This was the spur to European settlement of many parts. Rushes by people from Australia to New Guinea and adjacent islands were also important to the colonial history of Australia and the islands that became Papua New Guinea in the early twentieth century. As in Australia, gold was the motive for European entry into many places. The Wau and Bulolo goldfields began as old fashioned gold rushes. Waterhouse catches this story with intriguing detail.

Small scale mining could only scratch the surface at Wau and Bulolo. Large scale mining could carry the immense overhead costs of getting equipment and supplies into the goldfields. It could provide an incomplete security against the attempts of villagers to challenge the miners' presence. It could negotiate secure access to resources with governments far away.

But large scale mining was easier said than done. After the alternatives had been exhausted, it was decided that air transport was the cost-effective way to shift huge dredges and quantities of supplies into the high country where the gold was found — at a time when global commercial aviation was in its infancy. The large scale development of the Bulolo Goldfields required the pioneering of large scale air transport which was to make New Guinea one of the top loci of air freight in the world. Waterhouse's meticulous research allows us to know that between 1931 and 1938, the mass of airfreight in New Guinea was larger than in any country on earth and half as large as the five largest countries combined — the United States, Canada, Germany, France and the United Kingdom.

The innovations in human interaction were of similar dimension and challenge. The mining intrusion brought people of contrasting cultures into close contact — contact that was both destructive and enriching. One of Michael Waterhouse's special contributions is to tell parts of the story from the perspectives of participants from many backgrounds. Written records from official and private sources mean that stories from these perspectives are told in more detail than the Melanesian, but Waterhouse has succeeded in tracking down and telling Melanesian stories as well. His account is enriched by an extraordinary set of excellent photographs from the time of the action.

The result is a magnificent history of endeavour, and of interaction across cultural divides as wide as modern humanity has known. This is inevitably at times a disturbing story, as ignorance and insensitivity are always part of early contacts between humans of vastly different backgrounds. It is an important history for people everywhere.

The Wau-Bulolo Goldfields established the first substantial beachhead of modern economic activity away from the coasts of New Guinea. It was a forerunner of the great resource projects which have brought a modern infrastructure to isolated areas in Bougainville, Ok Tedi, Porgera, Kutubu and Lihir, and established the sinews of the economy of independent Papua New Guinea. It is of comparative interest from these contemporary perspectives, as well as for the insights into relations and contact between Australia and Papua New Guinea.

We now know that Papua New Guineans learnt quickly the value of gold and the techniques for locating and extracting it, but colonial law blocked them until 1957. In recent decades, the gold rush has flashed across the history of many regions of Papua New Guinea, most recently in the wastes deposited in the Ok Tedi and its tributaries. In some places, small scale mining is set to play an important economic role in the independent country. Near where the old Australian diggers and their Papua New Guinean workers plied their trades at Wau, a training centre for alluvial miners sponsored by the European Union and World Bank is now seeking to prepare a new generation of small scale miners for sustainable employment in an old source of livelihood.

Here we learn of the camaraderie of Australians together in a strange place in the generation after the reforging of the cultural institution of 'mateship' in a terrible war. The awful downside is the exclusion of non-Europeans from that camaraderie; a social exclusion reinforced by increasingly restrictive law.

We know too little of Australia's conduct of its League of Nations Mandate in New Guinea. We know less as a result of the destruction of records during the Japanese invasion; the beginnings of this historical turning point are described in the book as they would have appeared to people on the New Guinea goldfields. Waterhouse brings to this account early professional training in anthropology — how much, we wonder, inspired by his grandfather's experience on the New Guinea Goldfields? More rarely still, this background is joined in the same mind by deep professional experience in modern finance, from the author's years in the Australian Treasury and the old Australian bank Westpac. It is the latter background that leads him to attempt a reconstruction of national accounts for the Mandated Territory — an experience that leads to questions about financial dimensions of the Australian mandate.

The goldfields setting lays foundations for exploration of many other dimensions of Australia-New Guinea relations between the wars. We are fortunate that Michael Waterhouse's interest in his grandfather's story on the New Guinea goldfields inspired this sustained effort of scholarship. It is a wonderful book, rich in insights into the human condition, drawing from and contributing to insights from economics, anthropology and sociology, and political and administrative history. It is a good read. I commend it especially to Australians and Papua New Guineans seeking to understand some important and little known parts of their countries' stories.

Ross Garnaut
University of Melbourne
December 2009

EXPLANATORY NOTE

WRITERS OF COLONIAL HISTORY inevitably face the challenge of how to reconcile historical accuracy with modern sensitivities. Terms commonplace in a colonial context are now often discredited and may cause offence to many.

Recognising such sensitivities, I have avoided the use of 'native', preferring terms such as 'New Guinean', 'villager', 'carrier' and 'labourer'. However, I have retained 'native' where this occurs in extracts from letters, etc. or in an official sense, such as the *Native Labour Ordinance*. Terms such as 'kanaka', 'coon', 'boy' (a New Guinean man) and 'monkey' (a boy) were used widely on the goldfields in the 1920s and 1930s, but are similarly included only in extracts. They should thus be seen as reflecting the attitudes and perspectives of the time in which they were written rather than mine.

For reasons of historical accuracy, I have chosen to use 'Kukukuku' (pronounced kooka-kooka) to describe the people who live south and west of the Edie Creek-Watut-Bulolo area. Since the 1960s, anthropologists have referred to these people as 'Anga', because 'Kukukuku' is felt by some to have insulting connotations. However, 'Kukukuku' was used by Europeans pre-war, and the Upper Watut (Kapau) people today are comfortable with it and use it themselves.

First contact stories are intended to provide an insight into the effect of these dramatic encounters on New Guineans. Such incidents were often seen by Europeans as humorous, as indeed they usually are today by descendants of the New Guineans involved.

———

The following terms are also used and need clarification:

European	any white person
miner	prospectors, intending miners and those actually engaging in mining.
native foods	a generic term, covering the main foods grown by villages and eaten by carriers and labourers e.g. kaukau (sweet potato), taro, bananas.

A glossary in the Appendix contains relevant English and Melanesian pidgin English words in everyday use in the inter-war period as well as mining terms.

Though also listed on Australian stock exchanges, Bulolo Gold Dredging was incorporated in Canada. Unless otherwise indicated, dollars are Canadian and pounds, shillings and pence are Australian. A table in the Appendix provides the exchange rates prevailing in 1935. The value today of any specific amount mentioned in the text can be calculated at **http://www.rba.gov.au/calculator/annualPreDecimal.html**

Imperial measurements (ounces, cubic yards, feet, etc.) are used rather than metric; conversion details are provided in an appendix. However, consistent with practice at the time, all tons are 'short' tons (2,000 pounds) rather than the imperial 'long' ton (2,240 pounds) or metric ton (1,000 kg).

'Papua' in this book is, of course, the former Australian Territory of that name which, together with the former Territory of New Guinea, now form Papua New Guinea. It is not to be confused with the Indonesian province previously known as West Irian.

More information, including statistics, documents and additional photos may be seen on a companion website: **notapoormansfield.com**

INTRODUCTION

AS A SMALL CHILD, I was sometimes curious about two beer steins in a glass cupboard in our hall, each with a pewter flip lid, and bearing the image of a three engine, single-winged plane. One carried the name 'Peter', the other 'Paul'. I knew these were somehow connected with gold mining and the work of my maternal grandfather, Les Waterhouse, in New Guinea.[1] Les died of cancer on 27 November 1945, aged 59. I was not quite two years old and his only grandchild at the time. My mother spoke infrequently of my grandfather and his work, except to say he had been a director of Bulolo Gold Dredging (BGD) and its parent company Placer Development, which were involved in dredging for gold. Once, when pressed, she said she had flown in New Guinea on one of the planes as a schoolgirl in 1932. But she never elaborated, or if she did, perhaps I was preoccupied with the usual schoolboy things.

When I was a teenager, my grandmother gave me some New Guinea stamps, showing one of the planes on the beer steins flying over a valley. On either side of this scene was a Spanish galleon and a white man panning for gold. The meaning of the galleon was both puzzling and intriguing. She said the stamps were used to post to Australia gold mined at Bulolo—a name also on the beer steins. Other stamps used for airmail carried an overprint of an old-fashioned biplane, the meaning of which was no clearer than that of the Spanish galleon.

After my grandmother's death in 1981, there was no sign of any letters, diaries or other personal papers belonging to my grandfather. Nor were any forthcoming after my mother's death in 1998. Les had been a keen photographer but there were few photos, nor any sign of films taken by him in New Guinea which other, older, family members remembered seeing, long ago.

In 2001, I was asked to write an article on Les for *The Australian Dictionary of Biography*. I soon established that, although based in Sydney, he had visited the New Guinea goldfields regularly between 1929 and 1941,

Beer steins presented to Les Waterhouse on visit to Junkers aircraft factory, Dessau, 1936.

overseeing the direction and pace of development of BGD's operations, managing the many political issues that arose in Australia and New Guinea and acting as the link between Bulolo and the company's head office in Canada. He had also been a director of the main airline on the goldfields, Guinea Airways.

During my research, I uncovered many fascinating stories about what I came to know as the Morobe Goldfields. Two books written long ago revealed some of the history, but these have long been out of print. With the passage of time, and the destruction of most official and many private records by the Japanese, the story of the goldfields seemed largely to have been lost—despite being a dramatic and important part of the short but turbulent period when Australia was a 'colonial power'.

As I researched my article, the limitations of my knowledge about my grandfather became painfully obvious. Family members filled in some of the facts, enough for me to complete my piece, but I was left with a desire to know more about a man whose life had barely overlapped mine.

A sub-text to my research for this book, therefore, has been a journey to discover my grandfather.

1   My grandfathers were third cousins.

My intention was to write a book about the goldfields and the extraordinary mining and aviation achievements associated with them. But my focus has been not simply on the events—however interesting—but also on the people, many of whom such as Shark-Eye Park, Cecil Levien, Pard Mustar and Ray Parer, were compelling individuals. To convey a sense of time and place in this frontier society, I wanted to make use of the observations and recollections of people who were there. I sought out oral histories, diaries, journals, letters, official and unofficial documents, reports and articles from the time. These I supplemented extensively with personal interviews.

Having long ago been trained in anthropology, I was reluctant to write just another white man's story. The problem I faced, however, is that the times were documented almost exclusively by white men—or Europeans as they were invariably called. Villagers who lived near the goldfields and labourers who came from all over New Guinea left no written record of their experiences, while the stories handed down between generations have been variously integrated with legends and/or adapted to later political goals and so need to be treated with caution.

Nevertheless, I have been able to reconstruct the story—however imperfectly—of how villagers viewed early contact with miners and other Europeans by drawing on the few oral histories that exist, using their culture and beliefs in an attempt to interpret behaviour described at the time by Europeans, and by referring to similar experiences elsewhere in New Guinea. Information I have gathered, including from a few of the old people who remain and the next generation who knew the stories, has been amplified and clarified by three anthropologists who have done fieldwork in the area.

I have also reconstructed something of the experiences of indentured labourers by using a small number of interviews conducted by Ph.D students and others over many years and perceptive accounts by Europeans who were there, including those of an anthropologist who was later one of my university lecturers.

The product is far from a definitive history—if such a thing is possible even with a good written record. But it does provide an insight into the period that would otherwise remain beyond our knowledge.

I have taken a largely chronological approach in relating the gold mining story. I then look at the period through a series of different thematic 'lenses': aviation, the New Guinean experience, life and death of Europeans on the goldfields and the Australian Administration.

Initially, I had not intended to evaluate Australia's performance in administering New Guinea under a mandate from the League of Nations. However, the goldfields were central to the Territory's history between the wars, not least through their contribution to the Administration's revenue. Time and again, I encountered stories that raised serious questions about the Administration's activities and the constraints imposed on it by successive Australian governments.

The full story of the Australian administration of New Guinea between 1921 and 1942 has yet to be written. I have sought to shed light on how the Territory was administered, primarily through the prism of the goldfields. In discussing how the Australian Government and the Administration discharged their responsibilities, I have sought to address the question: How could so much have gone so wrong? Arguably, the answers have a bearing on PNG's post-war economic development.

Stamps used to post gold from Bulolo to Australia.

I have sought to do justice not only to the story of Bulolo Gold Dredging, but also to the stories of many others—black and white—who made the Morobe Goldfields such an extraordinary place in the 1920s and 1930s. By bringing their story to life, I hope to have reclaimed this small but fascinating part of Australian and Papua New Guinean history for this and future generations, while providing fresh insight into Australia's colonial experience in New Guinea.

Michael Waterhouse

PROLOGUE

21 JANUARY 1942: Bert Heath settled down to read his book, leaving his co-pilot to handle the Junkers G31 'Peter' on the short trip from Lae to Bulolo. It was just another routine flight taking in supplies to Bulolo Gold Dredging's airstrip, carved out of the jungle a decade earlier. What had started as a well planned if risky gold mining operation with two dredges in the early 1930s had expanded to eight dredges. These had produced 1.3 million ounces of gold, making it the second largest gold mining operation in Australasia.

'Peter' and its brother G31s 'Paul' and 'Pat', were amongst the largest freight planes in the world, and for years their record breaking role in supporting a remote mining operation had been the talk of international aviation and mining circles.

The laconic Bert took all this in his stride. As the co-pilot readied 'Peter' for its approach, he would take over the controls and land on the well-grassed strip. With level ground scarce, this had doubled over the years as a cricket field and golf course for BGD's white employees and a venue for its New Guinean labourers' free-spirited soccer matches and singsings. In future years a new aerodrome would be constructed, and this one in its turn would become fodder for the all-devouring dredges.

The Japanese had first attacked Rabaul early in January, with the latest and biggest attack, by 100 bombers and fighter planes, the day before. But for the moment all was quiet on the New Guinea mainland. Had Bert looked over his shoulder, however, he might have seen five Japanese Zeros tailing him as he approached Bulolo.

The plane circled the airstrip briefly while men cleared several steel cables laid across it to prevent enemy planes from landing. Bert then brought the plane in effortlessly, as he had so many times before. He taxied over to 'Paul' and 'Pat' and pulled up next to them on the edge of the airfield. Jumping down, he and his co-pilot strolled towards the mess to have lunch while the supplies were unloaded — including a much-anticipated hundred dozen bottles of beer for a thirsty mining community.

As they did so, the air was filled with a deafening whine as the Zeros attacked, machine guns spitting. Several explosions quickly followed as the fuel tanks on the planes were hit. In their two runs down the valley, the Zeros also targetted the wireless station. Alan Vagg, the operator, narrowly escaped by diving under a nearby water stand. Men working on or close to the airstrip leapt hurriedly into slit trenches prepared nearby for just such an occasion.

Within minutes the Zeros were gone, leaving the G31s burning furiously — though almost miraculously, nobody was killed or injured. Normal priorities quickly reasserted themselves, with several men trying frantically to rescue some of the beer from the flames.

The Morobe goldfields, on which BGD was by far the largest producer, had financially underwritten the Australian Administration during the 1930s. As such, they were central to Australia's most challenging colonial experience as it sought to administer a wild and inhospitable country, the majority of whose people had never previously seen white men and were less than enthusiastic about their presence.

Large and small miners alike had for years been supplied by a 'highway in the sky', as a motley collection of planes ranging from ex-World War I biplanes to large Junkers G31s met all their needs.

Junkers G31 'Peter' on Bulolo aerodrome, 21 January 1942.

Without these planes, there would have been no goldfields. Though the goldfields were only 32 miles from the coast, there were no roads and the only other access was over tortuous jungle tracks — a six to eight day trek.

Gold mining, with its high demand for labour, had led to the opening up of many new areas of the country for recruitment, drawing young men straight from their traditional villages into an economic system that was beyond their comprehension. Inevitably, this led to dramatic changes in traditional village life. Close to the goldfields, villagers were confronted with many more direct challenges, often with tragic consequences.

And so, at about 12.30 pm on 21 January 1942, the destruction of the three Junkers G31s marked the close of an era unique in New Guinea's and Australia's history — and indeed in world history.

Part 1
Discovery

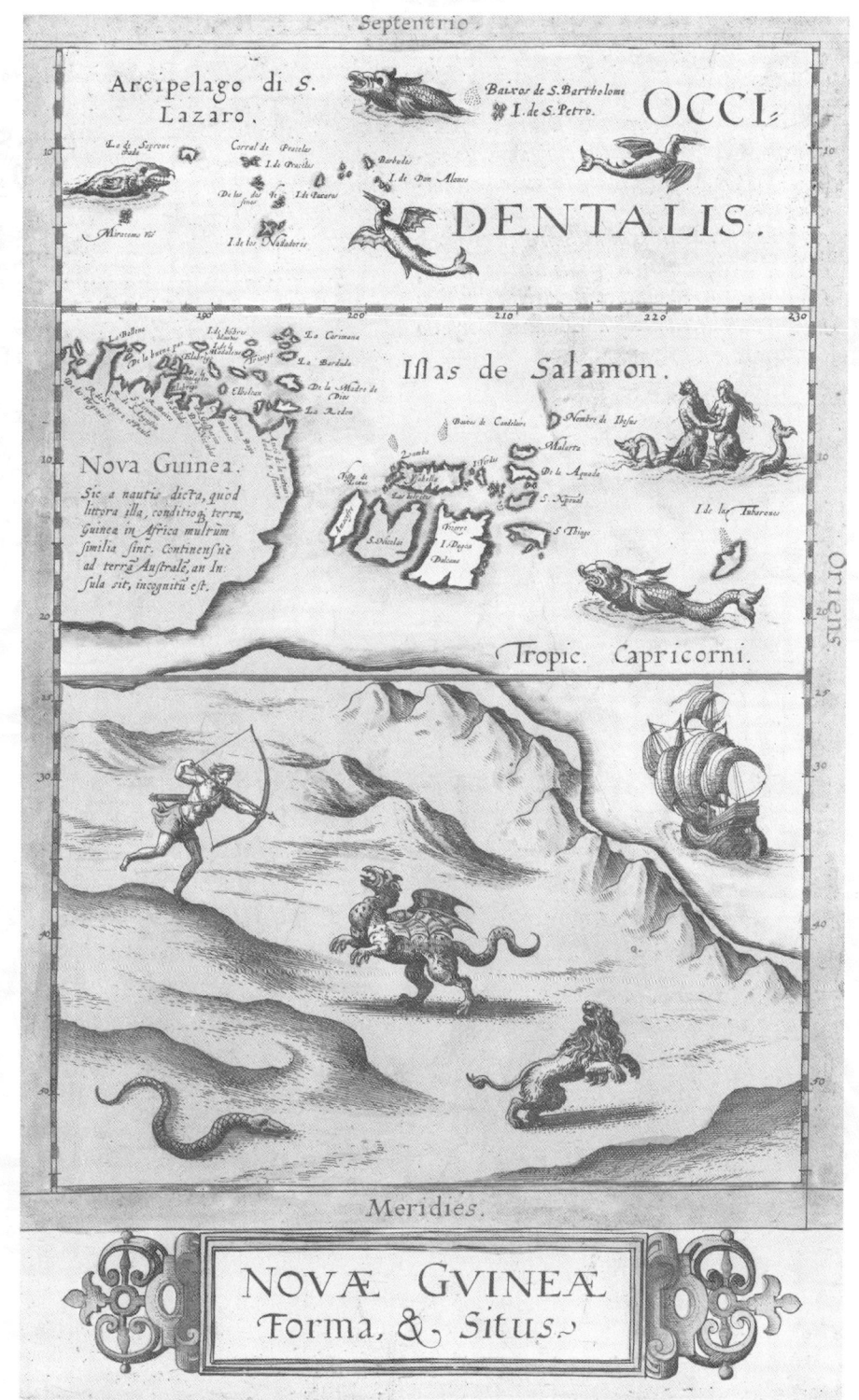

Speculum orbis terrae. Cornelius de Jode 1593.

CHAPTER 1
DREAMS OF GOLD

From as early as the 13th Century, when the Venetian explorer Marco Polo returned from China, a country in the approximate location of New Guinea had been inextricably linked with gold in the minds of Europeans.[1]

This legend inspired the Spaniard Alvaro de Saavedra, sailing eastwards from Tidore in the Moluccas (or Spice Islands) in 1528, to name an island he encountered *Isla del Oro*. In 1545, another Spaniard, Inigo Ortiz de Retez, sailing along an extended stretch of coastline in the same general vicinity, named it *Nueva Guinea*. While he did so because the inhabitants resembled those on the African coast of Guinea, it was no coincidence—given the Spanish obsession with gold—that Guinea had been a major source of gold for the Portuguese since the mid-15th Century. However, the hostility of the people they encountered in *Nueva Guinea* discouraged the Spanish from further investigation.

In the centuries that followed, the Dutch, French and English charted most of the coastline but made no effort to explore the interior. With mountains rising steeply from a narrow coastal plain, few natural harbours and aggressive inhabitants with (it was widely believed) a predilection for human flesh, the country and its resources remained almost unknown beyond the few bays and inlets where ships could anchor. Visitors soon discovered a further deterrent, rampant malaria quickly claiming many victims.

The Dutch laid claim to that part of the country west of the 141st meridian in 1828, but Europeans otherwise showed little interest in New Guinea until late in 1884 when the Germans and British claimed the north and south of the rest of the mainland. The Germans also took possession of New Britain, New Ireland and the North Solomons. They agreed to divide the mainland along its spine as far as the Dutch border, completing its partitioning between the three European powers.

Initially, the Neu Guinea Compagnie administered German New Guinea under an imperial charter, but this experiment in delegated government was not a success, and in 1899 the German Government assumed full responsibility for governing the colony. Both before and after this, the Germans' main interest was in developing copra plantations on New Britain and New Ireland and on some of the more accessible coastal areas of the mainland. After trying several different sites, Rabaul on New Britain was made the capital of German New Guinea in 1910. To the south, British New Guinea remained a British protectorate until 1906, with Port Moresby as its main town. In that year, Australia assumed responsibility for it under the new name of the Territory of Papua.

The association of gold with New Guinea was fuelled intermittently during the 19th Century by events both real and imagined. In 1852, a naturalist, John Macgillivray, visiting Redscar Bay on the survey ship H.M.S. *Rattlesnake*, noted flecks of gold in pottery, the source of which he believed was in the mountainous interior. As this was a time of major gold discoveries in California and Australia, his report failed to inspire any interest among prospectors.

On a more speculative note, a lecturer in Sydney in 1867 reported the story of a man shipwrecked in New Guinea who had travelled into the interior and *seen nuggets strewed about like potatoes on the banks of a stream*, concluding that *there can be no doubt that the auriferous deposits of New Guinea exceed the wildest speculation.*[2]

The first extensive efforts to find gold in British New Guinea occurred in 1888, following the discovery of gold on several islands in the Louisiade group off the south-eastern tip of New Guinea. Within a year, 700 miners had made their way to the field, many from the Palmer goldfields in Northern Queensland. They soon found the new field had little to offer. A discovery on nearby Woodlark Island in 1895 was more encouraging, with steady if not large amounts of gold being produced right through to 1914.

By the closing years of the 19th century, most exploration efforts had shifted to the mainland—with prospectors gradually moving north towards the border with German New Guinea. Alluvial gold was found on the Gira and Yodda Rivers in 1897, but in insufficient quantities to sustain more than a few miners. By 1905, others were pushing even further afield, up to the Waria River, most of which ran through German New Guinea. Gold was discovered in the Upper Waria by Matt Crowe and Arthur Darling in 1906, but mining it soon proved uneconomic, as the grade was low and costs high due to its remote location.[3]

Prospectors and miners, of whom there were rarely more than 300 on all Papuan fields combined, often endured extreme physical hardship. The terrain was mountainous, the climate hot and wet, and the inhabitants often hostile. Many miners and their carriers died in attacks or from malaria or dysentery. They often lacked money for food, equipment and medicine, but could not readily live off the land. On the Yodda and Gira fields, long supply lines meant it cost four times as much to feed a labourer as on the coast, making all but the richest patches uneconomic.[4]

After 1906, Papuan gold production declined and it became clear that the Waria River (or that part of it on the Papuan side of the border) was unlikely to become a significant new goldfield. With many miners at a loose end and a potential source of trouble, the Government in Port Moresby financed a prospecting party to search for a new goldfield. The highly experienced Matt Crowe was selected in a ballot of miners to lead the expedition, and he chose fellow Australians Frank and Jim Pryke to accompany him.

The three set out in June 1909 and after several months, and two fierce encounters with the Kukukuku,[5] they discovered gold on the Tiveri, a tributary of the Upper Lakekamu River, near the border with German New Guinea. The proclamation of the new field in December led to a rush of miners, and in turn a major outbreak of dysentery. Of 600 labourers, 255 died within five months. Again the field proved small, although some miners scratched out a living there for several years.

The discoveries of gold in British New Guinea, though limited in scale,[6] began to arouse the interest of the Germans. In 1896, an expedition found small amounts of gold in the Ramu River, but subsequent exploration failed to locate any significant deposits.

In 1901, the Huon Gulf Syndicate was granted an exclusive gold prospecting concession over the south-eastern part of the German New Guinea mainland, including all rivers running into the Huon Gulf. The Syndicate's main focus was on the Waria, where 'colours', or traces of gold, were found, though not in commercial quantities.

The Syndicate's prospecting efforts ceased in 1904, without any effort being made to explore the interior. This was despite a German geologist's prediction in 1903 that the source of the alluvial gold in rivers stretching from the Yodda to the Ramu would probably be found in the unexplored headwaters of the Markham River.[7] As the Huon Gulf Syndicate retained its concession until 1908, others were denied the opportunity to test this theory.

The German practice of granting gold prospecting concessions to syndicates contrasted with that in Papua, where Australian prospectors, working individually or in small groups, were highly mobile, pushing ever further into unexplored areas of the interior. They often strayed into German territory. As early as 1899/1900 the Annual Report for German New Guinea noted that *It can be assumed with some degree of certainty that Australian gold prospectors have crossed the German border without permission and are searching for gold on German territory.*[8] But given the terrain and its limited resources, the new German administration was in no position to do anything about this, and Australian prospectors knew it.

Over the years that followed, German officials made little effort to explore inland areas, beyond mounting intermittent punitive expeditions—usually with bloody outcomes—after raids by inhabitants of the interior on coastal tribes or attacks on the occasional European who ventured inland to shoot birds of paradise. Towering jungle-clad mountains rising steeply behind a narrow coastal plain posed an apparently impenetrable barrier along much of the coastline. Rivers such as the Waria and Markham were not navigable far upstream and the Ramu only with difficulty. Not that Lutheran missionaries were deterred. They first established mission stations on the mainland in 1886, and in the decade before 1914 undertook several expeditions, travelling long distances.

On a visit to the Waria River in 1907 to assess the extent of its auriferous deposits, the German Governor, Dr Hahl, encountered Frank Pryke, prospecting in German territory. Pryke later reported that *the Governor said he liked Australians to be prospecting because he*

recognised that they were the best men for opening up new country.[9]

The inability of German syndicates to locate gold and the success of Australian prospectors in Papua encouraged Dr Hahl in 1909 to issue prospecting permits to individuals, including Australian prospectors, following the expiry of the Huon Gulf Syndicate's concession. To monitor the movements of Australian prospectors, a post was also established at Adolphhafen, or Morobe as it was soon to be known, near where the Waria River emptied into the sea.

One of the first individuals to search for gold was an Austrian, Wilhelm Dammköhler, who had spent 30 years in Australia and New Guinea as a farmer, trader, explorer and prospector. In December 1907, while exploring the Markham valley, Dammköhler had detected 'colours' in a large tributary—later known as the Watut River.

In August 1909, together with a companion—Rudolph Oldörp—four horses, two carriers and

Miners on Woodlark Island, 1906.

arrows and Oldörp six, but the former's injuries were more serious, and he died two hours later.

Despite his wounds, Oldörp made a raft from tree trunks and floated down river for five days until he reached the Gulf. On the way, he lost most of his possessions in the strong current and nearly drowned.

Oldörp spent the next few months recuperating at a Lutheran Mission station, while planning a return to the Watut. He formed a partnership with a German settler named Broeker, in whose schooner they proposed to transport carriers and supplies to the mouth of the Markham after the wet season. On 14 April 1910, as they headed across the Gulf, their schooner encountered a fierce storm and sank. Oldörp and Broeker were drowned.

The next attempt to locate gold in the interior was unknown to the Germans, but also ended in disaster.[10]

Arthur Darling, a Canadian, had lived in Queensland for 20 years before finding his way to Papua in 1901 in search of gold. He was a small, wiry man and a crack shot. Unlike most miners, he didn't drink or smoke. Another miner, Les Joubert, described him as *good-looking, in a hatchet-faced way, but very tough. He had absolutely no fear, and was gamer than Ned Kelly.*[11]

Having been unable to sustain a mining operation with Matt Crowe on the Upper Waria in 1906, Darling had moved on, and in May 1910 was in Buna, down the coast from Morobe, in Papua, when he heard that Oldörp had drowned trying to get back to the Watut. Given the bloody outcome of the previous expedition, Oldörp's determination could only mean one thing, and Darling decided to go up the Markham himself. After recruiting 20 Orokaiva men as carriers—and for their fighting ability—Darling set off for the Markham in a two-masted whaleboat. As he had no permit from the Germans and was prohibited from taking Papuans across the border, he slipped past the new German post at Morobe in darkness and within a couple of days was on his way up the Markham and the Watut.

Precisely how far Darling travelled is unknown, though many old Papuan miners believed that he discovered gold. Later events suggest he reached Koranga Creek, a tributary of the upper Bulolo River, itself a tributary of the Watut, and close to Kukukuku territory.

provisions for three weeks, Dammköhler set off up the Markham in search of gold. A shortage of provisions soon forced the two carriers to return. The two men pressed on, up the lower reaches of the Watut River, finding good indications of gold.

At about 5 p.m. on 12 September, having set up camp on the river bank, Dammköhler and Oldörp were attacked by about 30 villagers, shouting loudly and shooting arrows from the middle of the river. The prospectors put up fierce resistance, killing about 25 of their attackers. Dammköhler was wounded by four

Feverish with malaria and short of supplies, Darling sent several carriers to look for a village that might provide food. While they were away, a number of Kukukuku attacked his camp. While he fought them off, he was seriously wounded by five arrows and several of his men were also wounded or killed.

On their return, the carriers made a raft and floated for some days downstream until they were close to the spot where Darling had left his whaleboat. At this point, the raft overturned in the raging Markham torrent. While Darling made it to the bank, more of his men were lost, leaving him with only three of the original 20. Despite their injuries and exhaustion, the four men managed to launch the whaleboat and make it out into the Huon Gulf, heading in the direction of Buna. They may not have survived had Les Joubert not encountered them in his schooner.

Darling remained in Buna for several months, recuperating, but determined to return. However a new expedition would cost money he didn't have. So making his way to Samarai, he met up with Matt Crowe and another old Papuan miner, Shark-Eye Park. He travelled to the Lakekamu goldfield with Park in the latter part of 1910, either to search for enough gold to finance a new venture or to cross the border in an effort to reach his earlier discovery from this direction.

But before he could progress his plans, Darling collapsed. Ill with tuberculosis, he made his way back to Port Moresby, and was put on the first available boat back to Australia, where he died in Townsville on 26 January 1911. Another miner on the Lakekamu, Joe Sloane,[12] believed that before he left New Guinea, Darling revealed to Park the location of his find.

In the last few years before the outbreak of war, prospecting by experienced Papuan miners continued in German New Guinea, both legally and illegally. One of the illegal miners, Albert Bethune, wrote of his experiences in 1953.[13] After finding a gap in the main dividing range north of Nepa on the Lakekamu goldfields around 1909, Bethune claims he took 15 well armed labourers and

> went through the gap and then downhill in a north easterly direction when I came to a fair sized river which I now know as the Watut, but I called it Murder Creek as we had a real good stoush up with the Kukus there and left 17 very dead corpses behind when they called it a day and bolted.

I found payable gold in some of the gullies on the eastern side of that creek, and … got 87 ounces of gold, but of very poor quality. I knew I was in German territory and had to keep very mum about it or our Administration would have thrown a fit if they knew I'd been over the border, and my returns were not very flash after all the risks.

Bethune mentioned his discovery to a mate, Jim Swanson, who then also crossed the border to try his luck. He was away a month before he returned, seriously ill. Before he was carried out, he exclaimed, *My God, Bethune, I've found it at last. I have found a creek that you can get more gold in the dish than wash.*

Bethune concluded that it was *absolutely certain that Jim had found what afterwards became known as Edie Creek.* However, seventeen years were to pass before the name Edie Creek was emblazoned over the pages of Australian newspapers. Shortly afterwards, Swanson died and the location of his discovery died with him.

As word spread that there was gold over the border, other prospectors followed, including Jim Preston, Matt Crowe, Joe Sloane and George Arnold. Arnold found and worked the upper reaches of a small creek, and in two trips took out 700 ounces of gold. Bethune eventually returned and after travelling for seven days through difficult country reached what he believed was Koranga Creek. *Someone had been there before me and I used their* [sluice] *boxes and before the tucker cut out I had 187 ounces of gold.* If Darling did in fact reach Koranga Creek, it would probably have been around the time Bethune arrived there.

Bethune summed up the pros and cons of crossing the border:

> There was very few of the old miners who did not know about the gold in the old German territory, but as the gold was low value and there were heavy transport costs getting supplies onto the Lakekamu field, then added costs getting supplies to where the gold was in the old German territory, with the risks of being caught by our own Government taking indentured boys across the border, never made it a very attractive proposition. Of course, we never found Edie Creek. Had it been found you could bet your life all that gold would have been worked by the Lakekamu miners before the Germans even knew it was there.

While the German Governor, Dr Hahl, was well disposed towards Australian prospectors there was no rush by them to take advantage of this. The attacks on Dammköhler and Darling, the long supply lines and high costs no doubt discouraged some, but since many prospectors were crossing the border illegally anyway, with little likelihood of being discovered, there was no incentive to apply for prospecting permits.

But there were exceptions. In 1912, Matt Crowe, Shark-Eye Park, Jim Preston and Edward Auerbach left Samarai on Auerbach's schooner *Niue* on a German Government-approved prospecting trip to the Markham. The Germans were doubtless unaware that Crowe and Preston had previously crossed the border from Papua, while Park may have had details of Darling's discovery. It seems probable that the group knew the approximate location of the latter and were seeking to confirm this and the richness of its alluvial deposits. They worked their way up the Watut and then separated. Years later Auerbach wrote that Preston had reached Koranga Creek and taken out 600 to 750 ounces of gold.[14]

In March 1913, Park, Crowe and Preston again went up the Markham, ostensibly to shoot birds of paradise, though almost certainly this was a cover for gold prospecting and perhaps mining. No details are known, but as this trip lasted six to seven months, it is safe to assume they returned with their pockets heavier than when they went in. The Draft Annual Report for German New Guinea for 1912/1913 reported the two trips in the following terms:[15]

A gold-prospecting expedition . . . to the upper Markham River by three experienced Australian prospectors who had been very successful in Papua, did not produce results. These men came back and later took up hunting for birds of paradise. It is probably mainly due to the failure of the expedition by these three prospectors that there has been no influx of Australian gold miners: these three men were in contact with almost all the alluvial diggers in Papua, and any new rush was dependent on the success of their expedition.

The evidence that Park, Crowe and Preston found and worked Koranga Creek, while largely circumstantial, is nevertheless compelling. Whatever they found and whatever their plans, they disclosed nothing to the Germans. A third officially sanctioned trip would have raised too many questions. Whether they resorted to further border crossings in the months leading up to the War is unknown.

For the Germans, as the outbreak of war approached, the discovery of gold on their territory seemed as far away as ever. However, in one final twist, a tantalising discovery: following a trip to the lower Waria River in July–August 1914, the Acting Governor and mining engineer, Dr Eduard Haber, reported the discovery of 'enormous quantities of precious metal' to the German Colonial Office.[16] At last, it seemed, the Germans had confirmation of their long-held suspicions.

But time had run out.

CHAPTER 2
THE SEARCH FOR KORANGA CREEK

At the outbreak of war on 4 August 1914, Germany had a significant naval force in the Pacific.

One of the coaling stations was at Rabaul, which was also part of a chain of wireless stations linked to Berlin. In response to the threat posed by this force and at the request of the British Government, an Australian Naval and Military Expeditionary Force (ANMEF) was despatched from Sydney to Rabaul on 19 August.

Arriving at New Britain on 11 September and finding no German ships, troops landed at Herbertshöhe (Kokopo) to capture the wireless station inland at Bita Paka. By the end of the day, it was in Australian hands, but at a cost of six men killed and four wounded—the first Australian casualties of the War.

The following day, the British flag was raised in Rabaul and, after some equivocation by the Acting Governor as to whether he had the authority to surrender German possessions, the Germans capitulated. The British flag was raised on the mainland at Friedrich Wilhelmshafen (Madang) on 24 September 1914, though not at Morobe until 11 January 1915.

A Military Administration comprising Australian military personnel (often disparagingly referred to as 'coconut lancers'), was now established; it was to administer New Guinea for the next 6½ years. Existing German laws and customs remained in force pending a decision about the future of German New Guinea at the end of the War. The Administration therefore did not grant mining rights, despite rumours and considerable interest in the possible existence of gold.[1]

At the Versailles Peace Conference in 1919, the Australian Prime Minister, Billy Hughes, argued vociferously with the United States and Great Britain for the full annexation by Australia of German New Guinea. While he was unsuccessful, it was agreed that Australia should be given a mandate to administer the Territory of New Guinea on behalf of the League of Nations. While falling short of outright annexation, the mandate permitted the application of Commonwealth laws to New Guinea.

Even before the mandate had been formally proclaimed, Australia moved to determine the shape of a future Administration. In 1919, a Royal Commission recommended that this should be separate to that in Papua, and that German property should be expropriated.

On 17 December 1920, the Council of the League of Nations formally conferred on Australia the mandate to administer New Guinea. The framework for this administration was laid down in the *New Guinea Act 1920*, which came into force on 9 May 1921. On this day, a new civilian administration, under Brigadier-General Evan Wisdom, took over from the Military Administration.

The new Administration faced an enormous challenge which it was ill equipped to handle. The Military Administration, under a series of ineffectual administrators, had done little to consolidate or extend control over the country. European influence rarely extended anywhere more than ten miles from the coast.

Australia had declined to build on its experience in Papua, where the Lieutenant Governor, Hubert Murray was regarded by many as being too soft on Papuans and insensitive to commercial considerations. The Administrator, Evan Wisdom, had no experience in colonial administration, although a number of personnel from the Military Administration remained in New Guinea as civilian employees.

Perhaps the greatest challenge the Administration faced was imposed on it by the Commonwealth Government—that it should be financially self supporting. In his 1921 Budget, Sir Joseph Cook proudly exclaimed:

> After considerable pruning, the expenditure estimates have been reduced to a sum not exceeding the estimated revenue. In accepting the mandate, Australia has entered upon additional responsibility, but no

stone will be left unturned to prevent further financial burdens being entailed thereby.[2]

This narrow-minded attitude persisted throughout the inter-war period, adversely affecting New Guinea's economic and social development.[3]

The Administration was in a cleft stick. On the one hand, it needed to promote the commercial exploitation of resources so it could generate revenue through associated taxation, import tariffs, etc. But on the other, it didn't have the financial resources to provide the infrastructure that would help achieve such an outcome.

The Territory of New Guinea was initially divided into ten districts, with a District Officer responsible for each. The Morobe District broadly encompassed all the territory south and east of the Markham River to the border with Papua. Morobe was retained as the administrative centre.

Despite its need for revenue, the Administration displayed little interest in facilitating activities that would generate it. It was more concerned with establishing the machinery of government, and it was not until October 1922 that a new Mining Ordinance was drawn up, based on that in force in Queensland. But as German claims in the Waria had not been settled, it was not proclaimed.[4] Thus while prospecting was permitted, for the time being mining was not.

Eventually, in December 1922, things began to move. A surveyor with some legal experience, Jack Lukin, was appointed acting Mining Warden and arrived in Morobe. Miner's Rights were issued from 1 January 1923, permitting applications to be made for a claim.[5]

The Morobe Goldfield was proclaimed on 30 January 1923. As there had been no known discoveries, this appears to have been intended as an 'open for business' signal to prospectors in Papua and elsewhere. At the same time, the Mining Ordinance was proclaimed to apply from 1 February, allowing mining claims to be worked, though only in a defined area around the Waria River — regarded as the most likely location for any gold discovery.

Finally, on 28 February, the Mining Ordinance was gazetted to apply to the rest of the Morobe District as from 1 April 1923. After this date, prospectors could apply for and work a claim measuring 40 feet by 40 feet or a dredging or sluicing lease of up to 240 acres.[6]

But not everyone had been sitting around waiting for the wheels of government to complete their slow grind.

During the War most of the old gold miners in Papua gave the game away, many drifting back to Australia, others joining the AIF and going off to fight in Europe. One who didn't leave was Shark-Eye Park.

Born in Dorset, England, in 1871, Park had been a gold miner in the Klondyke and in Western Australia before arriving in Papua around 1905. Matt Crowe named him the name "Shark-Eye" to distinguish him from another William Park on the Papuan goldfields, the sobriquet reflecting a squint in one eye. A small, slim man, he was clean shaven, apart from a straggling moustache, and had piercing black eyes. He wore the usual miner's attire of shorts and singlet, and an old hat. More unusual was his propensity for walking barefoot whatever the terrain; boots were reserved for his visits to missionaries or officials.

Park had little education and was solitary by

Morobe, c. 1924.

nature, not given to chatter and confiding in no one; he avoided the mateship and free spending for which miners generally are renowned. He was a kindly man, often helping others less fortunate than himself and always fair in his dealings with them. He also respected villagers and their culture, and was in tune with their way of living. He turned this to advantage, his willingness to share their food giving him considerable freedom of movement.

Little is known of how Park spent the years between 1914 and 1921. However, two letters written many years later shed some light. In the first of these, the old Papuan miner Albert Bethune claimed in 1953 that a track cut

> from Lakekamu to the Waria [was] the track Shark-Eye used all during the First War getting his gold in the old German territory and sending it out to Samarai through the Anglican mission at one of their stations and getting in his supplies the same way.[7]

Mining was not permitted in New Guinea, and the existence of an Australian military post at Morobe made surreptitious movement difficult between there and the interior, particularly if this involved the transfer of supplies for a team of labourers one way and gold the other. So access from the Papuan side was really the only option.

Nevertheless, Park visited Morobe periodically, no doubt to monitor developments which might enable him to start mining legally. His visits were recalled years later in the other letter, by the naval officer in charge of the wireless telegraph station at Morobe in 1918, James Twycross:

> Shark-Eye came in and out of Morobe several times during my term of 16 months … He was not very communicative regarding what gold he had found, except on the last occasion when he said, 'Well Jim, I don't know but I think I'm on to something at last.' … A number of his descriptions tally with the Bulolo Valley as I first saw it in 1927.[8]

Neither of the other two miners who knew of Koranga Creek before the War — Matt Crowe and Jim Preston — had any further involvement with it. Crowe is believed to have fallen out with Park on their 1913 trip. There is no record of his activities between then and his death in Samarai in 1925. Preston had planned to return, but developed cancer and died in the Trobriand Islands in 1922.

Thus, Shark-Eye Park had the secret of Koranga Creek to himself.

Shark-Eye Park.

Working alone between 1914 and 1920, or with the help of a few labourers, the time he could spend mining gold would have been limited by his need for supplies and to visit Morobe. The journeys from Koranga Creek to Samarai on the Papuan side of the border and to Morobe were long, over extremely difficult terrain, and time consuming. This would also have made the cost of supplies prohibitive. Thus, it is unlikely that the value of gold Park took out over this period was much more than the cost of obtaining it.

By 1921, feedback on the new civil administration during his visits to Morobe would have made Park realise that it was only a matter of time before mining was permitted. But by then he was broke and with little reason to wait.

To realise the potential of Koranga Creek, Park needed a partner to pay for and ensure a continuing flow of supplies; this would free him up to do the mining. A shorter way in to Koranga Creek than via the Waria or the Markham was also desirable to reduce the cost of supplies. In 1921, Park set about resolving both issues.

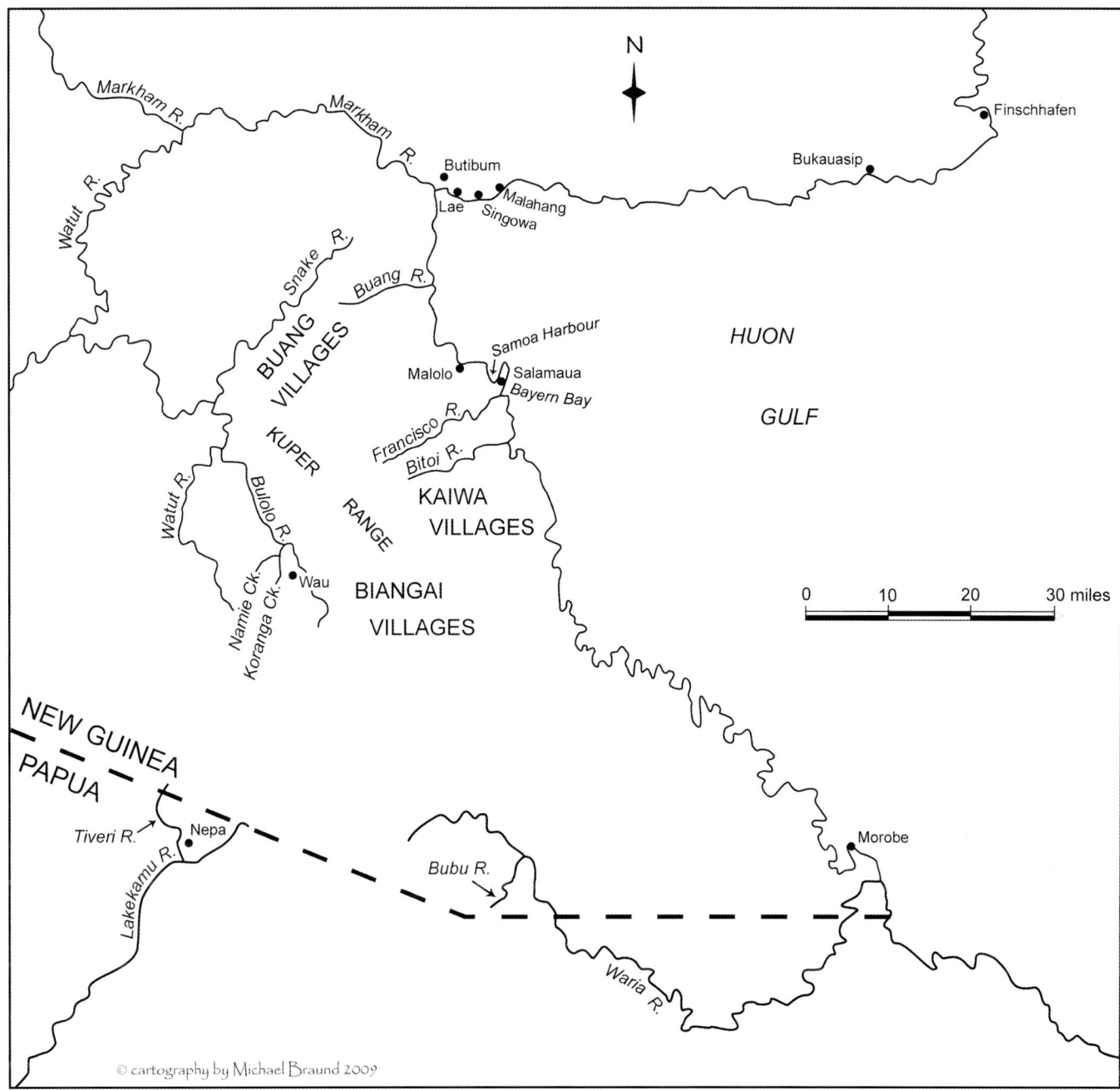

The Morobe District.

At this time, the long coastline between the tiny settlements at Morobe and Finschhafen was dotted with villages but virtually uninhabited by Europeans. There were Lutheran missions 64 miles up the coast from Morobe at Malolo, near Salamaua,[9] at Malahang plantation near Lae, a further 20 miles to the north, and at Bukauasip, east of Lae towards Finschhafen. There was no white settlement at Salamaua or Lae. The only visitors were labour recruiters, recruiting for plantations on New Britain and New Ireland, Lutheran missionaries and occasional Administration patrol officers.

There was even less contact with villages inland.

In 1916, a missionary at Malolo, Rev. Fritz Bayer, had walked inland from Salamaua with another missionary, Rev. Georg Pilhofer, reaching villages in the Kuper Range between the coast and the Bulolo Valley. As many prospectors and miners were later to find out, the route was irregular and time consuming due to the mountainous terrain and tracks that led from village to village rather than directly inland. By 1921, there were a few small mission houses scattered through the mountains behind Salamaua.

Salamaua was—and is—a picturesque, narrow, sandy isthmus joining a rugged volcanic island (known

Above: Logui Village.
Below: Salamaua from the air, 1932. Note Francisco River and aerodrome at bottom.

as Parsee Point) to the mainland; it provides protection from the strong prevailing south-east trade winds, and thus a natural—if shallow—harbour, on the northern side. No more than 100 yards wide at any point, and less over most of its length, it was dotted liberally with coconut trees and the sturdy *Calophyllum inophyllum*. These large trees grew close to the water's edge and were highly resistant to salt water, improbably reaching out in places to touch the breaking waves.

Bayern Bay is on the more exposed south-eastern side of the isthmus, a long beach stretching round to the Francisco (or Frisco) River, which drains the high mountain ranges behind. A village, Logui, was located close to the river mouth.

In a direct line (not that there is such a thing in New Guinea), Salamaua is closer to the Bulolo Valley than any other accessible point on the coastline, a distance of about 32 miles. Access via the Waria River, to the south, or the Markham and then Watut Rivers to the north, is far longer and more difficult.

Shark-Eye Park came into Bukauasip for supplies around the middle of 1921. A tall, thin Lancastrian, Jack Nettleton, ran the trade store here, buying copra from the local villagers and selling supplies to them. At 45, he was five years younger than Shark-Eye. He had enlisted in 1914 in the ANMEF and been police master at Morobe and subsequently in Madang. He had declined to join the new civil administration, preferring to open a trade store at this remote outpost.

Park stayed at Bukauasip for several months, during which time Nettleton agreed to join him prospecting over the watershed at the back of Salamaua. Park said nothing to him of his knowledge of Koranga Creek.

In 1919, Shark-Eye had made several visits to Karl Mailänder, the Lutheran missionary who started the Malolo mission 12 years earlier. No doubt Park was well aware of Fritz Bayer's trek inland in 1916, and from Mailänder gathered what information he could about the route. After an unsuccessful attempt to locate the track around Christmas 1921, Park met up with Patrol Officer George Ellis in Lae the following month. Ellis had just returned from a patrol inland from Salamaua and, in response to Park's request, drew a map of the route he had taken.

In May 1922, armed with the map, Park and Nettleton left Morobe for Salamaua and thence on a short prospecting trip inland. They travelled light, with just a few carriers, a single pick and shovel and two prospecting dishes. There was no need for more equipment, such as adzes to make a sluice box, as on

Koranga Creek. Shark-Eye Park's lease in foreground.

Sluice box being worked on Shark-Eye Park's lease. Note flume carrying water to sluice box.

this occasion Park was more interested in the path along the rainbow than what lay at its end. He knew that already.

While in Morobe, Park and Nettleton encountered another aspiring prospector, Harry Mason, who had arrived after resigning his job in Rabaul.[10] He was well into his 50s, unfit and with little knowledge of prospecting. Park talked Mason out of going up the Waria, though without suggesting any alternatives. Within a few days and with a companion, Ernie Dover, who had been with the Administration in Morobe, Mason decided to follow the District Officer's suggestion to prospect the Francisco River, and together they left on the next mission boat for Salamaua.

Over the next six weeks, Mason and Dover struggled through very difficult country. Mason's Diary records his experiences with leeches, steep and slippery ascents and descents, wading upstream over granite boulders, crossing unstable bridges of kunda cane perched high above roaring torrents, circumnavigating precipitous gullies and fighting his way through kunai grass between six and ten feet high. All without a sign of gold.

The only positive element was the attitude of local tribes—the Kaiwa and Biangai.[11] Far from being hostile, they carried his packs from village to village, for which he gave them sticks of tobacco, and when he was clearly struggling, they gave him sweet potato, cucumbers, taro, water melon and sugar cane.

Back in Salamaua on 10 July, Mason recorded that

we were surprised by a visit from Park, the prospector we met at Morobe. He was much surprised to see us here. He … has just come from inland prospecting, where he and his mate intend returning. I think they have found something for they are making great preparations and have 20 boys and full equipment. He is first waiting for his mate who is bringing provisions (in a whale boat they have) from Singowa.[12]

Now that he knew the way into Koranga from Salamaua and had Nettleton to maintain supplies, Park wasted no time. With a party of 40 men, including carriers from Logui village, he set off on 3 August 1922 for Koranga with one lot of supplies while Nettleton left for Morobe to secure more. Soon after his arrival, and despite the ban on mining, Park cut several sluice boxes from old tree trunks and began mining the alluvial deposits in earnest.

Meanwhile in Morobe there had been a changing of

Cecil Levien.

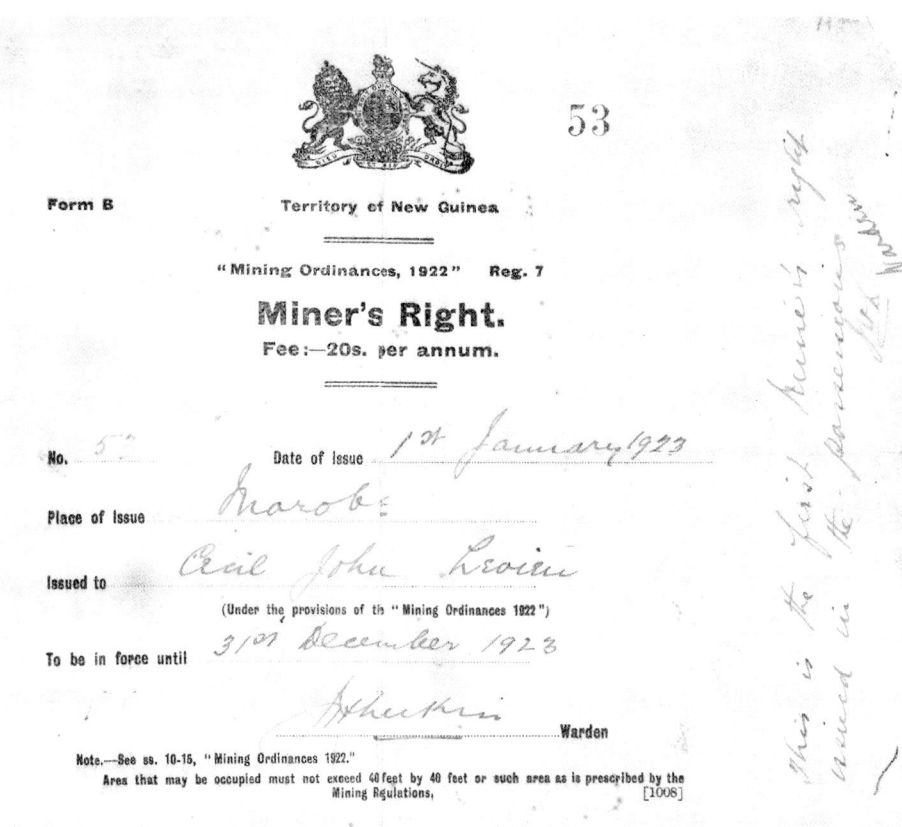

Cecil Levien's Miner's Right.

the guard, with a new Acting District Officer taking over on 3 July, a man whose vision and fierce determination were to change the course of New Guinea's history.

Cecil Levien was born in Drysdale, Victoria, on 4 January 1874. After attending Melbourne Grammar School, he worked intermittently, but with little success, as a gold miner in Western Australia between 1893 and 1906, before buying an 800 acre farm near Uranquinty, in southern New South Wales. While an extremely practical man and good with machinery, Levien was not a particularly successful farmer. In March 1917, aged 43, Levien joined the AIF and trained at the Royal Military College, Duntroon. He was discharged in February 1919 without serving overseas. The following month, he was appointed as a Second Lieutenant with the ANMEF and in May 1921 joined the new Administration. His appointment as Acting District Officer, Morobe, followed time as Deputy District officer on Buka.[13]

Levien was 5 feet 6 inches tall, of medium build and with brown eyes. He was variously described as having a strong personality and being a forceful speaker, shrewd, decisive and not a man to suffer fools—but at the same time kind, modest and without social aspirations.[14] As his later actions showed, he could also be passionate and manipulative. Above all, however, he was a visionary—though a practical one, drawing on his lengthy experience in mining and farming.

Nettleton came into Morobe for supplies only a few weeks after Levien started. He later observed: *I saw a lot of Levien when I was at the coast or Morobe. He had an idea that we were on to something and not in the bush for our health.*[15] When Nettleton reported later in 1922 that two Biangai men had been killed by Kukukukus[16] when on their way to Koranga, Levien sent George Ellis in on patrol to quieten things down. At Koranga, Ellis saw six bags of gold that Park and Nettleton had already accumulated. As the country was still closed to miners, he could have seized their gold; but he chose not to, instead reporting what he had seen to Levien.[17]

Soon afterwards, Levien decided to see for himself and on 14 December arrived at Koranga Creek. He spent three days there. What he saw made him realise that his future didn't lie with the Administration.

Park and Nettleton were in a bind. They couldn't use their gold to buy stores as mining was still illegal, and their main source of supplies in Rabaul, Burns Philp, had stopped their credit. Levien promptly solved their problem, offering to buy their stores for them and charge them 8% interest. They were stunned.[18]

When, two weeks later, on 1 January 1923, the new acting Mining Warden, Jack Lukin, issued the first Miner's Rights, the first issued was to Cecil Levien. Four others obtained a Miner's Right in Morobe that day: Park and Nettleton, and the only other two men on the field, Harry Mason and Ernie Dover. The latter two had found their way to Koranga in November, Park and Nettleton tolerating them rather than risk having them disclose what they had seen.

In February 1923, Levien left Morobe on a patrol to the Bubu River, a tributary of the Upper Waria. The author Frank Clune later concluded,

> Such a patrol would have the effect of distracting official attention at Rabaul, for the time being, from the Bulolo Valley [and] would forestall any possible request by Warden Lukin for an escort to visit Bulolo.[19]

It is easy also to see Levien's hand in Lukin's perception—expressed in a letter to his mother in February 1923—that *the country is all new and most of it entirely unexplored and inhabited by cannibals.*[20] Levien knew better, of course, but a possible encounter with cannibals was certainly a disincentive for Lukin to visit the Bulolo by himself.

In November 1922, a mining engineer, B.V. Barton, had arrived in Morobe to investigate a possible gold mining area on the Upper Waria River on behalf of Waria River Gold and Platinum Options N.L. Over the next five months, he tested the area, eventually concluding that it was uneconomic.

Whatever the real purpose of Levien's Bubu River patrol, he and Barton met somewhere on the Upper Waria.[21] It is likely Levien saw Barton as the key to a plan to acquire leases on the Bulolo River adjoining Park's and Nettleton's and on-sell these to a syndicate in which he retained a share.

Shortly after their meeting, Barton radioed his company on 16 April that he was returning to Morobe *where we are expecting to get* [an] *offer of valuable property in* [the] *same district.*[22]

By now, gold mining was legal. On 18 April, notice of application was given for four leases on the Upper Bulolo River on either side of its junction with Koranga Creek—to be called Kaili 1-4. The applications were made in the names of the wireless operator at Morobe, a doctor who was friendly with Levien, a landowner near Rabaul and Jack Nettleton—all apparently dummies for Levien himself. Several years later, the Mining Warden noted that Levien had prepared the plans in support of the applications, based on information supplied by Park, who had pegged the leases.[23]

It is likely that Park did this after Levien's December 1922 visit and his offer to purchase stores for Park and Nettleton. However, as the Mining Ordinance required leases to be manned and worked, they could not be applied for until someone could be found who would test them. With the Upper Waria ruled out, Barton was now free to do this.

On 18 June 1923, Barton radioed his company that he had arranged for an option over a property at an unnamed locality, though not on the Waria River.[24] Back in Melbourne late in July, he informed a meeting of

Waria River Gold and Platinum Options shareholders that he had secured an option over four leases, comprising 900 acres, and had applied for a fifth lease of 240 acres (Kaili 5). The option was free for six months with a further three months, if required, on payment of £50 per month. If shareholders agreed to the option, a company would be formed, in which the unnamed vendor would have 1,000 shares, for which he would pay £1,000. If the option were exercised, a new company would then be formed, with the vendor receiving a 25% interest and £10,000 cash.

Barton withheld details of the location as *The first man to get carriers had an advantage.* However, he provided a clue, saying that *One of the prospectors originally found gold 14 years ago, but had to get out. Later he went in again. The prospectors had now been working* [for] *a number of months.*[25] He subsequently reported that they had obtained about 7,000 ounces of gold from Koranga Creek.[26] In early August 1923, the option was taken up and Kaili Gold Options N.L. was formed.

At precisely the time the first four Kaili leases were applied for, in April 1923, another event occurred which increased the tension between Levien's role as District Officer and his growing passion for gold mining.

Assistant District Officer Sam Appleby, Acting Mining Warden Jack Lukin, miner Joe Sloane and labourers.

While prospecting had long been permitted, access difficulties and the ban on mining meant that other than Park, Nettleton and Dover, there was no-one on the field when the working of claims and leases was finally permitted on 1 April.[27] But this was about to change.

Joe Sloane was born in Ipswich, Queensland, in 1871 and had first come to Papua as a miner in 1893. He was well built, with the quiet, deliberate manner of a bushman. He was also very experienced, and had a lot of respect, if no great affection, for Shark-Eye Park, to whom he believed Arthur Darling had passed on details of his Koranga Creek discovery in 1910. Early in 1923, when in Port Moresby, he observed to Albert Bethune that Park had not been heard of lately, musing *I bet he has found a shorter route into that gold (behind Nepa on the Lakekamu) … and I'm going round to Morobe and see if they know of his whereabouts there.*[28] A launch took him as far as Mambare, where he acquired a canoe; two or three days later, on 18 April, he was in Morobe, where he encountered Levien.

Sloane later recorded:

He advised me not to go any further as Park was getting no gold, but I told him I was going to have a look for myself. I got a canoe and went from village to village up the coast as far as the Frisco. I landed at about 4 o'clock[29], got boys all ready and paid to carry me in. Levien arrived about an hour later at the Government Rest House (at Salamaua) and … not a nigger would come near me next morning as Levien had told them not to show me in. I was about six weeks (sic) trying to get boys to go in—walked about 10 miles where Levien had not got word in—got carriers and they took me from village to village.[30]

By early May 1923, despite Levien's obstruction, Sloane had reached Koranga and seen all he needed.

Sloane's arrival coincided with a sudden burst of lease applications on and around Koranga Creek. On 18 April, the day Sloane passed through Morobe, Levien progressed the applications for Kaili 1-4 and one by Nettleton for a 24 acre lease on Namie Creek, called "Nettlepark". On 16 June, Park applied for 48 acres on Namie Creek and the Bulolo, called "Koranga" and Sloane for 15 acres called "Gira", close to the boundary of Park's lease. Ernie Dover, who was by now employed by Park and Nettleton, also applied for a 15 acre lease on Namie Creek, called "Dovercourt". In December, Sloane applied for a further 20 acre lease adjoining "Gira", the appropriately named "Perseverance".

Meanwhile trouble was brewing between Jack Lukin,

the acting Mining Warden, and Levien. Lukin heard of Levien's attempt to stop Sloane getting in to Koranga Creek shortly after it happened. Coupled with Levien's efforts to discourage him going in to Koranga after he started as Mining Warden, it made him suspicious of Levien's relationship with Park and Nettleton. On 28 June, he made a number of allegations about this in a written report to his superiors in Rabaul.

This appears to have rattled Levien, who spent much of July trying to assess the strength of the evidence against him. The substance of Lukin's allegations was broadly correct, although Lukin and thus, presumably, the Administrator were unaware of the option deal with Kaili Gold Options. However, Levien was not yet in a position to resign. There was no certainty that the option over the Kaili leases would eventually be exercised. As well, he had mortgaged his house in Melbourne earlier in the year to help Park and Nettleton, and now had to contribute £1,000 for shares in Kaili Gold Options—the equivalent of nearly two years' salary.

While the Administrator was considering his report, Lukin went on leave. In a twist of fate, Levien was appointed acting Warden from 4 August 1923 – a position he had neither sought nor wanted. Kaili Gold Options, in which Levien had a beneficial interest, was being established and Wardens were not permitted to hold shares in mining ventures. In addition to the problems posed by Lukin's allegations, Levien knew he was now in breach of the Mining Ordinance.

Meanwhile, Administrator Wisdom had no doubt been making his own enquiries. Capable officers—and Levien was certainly one—were few and far between and he could not afford to let him go unless the allegations were proven. Then, in September, he summoned Levien to Rabaul and asked him to respond to Lukin's allegations. In a detailed report, dated 25 September 1923, Levien did so, refuting them in detail.

However, the Administrator was clearly unconvinced. It would not have been difficult for him to find out that Levien had paid Burns Philp in Rabaul for stores provided to Park and Nettleton, and to realise why he might have done so. The meeting concluded with Wisdom asking Levien to resign, which he did the following day.

Wisdom was later to describe Levien in disparaging terms as *a man of, to say the least, indifferent character.*[31] New Guinea had not heard the last of Cecil Levien, however, and for this the Administrator would one day be thankful.

CHAPTER 3
HARD TIMES

Within a few days of resigning, Levien left Rabaul for Melbourne on the return voyage of the ship bringing Barton back to begin a detailed inspection of the Kaili leases.

Levien carried with him 250 ounces of gold which, in an effort to whip up enthusiasm for the venture, were publicly exhibited in mid-October at the office of the Secretary of Kaili Gold Options.

After a brief stay, Levien returned to New Guinea early in November, intent on beginning mining activities while awaiting the outcome of Barton's assessment of the potential of the five leases and a further three for which application had now been made.

In January 1924, he applied for a lease of 63 acres on Namie Creek. Other miners were now beginning to appear on the field, one of whom objected to his application on the basis that it was alluvial ground, workable with a sluice box and dish.[1] Levien was not permitted to work the lease until the objection was heard, but nevertheless began shifting his supplies inland, negotiating with Park to work one of Park's leases. Nettleton had decided to leave the field, having made enough to set himself up back in England, leaving Park with more ground than he could work. By the time Nettleton left in March, his partnership with Park had provided him with a windfall of around £13,000.

The first half of 1924 was not a good time for Levien. After intensive investigation over several months, Barton concluded in March that all but two of the eight Kaili leases were uneconomic. The exceptions were Kaili 4, which he estimated to contain 1,103,000 cubic yards with a value of 1 shilling and 10 pence per yard, and Kaili 7 whose gravel had a value of 1 shilling and a penny. He suggested these were worth further consideration if a road could be constructed from the coast, though he believed this would take months and possibly years. In advising against acceptance of the option, Barton made a telling observation:

> The topographical conditions of New Guinea are exceptional and it is difficult to explain the almost impassable mountains one comes across, and to get to this area we have to cross a range 7,000 feet high, itself

no great difficulty, except that the slope of the hills is 45 degrees, and one goes up to 4,000 feet and down again at least three times on the way in.[2]

For Levien, Barton's report was a major setback, and it was soon followed by another. Although the nature of the ground he had applied for on Namie Creek was essentially the same as the leases being worked with sluice boxes by Park and Sloane, the objection against his application was upheld in May 1924.

In July 1924, Levien reapplied for his Namie lease, forcefully outlining the case for a lease rather than a much smaller claim in a letter to acting Mining Warden Lukin. He underlined how different mining conditions were in New Guinea from those in Queensland, on whose mining legislation the Mining Ordinance was based:

> In applying for a lease on Namie Creek, I would point out that, to outfit myself with stores, medicines, labour and transport for a 4 months stay cost me just short of £600 in cash, and unless it is possible to have sufficient ground to at least assure 12 months' work the position is hopeless, as the planting of native foods is imperative owing to difficulty and distance of transport.
>
> If the claims are limited to 200 by 100 [feet] in many cases it would only take 2–3 weeks to work out as there is generally only a few feet wide in the creek bed payable and most is useless ground. Therefore it will pay no-one to work as constant moving of camp and supplies would eat up any profit there might be.
>
> The cost of outfitting to get in and work will preclude any but those having a few hundred pounds … but may lead to some beachcombers battling in and being a source of trouble to both Govt. and legitimate miners.[3]

Despite their previous differences, Lukin was equally concerned about the possibility of an influx of small miners creating 'a community of paupers'[4]—and Administrator Wisdom even more so. This time there

Levien's camp at Koranga Creek, 1924.

was no objection, and his application was approved. By now, however, Levien was working Kaili 4 and had acquired a lease from Shark-Eye Park. He was therefore unable to work the Namie lease, letting it out on tribute for others to work for a share of the proceeds.

During 1924 and 1925, Levien won 1,700 ounces from Kaili 4 in 12 months—more than enough to keep him afloat. However, other events had been occurring which would create an opportunity that Levien quickly realised held far greater promise than anything at Koranga or Namie Creeks or on the upper reaches of the Bulolo.

In October 1923, as Barton began his investigation of the Kaili leases, another mining engineer, J.C. Coldham, arrived further down the Bulolo, prospecting on behalf of another mining company.[5] Coldham encountered an old miner from Papua, George Arnold, at the lower end of the Bulolo gorge, some distance below the Kaili leases. While getting good returns from the river beaches, Arnold was unable to reach bedrock in the fast moving river where the gold was more concentrated.

Below the gorge, the Bulolo opened out into a flat alluvial valley, a mile or more wide and ten miles long. It was heavily timbered, with the river winding along its eastern side. Over the ages, torrential rain had washed rocks, gravel and soil down from the mountains upstream, and these now comprised the valley floor. Coldham believed that gold was likely to be widely distributed across the valley. His testing showed the gold became more concentrated at depth, leading him to conclude that using large scale techniques, profitable mining would be a 'text-book certainty'.[6]

Coldham applied for three leases comprising 600 acres, and returned to Melbourne, only to find potential investors had been discouraged by Barton's negative assessment of the Waria and were not interested in the Bulolo leases.

No doubt as the result of his discussions with Coldham, George Arnold got a small syndicate together and applied for five leases near Coldham's, covering 1,120 acres below the junction of the Watut and Bulolo Rivers. His intention was to use them as the basis for floating a new company, but again investors in Australia simply weren't interested.

As he was working only a short distance up river, it is likely Levien met with Coldham late in 1923 or early 1924, and became aware of his views about the potential of the lower Bulolo Valley. It made sense to

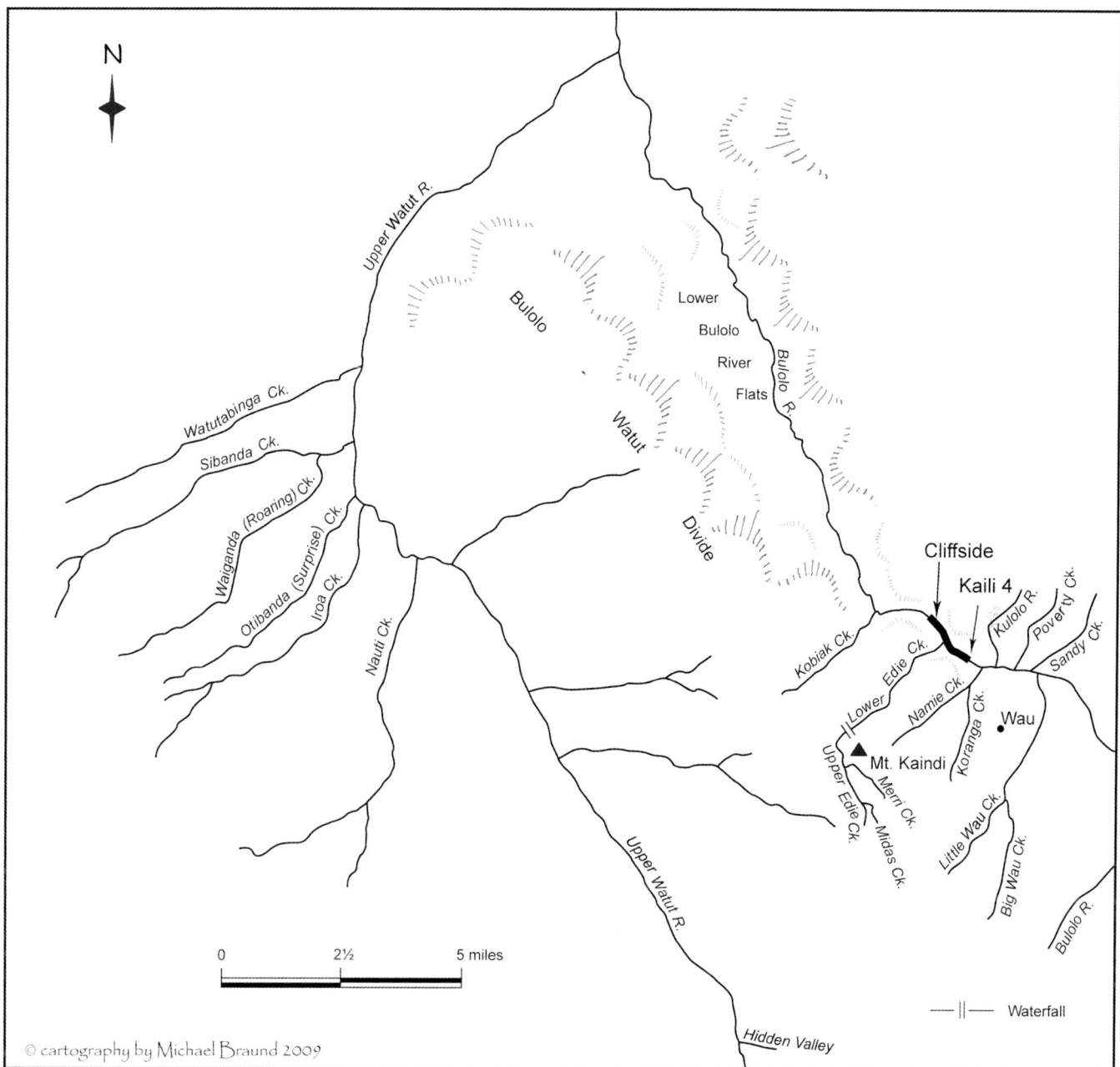

The Upper Watut and Bulolo Rivers.

him that gold brought down in the torrent of water in the Bulolo would settle once the river slowed on reaching the valley.

Levien bided his time until Australian investors passed up the opportunity provided to them by Coldham. By early 1925, the Arnold syndicate had also surrendered its leases, and the lower Bulolo Valley was finally open for Levien.

While his labourers continued working his sluice boxes at Kaili 4, Levien quietly slipped down to the lower Bulolo, and made his own assessment. He may have done his own testing or had access to Coldham's results. But either way, in April 1925, he felt confident enough to ask an Adelaide accountant, Charles Wells,[7] to approach the Melbourne stockbroking firm E.L. and C. Baillieu on his behalf with a proposal for a gold dredging and saw milling proposition.[8]

Levien said he could peg out more than 2,000 acres of river flat containing 20–23 million cubic yards averaging about 2 shillings per yard in gold. As evidence of the area's potential, he said that two parties working the river beaches with teams of seven labourers were getting up to eight ounces per day.

The absence of any reliable and efficient means of transporting men and materials from the coast represented a seemingly overwhelming obstacle to any large scale development involving the use of heavy mining equipment. While this may have daunted others, Levien articulated a remarkable vision.

He believed a light railway or road could be built via the Markham and Watut at reasonable cost. Indeed, there was *enough cedar on and adjacent to the proposition to pay for the railway, leaving the mining and pine timber as surplus.* Alternatively, aviation might be used to transport dredge machinery—although no plane had flown in New Guinea to that time. Finally, he suggested there was ample water to generate electric power for dredging or sawmilling.

Levien crisply concluded that *It seems a pity to see about £2,000,000 worth of gold go begging when at a cost of a little over half a million it could all be in someone's pockets.*

His efforts were to no avail; there was still no interest in Australia in gold mining in New Guinea.

As 1924 unfolded and word spread of the gold being taken out of Koranga, a small number of prospectors arrived at Salamaua. Most had been miners in Papua or thrown in their jobs with the Administration; many were First World War veterans. However, reports of the rugged terrain discouraged any influx of prospectors from Australia. The few who made it to Salamaua soon found there were insufficient carriers to take in their supplies or labourers to do their mining. This caused delays while they undertook recruiting expeditions to the Markham Valley, or waited for professional recruiters to obtain labourers for them.

In July 1924, the first woman arrived at Salamaua, heading for the field. Doris Booth, a former nurse, was accompanied by her husband Charles (whose nickname 'Yorkie' betrayed his English origins).[9] Although the trip from Rabaul should have taken only a few days, violent storms and protracted engine trouble meant it was six weeks before the small schooner carrying them finally limped in to Salamaua.

Getting this far was one thing, to the field another. While Doris and Yorkie brought some labourers with them, they had counted on obtaining others as well as carriers at Salamaua. They had brought two tons of stores, so the absence of carriers was a major problem, leaving them with little choice but to join the small but growing community of hopeful prospectors camping on the beach. Over the next few weeks, while Yorkie went recruiting, the stores were assembled into 150 packs and local villagers were persuaded to carry these

inland in relays as far as the Mubo Mission House. Here they were guarded as more packs were brought in until everything had been moved this first stage.

Doris and Yorkie then set out with 40 to 50 carriers and indentured labourers, many recruited from the Markham River area. Within a couple of days all but six had deserted. At this point, they decided that Yorkie should go on ahead and try to locate some rich ground, leaving Doris with most of the stores and two New Guineans, who would try and recruit some more carriers and labourers. Also left with her were a cat and a bulldog, the latter warily referred to by the carriers as 'mouth cranky'.

The journey was long and arduous, with periodic enforced spells of inactivity as more carriers were recruited. Eventually Doris arrived at the Bulolo River, five weeks after leaving Salamaua. After initially discouraging results, Doris and Yorkie obtained a promising lease below Kaili 4 on the Bulolo River, which they named Cliffside.

Towards the end of 1924, several more prospectors turned up at Salamaua, including members of the Alpha syndicate—Frank Chisholm, Dick Glasson, Bill Royal and Bill Stower. The main focus of their attention, as with most others, was the Namie/Koranga Creek area and the Bulolo down as far as the gorge, including the lower reaches of Edie Creek, which joined the Bulolo downstream from Koranga Creek. George Arnold and his partner continued mining the river beaches on the Bulolo where it emerged from the gorge—but the lower Bulolo Valley itself remained largely untouched.

Supplies were a major problem. Prospectors and miners had to bring everything they needed from Rabaul to Salamaua by whatever means they could in the absence of a regular shipping service, and then try and find sufficient carriers to carry their stores inland. Food had to be grown for their labourers, of whom there were now about 150 on the field. This included corn, kaukau (sweet potato), bananas and paw paw. Even prospectors planted gardens—the Alpha syndicate had 12-14 acres planted with corn, kaukau, tomatoes and beans. Food was sometimes bought for trade goods from villages, although such supplies were tenuous as villages often didn't produce more than required for their own needs.

At the end of 1924, there were 14 Europeans on the field, some mining, some hoping. Sharing both an obsession and the isolation, the small community supported each other wherever possible. Thus, when the first boat from Rabaul for five months failed to arrive, causing a serious food shortage, Park provided food to those in need. He had an established garden, ran a few fowls and was thus less dependent on supplies from Rabaul. Park sent Doris Booth some bananas, tomatoes, sweet potato and eggs.[10] And he followed up by providing Christmas dinner for all the Europeans, with roast duck and plum pudding with brandy sauce.

The growing number of people passing through Salamaua encouraged Bill Money, whose schooner had carried the Booths from Rabaul, to construct a small store on the beach early in 1925 using local materials, including sacsac (sago) palm leaves. However, it carried mainly trade goods and not much in the way of supplies for European use or consumption.

Bill Money was a resourceful London Cockney who migrated to Australia in 1913, aged 18, joining the AIF on the outbreak of war. He was wounded at Gallipoli, won the Military Medal on the Somme in 1917 and the Military Cross at Villers-Bretonneux in April 1918. After the war, he joined the Military Administration in New Guinea and was Assistant District Officer at Madang from 1920 to 1923, resigning to become a trader and recruiter of labourers, interspersed with occasional prospecting. Money had backed Dick Glasson financially, and with his ability to bring in supplies by schooner, as well as his knowledge of recruiting, he became a valued member of the Alpha syndicate.

On the field, 1925 was much the same as 1924. Shark-Eye Park continued to do well, although he was beginning to think of moving on as he had won a large quantity of gold from his Koranga leases[11] and was troubled by persistent ill health. Sloane was also doing well from his two leases and had a large garden providing food for his labourers. Cliffside was becoming very productive for Doris Booth, who learnt to manage her team alone, as Yorkie was invariably elsewhere prospecting.

Levien contained his frustration at the lack of interest Australian investors had in his vision, earned enough from Kaili 4 to pay his way, and waited. He did, however, put some of the building blocks in place to further his vision should circumstances change. As an army marches on its stomach, so he believed that the key to a successful mining venture was the development of large gardens to feed its labour force. These would improve labourers' diets and thus their productivity, reduce the cost of feeding them and free

Shark-Eye Park, Doris Booth and Frank Anstey M.H.R., 1925.

up men for mining activities who would otherwise be needed to carry supplies from the coast.

As any investors he succeeded in attracting were likely to have only limited capital, Levien also believed many labourers would need to be used to develop Kaili 4, generating the profits that would then meet the costs of testing the lower Bulolo leases.

Doris Booth.

While a few did well, the Morobe goldfield late in 1925 was no more than a backwater where a handful of prospectors and miners struggled to keep supplies coming from Rabaul, and thence along the tortuous track from Salamaua. High costs meant that nothing less than several ounces of gold per day was considered payable.

Communications were poor, with the nearest radio at Morobe, up to ten days away on foot and then by canoe or pinnace. The nearest medical assistant was also at Morobe—too far for help in an emergency.

There were no new discoveries and the uncompromising terrain raised serious doubts as to whether the field had a long term future. Miners used primitive means, mainly sluice boxes, to obtain gold.[12] And with much of the known gold-bearing ground tied up in large leases, there wasn't room for many more than the 14 or so hardy individuals who were there at year's end. The isolation and harsh living conditions took their toll; only half of those on the field at the end of 1924 were there a year later.

The Alpha syndicate was doing it tough. Bill Stower had given away prospecting to go recruiting. Bill Royal and Frank Chisholm were trying different stretches of the Bulolo with 40 labourers, while Dick Glasson and Bill Money were prospecting around the Buangs and lower Watut with another 25 labourers—all without success. Albert Royal, Bill's brother, was a fifth member of the syndicate though resident in Victoria, as he had agreed to guarantee Bill and Frank Chisholm up to £1,000.

Late in December 1925, Royal, Glasson, Chisholm and Money came together to assess their future. Royal and Chisholm were heavily indebted to Burns Philp, and could not afford further supplies. It was agreed that Glasson and Royal would make one final effort, leaving Chisholm at a base camp on the Bulolo, looking after what remained of their stores.

On the south-western side of the Bulolo, the country rose steeply from 2,500 feet to over 7,000 feet. One moun-

tain dominated the landscape, Mt. Kaindi, the slopes of which drained into Koranga, Namie and Edie Creeks.

While lower Edie Creek had not been encouraging, Glasson and Royal decided to prospect as far up it—and thus the slopes of Kaindi—as they could get. They worked their way upstream for about five miles from its junction with the Bulolo until they came to a series of three waterfalls, each about 300 feet high. After trying unsuccessfully for a couple of days to get past these, and with their food almost exhausted, Glasson agreed to take all the labourers except one back to the base camp, and return with fresh supplies.

While Glasson was away, Royal spent several days trying to negotiate a sheer cliff face, the terrain smothered with tangled vegetation, moss and roots, which often gave way at the slightest pressure; conditions were damp, misty and cold. A slip would have meant a 70 foot fall onto jagged rocks. Bill Royal later reported

I cut ten tracks, and each of them was probably a mile and a half long. Then we came to dead ends. It was too

Junction of Edie Creek (centre) and the Bulolo River (left to right). Mt. Kaindi in the distance.

sheer to proceed and we had to come back and start another one and try to get up that way. By the tenth track I cut I got up on to the spur above the waterfall. That took us away above the waterfall.[13]

It was 23 January 1926. Above the falls, at nearly 7,000 feet, Royal found that Edie Creek traversed a small, densely wooded plateau, fed in turn by several smaller streams, and falling only gradually from top to bottom. When Royal tried panning the creek, he couldn't believe what he saw. As he reported on his return to where Glasson was waiting, *It looks like gold, but it can't be. There's too bloody much of it.*[14]

With whatever containers they could carry, Glasson and Royal returned to the site. Clune later wrote:

> Incredulously, Royal and Glasson panned dish after dish that contained more gold than sand. Up and down …

they panned the sands for five days … They filled sugar bags with gold. They tied the legs of spare trousers, and the tails and sleeves of spare shirts, and filled them with gold. They had socks filled with gold, jam tins, beef tins, buckets filled with gold.[15]

A few months later, the mining engineer James Hebbard reported Royal as claiming that they often got 20 ounces per dish.[16]

It is unlikely Royal and Glasson would have known of the Papuan miner Jim Swanson's claim to Albert Bethune in 1909 that he had found a creek in German New Guinea with more gold in the dish than wash. But they had undoubtedly rediscovered the creek whose richness had so overwhelmed him. Only this time, the discovery was legal and was to be the catalyst for the development of a major goldfield.

Mt. Kaindi from Koranga Creek.

Part 2
Transition

Dredge No. 1 ready to commence dredging, March 1932.

CHAPTER 4

THE RUSH

*As they filled their containers, Royal and Glasson set about pegging four leases covering
81 acres on what they believed were the best stretches on Edie, Merri and Midas Creeks.*

The leases were called the Royal, the Chisholm, the George (each 22.5 acres) and the Glasson (13.5 acres). It was later agreed that all members of the syndicate would share equally in all the gold won from the four leases.

Royal and Glasson then set out for Koranga Creek, arriving at Joe Sloane's lease eight hours later. They had made the richest alluvial gold find ever on the mainland, but didn't have the £150 necessary to pay the application and survey fees. Joe Sloane had previously helped them with food and advice, and now agreed to provide money for the fees, as well as making available his large vegetable gardens—essential if the leases were to be worked efficiently as it was too cold to grow food in sufficient quantities at Edie Creek's higher altitude.

As none of the syndicate members were experienced miners, Royal and Glasson realised they would need someone with Sloane's mining skills and therefore invited him to become a member of the syndicate or, as they were soon to be known, the Big Six.

The next day, Royal headed to the coast to apply for the leases. Each was considerably smaller than

Bottom end of the Royal Lease, 1926.

the maximum 240 acres permitted, and he therefore expected no problems in having the applications approved. On the way, he saw or passed a message to most of the other miners on the field, so they could peg leases or claims before news of the discovery broke in Rabaul and Australia.

While Royal was away, Sloane went up to the new field with Glasson. Clune later wrote that together they extracted 7,600 ounces of gold in six weeks, worth about £15,000. He quoted Dick Glasson as saying: *Midas Creek was only a yard wide, but it was a good little creek. In one day's work, Joe and I took out three hundred ounces of gold, which was all our sluice-boxes would hold.*[1]

The richness of the find was as unexpected as it was extraordinary. The values in Lower Edie Creek had not been good, so there was no reason to believe they would be dramatically higher upstream. Only later did geologists realise that a massive natural bar of silicified slate above the falls had trapped most of the gold which had leached into Upper Edie Creek and its tributaries from the surrounding hillsides. The fact that it fell only gradually over its length had allowed the gold to settle in the alluvial wash, with little finding its way over the falls into Lower Edie Creek.

When the news reached George Arnold further down the Bulolo, he headed to Edie Creek to see for himself. He had some idea of what to expect, having crossed the border from the Lakekamu before the war and worked the upper reaches of what he now realised was Merri Creek. Even so, he was stunned by the richness of the find, reporting to Levien that the values were 'phenomenal'.

Royal had called at Levien's workings on his way down, and met with a surprisingly uninterested response. But Levien's attitude changed immediately on learning of Arnold's reaction. Realising that when the news broke in Australia the publicity would provide a new opportunity to attract Australian investors, he set out for the coast. On 22 February, he sent an urgent coded radiogram to Charles Wells in Adelaide: *Phenomenal alluvial gold has been found at Edie Creek 5 miles from Kaili. Believe reef also. Get busy. Cecil.*[2]

In direct contrast to the views he expressed in July 1924 in support of leases rather than claims,[3] Levien now set about promoting the idea that the lease applications should be refused, with claims under Miner's Rights being issued instead. In a letter to Lukin on 27 February, Levien claimed to have a letter from another miner *who states that he estimates the ground at about 4–500 claims and*

all seem to be of exceptional value. You will gauge by all the indications the importance of this find, and should the leases be refused there will be a very big rush …[4]

Levien followed up his cable to Wells with a letter authorising him to give an option over Kaili 4 for a quarter interest in a company with a fully paid up capital of £10,000.[5] Levien was trying to keep several balls in the air at once, as he was only permitted to hold 240 acres in total and had to work the ground he held. He was in the process of acquiring Park's Koranga leases, and while he wanted to acquire some claims at Edie Creek if the lease applications there were refused, he didn't want to relinquish Kaili 4, from which he was clearing £2,000 a year. And he still regarded the lower Bulolo leases as 'a wonderful proposition'.[6]

It was no doubt with the latter in mind that he now wrote to Australian Airways in Melbourne enquiring about the possibilities of establishing an aerial service. In his usual practical, no-nonsense way, he said:

> A landing ground is quite feasible at the coast and good landing grounds could be made on Bulolo River flats— but between these points … and in case of forced landing it would be a clean case for inquests.[7]

Although the Administration had proclaimed the Morobe Goldfield three years earlier and appointed a Mining Warden, it was completely unprepared for a major find. It was now found seriously wanting on two fronts: its administration of mining and its readiness for a possible rush by prospectors. Its actions (and inactions) were a precursor to years of bungling and inefficiency which constrained the development of the goldfield and wasted the opportunity to establish a platform for later economic development.

In the first of many misjudgements, the acting Mining Warden, Jack Lukin, despite lacking prior experience in mining administration, saw no need to visit Edie Creek before recommending that the whole area applied for by the Big Six be granted. Despite Levien's assertions about the richness of the field and its ability to sustain many claims, Lukin concluded that the ground was patchy and not particularly valuable—similar to that for which leases had previously been issued on the Bulolo.

In mid-March, P.L. Madigan, a Rabaul solicitor, lodged objections against the Edie Creek lease applications on behalf of several unnamed persons. Levien later admitted having instigated this as *the more miners that could get in, the more publicity it would get, and the better advertisement it would be for the ground lower* down.[8] A new employee of Levien's, Harry Costello, also lodged an objection.[9] The principal reason for the objection was that, given their value, the areas applied for were excessive. Lukin heard the objections on 19 April, and dismissed them.

But this was far from the end of the matter. On 3 May, 22 miners signed a letter to the Administrator, initiated by Levien and claiming that as the leases were alluvial they should be worked as claims. This again highlighted the failure of the Administration to establish the circumstances in which dredging or sluicing leases should be granted. 'Dredging' and 'sluicing' are at opposite ends of the scale of alluvial mining operations, so their linking in the Mining Ordinance provided fertile grounds for dispute. The uncertainty surrounding this had already been highlighted in 1925 by the rejection and subsequent acceptance of Levien's application for a lease on Namie Creek. But more than six months later, the Administration had done nothing to clarify how the provision in the Mining Ordinance should be applied.

On 10 May, Lukin set down the facts of the situation as he saw them in a memo to the Administrator. He argued, not unreasonably, that

> The field up to the present has been worked in a steady and systematic manner owing to the policy of granting leases. The miners have been well enough off to treat their labour well, and lessees have had such permanent camps that they have been able to plant large gardens of native foods.[10] He also advocated that the Mining Ordinance be amended to permit miners who were intending to use box sluicing to apply for leases of up to 20 acres.

Lukin was particularly dismissive of the alleged value of the discovery, suggesting that *the applicants would be very lucky to wash £100,000 worth of gold from the property*. His antipathy for Levien then got the better of him. Accusing him of deliberately stirring up trouble among the miners, he claimed that *Levien's lust for gold amounts almost to a mania and he is prepared to do any dishonest or dirty trick to attain it, provided it can be done with reasonable safety.*

Lukin's assessment of Levien was perceptive. In a letter to Wells at around the same time, when it seemed likely he would get some claims at Edie Creek, Levien wrote

> If so, there is no telling where we will end for cash, as the possibilities are enormous; it has been a very strenuous time and I have had to watch my step, but when it comes to manoeuvering practically I can quite

hold my own with the mob here and this has proved it. I will tell you quite a lot of the history of here some day and you will see that I deserve all I can get, if not jail.[11]

Following an appeal to the Central Court, Lukin's decision to dismiss the objections was quashed on a technicality, leaving the matter to be resolved by the Administrator.

———

Back in Australia, Levien's radiogram to Wells, combined with growing press coverage of the Edie Creek discovery, was bearing fruit. Wells finally managed to attract several investors, and on 18 May 1926, Guinea Gold NL was registered with a nominal capital of £2,000 and Wells as Chairman. It accepted a six month option over Kaili 4 and sent a mining engineer, James Hebbard, to New Guinea to inspect the property. A cable was also sent to Levien requesting that he peg all the best alluvial land in the lower Bulolo Valley.

Hebbard arrived at Levien's camp on 15 June, and proceeded to investigate Kaili 4. Using Barton's earlier test results and Doris Booth's experience at Cliffside, he concluded that the value of the lease was considerably greater than Barton had estimated, and cabled Guinea Gold on 27 July recommending that the option be exercised.

Hebbard then visited Edie Creek and was impressed with what he saw, forecasting an enormous output if Miner's Right claims were allowed. He had met Coldham, an old friend, in Rabaul on his way to Koranga, who convinced him of the extent and richness of the lower Bulolo Valley, the main problem being its inaccessibility and the extreme difficulty of transport.[12] He conveyed this information to Guinea Gold, but didn't have time to see for himself.

Early in June, Levien had pegged and applied for six leases (Guinea Gold 1-6) covering 1,050 acres in the lower Bulolo Valley. With Hebbard's encouragement, more leases were pegged in the following months so that, by year's end, Guinea Gold had taken the first steps to implement Levien's vision, with leases totalling 1,650 acres.

Hebbard's enthusiasm meant Levien had little trouble convincing him of his ideas for their development. In his report,[13] Hebbard confirmed there were numerous opportunities for hydro-electric power and large quantities of cedar and pine in the area. He suggested addressing the transport problem with a narrow gauge railway from Salamaua, while noting that he understood *there is serious talk of a company being formed to establish aerial transport to a point near Mr Levien's camp where good natural landing ground exists.* Citing Levien's experience, he also concluded that *practically the whole of the food required by native labour can be grown on the leases at very nominal cost.*

Things now moved fast at Guinea Gold—or as fast as communication difficulties allowed.[14] On 27 July the company's authorised capital was increased from £2,000 to £10,000, and then to £50,000 early in September. On 12 August, the Board formally agreed to exercise the option over Kaili 4, giving Levien 25% of the enlarged company. It also agreed to acquire the Koranga leases and stores from Levien for £9,800, and appointed Levien as its General Superintendent on the field, at a salary of £1,000 per annum.

During the first half of 1926, aspiring miners from around the Territory made their way to Salamaua in twos and threes in all manner of craft, even canoes, which were often barely seaworthy. While the majority were former Administration employees, or plantation owners and employees, and were used to using New Guinean labourers, most were unfamiliar with living and working in the bush and knew little about mining.

During Lukin's absence on leave in May, Ward Oakley was appointed acting Mining Warden, although—like Lukin—he had no experience in mining administration. After visiting Upper Edie Creek, Oakley concluded that reports as to its richness were 'wild exaggeration'.[15] He believed a rush would result in chaos with a lack of proper housing and food for labourers, who would be working in icy cold, wet conditions.

Nevertheless, by July a rush mentality had taken hold in Rabaul, with more Administration employees forming syndicates or resigning to go to the field. 25,000 ounces had already been produced at Edie Creek, in addition to 35,000 ounces elsewhere on the field to that time.

But this heightened activity had no impact on the Administration's planning. The administrative centre remained eight to ten days travel away at Morobe, requiring miners to travel there to obtain Miner's Rights, sign on indentured labourers and transact other business. In his report to Guinea Gold, Hebbard expressed surprise

that the Government had not yet recognised the importance of the industry by improving the track (in from the coast), establishing means of communication, and installing officials nearer than Morobe, 90 miles away by track and sea.

In a separate letter to Guinea Gold's Secretary, his assessment of Administration indolence was less diplomatic: *The dilatory ways of the officials are unspeakable. I think they amend the axiom don't let business stop golfing, only they substitute ... ing.*[16]

As well as the problems identified by Hebbard, there was still no hospital at Salamaua and no effort to protect the health of those on the field or travelling to it. This was despite the fact that, as the Government noted in its 1926/27 Annual Report to the League of Nations, *The experience of gold mining in other parts of New Guinea has always been that bacillary dysentery has quickly made its appearance on the fields in epidemic form ...* [17]

While there were still only 50 Europeans on the field or at Salamaua in July, 1,300 labourers and carriers were working sluice boxes or moving back and forth on the track in from the coast. The discovery was by now attracting huge publicity in Australia, with newspaper headlines such as 'Phenomenal New Guinea Goldfield', 'Gold Madness Grips New Guinea' and 'Gold Fever. New Guinea Infected'. Such reports made inevitable a substantial influx of prospectors from Australia. But instead of accepting this and making preparations, the Administration simply intensified its efforts to avert it.

Administrator Wisdom was concerned that public comments by Hebbard and Levien on their return to Australia would inflame the situation, something he wanted to avoid at all costs. In correspondence with the Department of Home and Territories, in Melbourne, he argued that Edie Creek was 'not a poor man's field'—a term that was to feature regularly in Government-inspired press reports. He later explained that

A poor man's field in Australia is understood to be a field to which a man without anything can go with his swag and live by the gold he gets from the field; he is not dependent upon anyone helping him. He can go out with a swag and a tin of 'dog' and get enough gold to keep him going. But you must have natives here to help you, and money to pay them, money to carry you there, and on when you get there; therefore it is not a poor man's field ... A man cannot carry a swag in this climate over that country.[18]

Wisdom believed a man operating by himself would need £1,000 in capital to keep him going for six months. This reflected the high cost of acquiring and maintaining 20 carriers and labourers and of obtaining provisions and equipment from Rabaul. With reports starting to filter through that many men were likely to arrive from Australia in the next few months, he advocated press propaganda deprecating a boom, and reiterated an earlier request for a Mining Registrar and some police.[19] Shortly after, *The Argus* reported advice the Department had received from 'residents' about the danger of the journey to the field, its remoteness and inaccessibility and the improbability of success once prospectors got there.[20]

Widsom's fears about Hebbard and Levien's public comments were well founded. On their arrival in Australia, each gave lengthy interviews to newspapers. Levien claimed that *the Edie Creek field was probably the richest in the history of the world*, and to support this put 900 ounces of gold on public display in Sydney. [21]

Hebbard reported that:

the field was yielding at least 1,000 ounces a day on the labour of about 100 'boys'. I saw one washing, from the labour of not more than 10 'boys', who could not possibly handle more than 1½ cubic yards (of wash) a day, which yielded 270 oz of gold.[22]

He further claimed there were at least 50,000 ounces of gold stored on the field—a view anecdotally confirmed by the first wireless operator, Ted Bishton, who arrived there in September: *We used to get our flour in twenty-five pound tins and I've seen eight or nine of these tins, full of gold, in Bill Royal's hut.*[23]

While their intention was to talk up Guinea Gold's prospects by suggesting that Edie Creek was the source of gold on its leases, Hebbard did at least try to paint a balanced picture. He acknowledged that it was not a poor man's field, referring to the costs and difficulty of getting there—much of the walking being 'as steep as a steeple'—and that all the known ground at Edie Creek was already occupied. Levien likewise noted that it was not a big field and could not support an unlimited number of prospectors. Nevertheless, Wisdom's worst fears concerning a rush were soon to be realised.

In August 1926, the number of Europeans on the field or in Salamaua rose from 50 to 80—not a large number, but supporting them were 1,740 carriers and labourers. News that another 40 or so men were on their way from Australia on the *Montoro* was the signal for panic stations by the Administration. It hastily decided to transfer the District Office (but not the radio station)

from Morobe to Salamaua, and the Commissioner for Native Affairs, Henry Cardew, and Director of Public Health, Raphael Cilento, headed there as quickly as possible in the Administration's schooner, the *Franklin*.

On their arrival on 29 August, Cardew and Cilento found a small but growing number of Europeans camped in tents along the beach towards the mouth of the Francisco River, with several hundred carriers who had just returned from the field or were waiting to go there. The only water supply was a soak at one end of the isthmus and a small stream some distance away on the mainland. At the back of the beach was a mosquito-infested swamp. There were no sanitary facilities or medical services, and the few buildings were made of bush materials and in dilapidated condition.

Cardew and Cilento quickly laid out a rough plan for the future siting of buildings for the Administration and residents, established a compound for carriers and labourers and two police posts, as well as arrangements for weighing all packs being carried to the field, to prevent overloading. They also fixed the price for canoes ferrying miners across the Francisco River, in response to complaints about the amount charged by Logui villagers.

On 3 September, the *Montoro* arrived in Salamaua with 40 miners and 300–400 carriers and labourers. Mick Leahy was one of the 'new chums' who arrived that day. Aged 24 and after eight years as a railway clerk in Townsville, the prospect of joining a gold rush was exhilarating:

We were the vanguard, sailors, traders, clerks and roustabouts—everything but miners—most of us unattached young men who had dropped everything to catch the first boat.[24]

Once it realised that nothing was going to stop the influx, the Administration proclaimed the goldfield an Uncontrolled Area, entry to which required a special permit. New arrivals had to lodge a deposit of £50 with the Administrator against any breach of conditions and to meet the cost of their fare back to Australia. They must also have arranged transport from Salamaua to the field and have sufficient financial backing to enable them to operate there, including paying the carriers and labourers they employed. Finally, they were required to pass a medical examination and be inoculated annually against typhoid. Detailed requirements also applied concerning the welfare of those carrying to and working on the field.

However, the lack of preparation quickly caught up with the Administration. Toward the end of September, a dysentery epidemic broke out at Salamaua and on the Gadagadu track. A medical officer, Dr Ian Dickson, had just arrived in Salamaua, and he immediately closed the track, quarantining those coming down it. He then proceeded along it, burning and rebuilding rest houses, erecting latrines and ensuring a good water supply nearby. New Guinean police were also stationed at each camp to supervise the use of latrines and water collection. Later, efforts were also made to stagger parties travelling along the track at intervals, to avoid overcrowding at camps.

When Dickson reached Edie Creek in late September, he found about 150 Europeans and 1,500 labourers—but no sanitary arrangements. While there was no sign of the dysentery epidemic, he immediately specified actions miners should take to avoid an outbreak.[25]

Up to this time, the burden of caring for those afflicted with dysentery fell on Doris Booth at Cliffside, past whose lease the track to Edie Creek ran. Doris had been a nurse, and as cases began to arrive, she quickly erected a primitive bush 'hospital', in which she cared for about 130 carriers and labourers over the next two to three months.[26] Hastily trained orderlies proved of little use and she had to do nearly everything herself. On several occasions she sent out her own labourers to bring in sick carriers on improvised stretchers made of saplings and copra bags.

Doris also had a 'private hospital' in her house for a small number of Europeans, and a third building for general cases, such as pneumonia. Once the miners heard about her 'hospital', they sent their carriers and labourers to her for help whatever their illness, and within a short time she found herself treating or caring for many with a range of other medical problems. The miners were soon calling Doris 'the angel of Bulolo' and she was later awarded the OBE.

With the epidemic spiralling out of control, the Minister for Home and Territories made one final effort to discourage travel to the goldfields. In a press release in October, he warned that *the field is not a poor man's field, and it would be most inadvisable for any person to proceed there unless he is in possession of between £500 and £1,000 capital.*[27]

Curiously, however, it made no mention of the epidemic, which reached its peak in November at Salamaua. Thereafter it gradually diminished as containment measures took effect. Early in December the Administration belatedly established a small hospital in Wau,[28] upriver from Cliffside, though it was staffed only by a medical assistant, with a second assistant being sent to Edie Creek the following month.

The Administration later took pride in the fact that only 29 carriers and labourers died within a five month period, or less than 6% of those who were infected, compared with 57.5% of those on the Lakekamu in 1910 over a similar period.[29] While Dr Dickson's efforts were effective in containing the outbreak, greater anticipation and preparation would almost certainly have prevented the epidemic in the first place. And without Doris Booth's improvised hospital care, the Administration would have had less reason to be satisfied with the outcome.

The Minister's October press release did nothing to stem the tide, and by December there were 280 Europeans and 3,350 carriers and labourers in Salamaua, on the field or somewhere in between.

At Midas Creek, Sloane and Glasson averaged 100 ounces a day for six weeks as new arrivals drifted in and began to peg the terraces alongside the Big Six leases—the remains of former creeks 50 to 60 feet above the existing creek beds, and comprising gold-bearing alluvial wash. Before long, some were recovering up to 50 ounces a day.

One of the early arrivals, in June 1926, was Harry Darby. Harry was born in 1900 and taken in as an orphan by the Anglican Brighton Babies Home, Victoria. After two years in the AIF, he found his way to Rabaul, where he worked with the Administration as a sanitary inspector and then as a labour overseer. Harry was a lover of life, reckless, likeable and generous—a man who never forgot his origins or those who helped him. Harry struck it rich on his appropriately-named Eldorado lease, and within three years took out an estimated £100,000 in gold.

More modest, but still very rewarding, was another claim that produced 2,300 ounces in six months. As well as fine alluvial gold, miners often found specimens of gold embedded in quartz. The largest of these, weighing 300 ounces, contained about 70% gold.

Despite all the warnings, many who joined the rush confronted reality only when they arrived at Edie Creek. Before long, a trickle of miners was returning to

Australia disillusioned by the small size of the field, the difficulty of getting there and the costs involved. Nor did it help that, being inexperienced, many of them missed much of the gold that was there, while its high silver content reduced the value of what they did get.[30] Gold declarations for the period November 1926 to July 1927 suggest that no more than one third of miners were on payable gold.

While some miners were returning to Australia, others were arriving, and when they realised there was no ground to be worked, they needed little encouragement to join a growing throng of miners agitating for the Administrator to change his decision to grant leases to the Big Six. On 8 July 1926, in an effort to calm an increasingly tense situation, he granted the four leases, but arbitrarily reduced three of them by 50% and one by 80% — and the total from the original 81 acres to 33 ¾ acres.

The Administrator's decision had little effect. The objection that the Big Six leases were 'excessive', while a strong emotional justification for the miners' resistance, had by August given way to a more substantive and thus arguable objection: that the Mining Ordinance permitted dredging or sluicing leases to be approved only for working by hydraulic sluicing, and yet the ground awarded to the Big Six was being worked by 'boxing'.[31] The miners were also concerned that another 21 leases had been applied for covering about 100 acres. Pending a decision, this ground could not be worked as claims.

However, as a man who believed that acceding to pressure was a sign of weakness, the Administrator refused to make further concessions.

The miners were by now becoming increasingly well organised. The Morobe District Miners' Association was formed in September 1926, a meeting of its members resolving that, if the Administration did not redress the situation, the Big Six leases (other than those belonging to Royal and Glasson) should be marked off in claims to be allotted among miners by ballot.[32] This ultimatum was duly conveyed by Oakley, the acting Mining Warden, to the Administrator, along with a request for an early decision on the 21 leases.[33]

Oakley had issued a stiff warning in May that miners attempting to work any ground within the Big Six leases would be prosecuted. However, confronted with increasingly aggressive tactics and isolated at Edie Creek from others in the Administration, Oakley was finding the volatile situation difficult to handle. Radio

Harry Darby.

communications with Rabaul were unreliable at best and Wisdom made no effort to visit the field to see things for himself.

On 5 October, the Administrator radioed Cardew (via Morobe — there still being no radio communication with Salamaua) but not Oakley (though there was a radio at Edie Creek) that he had refused applications for the 21 leases at Edie Creek on the grounds that they could be profitably worked by claim holders. Although this may have reduced the tension, Oakley was not advised until 19 days later.

On 11 October, believing the arrival of his successor was imminent,[34] Oakley responded to the miners' threats, saying that he was not the Warden, and would refer the matter to the new Warden on his arrival at the field. This response only inflamed the miners and on 24 October, 141 of them held a ballot for claims on all ground at Upper Edie Creek, including the Big Six leases.

Meanwhile, Wisdom had written to the Department on 16 October, haughtily dismissing the miners' concerns, claiming that the agitation had petered out and that anyway *The noisy section consisted of a few of the men only — the better class being quite satisfied with the fairness of the grant to the finders*.[35] Whether due to ignorance or defiance, such a statement showed how out of touch Wisdom was with the mood at Edie Creek.

On 5 November, the Association cabled the Prime Minister, requesting a Commission to investigate the

Miners' Association meeting, Edie Creek, 1926.

actions of the Administrator regarding the Big Six leases, the absence of a Warden and the lack of medical facilities. However, the replacement of Oakley as acting Mining Warden in mid-November by W.E. Grose, an experienced Administration officer with the powers of Deputy Administrator, soon saw an end to civil disobedience. Several men who had begun working claims on the Big Six leases were prosecuted and fined £25 — these fines being paid by the Miners' Association.

In an extraordinary decision, reflecting his desperation to placate the miners without being seen to back down on his decision to grant leases to the Big Six, Wisdom amended the Mining Ordinance in November allowing the Warden to permit holders of Miner's Rights to peg claims on leases where the ground was subsequently found to be suitable for working by hand appliances. The effect was to allow claim holders to work the Big Six leases side by side with the Big Six.

Following this amendment and with an experienced official acting as Mining Warden, an ebullient Wisdom reported to the Department on 30 November that *the trouble was practically over*.

Again his optimism was unfounded. The miners could sense victory, and on 20 December the Miners' Association again cabled the Government, this time pressing for a broad-ranging inquiry, and followed up with a delegation to the Minister for Home and Territories.

The Minister and his Department were clearly becoming increasingly frustrated with the Administrator's inadequate responses to their questions, and no doubt at the frequency with which he seemed out of touch or misinformed. Nor did his unwillingness to visit Edie Creek throughout the dispute enhance his credibility.

The Australian Government was faced with a situation where the antagonistic mood of the miners towards Wisdom's autocratic approach echoed — and not so faintly — that of miners prior to the Eureka Stockade in 1854. There was no suggestion of an armed insurrection, but in an atmosphere of claim and counter-claim, where clearly there was substance to the miners' complaints, a circuit breaker was needed.

On 2 March 1927, the Government appointed a Royal Commissioner to inquire into and report upon all matters connected with the Big Six leases. Specifically included in the terms of reference were the exercise by the Administrator of his powers under the Mining Ordinance and whether reasonable provision had been made for the administration of the Edie Creek locality, and in particular for the medical requirements of Europeans and New Guineans on the field.

This gave the Miners' Association everything it wanted and was clearly not a vote of confidence in the Administrator.

CHAPTER 5
NOT A POOR MAN'S FIELD

Whatever his mistakes in preparing for the rush, the Administrator's assessment of the challenges facing new arrivals was accurate.

This was a gold rush unlike any other. It was impossible for individual miners to get to the field by themselves: a man could not carry his equipment and enough food for the trip in, let alone food to sustain him once he was there. If he didn't have labourers, he couldn't operate a sluice box and he couldn't get enough gold panning by himself to meet the cost of obtaining his supplies.

It was a triumph of tenacity and, of course, luck that many miners overcame the challenges they faced and made a living. However, carriers and labourers, particularly those employed by inexperienced miners, were often less fortunate.

In the early days, even getting to Salamaua was difficult. Until a regular shipping service began in September 1926, one had to get there any way one could. If an aspiring miner could find his way to Morobe, he might travel on the government pinnace or take his chance in a canoe going from village to village up the coast. Travel was also possible on small inter-island vessels and plantation schooners which occasionally visited Salamaua, or the mission boat, *Bavaria*, bringing supplies to Malolo mission.

Before the rush, men going to the field relied mainly on carriers recruited casually from Logui village. They would carry in on the Gadagadu track as far as the boundary of the Kaiwa people, who would then carry as far as Biangai territory, whose villagers would carry through

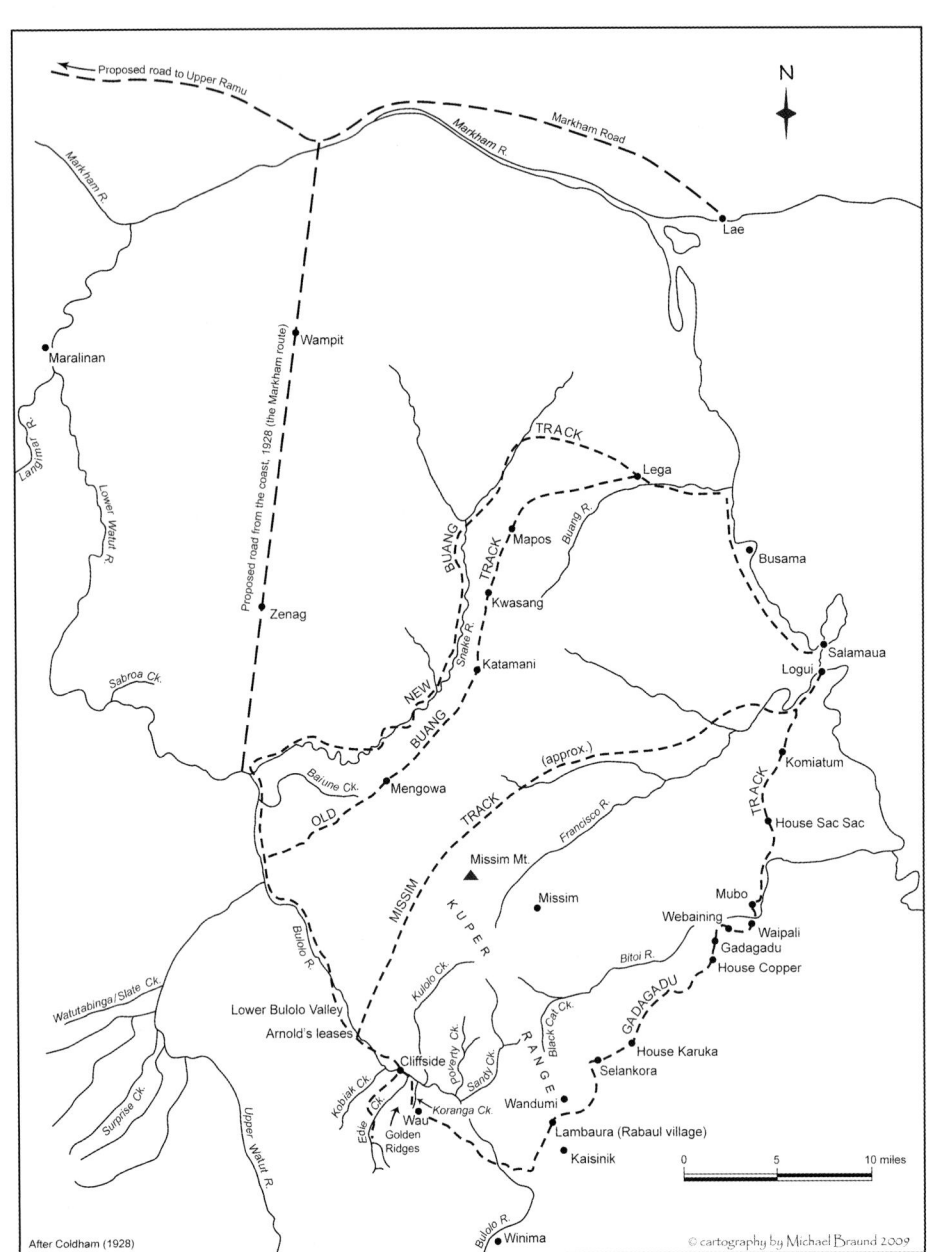

The tracks and proposed road from the coast.

Carriers leaving Salamaua for Edie Creek.

to the Bulolo. It was a slow process. When one group was paid off, travellers might have to wait several days until enough villagers were found to carry the next leg. The cost was about 10 shillings per 50 pound pack into the field. However, once the rush started, the price trebled and finally it became almost impossible to get carriers on a casual basis at any price.

In January 1927, the Mining Warden estimated that each miner needed eight men to work a claim and 16 carriers to keep them supplied with stores. If a miner didn't bring carriers and labourers from elsewhere with him to Salamaua, and most didn't, he was dependent on recruiters to find them. As demand increased, the cost of recruiting rose dramatically, from £5 per man to as high as £30 — the shortage compounded by the reluctance of villagers to work at Edie Creek once they heard about conditions there. Those who did agree, signed on initially for a maximum of two years.

As delays in getting carriers and labourers increased, the number of men forced to wait on the beach grew. The line of crudely built huts of sago palm wood and leaves, some with hessian and corrugated iron, eventually stretched along the beachfront on Bayern Bay almost as far as the Francisco River.

For men impatient to get to the field, a wait of six weeks or even longer was frustrating, though it gave 'new chums' time to learn a few things from more experienced men before they set out. For some, it was

all too hard, and they returned to Australia without ever reaching the field.

Some new arrivals, however, struck it lucky almost immediately. Years later Bert Weston recalled that:

> It was not at all uncommon for a man to step off the steamer at Salamaua, … and within hours to be befriended by a successful miner and given a claim to work on shares. This was not always entirely altruistic as a mining claim, once pegged and recorded, had to be manned and worked after a stated time or otherwise forfeited.[1]

There were two main tracks from Salamaua, the Gadagadu track and the Buang track. The former was the more direct route to Edie Creek, while the latter involved travelling up the coast a short distance and then striking inland.

Neither was a track in the normal sense, but a series of paths running haphazardly between villages. Wherever the deeply folded terrain permitted, these tracks followed spurs and ridges, many of them razor-backed, before plunging down one mountain side and up another. As inland tribal groups traded only with their neighbours, there was no reason for a direct route linking the coast with the interior.

Shark-Eye Park had made his way into Koranga Creek via the Gadagadu track, as did all early travellers. It became one of legend. Some claimed that over six to eight days they travelled further vertically than horizontally, others that they had to climb 30,000 feet for a net gain in altitude of 3,500, which was perhaps closer to the truth. The Mining Warden clinically referred to this as *lost climbing — i.e. climbing up and down without attaining any appreciable difference in altitude …* [2] Frank Pryke, a miner for 30 years in Australian and Papua, claimed the track *was the worst road I had seen food packed over to a goldfield.* [3]

In July 1926, A.A. Chauncy, the Administration's senior surveyor, walked in on the Gadagadu track. He subsequently recalled:

> For five days we clambered up steep mountain ranges and down into what seemed bottomless gorges. We waded knee deep for miles in mountain torrents. The rain pattered down almost incessantly, and we were wet to the skin all the time. The timber was all wet and sodden, so that a decent fire could not be made, and at times it was bitterly cold. [4]

To ensure carriers were not forced to carry packs beyond their physical limitations, the Administration set a maximum limit of 50 pounds; each carrier also had to have a chest measurement of at least 31 inches. [5] Leaving Salamaua, miners first had to cross the Francisco River. After an Administration officer checked they had not overloaded their carriers, 'Old Charon' would ferry them across in a large canoe. He was well named, given the terrain that lay ahead.

The first leg was a 1,400 foot climb to the village of Komiatum. For some, the climb was steep but beautiful, with many different types of orchids and birds to admire. For others, it was a killer climb. As miner Jack O'Neill noted,

> This 'thing', … which had been the subject of such harrowing tales in the pub bar, reared up out of the narrow coastal plain, and it needed little imagination to appreciate why the old timers dreaded their first day's walk 'in', with Komiatum for a pipe opener. And they

Kunda cane bridge on Gadagadu track.

Mountain and ravine on Gadagadu track, 1924.

Carriers crossing a river.

Up and up and at last we would see daylight through the tree-tops ahead, but it wouldn't be the top, just a slight flattening of the grade and too soon up we'd go again.[8]

Gadagadu was four days from Salamaua and about halfway to the field. Royal, Money, Levien and Darby, amongst others, had store houses here which gave them greater flexibility in moving their supplies to the field. By May 1927, there were also 15 or so roughly built shacks owned by various miners, but used by all and sundry.

Gadagadu also offered a last chance to look back. Doris Booth recalled

From the summit … one saw some of Nature's wonders—a panorama of mountains, cascades, and valleys, clouds and mists; and in the distance the shimmering sea. These were scenes of indescribable grandeur.[9]

As the track climbed beyond Gadagadu, the jungle transformed into a moss forest enveloped in a thick mist or cloud silently dripping its moisture. One traveller recalled:

Here … every tree trunk and bough was moss or lichen covered. Leaf-mould and moss covered the earth several feet deep, between the aerial roots of the trees. Walking became a nightmare—just stepping from one slippery, moss-covered root to another. It was necessary to place the foot cautiously so that the waist of the boot gripped the root; even so, falls were numerous … The whole forest was damp, dank and eerily silent. No life was in evidence, except our unhappy selves and our miserable carriers, who seemed too impressed, or depressed, to utter a word … A stick was of little assistance as, once weight was placed on it, it sank through the moss and leafage some distance before reaching the ground.[10]

didn't need a thick aching head and a booze-saturated body to get murdered by that climb up a grass covered, shadeless spur during the hottest part of the day. They didn't need those handicaps but they usually carried them.[6]

A day and a half out, House Sacsac—a hastily constructed hut roofed with sago palm leaves—offered a respite, but most pushed through to Mubo where there was a Lutheran mission house of dressed timber, with four rooms and a verandah. At 2,400 feet, there were no malaria-carrying mosquitoes here, though rats and their attendant fleas were plentiful. In 1924, Doris Booth was taken with the balsams, orchids, staghorns, ferns and beautiful birds of paradise round Mubo, while *wonderfully marked butterflies fluttered like fairies across the mountain paths.*[7]

From Mubo, the track descended 1,000 feet to the Bitoi River, across which a two foot wide bridge of kunda cane was suspended precariously like a giant spider's web above the raging torrent. As travellers made their way across it one at a time, the bridge swayed alarmingly.

Safe on the other side, they resumed their climb, often under a scorching sun, the track a seemingly interminable switchback, until Waipali was reached at 2,900 feet. Before being cleaned up in September 1926, the village here was filthy and flea infested, and many pushed on the short distance to Webaining.

The stretch to Gadagadu (4,075 feet) was regarded by many as the worst on the track—a near perpendicular climb for five hours, its difficulty accentuated by a series of false summits. O'Neill:

The track continued to climb until House Copper was reached at around 6,000 feet. This camp was the boundary between the Kaiwa and Biangai people, and took its name from a hut comprising a few sheets of galvanised iron previously abandoned by carriers. Shortly afterwards, the highest point on the track was reached, at around 6,700 feet. Not that things then became any easier. To reach the next camp, House Karuka, at 6,000 feet, travellers found themselves wading up to their waists for up to two miles through a rapidly flowing creek before a final steep ascent through the pervasive moss forest.

From here the track downhill crossed a number of spurs. A descent of 1,000 feet was often followed by an ascent of 800, with roots for footholds going down and for hanging onto when climbing. After many hours, weary travellers suddenly and unexpectedly emerged from the steep canyons through which they had been descending into undulating grass-covered country, spreading away to the north. The effect on travellers of this open, sunny vista following the claustrophobia of the moss forest was dramatic:

> After days of rank tropical bush and dank mountain forests, the sight of the glorious Bulolo valley from this vantage point was breath-taking. We sat and contemplated it for an hour, whilst our clothes dried in the warm sunshine.[11]

From this point, the going became easier, a long descent along marbled ridges bringing travellers to Selankora and then Lambaura village. On reaching the Bulolo, Biangai carriers were often reluctant to go any further, and travellers would find themselves with no-one to carry their supplies through to Koranga or Edie Creek. Koranga Creek was a few miles downstream, past the future site of the township of Wau, and Cliffside a short distance beyond this — the starting point of the final leg for most, the climb to Edie Creek.

On the old Buang track. Two figures on razorback ridge provide perspective.

In 1926, the track was ill prepared to handle the large numbers who traversed it after the rush began. There were no sanitary arrangements and little shelter at most camps, just lean-to's of rough timber and leaves. Dr Dickson burnt these during the dysentery epidemic

Mule train on the new Buang track. The first mules to reach the field, 1929.

in September, and in several places cleared the ground and built houses for 40 or 50 carriers and labourers and about five whites. But nothing was done to make the track easier. As most travellers were barely able to communicate with their carriers and labourers, progress was slow and difficult. Desertions were frequent.

The Buang track was a different experience, though hardly less demanding. It was first used when the Gadagadu track was closed during the dysentery epidemic. Having sailed or walked up the coast from Salamaua to where the Buang River entered the sea, travellers headed inland. After a few miles, the River was crossed at a point where it was about 200 yards wide. It was not fast flowing, but deep, forcing carriers to cross with their packs on their heads. The track then wound upwards, passing through the villages of Lega and Mapos on the range dividing the Buang and Snake Rivers at a height of more than 5,000 feet. Here villagers had gardens of kaukau and taro which travellers could trade for salt and matches.

Beyond Mapos the terrain became more rugged. Patrol Officer John Murphy later described the country as

very grand [with] rolling kunai hills, deep sheer valleys and limestone cliffs, high rugged mountains shepherding the Snake River along a deep, tortuous valley … little stockaded villages are on the peaks and hillsides.[12]

At one point, a waterfall 2,000 feet or more in height erupted spectacularly from the hills to feed the Snake River far below. Ted Bishton provided a vivid account of this part of the track:

We generally travelled on the tops of these mountains and some of them were real razorbacks. I remember going along one … it was so narrow, about eighteen inches to two feet wide. The native carriers were so sure-footed they thought nothing of it, but I handed my rifle to my boy and got down on my hands and knees. I must have travelled for some hours like this, but I was not game to stand up, especially after seeing one of the carriers drop his pack, which careered thousands of feet down below … Some mornings we would start off from a mountain peak and fall, or slide down for five or six thousand feet, then ascend the opposite mountain by climbing and pulling ourselves up on vines. By evening, when we would have reached the top, looking back to where we had started from in the morning seemed only a stone's throw … [13]

In the early days, villagers inland from Mapos showed considerable disquiet at the passage of the intruders. Bishton reported villages of up to 400 or 500 huts that were deserted, but as soon as they left drums would communicate with a village further ahead. Kwasang was one such village, and further on Katamani, perched high on cliffs above the track. Here his team awoke one morning to find several hundred *wild looking cannibals watching us from a knoll 300 yards away*. Over several days they moved closer, and when Bishton's party left they looted and burned their camp, firing a volley of arrows after them.

It wasn't long, however, before the desire for trade goods overcame the fears and suspicions of Buang villagers, as subsequent travellers found them willing to sell kaukau and other local foods. These parties tried variations to the track Bishton and other early travellers took, to avoid the worst stretches, and gradually a passable route developed that followed the Snake River. During the next few years, small numbers of mules, donkeys, horses and cattle were driven along the new Buang track.

Reaching the Bulolo, close to its junction with the Watut, travellers followed it upstream, across the leases pegged by Levien in the lower Bulolo valley, past Arnold's leases at the entrance to the gorge and up to Cliffside.

Whichever track they travelled, by the time they reached Cliffside, miners heading for Edie Creek had experienced a gruelling trip of several days. They now faced the final stretch up Mt. Kaindi to Edie Creek. The main route in the early days was a narrow track cut by Yorkie Booth through dense bush and involving an exhausting nine hour climb of 4,000 feet over difficult terrain and across 13 small creeks. About half way, he'd cut a lookout through the trees, which came to be known as 'Booth's window', with a wonderful view over the upper Bulolo valley. The ashes of many campfires attested to the popularity of this welcome break in what otherwise seemed a never-ending climb.

As travellers approached Edie Creek, it became colder and wetter, a tangled mass of roots and thick

Cliffside on the Bulolo River; 1929. Those travelling the Gadagadu track approached Cliffside from the left, and those using the Buang track from the right. Yorkie Booth's track up Mt. Kaindi began behind the houses.

moss making it hard to keep one's footing. For Ward Oakley, this last stretch was the hardest encountered in six years patrolling.[14] It was always with a deep sense of relief that miners arrived at their destination.

At up to £30 per man, the recruiter's fee for eight labourers and 16 carriers made a significant dent in the £1,000 Administrator Wisdom suggested a miner would need for the first six months. So did the cost of getting supplies continuously to the field. While the maximum load was 50 pounds, the effective load was about half this, as food had to be carried for the 12 to 14 day round trip — with each carrier eating about 1½ pounds of rice per day. As well, there were losses from water damage and pilfering. In December 1926, Levien estimated that the cost of getting a 50 pound load to Edie Creek was £1/15 shillings to £2/15 shillings.[15] Thus a 50 pound bag of rice that cost 12 shillings and 6 pence at Rabaul, and 15 shillings and 6 pence at Salamaua[16] cost miners as much as £3/10 shillings at Edie Creek.

The minimum wage for a New Guinean engaged as an indentured labourer for mining or carrying was 10 shillings per month, half paid monthly and the balance at the end of his contract, when miners also had to bear the cost of repatriating them to their villages.

The various requirements to which miners were subject in respect of their labourers also added to their costs. Each had to be supplied with two blankets if working above 2,000 feet and three above 5,000 feet, a box for his possessions, a bowl and a spoon. But the devil was in the detail. Not unreasonably, the minimum weight, length and breadth of blankets was specified. Diet scales for all labourers were also specified in great detail, with extra rations for those engaged in mining and carrying.

The Rabaul bureaucrats left little to chance, specifying the inside measurement of boxes, the depth of the lid, sides, ends and bottom, the dimensions of the blocks under the bottom corners, the stops inside for the lid, and even the size of the handles, hinges and screws. Bowls were to be 7 inches in diameter, 3 inches deep (though 2 ¾ inches was later deemed acceptable), made of blue or white enamel and weigh 8 ounces. Spoons were to be metal, 8½ inches long and weigh 1½ ounces. The issuer of any article not meeting these specifications was potentially subject to a £50 fine or six months imprisonment.[17]

The Mining Warden estimated the cost of employing

Gorge near Cliffside.

24 carriers and labourers at around £28 per week.[18] After allowing £4 a week for European rations and with gold returning about £2 per ounce after direct expenses (gold royalty, shipping costs and insurance), a miner needed to recover at least 16 ounces a week to break even.[19]

In the absence of any shops on the field in the early years, miners were critically dependent on an uninterrupted flow of supplies from Salamaua. Mick Leahy noted that

> food was the one thing that money couldn't buy on Edie Creek. The prospectors who were making a go of mining were mostly working in pairs, employing native contract labour. One man, with a line of boys, would work the claim, while his partner, with another line of boys … would be packing out stores from Salamaua.[20]

Others relied on an agent at Salamaua to acquire the food and other supplies they needed, pack them and despatch their carriers back to Edie Creek. Clem Hendry told the 1927 Royal Commission: *I handle all the boys that come down from the field, make ready their cargoes and pack them out again … for 27 different partnerships and individuals.*[21] This involved handling about a ton of food

Chisholm's house and miners' tents, Edie Creek 1926.

a week which had to be sourced wherever he could get it. Well over 1,000 carriers were despatched to the field in this way each month.

With supplies often difficult to obtain in the vicinity of Salamaua and ships arriving only infrequently, food shortages were common at Edie Creek. The lack of carriers necessary to transfer large volumes of food and other supplies needed on the field added to the miners' frustrations. The *Marsina* unloaded 61 tons of cargo at Salamaua in October 1925.[22] With an effective carrying rate of 30 pounds per carrier, 4,500 carriers would have been necessary to get this to Edie Creek. As a result of such logistical problems, food and other shortages persisted for quite some time, even after the commencement of air transport in April 1927.

Mining usually involved the use of sluice boxes. Each miner employed about eight or ten labourers stripping back the bush and overburden on his claim, digging or constructing water races, making sluice boxes, shovelling gravel through them and removing the tailings—all in extremely inhospitable weather.

Frank Pryke described Upper Edie Creek as 'a miserable kind of place'.[23] The sun shone weakly for no more than two or three hours a day, and when it wasn't raining it was cold and misty, the dense canopy perpetually dripping moisture in the still air. Labourers worked continually in cold, muddy conditions, the fortunate ones wearing oilskin coats and hats. The nights were intensely cold and uncomfortable; all firewood had to be fire-dried before it would burn.

Dysentery was endemic. In evidence to the Royal Commission in May 1927, the Director of Public Health, Dr Cilento, put this down to the predisposing factors of overwork, over-exposure and inadequate diet.[24] He expressed concern that most deaths were among labourers employed by Europeans who had no experience in mining.

After his arrival at Upper Edie Creek in mid-September 1926, Oakley saw some labourers

> sleeping on the wet ground, with a sail or tarpaulin over them. In some instances the boys were sleeping on pieces of wood, but the wood was directly on the ground which was wet. The whole place after 4 p.m. was enveloped in mist, and it was damp continually … from a native labour point of view, conditions could not have been worse.[25]

With labourers crowded together in inadequate, damp living quarters, it was hardly surprising that pneumonia was also rife.

Dr Dickson had specified that housing for labourers should be weatherproof and provide a place for a fire and a drying rack. These requirements later formed the basis for minimum housing arrangements prescribed under the Native Labour Ordinance. However, compliance with these requirements was rarely, if ever, supervised during the early years. Nor were the working conditions of labourers at Edie Creek monitored, much less controlled.

The mortality rate of labourers[26] in the Morobe District was 4.8% in 1926/27, compared with 1.9% elsewhere in New Guinea. Somewhat perversely, the Administration trumpeted in its 1932/33 Annual Report that, while pneumonia accounted for 37% of deaths, this was comparable with elsewhere in the Territory. This was

> actually gratifying evidence of the fact that the miners have made provision against the cold and wet conditions under which natives must work to a degree that has protected them from any increase in mortality rate from this disease.[27]

Aside from the fact that one might have expected better accommodation and less over-crowding to have led to a lower pneumonia mortality rate, six years after Dr Dickson's visit the overall mortality rate in the Morobe District, at 3.2%, still compared unfavourably with 1.2% elsewhere in New Guinea.

It was too cold to grow much food at Edie Creek, and fresh food was often unprocurable, making a mockery of the Administration's well-meaning dietary formulations. As most miners had small claims which were quickly worked out, there was no incentive for them to grow food such as kaukau, taro, etc. at lower altitudes.

Labourers were thus often dependent on white rice, resulting in a high incidence of beriberi that contributed directly or indirectly to the high mortality rate. The Administration endeavoured to induce miners to substitute beans, nuts and wheat flour for the rice, and supplement their diet with cod liver oil, malt or marmite, but with limited success. Even when such items were available, their cost discouraged miners from providing them to labourers, particularly the two thirds who were not on payable gold. In its 1932/33 Report, the Administration rationalised the high mortality rate, in part, as being due to *the rejection of food essentials provided by the white miner, but foreign to the native and hence suspect.*[28]

⸺

While not a poor man's field, Edie Creek attracted many men who had neither the financial resources to sustain themselves nor the experience to manage a team of labourers in difficult circumstances. The Administration was undoubtedly concerned at the plight of labourers, but particularly in the early years its efforts to deal with the causes met with limited success.

In later years, companies employed most of the labour on the field, and in general they were better at caring for their workforces. By this time the Administration was also better organised, and it became more successful in ensuring compliance by all miners with requirements that would ensure acceptable living and working conditions for their labourers and carriers.

CHAPTER 6
COMPANIES AND CAPITAL

The Royal Commissioner appointed to enquire into the Edie Creek leases, Peter MacGregor, held 26 sittings at Rabaul and Salamaua in April–May 1927, at which 48 witnesses appeared.

In his evidence, the Administrator argued that the Mining Ordinance made inadequate provision for the discoverers to be rewarded, and that he had granted the Big Six an area that was less than half the area for which they had applied.

In his Report, published in August 1927, MacGregor noted Wisdom's view, but concluded that the grant of 33¾ acres as a reward was *clearly excessive*,[1] that only Royal and Glasson should have been ranked as discoverers and that a considerably smaller area *would still have been a generous recognition of the efforts and expenditure of the six members of the party*. However, he made no recommendation for a further reduction in the area granted.

MacGregor was not required to, and thus did not, adjudicate on the issue at the centre of the furore: the lack of a clear policy on the circumstances in which dredging or sluicing leases should be granted. He did, however, note that the Queensland Ordinance, on which the Territory's Mining Ordinance was based, reserved ordinary alluvial ground for the holders of Miner's Rights, *a well known practice under all mining laws*.[2] He added that it was difficult to avoid concluding that the provision giving the Administrator discretion to grant a dredging or sluicing lease, which was not in the Queensland Ordinance, had been *somewhat hastily inserted*.[3]

Nevertheless, he accepted that, as many difficulties associated with the field had been lessened by the granting of leases rather than claims, the Administrator had acted reasonably in this regard.

MacGregor concluded that *there was no lack of attempt to provide adequate administration*.[4] He sidestepped the issue of why an experienced Mining Warden had not been requested from Australia until well after the rush started, simply noting that staff shortages had *prevented the intended establishment of a competent officer on the field ... for some months prior to November 1926*.

Finally, despite the lack of preparation to meet the likely medical needs of miners and their labourers, and thus the Administration's dependence on Doris Booth's improvised hospital during the dysentery epidemic, MacGregor concluded that provision for the medical requirements of Europeans and natives *was not only complete and efficient but exceptionally so in view of the difficulties of such provision in the Territory*.[5]

Thus, apart from a slap on the wrist over his generosity to the Big Six, MacGregor broadly exonerated the Administrator. Whether political sensitivities discouraged a more penetrating assessment of Wisdom's performance is open to question. The Royal Commission had given the miners a forum to express their views, providing both a valuable safety valve and time for the Administration to take further action to defuse the situation. By the time MacGregor reported, the pressure for change had abated. A report criticising the Administration more directly may simply have reignited tensions and invited criticism from the League of Nations.

Despite the unrest, nearly 40,000 ounces of gold were produced during the last three months of 1926, mostly at Edie Creek. Miners continued to arrive, the number on the field peaking at 250 in January 1927, with a further 45 waiting at Salamaua. 3,250 New Guineans were mining or carrying in supplies.

By this time, most of the easy gold had been won and the high costs and difficult conditions at Edie Creek were taking their toll, particularly among less experienced miners. An exodus began, and by April, the number of Europeans had dropped to 160. The new Warden, J.D. McLean, who arrived in December 1926, observed a few months later that *many disgruntled miners have left the field declaring that all alluvial ground has been worked out. It is now apparent*

Merri Creek, near junction with Edie Creek, 1928-29. Day Dawn reef was discovered on hillside in trees behind tents, centre of picture.

that returns will only be made by competent miners.[6]

One of the major problems miners faced was obtaining an adequate supply of water for their sluice boxes. Over geological time, many small creeks on the Upper Edie Creek plateau had gradually cut their way down through the ground, leaving terraces of alluvial gravels high above the existing creeks. For miners willing to make the effort to bring water to these terraces there was good gold to be won.

To do this, they constructed races and flumes, often over considerable distances. One miner brought water 1½ miles through hollowed out karuka palms across other claims to his terrace, 30 feet above the bed of Edie Creek.[7]

Pandanus (karuka) palms grew up to 100 feet tall near the top of the Edie Creek-Watut divide. Jack O'Neill described how they were used for fluming: *The trunk was split into halves and the fibre within it knocked out with the back of the axe, leaving the strong semi-circular section shell, which is characteristic of palms.*[8] These could be laid on the ground the ground end to end or used to bridge uneven ground.

In April 1928, the Warden reported that ten men had banded together to construct a race about three miles long to get water onto their claims. It took six months

and cost £3,000. Such activities gradually led to the plateau being criss-crossed with water races.

But if water was the field's life blood, it was also a curse. The catchment area at Edie Creek was small and the run-off rapid, so that water shortages often hampered mining operations. Conversely, land slips due to heavy rain regularly demolished races and smothered claims with thousands of tons of debris. Sudden storms would result in a torrent of water, rocks and logs carrying all before it, not least miners' sluice boxes and other equipment, and smashing dams used to divert water from workings. Time and again, miners had to restart from scratch.

By early 1927, the hunt was on for the source of the alluvial gold—the mother lode or reef, though thick vegetation and the moss-covered ground made prospecting difficult. Each discovery of specimens where the gold was coarse—sharp and angular, unweathered by water action—brought a scramble of miners in the belief that the source was close by.

Finally, in May 1927, a gold bearing vein of quartz was discovered on the Royal lease, and in June, the rich Day Dawn reef was located about 300' above Merri Creek, near its junction with Edie Creek.

Ted Bishton recounted the story of its discovery:

One day Normie Neal came to me and showed me a lump of quartz about the size of a football. It was impregnated with gold and ... looked as though it had just broken off a very rich reef, as it was not water worn and had not travelled any distance.

After pegging six leases in the surrounding area,

we went prospecting to try to locate the lode. We were working up the side of the mountain, when my stick struck something hard. I thought it was the root of a tree, but looking around could see no tree near enough, so I raked away the moss, which was about three feet deep and there was the lode; my stick had struck an outcrop of the reef ... We broke off a lump of the reef and got

old Jimmy Jones to assay it for us. He said, on a very rough assay, it was 365 ounces to the ton, an ounce for every day of the year.[9]

Bishton washed a dish of rubble from the surface; it produced 19 ounces of gold.

The Day Dawn discovery generated a new burst of frenetic prospecting activity, and in the following months applications were made for several hundred gold mining leases. Before long several more reefs had been located. The likelihood that lode mining would augment alluvial mining looked encouraging.

Nevertheless, numbers on the field continued to dwindle. By November 1927, there were fewer than one third as many miners — around 75 — as there were on the field or at Salamaua in January, with a similar fall in the number of carriers and labourers, to about 850. Despite this, more than 100,000 ounces of gold were produced on the field during 1927, 95% of it in the upper Edie Creek area. The two largest producers were Edie Creek Pty Limited, which had been formed by the Big Six to work their leases, and Harry Darby. These two aside, each miner produced, on average, a reasonable 670 ounces, with nearly half producing 455 ounces, or about £1,000 in gold during the period.

Contributing to this outcome was the bizarre amendment to the Mining Ordinance in November 1926 to appease the miners, authorising the Warden to permit holders of Miner's Rights to peg claims on leases where the ground was subsequently found to be suitable for working by hand appliances. Any system which enabled ground to be worked by two different parties was clearly unsustainable, and was opposed by the new (and experienced) Warden, J.D. McLean. However, shortly before he arrived in December 1926, the Administrator directed that the new arrangements should apply to all leases in the Edie Creek area, leaving McLean with little choice but to issue permits where the circumstances warranted. In consequence, throughout 1927 the Big Six had to work their leases side by side with as many as 60 claim holders.

Mining techniques remained fairly primitive. The prohibitive cost of transporting petrol to the field and absence of electricity limited the use of machinery. While sluice boxes continued as the main method of winning gold, Edie Creek Pty Limited began using pipes and nozzles[10] late in 1927 to break up the ground by applying water under high pressure. These relied on gravitational feed rather than pumps.

Ground sluicing on South and Mateer's claim, Merri Creek, 1928.

By early 1928, little new alluvial ground was being discovered—though there were exceptions. During the first half of 1928, Clarence Williams and Frank Hunt, working an amalgamated claim of 400 by 100 feet, produced 7,088 ounces and 654 ounces of specimens in 84 days, with an estimated value of £16,602.

While many individual miners were drifting away, another 'rush' was beginning—one by wily promoters to float companies in Australia with a connection (real or imagined) to the Edie Creek discovery. At least 26 new companies were formed between 1927 and 1929, attracting a stream of investors eager for a share in the excitement, if not the discomfort of the field itself. The Manager of the Bank of New South Wales at Salamaua, Harry Johns, reported that many new companies *whose main asset is hope have been formed and shares sold without even preliminary investigation as to the gold content.*[11]

Some of these companies acquired claims from prospectors; others sent 'mining engineers' to New Guinea to locate prospective ground. Locals also got in on the act. Alice Innes, who managed the Salamaua Hotel, recalled some years later that

> a number of Administration officials on leave would pop out to Salamaua—en route south—peg and lodge a claim and then one would be amused to read the amazing reports in southern papers of their 'Adventures in the wilds of New Guinea' (rarely more than a toddle

over the nearest hill between drinks!) and the imposing looking mining prospectuses that evolved.[12]

While floats often closed heavily over-subscribed, few ever produced meaningful gold.

However, beneath such froth and bubble, a serious shift in mining activities was occurring, as Mick Leahy noted when working briefly as barman at the Hotel Salamaua on his return from Australia late in 1927.

> As I listened to idle gossip over the bar, I began to understand the extent of changes that had taken place in New Guinea during my absence, and others now in the making. The gold rush was over, and mining was entering on a new phase—that of big business. The talk was now mostly about dredging leases rather than claims. It had begun to appear that large, low grade deposits of alluvial gold along the larger streams, that could be worked with modern machinery handling hundreds of tons of gravel a day, were of much greater importance than rich but limited deposits on the creeks.[13]

This brought a new twist to the view that this was not a poor man's field. While individuals might eke out a living, companies with their greater capital were more likely to prosper. Political considerations may have induced Wisdom to adopt a more accommodating tone towards individual miners as a group, but he never wavered in his belief that ultimately the success of the field (and thus the potential growth of the Administration's revenue base) lay in the hands of companies, not individual miners.

Nevertheless, while capital improved the odds, it didn't guarantee success. One company with more than its share of water troubles was Upper Watut Gold Mining Pty Ltd. The firebrand deputy leader of the Australian Labor Party, Frank Anstey, and his close friend, the wealthy entrepreneur and gambler John Wren, were shareholders and Anstey made several trips to New Guinea in connection with its activities.

From early 1927, the company actively tried to develop

Hydraulic sluicing with nozzle or monitor.

Charles and Doris Booth, and Frank Anstey M.H.R., 1925.

an alluvial mine on the Watut, and over the next three years constructed a 5½ mile water race to provide water under pressure for two hydraulic jet elevators. But early in 1930, a flood swamped its workings. With the damage repaired, mining stopped in November because the river was too low to provide water to work the elevators. Then in February 1931, heavy rain caused two enormous landslips onto the race. By the time these had been cleared, the river was low again. Shortly thereafter its operations ceased and the company quietly disappeared.

Development of the reefs discovered during 1927 required more capital than individual miners could provide. It was therefore convenient that their discovery was followed by a visit in April 1928 of the mining engineer, W.H. Corbould, on behalf of the London-based Ellyou Goldfields Development Corporation. He arrived with an ambitious plan: to acquire options over alluvial and reef claims and leases right across the Edie Creek plateau and to use large scale capital to work them effectively.

Ellyou was a subsidiary of Russo-Asiatic Consolidated Ltd, which at this time was developing the large Mount Isa copper mine in North Queensland. The Chairman was Leslie Urquhart, from whose initials (LU) the company took its name.

Corbould spent several weeks in New Guinea acquiring options over leases and claims covering about 8 square miles, including the Big Six leases of Edie Creek Pty Ltd. His vision for their development matched the scale of his acquisitions: a company with a capital of at least £2.5 million, of which £1 million would be in working capital; a light railway from the coast to transport the heavy machinery required to develop the field; and a hydro-electric plant to generate the power required.

For miners with little capital, making do without power or decent mining equipment, Corbould's plans were breathtaking. The prospect of sharing in the benefits generated a sense of euphoria, convincing miners to accept shares in the new company rather than cash. However, realisation of Ellyou's vision was to prove infinitely more difficult than its conception.

The Warden was particularly enthusiastic about this new turn of events, observing in his April report that *this portion of the field is now entering upon the second phase of its existence, development by mining companies.* He refused applications thereafter from the holders of Miner's Rights for permits to enter and mine on dredging or sluicing leases as they clouded lease title, making it difficult for owners to dispose of their leases or to obtain capital to develop them.[14]

The appointment of Levien as Guinea Gold's Field Superintendent, in late August 1926, was soon followed by that of J.C. Coldham as the company's Mining Engineer. It was Coldham who had first tested the lower

Bulolo leases two years before, aroused Levien's interest in them and convinced Hebbard of their richness and magnitude. On 9 September 1926, Levien transferred Kaili 4 and the Koranga Creek leases to Guinea Gold. Acting with unusual speed, the Administrator agreed on 5 October to consolidate these into a single lease designated 'Guinea Gold'.

Levien was then allocated 6,500 £1 shares in the company, one quarter of the 26,000 shares on issue. Three weeks later he was appointed a Director.

Levien's plan was to work the Kaili and Koranga leases intensively to generate sufficient funds to cover the cost of testing and eventual development of the lower Bulolo leases. Within days of his appointment, he was moving to address issues he saw as critical to this outcome: the recruiting and feeding of labourers, ordering pipes and pumps so the leases could be worked more efficiently and establishing an aerial transport service.

By early November, he had recruited 73 labourers, in addition to the 70 already employed. He had 50 acres planted with corn, yams, bananas and kaukau, though until the crops matured Guinea Gold would be dependent on higher cost rice and other imported food. Levien's emphasis on food production was understandable, as each labourer consumed 8 to 10 pounds of kaukau daily — nearly ¾ ton of food.

In the absence of aerial transport, getting equipment to the leases was a major problem. Levien advised that the pipes should be in 5 foot lengths, weighing 50 pounds, the maximum permitted load. However, the Board decided to order them in 10 foot lengths, as this would halve the number of joints required. This was the first of several occasions when the Guinea Gold Board made decisions in the comfortable ignorance of their Adelaide boardroom without any real appreciation of circumstances on the field. Levien aside, none of the Board had ever been to New Guinea nor had any appreciation of how impractical it was for two carriers to manoeuvre each 10 foot pipe over the Gadagadu track.

Nor did the Board share Levien's enthusiasm for air transport. In August and again in October the Larkin Aircraft Supply Co. approached Guinea Gold, apparently at Levien's instigation; but its proposals were politely rebuffed as being too costly. However, two airmen, R.L. (Nobby) Clark and Ray Parer, were each proposing to establish a service to the goldfield if they could get the necessary financial support. Levien urged the Board to consider Clark's proposals, describing the potential profits as 'quite startling'.

It was perhaps inevitable that the Board's expectations and Levien's priorities would soon diverge. In November he reported that a large area of native foods had been planted as

> it is wasted effort to carry rice and food from the coast when, by organising a little less hastily, we can reduce our labour costs at least 40 per cent. I place our requirements at present in the following order: recruiting labour, food supplies, staff organisation, prospecting and testing wash, carrying in machinery, etc., and gold production.[15]

OFF TO NEW GUINEA GOLDFIELDS.—Mr. C. Levien and Mr. J. Coldham.

Cecil Levien and J.C. Coldham.

This obviously elicited a sharp response from Adelaide, as a month later he reported

> You are giving me a difficult job to keep gold production and such heavy developmental work going at the same time with the present amount of labour, but we will do our best.

Reiterating the importance of addressing the 'native food supply' issue, he added

> This is a country in which … work cannot be rushed, but must move along in unison with supplies … Unforeseen difficulties arise due to our lack of communication, and one must not gauge our work by southern times and methods. Organisation and production take time here … owing to our primitive and slow methods of transport.[16]

Never one to miss an opportunity, Levien also observed that

> only 17% of labour can be spared for gold production, but if the proposed establishment of an air service is realised, that proportion will be greatly improved. The cost of carriage would be reduced by nearly 90% and development and production greatly accelerated.

By December, the Board seems to have accepted that however rich the lower Bulolo leases may be, they would never be developed until there was an efficient transport link with the coast. It had a choice: wait until a road was constructed or adopt Levien's proposal to become involved in air transport. With the Administration showing little sign of commitment to a road, it finally bowed to Levien's pressure and on 30 December 1926 agreed to purchase a small De Havilland 37 biplane and ship it to New Guinea.

The other impediment to developing the leases was their ownership structure. Through options over leases held by nominees, Guinea Gold controlled about 11½ miles of the lower Bulolo River downstream from where the river emerged from the gorge. To develop them, however, the leases would need to be registered in Guinea Gold's name.

This posed a problem. While under the Mining Ordinance, the Administrator could not grant a lease of more than 240 acres, he could permit a party to hold any number of leases, without restriction as to the total area. However, this would require Guinea Gold to observe labour manning requirements on each lease rather than developing them as a group.[17] Alternatively, the Administrator could authorise the consolidation of holdings through the union of two or more contiguous leases so they could be worked more effectively. It was the latter power he had used in September 1926 to authorise consolidation of the Kaili and Koranga leases. Early in 1927, Guinea Gold's Chairman, Charles Wells, called on the Administrator when he was in Melbourne and sought approval for this.

While Wisdom was keen to assist, authorising the consolidation of ten leases for one company at a time when his decisions regarding the Big Six leases were about to be scrutinised by a Royal Commission would inevitably attract further criticism. However, he agreed to Guinea Gold holding the leases through three subsidiary companies. Thus in March 1927, Guinea Gold South N.L., Guinea Gold Central N.L. and Guinea Gold North N.L. were registered, with the Administrator subsequently approving the transfer of the leases to them. In July, nominees of Guinea Gold applied for a further 5 leases, and later these also were transferred to the three companies.

Guinea Gold's limited capital meant it relied on gold produced from the consolidated Kaili/Koranga lease to generate the revenue necessary to test the lower Bulolo leases—as Levien had always envisaged. To work the lease efficiently required a considerable head of water to allow the use of monitors or nozzles under high pressure. To this end, by early 1927, Coldham was constructing a water race to bring water three miles to Kaili from the Kulolo River, an upstream tributary of the Bulolo. This was no small engineering challenge, having to be constructed through dense jungle, on fluming across ravines and in places even suspended on the edge of precipices.

Before long, however, construction of the water race, as well as airstrips on the coast at Lae and on the field at Wau, was diverting labour from gold production, and stretching the company's financial resources to breaking point. Levien suggested calling up all the remaining capital, but the ever-cautious Board decided to issue a limited number of shares to existing shareholders, at a £1 premium, while seeking to contain costs.

With financial pressures intensifying, Guinea Gold accepted an offer in April 1927 from a Sydney-based syndicate, Territory Investments, for an option over the GG North leases. Its intention was to float a company in which Guinea Gold would retain an interest. Tom Horton, a mining engineer with considerable dredging experience in Malaya, assisted by another experienced miner, Tom Yeomans, were sent to undertake an independent valuation of the properties. They subsequently advised Territory Investments to replace this option with one over the Guinea Gold South leases, which were closer to Wau with its new aerodrome and thus more accessible. This was agreed, and an expiry date set for the option—31 March 1928.

Coldham was now transferred from his race construction activities to undertake the testing, with Horton checking his calculations and conclusions. On 6 June 1927, the Adelaide *Register* reported

> Intense testing of the wash on the large areas of the lower Bulolo Valley is now proceeding. To enable this work to be accelerated, all the company's engineers and white staff and the whole labour force of 150 natives is being employed.

By diverting its labour force from other activities to the Guinea Gold South leases, Guinea Gold was now effectively placing all its bets on Territory Investments' option being exercised.

In July, the continuing deterioration in Guinea Gold's financial position finally compelled the Board to issue the balance of its unissued capital. Knowing that it did not have the resources to develop the central and northern Bulolo leases in its own right, and encouraged by Territory Investments' option over the southern leases, it actively solicited the interest of London investors in the other leases, but without success.

Testing the leases was difficult and time consuming. Initially, it involved sinking about 50 shafts using hand pumps. When these were found to be ineffective below a depth of 8 to 10 feet, power pumps were brought in, enabling some shafts to go deeper. Finally, in late September, Coldham reported that Guinea Gold South had 400,000 cubic yards valued at 5 shillings per yard, and 5 million cubic yards at 2 shillings and 6 pence per yard. There was insufficient time to test a further 4 million yards, but he believed most of this was likely to be payable. In his final report in November, Coldham estimated that, with a dredge capable of handling 80,000 cubic yards per month, working costs were likely to be 6 pence per yard.

On 29 September 1927, after just a year as Director and Field Superintendent, Levien resigned both positions. His resignation as Field Superintendent was explained as being due to conviction that technical control was rapidly becoming essential. Coldham's role was also coming to an end amid ill-informed board frustration at the slowness of his work. Some months earlier, another mining engineer, E. Broughton Jensen, had been appointed to Guinea Gold's New Guinea staff, and he now took over from Levien as Field Superintendent.

With testing completed, Territory Investments and Guinea Gold agreed in early November 1927 on terms for a new company to acquire the Guinea Gold South leases. Territory Investments was to arrange for the float to be underwritten and for the company to be listed on the Sydney Stock Exchange. This would be conditional on receipt of an assurance from the Australian Government that a road would be constructed from the coast to the field without delay.

The outlook seemed positive and Guinea Gold now resumed construction of its water race to the Kaili lease, while continuing to work the Koranga leases with simple sluicing equipment.

But two major problems soon loomed. In early February 1928, Jensen informed the Board that the water race Coldham had designed and which was nearing completion was useless. Instead, he proposed that Guinea Gold should consider using an experimental aerial dredger he had invented to work the Kaili and Koranga leases.[18] At the same time, Territory Investments was having difficulty finding an underwriter for the float.

These events sent the Chairman, Wells, into a fit of depression and recrimination. On 13 February, he wrote to Levien:

> We have very largely been the victims of our advisers in this whole business. Coldham and Hebbard made a ruinous mess of our plant requirements … Kaili seems another mare's nest … As for the lower leases, we find they can't be sluiced or boxed payably. Alternative? A dredge. Cost prohibitive. Transport as experimental as Jensen's dredger and even less likely to succeed … Evidently the prime drawback has been, is now, and always will be the scarcity of boys … whereas one tenth of the cost of Coldham's blunders would have fitted out the most elaborate recruiting expeditions ever seen in N.G.[19]

In fact, Jensen appears to have contributed significantly to Guinea Gold's misfortunes.[19] While he was meant to be producing gold from the Kaili/Koranga leases, he devoted all his energies to experimenting with his aerial dredger, building a bridge across the Bulolo and organising food production.[20] He even went so far as to propose that Guinea Gold should divert labour to food production to meet the needs of the Edie Creek field, as this was more profitable than gold mining.[21]

On 13 March 1928, unable to arrange an under-

Guinea Gold's camp on the Bulolo, 1928.

writer for the proposed float, Territory Investments surrendered its option over Guinea Gold South.

Guinea Gold's solvency was now on the line. It was spending about £2,000 per month, and its reserves had dwindled to £5,000. Although earlier efforts to attract the interest of investors in London had been unsuccessful, the promising test results from the southern leases encouraged the Board to send one of its Directors, Dick Lapthorne, to London one last time to try to interest potential investors.

The mining expert who had advised Territory Investments, Tom Horton, regarded the southern leases as the richest gold-dredging proposition he had ever seen. Following the surrender of Territory Investments' option, he approached an Australian businessman, Addison Freeman, who was President of a small Canadian-based mining company, Placer Development. Horton knew Freeman well, having jointly owned a goldmine on the Coolgardie goldfields with his brother in the 1890s. He had also been closely involved with Austral Malay Tin, of which Freeman was a Director. Freeman listened, and was soon convinced.

On 26 April, the day Lapthorne was to leave for London, Freeman quietly appeared in Adelaide to meet with the Guinea Gold Board. Within 24 hours, Placer had secured a nine month option over all the lower Bulolo leases, for which it paid Guinea Gold £2,000. If exercised, Guinea Gold was to receive £50,000 (of which the £2,000 was part) and 10% of the issued capital of any operating company established to work the area.

Placer Development's option was the saviour of Levien's vision. Guinea Gold had tried hard but been ineffectual in progressing his ideas; it was simply too poorly capitalised and its Directors too inexperienced. However, the Placer Board comprised several mining engineers and, if it exercised its option, the operating company would be much larger than any Guinea Gold could have established.

Coincidentally, at precisely this time, W.F. Corbould was negotiating options over large tracts of upper Edie Creek, as well as Guinea Gold's Koranga and Kaili leases.

So, within the space of a couple of months, two companies acquired options over the main gold-bearing areas on the Morobe goldfields. The two operating companies they established were to dominate the field up to the War, though their fortunes could not have been more different.

CHAPTER 7
TRANSPORT TRIALS
AND TRIBULATIONS

The difference between the Guinea Gold Board, which lacked anyone with mining experience, and the Placer Development Board could not have been more stark.

Placer had been formed in Canada in May 1926 with an Australian, Addison Freeman, as President and the New Zealander Charles Banks as Managing Director.[1] Freeman was a businessman with long experience in mining and a director (later Chairman) of Austral Malay Tin, which dredged for tin in Malaya. Banks and the other Board members were all experienced mining engineers: two Americans Frank Griffin (an expert in dredge design) and Frank Short (an expert in gold recovery), and an Australian, Leslie Waterhouse, who joined the Board shortly after Placer acquired its option over the lower Bulolo leases, having held various technical and senior managerial mining positions.

Placer made the exercise of its option over Guinea Gold's leases conditional not only on confirming their value by further testing, but also on satisfactory resolution of the transport problem. Without efficient transport, it would be unable to import dredging and other equipment necessary to work the leases on a large scale.

While the distance from the coast was not great, any road to the Bulolo Valley would have to bridge many fast-running streams and skirt or climb jungle-clad mountains that were prone to landslips due to frequent earth tremors and high rainfall. The engineering challenge and uncertainty as to the Administration's attitude prompted Placer to insist on the right to extend its option by up to 18 months in the absence of an adequate transport link, after which it would be entitled to a refund of its £2,000.

In April 1928, air transport in New Guinea was barely twelve months old. Comprising a few small ex-World War I biplanes, there was no reason to believe aviation offered an effective alternative to road transport. A fortnight earlier, a new plane—a Junkers W34—had made its maiden flight in New Guinea. However, its payload of 2,000 pounds, though larger than that of the biplanes, was still much too small to carry heavy dredging machinery.

Placer's option included 17 leases covering 2,509 acres along 11½ miles of the Bulolo River. The property comprised two sections, the upper or southern flat and the lower or northern flat, separated by a gorge. Over millions of years, the southern flat was a catchment area for alluvial wash brought down river along with gold eroded from the reefs high up on Mt. Kaindi and extruded through Koranga and Edie Creeks. The river slowed on leaving the gorge, allowing the gold to settle, and as it meandered across the valley, changing its course periodically over many years, the gold was distributed widely. Payable concentrations were found later on terraces at the margins of the valley, the residue from a time when the river was much higher.

In June 1928, Placer despatched two experienced American mining engineers, Louis Decoto and his assistant Louis Joubert, to test the ground. They arrived in September at Wau, the location of the only airstrip on the field, with a considerable quantity of drilling equipment, which they then carried down through the gorge to the southern leases, a day's walk over a rough and difficult track. Decoto's task was to establish whether there were sufficient reserves to justify Placer exercising its option and establishing an operating company to mine them. His drills were all hand drills—hardly ideal, given their limited ability to drill at depth; but in the absence of any power other than manpower, he had no choice.

Dense jungle made moving equipment around the leases difficult, although the altitude, 2,250 feet, largely spared them the high temperatures normally associated with the tropics. Testing proceeded slowly, to Decoto's frustration. By April 1929, however, values were exceeding Placer's expectations. The fact that they were very even across the testing area meant fewer drill holes were needed and engendered greater confidence in the accuracy of his results. This encouraged Placer to apply for leases over a further 728 acres to the west of the Guinea Gold leases.

In his report dated 22 August 1929,[2] Decoto estimated that the southern leases, which covered 1,102 acres over 4½ miles of the Bulolo River and surrounding flats, contained 39 million cubic yards of dredgeable gravel, with an average depth of 22 feet and recoverable gold of 2 shillings and a penny per cubic yard.[3]

He strongly recommended that Placer exercise its option over the property, which he said was sufficiently large to justify two dredges, each with 8½ cubic yard buckets. Together they would handle 3 million cubic yards per year, at a cost not exceeding 7 and a half pence per cubic yard. Decoto suggested any testing of the northern leases be delayed until a permanent camp had been established.

The transport problem remained unresolved. The issue of a road from the coast had troubled the Administration since 1925, when it first made a budgetary provision of £500 towards this. In November 1926, surveyor Ted Sheldon undertook a preliminary assessment for the Administration and determined that it was possible to construct a 45 mile road from Salamaua to Wau with a 1:12 grade. Six months later, he started surveying the route. But in August, as he was nearing the end, the Administrator suddenly (and apparently unilaterally) decided that a road following the Buang track would present fewer difficulties—although no survey of the route had ever been undertaken. Before long 400 labourers were working on the road, and the Administrator was giving public assurances that the Buang road would be ready to carry heavy wheel traffic by the end of 1928.

In fact, the road was a fiasco. Several men tried to progress the work and failed. A road master who inspected the route early in 1928 concluded that to construct it would require 32 bridges. A surveyor was even more scathing, claiming that it was impractical economically and an engineering impossibility.

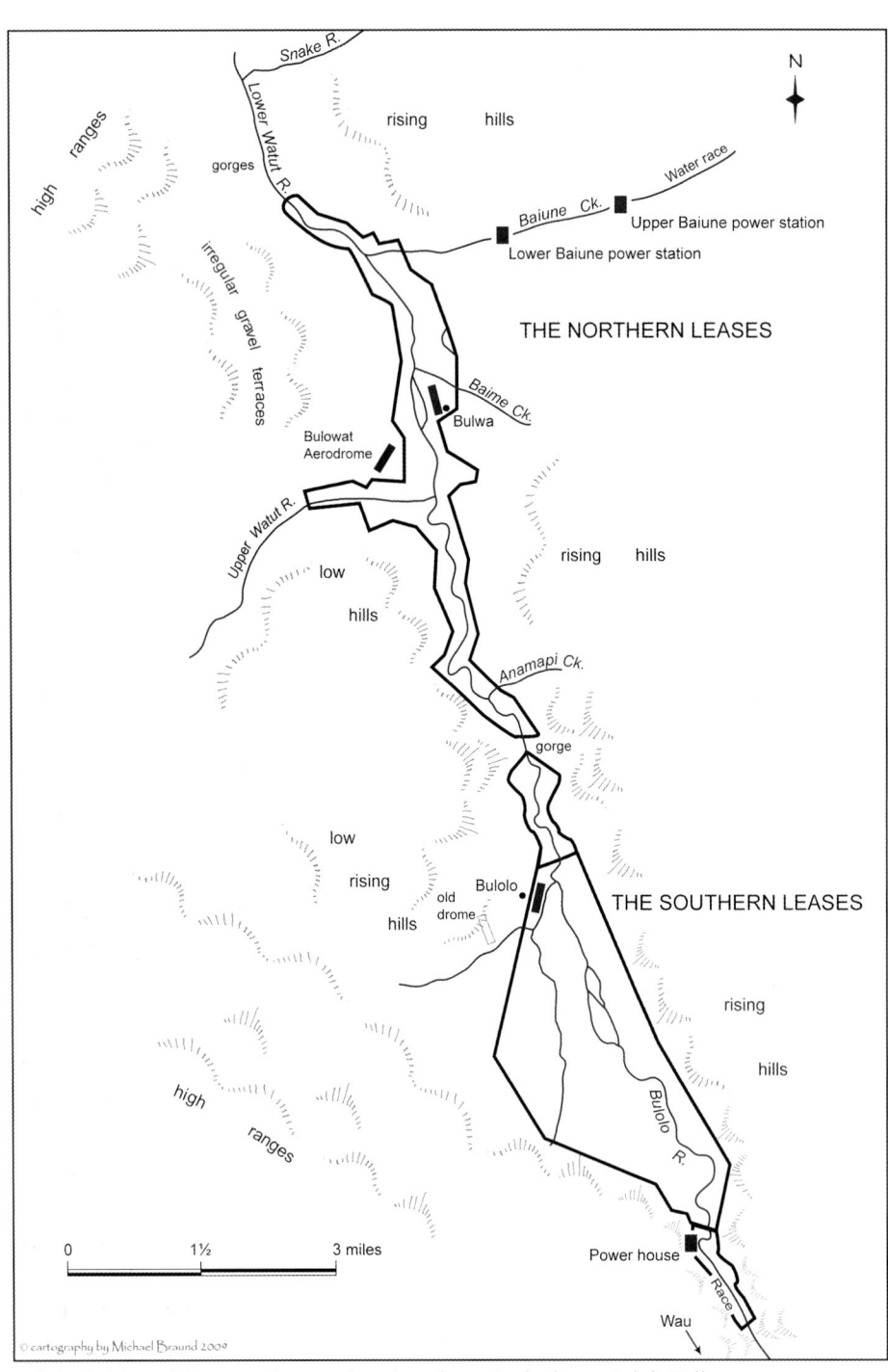

Bulolo Gold Dredging—southern and northern leases in the lower Bulolo Valley.

Bulolo Central Camp, 1929.

In February 1928, the Administration took the opportunity afforded by the absence in Australia of many individual miners during a period when manning requirements had been suspended, to increase the royalty on gold from 1% to 5%.[4] It gave as the reason the need to meet the costs of administering the goldfield and the construction and maintenance of roads – which was widely interpreted to mean a road from the coast.

The Miners' Association tartly cabled the Minister for Home and Territories: *We have witnessed abortive efforts of Administration here trying to construct roads during past twelve months. To date not a foot [of] any useful road is available.*[5] But at least it appeared that the Administration was finally serious about moving things forward.

Nothing could have been further from the truth. Wisdom's frustration with the Buang road, with criticism of the gold royalty increase and with the financial straitjacket in which his Administration was forced to work, spilled over in a radiogram to the Minister on 14 March: *Edie Creek cannot be regarded as having [a] long life. Reef or lode not proved and may not develop. Nothing therefore on Edie Creek warrants large expenditure on road.* [The Bulolo and Watut] *area is also not proved and is of doubtful payabilities* [and] *does not warrant heavy expenditure on road.*[6]

The Buang route was

impassable [for transport of machinery] in reasonable time or at a reasonable cost. Work has consequently been stopped ... [I have] personally visited [the] area ... and have reorganised [the] whole plan with [the] object [of] get[ting] [a] location for [a] rough tractor or caterpillar road within our means ... Remember we have no money [for] these works nor for [a] wharf which [is] of much greater importance to [the] Territory.

Wisdom was uncharacteristically emotional about what he regarded as a lack of support from the Commonwealth:

This territory cannot finance heavy expenditure on such roads, even if justified by development. Your Government will not help though deriving nearly all the benefit from gold produced ... If we are expected to do things [we] must be given means to do them [or be] allowed to create means. [The] Government has so far denied us both ... [The] only substitute for [a] royalty is [a] grant from the Commonwealth.

This tirade led the Department of Home and Territories to remind Wisdom that the Minister had promised several mining companies that every effort would be made to expedite construction of a road to the goldfields, work that was now urgent if faith were to be kept with them.[7] Wisdom acquiesced, saying that, given the royalty increase, it was likely a considerable sum could be provided for the road in the following financial year.

Soon afterwards he selected a new route—again apparently without any detailed assessment or advice. This time, the road was to come up the coast from Salamaua to Lae, into the Markham Valley, through the Wampit and Zenag and on to the Bulolo Valley and Wau. Wisdom advised Placer Development of this new proposal on 10 May 1928.

Surveyor Sheldon, who had been shuttled back and forth between the three alternative routes and was getting increasingly frustrated at the Administrator's indecisiveness, estimated that the road would be about 100 miles long and involve expensive engineering, particularly the crossing of the Markham River.[8] It would have to cut through 18 miles of granite outcrops and traverse swampy flats. Nevertheless, 160 labourers and two Europeans were working on the new road by the end of May.[9] Six months later, the Administrator reported that considerable preliminary survey work had been completed, and jungle cleared over a 26 mile stretch from Lae.[10]

The Administrator's commitment to the road was, however, always open to doubt. So when Ellyou submitted a formal proposal in December 1928 for a light railway from Salamaua broadly following the same Markham route, and set about surveying it, the pressure to build a road eased—in Wisdom's mind, at least. While some work on the road continued during 1929, little tangible progress was made.

In December 1929, Levien walked back to Lae from a prospecting expedition to the Upper Ramu, so he could assess progress on the road. He was horrified by what he saw:

> I regret to report that in the whole trip the worst walking and roads I encountered were on this supposed strip of much advertised road. For gross incompetence, waste of money, lack of brain, local knowledge, commend me to the powers that be. This road is a monumental example of the above qualities … [The road] starts at about 22 miles from Lae … On this stretch there are 80 natives and 3 whites and as all the foodstuffs and supplies have to be portered by boys from the beach [Salamaua] you can see the absurdity of starting a road in the middle … Why on earth the Govt. do not start the road at the beach end and make it as they go and use the tractors and motor lorries on it as it progresses is not quite patent … After 5 years of much advertised effort a motor lorry can go up the road in fine weather about 2½ miles with

a load and in wet weather cannot be taken out of the shed, and this after an outlay of well over £30,000 …

Levien had little doubt about where the blame lay:

> … until we get an Administrator with a mind larger than that of a cockroach and a vision in proportion we shall retrogress.[11]

By April 1929, Placer was becoming increasingly alarmed about the transport issue. Freeman and Waterhouse held separate meetings with the Administrator, but were left with little confidence that they could expect satisfactory progress with the road. Freeman went so far as to cable Banks in Vancouver suggesting that Placer should seriously consider abandoning the project.

But Banks was not one to give up so easily, particularly as the initial testing was so encouraging. He therefore decided to visit New Guinea with Frank Griffin to see things for himself. At the same time, Placer sent a leading Australian road engineer to New Guinea to review the Administration's Markham route. By early October, he had reported that the 90 mile road would take two years to complete and cost £225,000.

Banks arrived in Australia in September 1929 and, before leaving for New Guinea, had discussions with Pard Mustar, the pilot who had begun Guinea Gold's air service in New Guinea 2½ years before. Ill health had forced Mustar to resign earlier in the year, though he was still an adviser to the Board of Guinea Airways (as Guinea Gold's air service was now known). On a trip to Germany late in 1927, Mustar had been shown drawings of a new three engine passenger aircraft, the Junkers G31, which Junkers's design staff believed could be reconfigured to lift three tons, loading through a hatch on top of the fuselage. This had convinced him that air transport was the key to future large scale development of the field.

Mustar told Banks it would probably take three years for the road to be constructed and its cost would far exceed that of improving the aerodrome at Lae, building a new one at Bulolo and purchasing two G31 aircraft and spares. Using aircraft, revenue would also be earned much earlier, as the first dredging plant would begin arriving at the site within a year of being ordered. In New Guinea, Levien met with Banks and Griffin, and echoed Mustar's views, strongly advocating that Placer should come to a working arrangement with Guinea Airways.

Despite Mustar's and Levien's enthusiasm, Banks remained committed to a road. He was well aware that aviation had never been used anywhere on the scale necessary if Placer were to adopt their proposal. In October 1929, he wrote to Wisdom proposing that, if the Administration waived gold royalties for 13 years, Placer would construct a road costing £200,000 and capable of carrying individual items of up to 5 tons.[12] The estimated present value of these royalties was £102,000, so Placer would end up paying about half the total cost. Wisdom flatly rejected this proposal.

Back in Australia the following month, Banks and Griffin met with Prime Minister Scullin, who agreed that the Government would make £40,000–£50,000 available towards the cost of the road. A few days later, Banks informed a meeting of Placer Development shareholders that the company had agreed to construct the road over two years at a cost of not more than £225,000, and that an operating company to mine the leases would be formed immediately.

By this time, however, world stock markets were in freefall following the collapse of Wall Street in the last week of October 1929. This introduced an entirely new consideration. In normal times, investors might be prepared to invest in a new operating company and wait two years or more for a road to be built through difficult country so that dredging equipment could be brought to Bulolo. But in such uncertain times this was unlikely. The aviation option offered the prospect of an earlier return and so was likely to be more attractive to risk-averse investors. Accordingly, on 4 December, Freeman wrote to Guinea Airways enquiring about the possibility of transporting dredging machinery of up to 5 tons by aeroplane.

Meanwhile, Mustar, in the course of a private flying engagement, found himself at the Hotel Australia in Sydney, where Banks and Griffin were staying.[13] At a breakfast meeting on 8 December and again the following day, Mustar answered innumerable questions put to him by four Placer Directors — Freeman, Banks, Griffin and Waterhouse. Mustar believed the air operation would cost no more than £80,000 to establish, compared with £250,000 for a road, and the dredges could be earning revenue nearly two years sooner.[14] He didn't know whether the Junkers G31 aircraft could be modified to handle the weight and awkward shapes of some dredge parts, but agreed to cable the Junkers factory to find out.

Years later, Mustar told Ian Grabowsky that

Banks advised him confidentially that, due to the world depression, isolation of Bulolo, and failure of other parties to agree to share the costs of road construction, many of his other financial associates had gone cold on the whole proposal.[15]

Grabowsky recorded that Banks

was now prepared to drop the road scheme and go all out for air transport, but to justify such a decision, he needed Mustar to convert Freeman, Waterhouse and Griffin, so that a unanimous recommendation could be presented to their financial associates.

On 19 December 1929, the Placer and Guinea Airways Boards met in Melbourne to discuss the basis for a working arrangement should air transport be used. They agreed in principle that Guinea Airways would supervise the transport to the Bulolo of two dredges and one power plant weighing approximately 2,500 short tons on two G31s. For this Placer would pay a management fee of £12,500 or £5 per ton.

On 22 December, Mustar attended a breakfast conference with Banks and Griffin at the Menzies Hotel. He conveyed advice from Junkers that they could adapt the G31 to provide a cargo cabin capable of carrying up to 7,000 pounds of freight with a large hatch in the roof of the cabin, allowing it to be loaded by crane. The first plane could be delivered in six months, the second two months later, each at a cost of £31,000.

Discussion then turned to whether the main dredge pieces, the shaft and tumbler, which were usually cast in one piece and weighed between 7 and 8 tons, could be made separately, flown in and then assembled on the field, and whether the planes could carry these and several large gear wheels, because of their dimensions.

Griffin, the dredge design expert, conceded that the tumbler and shaft could be made separately and assembled without loss of strength. But whether they and the other items could be flown in on a G31 was less easily resolved.

Mustar realised that a scale model was the only way to break the impasse. He worked into the night with the Junkerss representative in Australia and a professional model builder and at breakfast the following day presented a model of the plane's cargo compartment and dredge pieces. For the next hour and a half, Banks and Griffin played like boys with a Meccano set, loading and unloading dredge pieces suspended by cotton thread, taking care to ensure they could be loaded over the plane's centre of gravity.

Finally Griffin was satisfied. In response to his

Railway survey party, Zenag, in the Buang mountains.

further question, Mustar said it should not take more than 15 minutes to load or unload the plane, though a high speed pressure refuelling system would need to be installed at Lae or refuelling would take longer than loading. With the Lae-Bulolo leg taking 45 minutes and Bulolo-Lae 30 minutes, a round trip should take 1¾ hours, permitting several trips a day.

Banks now had the full support of Freeman, Griffin and Waterhouse for the air transport option. It was a dramatic and courageous decision, as the success of the project would depend critically on whether two planes could fly in an enormous quantity of plant and equipment on a tight timetable. Such a task had never before been achieved anywhere in the world.

While the Placer Development transport story was playing out, Ellyou was confronting its own transport issues, but in a very different way.

In April 1928, Corbould met with Mustar and proposed a two year contract for Guinea Airways to carry all the freight of the proposed operating company at 6 pence per pound, or half the prevailing rate.[16] Corbould threatened that, if it did not agree, Ellyou would buy its own aeroplane. When this 'offer' was rejected, Corbould switched his attention to the possibility of a railroad to transport heavy machinery from the coast. Broughton Jensen, Guinea Gold's Field Superintendent, wrote to the Secretary of Guinea Gold on 11 May 1928, *He has adopted my strong recommendation to build a jetty at Salamaua and put in a railway from that point via the Markham valley, Wampit valley and Bulolo valley right up to Wau and later from Wau to Edie.*[17]

Ellyou never set out to do things by halves. From the outset, hubris was characteristic of the company's actions. It had grand plans and was not reserved about publicising these. Guinea Airways had got an early taste of its arrogance and the Administration was soon to experience it as well.

Following Corbould's arrival back in London, Ellyou decided to send one of its directors, the mining engineer Arthur Dickinson, to investigate the Edie Creek area further, as a prelude to floating an operating company. Arriving in September, Dickinson was excited by the field's promise, and proceeded to acquire further leases both on the plateau and in an area below it and closer to Wau. By the time of his departure in late January 1929, he had increased the area over which Ellyou had options from around 8 to more than 13 square miles.

Dickinson's other objective was to sort out the transport problem. He held further—equally unproductive – discussions with Guinea Airways, rejecting not only compromise terms of 9 pence per pound but also an offer to become a major shareholder in the airline and take a seat on the Board.

Another major sticking point arose from the fact that, while Lae's aerodrome was located close to the waterfront, ships were reluctant to offload cargo there due to its lack of a natural harbour. They preferred the sheltered, if shallow, waters of Salamaua, though the only room for an aerodrome there was a small flood-prone area near where the Francisco River emptied into Bayern Bay. While Ellyou baulked at the cost of trans-shipping goods to Lae for on-forwarding by air, Guinea Airways was unwilling to operate from an aerodrome at Salamaua in such an unsuitable location.

Dickinson disagreed with Guinea Airways' assessment, and decided that Ellyou would construct an aerodrome itself at Salamaua, for use by its own plane, and would survey the route for a light railway, along the route proposed by Corbould and Jensen. By January 1929, construction of the aerodrome was under way.

In November 1928, Jensen had advised the Guinea Gold Board that he would be resigning as from 1 January to undertake the survey of the proposed light rail route for Ellyou.[18] Dickinson wrote to the Administrator on 5 December, seeking permission to construct and operate the proposed line.[19] Arguing that it would open up not only a rich goldfield but also country with great agricultural and timber possibilities, he sought various concessions in compensation for the large financial risks involved. In particular, the proposed operating

company should have a right of way 1,000 metres wide between Salamaua and Wau, with the company having the right to all minerals within its boundaries. It would also have free use of timber, stone and other materials necessary for the line's construction and maintenance, and absolute discretion over freight charges.

Dickinson concluded:

I regret extremely that I have still not had an opportunity to meet your Honour and to discuss the various matters that we should be mutually interested in, but it is quite impossible for me to leave the field until my return to England.

His imperious manner and list of demands were hardly likely to endear him to the status-conscious Administrator, who was used to those wanting concessions beating a path to his Rabaul door.

After Dickinson's departure in January, Ellyou had no senior representative on the field. Nevertheless, Jensen's survey continued, taking about nine months. However, with a length of 166 miles, much of it through country prone to landslips, and involving many bridges and tunnels, it became clear that the cost of construction and maintenance would be far too great. Ellyou briefly considered the possibility of an aerial ropeway over the mountains, capable of carrying 2,000 tons per day, and linking with a tram line at the Salamaua end, but in the end concluded that this too was unlikely to be financially viable.

In the continuing absence of meaningful progress with the Administration's Markham road, but with an aerodrome under construction at Salamaua, Ellyou

The Handley Page Hampstead.

decided in March 1929 to charter a 14 passenger, three engine Handley Page Hampstead biplane which had been flying on the Paris-London route and was renowned for its speed in level flight. This plane was soon to provide the new operating company with a lesson in aviation economics.

Ellyou's long-awaited operating company, New Guinea Goldfields (NGG), was incorporated in Sydney on 25 July 1929, with authorised capital of £5¼ million—the largest mining company ever floated on an Australian stock exchange. In the following months, most of Ellyou's options were exercised and transferred to the new company, with the vendors usually paid in NGG shares. Major G.A. Harrison was appointed its first General Manager.

Mustar maintained that the most critical issue for the efficient transport of air cargo was ease and speed of loading and unloading, minimising time on the ground.[20] Given the mountainous terrain, he also believed speed of level flight was less relevant than the rate of climb. The Handley Page was to prove him right on both counts.

The plane was crated to Port Moresby, where it was assembled before being flown to Salamaua early in September. It had a 79 foot wingspan and a maximum payload of 3,200 pounds and could do the Salamaua-Wau trip in 25 minutes. However, it was deficient in the two elements Mustar believed were the most important.

First, the Handley Page was designed to carry passengers rather than freight and had not been modified for the latter. Loading and unloading were through the passenger door on the side of the fuselage, limiting the scope to use a crane and requiring considerable time and manual effort. Second, the plane had a slow rate of climb, a major disadvantage given the high mountains between Salamaua and Wau. As a result, it could only fly an average of two round trips per day.

In his discussions with Banks, Mustar was at pains to emphasise that the Handley Page was far from what he had in mind when advocating air transport to meet Placer's needs.

Already critical of Ellyou's lack of co-operation with Guinea Airways, Levien was scathing of NGG's aviation venture. In July 1929, he reported to Guinea Gold that Salamaua aerodrome had already cost well over £11,000 and could only be used for a few months a year, due to flooding by the Francisco River.[21] In October, a month after the Handley Page had begun flying, he reported that it was costing NGG up to 2 shillings per pound, three times the rate charged by Guinea Airways.[22] Before long, NGG sought Guinea Airways' assistance with its freight, and in the first four months of 1930, Guinea Airways earned one quarter of its gross revenue carrying freight the Handley Page couldn't handle.[23] The poorly conceived attempt by NGG to carry its own airfreight ended when the plane crashed, without loss of life, between Salamaua and Wau on 31 May 1930.

This less-than-happy experience discouraged NGG from acquiring another plane, reducing its options to one: Guinea Airways. A deal was soon done for Guinea Airways to fly all of NGG's requirements at the rate of 6 pence per pound. Although none of its competitors had the capacity to meet NGG's requirements and it could have set a higher rate, Levien persuaded Guinea Airways to take a longer term view. But even this lower rate did not make for a comfortable working relationship, with NGG continually pressuring Guinea Airways for lower freight rates in the years that followed.

NGG did make one last effort to free itself from dependence on others for its transport needs when, in August 1930, it proposed a similar arrangement to the Administration to Placer Development's proposal in October 1928—to pay for half the cost of a road subject to a release from royalty payments. The Administration was no more sympathetic than it had been to Placer.

Had NGG agreed with Placer to share the cost of a road at that early stage, the goldfields story during the 1930s would have unfolded very differently.

CHAPTER 8
GEARING UP

1928 and much of 1929 provided a last opportunity for those miners who had given Ellyou options over their claims and leases.

They were still entitled to work them and, not unreasonably, wanted to leave as little gold as possible for their new owner. So for 15 to 18 months the goldfields were a hive of activity. Although only 67 miners made gold declarations at Edie Creek in 1928, half as many as in 1927, gold production was only slightly less for the whole district, at 104,504 ounces.

Edie Creek Pty Ltd, which the Big Six had formed to work their leases, produced a stream of gold. Month after month, the Mining Warden reported excellent, if uneven, returns. Thus, in September 1928, the Glasson lease yielded 1,215 ounces from 1,410 cubic yards, the Chisholm lease on Merri Creek 1,637 ounces from 3,830 yards and the George lease 443 ounces from 4,600 yards.

Miners still very much in business included Harry Darby, with his Eldorado lease, Hector Wales, who owned the Cleopatra lease and Yorkie Booth, who worked the neighbouring Queen of Sheba lease, while Doris continued to work Cliffside down on the Bulolo. Nevertheless, the number of miners declaring gold at Edie Creek declined further to 33 in 1929, with gold production falling 30%, to 72,623 ounces, most of which was mined prior to NGG exercising its options.

Ellyou's main priorities in 1928 were to sort out its transport problems and extend the area over which it had options. From early 1929, it shifted to establishing the infrastructure needed to begin mining activities.

Edie Creek, 1928. The offices of the 'Big Six' are on the right.

Doris Booth, Hector Wales and carriers.

The six months prior to the formation of NGG in July was a period of great activity. Forty five Europeans and 324 labourers were employed at Wau and Edie Creek constructing stores, offices and accommodation. At Salamaua, construction proceeded on a wharf and the new aerodrome; the railway survey was under way, while a mule track was being cleared on Mt. Kaindi between Wau and Edie Creek.

In the latter half of 1929, NGG set about exercising its options over leases and claims. It was said to have paid £1½ million for these, mostly in shares, including £500,000 for the Big Six leases, while Guinea Gold received £90,000 in shares for its Kaili and Koranga Creek leases and others it held at Edie Creek.

Having exercised its options, NGG was confronted with manning requirements imposed under the Mining Ordinance. Leslie Urquhart highlighted their archaic nature when he claimed in August 1929 that, if these were enforced, NGG would need to employ 809 Europeans on its leases.[1] He bluntly asserted that it

could not undertake to spend the capital it had raised so long as its leases were liable to forfeiture through the imposition of such requirements.

Urquhart requested that the Ordinance be amended to enable mining tenements with an aggregate area of not less than 5,000 acres to be proclaimed a 'special area' and exempted from normal labour covenants. The Administration was already well aware of the problem; over the previous 18 months it had fielded a steady flow of Guinea Gold applications for exemption from manning requirements on its lower Bulolo leases.

With the Depression beginning to bite, the Administrator realised that if he did not co-operate, there would be no golden egg — no large future royalty stream — from this particular goose. The Mining Ordinance was duly amended in February 1930, enabling the Minister (rather than the Administrator) to declare tenements of not less than 2,000 acres to be a Special Area where he was satisfied they could only be developed on a large scale. The holder of such an area would be required to spend at least £3 per acre per annum on mining operations or development work.

In April 1930, the Administrator wrote to the Secretary, Prime Minister's Department, supporting NGG's application for its tenements to be declared a Special Area, as this would enable the leases to be developed *as one big proposition – to my mind the only effective and economic method reasonably possible.*[2] It was not until August 1931, however, that the Minister finally declared NGG's holdings as a Special Area. In the interim, the Administration provided NGG with all the manning exemptions it required.

The delay was due to the difficulty assessing just how large an area NGG had acquired. It owned more than 200 claims and leases, but these were of several types and many different shapes and sizes. An inquiry into the mining industry concluded in June 1931 that NGG's holding was 5,000 to 6,000 acres rather than the 10,000 acres it had paid for.[3]

The problem stemmed from the lack of adequate surveys. Applicants for claims and leases had to pay a survey fee, but there was a long delay before surveys were done, if indeed they were ever done at all. The Administration found it difficult to attract sufficient surveyors to New Guinea, even after the onset of the Depression. The 1931 Inquiry also pointed to difficulties associated with the irregular pegging and over-pegging of leases by the original holders, noting that *the ruggedness of the landscape features and the dense jungle ... makes the progress of surveying operations very slow and difficult.*[4]

The effects of the surveying problem had been highlighted three years earlier, when *The Bulletin* reported that

> the map of the field represents a crazy patchwork quilt, with dredging and sluicing leases covering it at all angles and running in every direction while, following on discovery of lode near the falls on Glasson's lease, a rush of gold mining lease applications occurred and were squeezed into every nook and interstice. ... The most recent map of the field shows some of the areas applied for, or even granted, overlapped by as many as six others.[5]

While this was being sorted out, NGG commenced extensive testing of its leases. In a speech in London in November 1929, Leslie Urquhart was enthusiastic about NGG's prospects.[6] On the Edie Creek plateau, the area close to Wau and the intervening hillside,

> many gold veins have been found varying in width and richness. Our exploration work [has] ... revealed formations which promise to develop into important ore bodies, while the high values of the ore thus far found place this field in an exceptional class.

> We are pressing on with ... the work of systematically filling in and correlating the many exposures on the lines of strike of the different ore bodies, proving their lengths, average widths and depths by underground work ... The company is concentrating on proving tonnage by sinking prospecting pits and tunnels and drives, to expose ore formations, though there is a thick overburden of roots, moss and trees which makes prospecting work slow and difficult.

What Urquhart didn't say was that gold production had virtually ceased on NGG's leases. Given the scale of its holdings, the effect was a rapid slowing of activity on the field from mid-1929.

Faced with the prospect of joining growing unemployment queues back in Australia, many miners who had sold out to NGG sought and obtained employment with the company. But for others, the lifestyle of the independent miner continued to exert a strong pull. There had been a widely held expectation that NGG would lease to tributers whatever alluvial ground it didn't work itself – letting miners work the ground for a percentage of the gold won. Its decision not to do so aroused much antipathy among miners towards NGG and also towards the Administration for condoning this by exempting it from manning requirements.

With little mining possible around Edie Creek, many miners began to look further afield – in the process exploring country never before visited by Europeans. In September 1929, Bill Chapman discovered gold at Hidden Valley, at 8,500 feet, about 15 miles south-east of Edie Creek, near the headwaters of the Watut River. Forty or so miners trudged for three days through difficult country to get there. However, few stayed long, as there was little gold, the conditions were unbearable – with intense cold and constant rain – and most of their labourers deserted. Other miners moved further down the Watut River and began exploring its tributaries, with limited success.

In August 1930, Bill Anderson reported the discovery of payable gold on a tributary of the Bitoi River he named Black Cat Creek. It was a narrow creek winding through dank jungle for about 3½ miles on the coastal fall of the Kuper range, east of Wau towards Salamaua.

Looking down Merri Creek, 1928. Day Dawn workings on left.

Word rarely travels faster than when gold is discovered, and about 30 miners had pegged the whole creek by the time the Assistant Warden, Harold Taylour, got there two days later. The gold was of high quality, worth £3/15 shillings an ounce, compared with £2/4 shillings at Edie Creek.[7]

To the authorities' consternation, the small community at Black Cat Creek, led by a wild, rum-loving Irishman, Harry O'Kane, often seemed more intent on having a good time than seriously mining for gold. In August 1931, the Mining Registrar reported to the Warden on the activities of miners there. One miner, James Wilton,

> gave me the impression that he was not very anxious to do any work himself. If his boys could get gold it was OK, if not, well he could get an existence and he is apparently satisfied with that.

The Registrar concluded that

> The general rule on this section of the field is for the men to leave gold winning to the boys, while they hold parties in the various houses ... I warned a number of the residents ... that should a serious accident occur to any of their boys and it was shown that the miner on whose claim the accident occurred was absent from the actual work at the time, he would be liable to a severe penalty.[8]

When Corbould visited Edie Creek in April 1928, he took an option over the 200 acre lease covering the rich Day Dawn Reef, close to Merri Creek, for which he paid £25,000. This option expired in April 1929 without being exercised. An Australian company subsequently acquired a 50% interest in the lease, established Day Dawn (New Guinea) Ltd in November 1929 and floated it on the stock exchange. There were three veins on the property, of which the main one was 3 feet 6 inches wide with values exceeding one ounce to the ton over a strike length of 450 feet.[9]

To process the ore, Day Dawn imported a 27 ton wood-fired boiler, designed for an altitude of 7,000 feet, and a crushing and grinding mill capable of crushing 50 tons per day. These were made in sections with dimensions and weight that would enable them to be flown from Salamaua to Wau in a Junkers W34. These and other items such as thousands of fire-proof bricks, pumps, electric light plant and corrugated iron, weighed around 100 tons.

On reaching Wau, everything had to be carried up the poorly graded mule track clinging precariously to the side of Mt. Kaindi, which climbed more than 4,000 feet over its 11 miles to the mine. Some items were

Carriers on the Wau-Edie Creek track, 1931.

carried by mules, with the largest attached to long timber poles enabling them to be carried by teams of up to 20 carriers.

By the time they arrived at Day Dawn, most items had been carried by ship, plane, mules and carriers.

The first material arrived at the Day Dawn mine site in December 1930, and milling operations commenced on 18 May 1931—the first lode mining on the field. This, and the flow of royalty payments it represented, was welcome news for the Administration.

The lack of a serviceable road from Wau to Edie Creek also posed major problems for NGG. Although the Administration had justified the higher royalty on gold in 1928 by the need to construct and maintain roads on the goldfields, it ignored frequent requests to construct one up Mt. Kaindi. NGG was therefore forced to divert resources from its other activities to cut a track through to Edie Creek. It was, however, narrow and prone to landslips, with travellers facing the ever present prospect of suddenly disappearing over the edge and into the valley far below.

Late in 1929, bullocks were driven in to Wau over the new Buang route, with a view to pulling wagons to Edie Creek. However, the track was not wide enough, and from 1931 they were used instead to carry equipment between the aerodrome and a new mine NGG was developing at Golden Ridges, three miles from Wau. The track to Edie Creek was so poor that, as late as February 1932, NGG was transporting machinery and stores up Mt. Kaindi using pneumatic-tyred carts hauled by New Guinean labourers.

In providing NGG with manning exemptions while its leases were consolidated into a Special Area, the Administration apparently expected that alluvial mining would continue more or less as before and that lode mining would begin once sufficient reserves were proven.

However, 1930 passed with a steady flow of test results, but no apparent move by NGG to resume alluvial mining or commence lode mining. Gold production in 1930 was half that in 1928, with revenue from gold royalties similarly affected. Finally, the Administration decided it had had enough, and insisted on NGG's alluvial areas being manned. As it didn't have sufficient employees to work all the leases itself, NGG had little choice but to let out most of them on tribute to individual miners for twelve months from the end of January 1931.

Although pressured by the Administration to begin mining in its own right, NGG continued to place testing ahead of production. An exception was its decision in mid-1931 to establish a mill at Golden Ridges on the lower slopes of Mt. Kaindi behind Namie Creek, to treat a flat ore body of 100,000 tons, assaying £5 per ton. Ore production and milling commenced there in August 1932.

By December 1931, the Administration's restlessness had spread to NGG shareholders. More than two years had passed, and there was little sign of it commencing mining on a scale commensurate with its size. Its £1 shares were trading at around 4 shillings and 6 pence, to the consternation of miners who had been paid for their leases in shares. However, NGG ignored the growing discontent, continuing to test its ground and develop its infrastructure.

In April 1932, the Salamaua Manager of the Bank of New South Wales crystallised the frustration widely felt towards NGG, when he reported that

The bulk of the gold produced [on the field] has been won by tributors from the Edie Creek leases held by NGG which tributes expired on 1st February last, and have not been renewed. The company, which has built up no organisation to carry on production, should re-commence operations next month ... To test the Edie Creek lodes at depth, made impossible by strong water flow, NGG have installed a power plant ... On the proving of these lodes hinges the future of this company at Edie Creek, but even if the most favourable values are disclosed, we do not look for bulk production [in] under three years.[10]

On 16 January 1930, barely two weeks after its decision to use Junkers G31s, Placer Development announced that a new operating company, Bulolo Gold Dredging (BGD), would be established with nominal capital of $C4 million, comprising 800,000 shares of $C5 each.

Bulolo valley (looking towards Wau), 1931. Dredge under construction to left of aerodrome.

Hand operated crane, Bulolo, 1931.

224,000 shares were allocated to Placer Development, together with $C605,000 in cash, as payment for the southern Bulolo leases. From this, Placer was to pay 70,000 shares and £50,000 to Guinea Gold. 476,000 shares were offered for public subscription.

Placer also announced that two 10 cubic feet bucket dredges would be constructed, to be powered by hydro-electricity. The first dredge would commence operating within 21 months of BGD being floated. A 10% dividend was predicted in the first year, with annual dividends of 28% thereafter for 11 years.

BGD was incorporated in Vancouver, British Columbia, on 14 February 1930, and a prospectus issued a couple of months later. In it, Tom Horton was quoted as regarding the Bulolo leases *as the world's most important placer (i.e. alluvial) deposit located since Klondyke, or say, for the last 25 years. There has been nothing in Australia like it* … This assessment from a man with 50 years' mining experience, together with the expected early start and promised dividends, enabled BGD to raise the money it was seeking without difficulty, despite the Depression. BGD received its certificate to commence business on 11 June 1930, setting 11 March 1932 as the date for the first dredge to begin operating.

This was an audacious forecast. To achieve it, several thousand tons of material would have to be ordered and shipped in from around the world, flown in on planes it didn't have, to an airstrip that didn't exist. A huge dredge and a hydro-electric power plant would have to be constructed by a labour force that hadn't been recruited. Roads would have to be cut through dense jungle linking different parts of BGD's operations. The list of challenges seemed endless.

Placer wasted no time. After helping Tom Horton assess the lower Bulolo leases for Territory Investments, Tom Yeomans had been mining at Edie Creek, regularly producing 30 ounces a day. A kindly and immensely practical man, Yeomans agreed when Placer asked him in January 1930 to construct an aerodrome at Bulolo. The main flats—the logical place for an aerodrome—were covered with thick jungle. Yeomans therefore set about constructing a small temporary airstrip on kunai grass-covered flats nearby. This would enable a large tractor to be flown in on a W34—in sections for reassembly—to be used in clearing and levelling the main aerodrome. Another high priority was a sawmill to enable the construction of buildings and fluming, using klinkii and hoop pine and cedar, all of which grew prolifically around Bulolo.

Yeomans had the airstrip operating by 17 February and before long work was under way carving the main aerodrome out of the jungle. This was located next to

Fluming for powerhouse head race being constructed next to the Bulolo River.

where the two dredges were to be assembled, so that construction material needed no further transport. On completion, the airstrip was 1,150 yards long and 120 yards wide, and planted with couch grass.

The main development work at Bulolo began in June 1930, when an American mining engineer, T.D. Harris, arrived as BGD's General Manager. Arthur John, his personal assistant, described Harris, a man in his 60s, as *tall, lean, balding, with a friendly smile and gentle manner*.[11] His challenge was to prioritise and co-ordinate air freight from Lae and ensure that construction of the dredges and power house at Bulolo progressed smoothly, while oversighting a test drilling program elsewhere on Placer's property. Although Harris could be uncompromising when circumstances demanded, he was considerate and supportive, attributes that enabled him to forge a disparate group of Australians, Americans and Englishmen into a highly effective team.

He was ably supported by another American, O.B. Hart, a construction engineer, who could turn his hand to anything and was, in the words of Australian welder Arthur Ives, a tough *fiery little bugger* but *a hell of a good bloke once you got to know him*.[12] Hart had the daunting challenge of building dredge No. 1 and the power house to meet the March 1932 deadline.

By August, the office, first aid post, mess house and living quarters for white men and labourers, had been constructed on the western side of the new aerodrome at Bulolo. Thatched with sacsac, they were rough but functional. All machinery for the hydro-electric scheme and the dredges had been ordered and contracts let for the manufacture of two dredge hulls and super-structure. Two steel barges or lighters, each capable of carrying 50 tons, were under construction, along with a wharf at Lae, and a self-propelling steam crane was on its way.

This crane—an improbable piece of machinery resembling a Heath Robinson prototype—was to be a linchpin of BGD's operations in Lae. It was mounted on a broad gauge railway running from the new wharf to the aerodrome ¾ mile away. It could lift items weighing up to 10 tons from the lighters, transport them to the aerodrome and then load them directly onto planes.

Co-ordinating the supply of machinery, equipment and people from all over the world was a major logistical exercise—and one not made any easier by poor communications. Contact with the outside world was confined to radiograms sent to Salamaua, which were then carried to Bulolo by plane. The dredge hull and superstructure were made in Sydney, dredge machinery came from San Francisco, turbines from Sweden, alternators and other electrical equipment from England, electric motors from Switzerland and, of course, the G31 planes from Germany—with American engines.

The first Junkers G31 made its inaugural flight to Bulolo on 31 March 1931, carrying a sectionalised hand-operated derrick for future unloading. The second G31 made its first flight shortly afterwards, and within a few weeks most of the equipment needed to begin dredge construction had been flown in.

By May 1931, much of the initial preparatory phase had been completed. Equipment for unloading and handling freight was in use at Lae, including a 75 foot long wharf, the railway line and locomotive crane, a warehouse and, at the aerodrome, a concrete loading apron, weighbridge and an automatic aircraft refuelling system. The Bulolo valley was criss-crossed with rough but serviceable roads and 6½ miles of telephone line connected the main office with outlying camps. The pits for the hull of No. 1 dredge had been excavated, a 100 foot steel boom derrick erected to handle dredge parts during construction and three wood-fired boilers were being assembled that would provide power for the compressors and other equipment needed to construct the dredge.

The second phase involved construction of the power house and the first dredge. It was decided to locate the power house where the river left the gorge at the southern end of the Bulolo flats, with a head race drawing water from 1.5 miles upstream to drive the turbines. Construction of this race had commenced on 1 August 1930. It involved driving a tunnel by hand through the side of a mountain that was 1,637 feet long and 8 feet by 8 feet in cross-section, constructing 3,173 feet of cedar fluming, measuring 8 feet by 5 feet, and digging an open ditch 2,900 feet in length. By mid-1931, work was well advanced, with machinery and equipment for the power house already in BGD's warehouse in Lae awaiting transport.

The dredge hulls and superstructure were built by shipbuilders Poole and Steel at Balmain in Sydney, where they were test-assembled before being dismantled for shipment to New Guinea. Erection of the first dredge began on 22 June 1931.

Each dredge hull was assembled in a large rectangular pit which, when completed, was filled with water to a depth of about 10 feet. The superstructure was then completed and dredging machinery installed. It was hot, exhausting work.

Jack O'Neill later worked on the hull of another dredge, describing it as

Dredge under construction.

Dredge buckets on digging ladder.

A huge rectangular frying pan— a hot frying pan. All around it on the edge of the pit were stacked the steel plates, cut, numbered and already drilled for the rivets, pieces of a 'Meccano Set' ... My first step was onto that frying pan, which, situated only a few degrees below the equator, was at a good cooking temperature ... Soon there were red-hot rivets flying through the air from the forges up above to the riveters' off-siders, who caught them in steel funnels and poked them through the holes ... The sweat dripped off our noses and sizzled to nothing on the hot steel. We were building a huge, rectangular, ugly, flat-bottomed boat and as day followed day the frying pan became a series of ovens as the sides and bulkheads went up; we were the roast.[13]

Despite such uncomfortable working conditions, BGD had little trouble attracting the skilled workers it needed. In 1931, work was coming to an end for many metal workers employed constructing the Sydney Harbour Bridge. Economic activity in Australia was heading towards its low point, unemployment reaching 27%. The first dredge at Bulolo was one of the few large capital projects offering employment, and many of those who worked on the Bridge were recruited to work on its construction.

On 19 July 1931, M.V. *Carisso* arrived at Lae from the USA, with 500 tons of dredge machinery, 500 tons of petrol and large quantities of dredge buckets and steel plates for the dredge hull. Teams of labourers unloaded the cargo over six days onto lighters which a pinnace then towed to the wharf. The next six months saw many such deliveries to Lae. From there BGD's two G31 work horses, often making five trips to Bulolo daily, ensured that whatever parts were needed in Bulolo were on hand when required.

About 70 white men were engaged in constructing dredge No. 1, including five rivetting gangs. In September, the Mining Warden reported that 65,125 rivets had been driven into the hull and superstructure, and by October the dredge was floating in its pit.

Dredge No. 1 ready to commence dredging, March 1932.

Power House (c. 1935)
By the time this photo was taken, two more pipes had been laid, to feed two additional turbine generators.

Construction of the power house was well advanced, with work on the head race also nearing completion. At the end of the race was a surge tank, from which two massive steel pipes ran down the hill to the power house, feeding two 1,000 h.p. turbine generators, with provision for two more when needed.

Power was to be transmitted at 6,600 volts to the dredges and main camp, a distance of about five miles, where step-down transformers would reduce it to 440 volts for power and 110 volts for lighting. The head race was finished on 12 March 1932 and the first turbine began operating four days later.

By 16 March, less than a year after the first flight by a G31, dredge No. 1 was also finished. It was 106 feet long, 50 feet wide, with a 9 foot draught. Its total weight was 1,050 tons. The digging ladder was mounted with 63 ten cubic feet dredging buckets, each weighing 1½ tons, capable of gouging the alluvial gravels to a maximum depth of 29 feet, at the rate of 23 buckets per minute. After being dumped in a hopper, the gravel passed through a revolving perforated screen 40 feet in length and 7 feet in diameter, where it was washed by water under high pressure. The fine material passed through the screen and over gold saving tables where the gold was trapped by riffles and amalgamated with mercury. The larger tailings were dumped well astern of the dredge via a conveyor belt on the stacker.

However efficient BGD was, one issue could have made life very difficult for it: the rights of nearby villages to compensation in relation to land used for dredging. Given the magnitude of land degradation dredging caused, this was not simply an academic issue.

Whether they had rights to compensation hinged on the relationship villagers had to the ground concerned. In 1921, and again in 1923, the Administrator said that *the natives should be secured in all the land occupied or used by them.*[14] The 1922 Land Ordinance applied this broad definition of 'ownership', embracing the concept of 'use'. Land *of which there appears to be no owner* was deemed to be *waste or vacant* and could be proclaimed as Administration land. The Ordinance required the proclamation to include a statement showing *how long* [the land] *has been unused by natives*. However, the Mining Ordinance took a narrower approach, providing for compensation only for damage to land *owned and occupied by natives*.

While there were no villages on any of BGD's leases (and so no compensation payable under the Mining Ordinance), it is likely that people living on either side of the lower Bulolo Valley—the Buang to the east and the Kapau and Langimar (or Angaatiya) people to the west—hunted in the valley. If the Administration were aware of this, it would not have been able to declare the land concerned to be 'waste and vacant'.

There is no evidence that investigations to establish 'use' were ever undertaken in connection with lease applications elsewhere on the goldfields. In any event, times had changed since the early 1920s and the Administrator could ill afford any suggestion that the land was not the Administration's to confer on

BGD, which might have delayed the commencement of its new revenue stream from Bulolo. In July 1932 it therefore proclaimed BGD's land to be waste and vacant on the grounds that *there appears to be no owner* and that *the said land has not, as far as is known, been used or occupied by natives.*[15]

While work progressed inexorably toward the commencement of dredging, Levien continued as a director of Guinea Airways, as passionate as ever about the role of air transport in New Guinea's development. After years of effort, he was on the verge of realising his vision for unlocking the value of the lower Bulolo

Launch of Dredge No. 1, 21 March 1932.

leases. With 25% of the shares of Guinea Gold, his insight, energy and perseverance would soon reap their reward.

However on 20 January, two months before the launch of dredge No. 1, Levien died suddenly of meningitis while on a visit to Melbourne. He was 58.

On 21 March, only ten days later than the original date set 21 months earlier (and two days after the opening of the Sydney Harbour Bridge), the Administrator started dredge No. 1 in the presence of 300 Europeans, many of whom had flown in for the occasion, dressed in their tropical whites. Arthur John recalled:

> The superstructure of the dredge was covered with bunting and speeches delivered from a platform on the dredge itself. General Wisdom was followed by our Managing Director, Charles Banks. Mrs Banks broke the traditional bottle of champagne over the digging ladder and declared the dredge launched.[16]

Wisdom's address concluded with an unexpected acknowledgement:

> I cannot close without reference to the late Mr Levien. Every one of you, I am sure, will regret very deeply that he did not live to see the consummation of the first stage of an enterprise for which he was, in a large measure, responsible.[17]

Having described Levien in official correspondence a few years earlier as *a man of, to say the least, indifferent character*, it was a turnaround that was both surprising and gracious.

In his diary, the Chairman of Guinea Airways, Charles Wells, described the moment for which everyone had waited:

> She rocked and groaned and up came the gravel and rocks and round the cylinders spun and boulders toppled over the back and the riffles simmered and splashed while the flags fluttered above.[18]

Later, he referred to the dredge as *a relentless gouging, groaning, splashing, ponderous thing.* Not pretty, just effective. In its first three months, working three eight hour shifts a day, the dredge recovered 14,192 ounces of bullion from 733,100 cubic yards of alluvial gravel.

Two days after the launch of dredge No. 1, Wells brought this chapter in Bulolo's history to an end. As he noted in his diary:

> Beautiful fine day. Took CJL's ashes and with Cross' assistance scattered them over the Bulolo valley. Vale CJL.[19]

PART 3
GROWTH AND DEVELOPMENT

Dredge No. 1 at southern end of Bulolo valley. Road at left links the Power House (left, out of picture) with Bulolo township (in distance).

CHAPTER 9
NO STONE UNTURNED: THE BGD STORY

A dredge is not unlike an ordinary ship, with a dredgemaster (the captain)
and winchman (the first mate).

The winchroom—effectively the bridge—overlooks the digging ladder and is the dredge's control room. At Bulolo, the dredgemaster was responsible for its overall operation and for throwing mercury on the gold saving tables every day or so.[1]

The dredges operated three eight hour shifts, 363 days a year—Good Friday and Christmas Day being the only days of complete shutdown. The crew for each shift was surprisingly small: a winchman, responsible for keeping the dredge running smoothly, bow and stern 'oilers', who had the never-ending, unpleasant job of applying grease from 44 gallon drums to ease the friction of the many moving parts, and a jig oiler to keep the jigs (or secondary gold saving devices) working efficiently. A dayman also undertook minor repairs and maintenance.

Working ahead of each dredge was a shoreman, with a dozen or so labourers. They cleared the jungle—often difficult in wet weather and, with the early dredges each 'consuming' 6 to 8 acres per month, always with the pressure of not delaying their progress. They also dug 'deadmen' holes, filling each with a log to which steel hawsers were attached to stabilise the dredge as it gouged the bottom of the pond.

The noise of the dredges—steel on steel, rock on steel—was never ending, and could be heard miles away. Former District Commisioner Jim Sinclair later wrote

> No-one who has ever stood on the high control deck of a Bulolo dredge in operation is ever likely to forget the experience. Beneath one's feet the steel deck throbs and pulsates as the great manganese steel buckets,

moving in a continuous line at some 22 per minute, drive into the gravels far below the surface of the dredge pond, discharging their loads into a great hopper and going down for more, hour after hour, all day and all night ... Through the hopper the rocks and gravels thunder down into the bowels of the dredge, where the gold ... [is] extracted. A constant stream of waste material pours out over the stern by conveyor belt. The noise is shattering—a never ending screech of metal, thumps, bangs, groans and bellows.[2]

A counterpoint was the eery silence when a dredge stopped suddenly due to an electricity supply failure. Geoff Baskett, who worked as a jig oiler on No. 4 dredge, later recalled the sensation:

> One moment the lights would be glaring out into the darkness, the bucket line would be jolting and bucking, the revolving drum clanging and ringing as the rocks fell against the steel sides, and I would probably be singing at the top of my voice knowing only too well that no-

Winch room of a dredge.

The digging ladder, with full dredge buckets.

one else could hear. Then in the midst of all this bedlam there would be a sudden blackout. Complete darkness and a deathly silence broken only by the clanging of the odd rock or two falling through the now stilled drum … We just had to wait and enjoy the stillness of the night until power was restored and the dredge started chewing its noisy way into the river bank again.[3]

Most of the early dredge masters and winchmen were Americans working under a dredge superintendent, Chester Mayfield—also an American, with great experience in the Klondyke and California. Mayfield was outstandingly successful in training and making effective teams out of the many inexperienced men lining up for jobs during and after the Depression, and Australians who had started off as ordinary dredge hands gradually replaced the Americans.

The dredges travelled up to a mile in a year,[4] leaving in their wake massive piles of recycled rock, gradually converting a jungle-covered valley into what patrol officer Ian Downs later described as *a moonscape of bare boulders, stones and slag that covered every square centimetre of soil and smothered every form of vegetation.*[5] The devastation provoked Arthur John to ask, perhaps on behalf of future generations, *how green was my valley?*[6] By the time BGD eventually finished dredging, it was certainly 'waste and vacant'.

Bulolo Gold Dredging's experience during the 1930s is unique in Australian mining history. Initially a two dredge operation, it expanded progressively until the eighth and final dredge began operating late in 1939. From the launch of the first dredge on 21 March 1932 to the cessation of operations after the Japanese attack on Bulolo on 21 January 1942, these dredges handled 119 million cubic yards of alluvial gravel, producing 1.3 million ounces of gold and 576,000 ounces of silver. Even by early 21st Century standards, this was a large scale operation.

BGD started with known reserves of 40 million cubic yards with an average recoverable value of 2 shillings and a penny per cubic yard. By opening up new ground—both vertically and horizontally—it had increased this to 150 million cubic yards at the outbreak of war, with an average value per yard of 1 shilling and 11 pence.

Dredging at night.

To support its operations, BGD constructed three hydro-electric power stations and established two townships, catering for the needs of a labour force of up to 330 white employees and their families and 1,525 indentured labourers. With the exception of local timber, everything required was flown in without major incident—mainly on the two Junkers G31 aircraft 'Peter' and 'Paul'.

It was an extraordinarily profitable operation. In eight years, BGD paid out $C22 million in dividends, or $C22.50 per share. A further $C3.5 million was paid in royalties and, from 1939, Australian gold tax.[7]

There was an element of good fortune—notably higher gold prices—but the real key to BGD's success was the quality of its Board and management. Even today, the BGD story stands out as an example of best practice mining in a remote location.

Inevitably there were initial teething problems with No. 1 dredge, recovery rates being lower than forecast. The ground was easier to dredge than expected, and it was soon digging well in excess of planned levels, overloading the gold saving tables. As the gold was very fine, some escaped in the tailings. The digging rate was reduced and the dredge's operation gradually refined to increase recovery rates.

Construction of No. 2 dredge began immediately after No. 1 had been launched, and it was christened on 15 October 1932 by Dorothy Waterhouse, the wife of director Les Waterhouse, in the presence of about 200 Europeans. Its specifications were broadly the same as No. 1 dredge, also dredging to a depth of 29 feet.

Meanwhile, testing of the northern or Bulowat leases since early 1931 had revealed the presence of gold in commercial quantities at depths of up to 65 feet. The leases were estimated to contain 50 million cubic yards of gravel with an average recoverable gold content of 1 shilling and 4 pence a yard—not as rich as the southern leases, but with dredging costs of only 6 pence per yard, still very profitable. In December 1931, even before the launch of No. 1 dredge, BGD decided to construct two more to work the northern leases.

Launch of Dredge No. 2, 15 October 1932.

These were to be located near the junction of the Bulolo and Watut Rivers, about 7 miles down river from the main Bulolo camp. Building an aerodrome at the site of what was to become the township of Bulwa was the first priority, as the area was separated from Bulolo by Anamapi Gorge and could only be reached on foot along a rough bush track. By July 1932, it was sufficiently advanced for small planes to land. Sawn timber for use in building a construction camp and the formwork for No. 3 dredge was floated down river from Bulolo. There was a hiccup at Lae in September when 5 acres of land, the wharf, crane, three sheds and 100 yards of railway line unexpectedly slid into the sea, but this had little impact on progress.

In November, a road was blasted through the gorge,

enabling power lines to be extended to the new camp, and in December the Bulwa 'drome was able to take its first Junkers G31. By early 1933, material was pouring into Bulwa from Bulolo by road and from Lae by air. In February, the two G31s made 143 trips carrying 390 short tons—mainly material for No. 3 dredge. Progress was rapid. The first hull plates were laid in March, it was floated in July and began operating in November 1933. Construction of No. 4 dredge then commenced; it began operating in August 1934.

These two dredges had larger hulls than the first two, enabling a longer digging ladder to reach the deeper gravels. No. 3 could dig to a depth of 52 feet below water level, and No. 4 to 59 feet.

The gold at Bulwa was even finer than at Bulolo, making it difficult for it all to be captured. Following experiments on No. 2 dredge, pulsating jigs were installed which were successful in trapping gold that would otherwise have escaped.

Maintaining a reliable power supply to the dredges was critical. It was therefore of great concern when, as early as June 1932, the power station encountered problems with silt from mining operations upstream at Koranga and Edie Creeks. Then in November flood debris blocked the intake. A settling tank was installed to catch most of the silt and screens used to trap river debris. But with four dredges and rapidly growing communities at Bulolo and Bulwa, there was a risk that everything would grind to a halt if a major flood damaged the turbines. As well, white ants were making rapid inroads into the 6,600 wooden poles used to carry the power lines down the valley.

Late in 1932, BGD therefore decided to construct a second power station at Baiune Creek, down river from Bulwa. With no mining activities upstream, the Baiune's water was crisp and clear, substantially reducing the risk of power failures. It also decided to replace the wooden power poles with 11,000 steel ones. With global economic activity now at its low point, BGD acquired all the machinery and equipment required for the new power station for one third of what it would have cost in 1930.[8] Construction of the two mile long cedar water race feeding the Baiune power station began in September 1933, and the station itself, with four 1,000 h.p. generators, began operating in November 1934.[9]

With two dredges operating, a third under construction, and a new power station under way, the Bulolo Valley was the centre of great activity during 1933. Further testing of the southern leases was also progressing. In 1929, Decoto had only been able to test these using small hand drills. The availability of electricity now meant that a powerful Keystone electric drill mounted on caterpillar tracks could be flown in and used.

Dredge No. 4, 1934.

Keystone drill, 1934.

By early 1934, it was obvious that, with his limited equipment, Decoto's drilling had hit a false bottom at around 22 feet, and that economically payable gravel extended to a much greater depth. Dunkin noted that,

An intensive drilling campaign was therefore started with three Keystone drills, working two shifts each … Although gold bearing horizons of good grade existed as far as 200 feet below ground level, the most favourable depth to dig … was 125 feet … [10]

The first two dredges could only dig to 29 feet and dredges 3 and 4 to less than 60 feet. BGD therefore faced a new challenge: whether to build new deep-digging dredges that would need to be amongst the world's largest, sectionalise them and fly them to the field for reassembly, or pass up the opportunity to extract a potentially enormous quantity of gold. Dredging gold at such depth would be costly, but a rising gold price improved its potential viability. Then, in January 1934, the US dollar was devalued against gold, lifting the price from $US20.67 to $US35 per ounce.

Further testing during 1935 confirmed an additional 90 million cubic yards with a working profit of 38 cents per yard, and 80 million yards of deeper gravel with a profit of 20 cents. With such large reserves, BGD decided in November 1935 to construct two additional dredges.

No. 5 dredge was designed to dig 85 feet below the water line and carry a bank of 40 feet, making a total dredging depth of 125 feet. At 2,500 tons, it was more than twice the size of the first dredge and its digging ladder operated with 118 buckets, each with a capacity of 11 cubic feet and weighing more than 1½ tons; the pins holding them on the digging ladder each weighed 260 pounds. The buckets would pass a given point at the rate of 24.5 a minute and be capable of digging 250,000 cubic yards a month.

Construction began in September 1936, though progress was delayed early in 1937 by a US Pacific Coast marine strike and then by the loss of machinery and equipment when the ship carrying them sank on its way to New Guinea. It eventually began operating in December 1937.

The second deep digger was originally planned to be even larger, capable of digging to a total depth of 165 feet. However, the tumbler shaft would have been too heavy for the Junkers G31s, and the dredge considerably more expensive to build. In such a remote location, it would always be difficult to obtain parts if something were to go wrong. BGD's practice was to reduce risk by standardising parts wherever possible. It therefore decided to duplicate No. 5 dredge, even though this would mean sacrificing 10 million cubic yards of reserves. Construction of No. 7 dredge began in early in 1938, and it began operating in June 1939.

It was a mark of the company's propensity to leave no stone unturned that, while planning to build a couple of the largest gold dredges in the world, it was also focused on an alluvial deposit that would require one of the smallest. Late in 1934, BGD acquired an option over leases in the Wau-Koranga Creek area, about 6 miles up river from its southern Bulolo leases. Testing revealed a shallow alluvial deposit of 6.3 million cubic yards with the potential to generate a profit of 8.9 cents per yard and the option was exercised.

Even though the site was less than ten miles from Bulolo, access was difficult as there was still no road through the gorge between Bulolo and Wau. Instead, dredge components were flown to Wau and everything required to build a 1,000 ton dredge with 77 six cubic feet buckets was then laboriously transported on a single five ton truck over a difficult track through jungle to the construction site. Living quarters were built for New Guinean labourers and the Europeans who constructed and then operated the dredge, and a large area of jungle was cleared for the planting of native foods. Fortunately, it was easy to get power to the dredge site, as BGD had been supplying NGG at Wau and Edie Creek from its Baiune power station since 1935. Construction started early in 1937, and dredge No. 6 was operating by March 1938.

BGD progressively acquired other new areas through the 1930s, the 5,750 acres it had when its leases were consolidated into a Special Area in 1932, increasing to 9,360 acres by 1939.[11] It developed a symbiotic relationship with individual miners working ground at the fringe of its leases. BGD would acquire leases from them when they didn't have sufficient capital to develop them, or sell ground where it could be more easily worked on a smaller scale.

BGD would also occasionally let some areas out to tributers, providing them with 75% of the value of gold won. One such area were Arnold's leases, near the Power Station at the exit from the gorge. These had been worked by the old Papuan miner, George Arnold, since Coldham first surveyed the southern Bulolo leases in 1923, and were acquired by Placer in 1930. The river here was unsuitable for dredging due to the many large boulders, but lent itself to hydraulic sluicing.

By the late 1930s, BGD had extended its operations to Bulwa and even further downstream, at greater depth across the southern Bulolo leases, as well as upstream near Wau and Koranga Creek. The final piece of BGD's plan was now to dredge the lower reaches of the Watut River above its junction with the Bulolo. It commenced constructing an eighth dredge, before deciding to use this on the Bulolo above the junction while repositioning No. 3 dredge to work the Watut leases. No. 8 dredge began operating in November 1939.

The ever-expanding dredge program led BGD to add a fifth generating unit to the Baiune power house in 1937, increasing its output to 5,000 h.p. By 1938, barely six years after its construction, the original power house was no longer a reliable source of electricity, and was on 'care and maintenance'. NGG's electricity requirements now frequently exceeded what BGD had agreed to supply, putting at risk the latter's dredging operations. With two more dredges due to begin operating in 1939, a long dry spell rang alarm bells.

BGD responded cleverly, deciding to construct a new power station two miles upstream from the existing Baiune power station, capable of generating 2,800 h.p. After generating electricity at the new power station,

Dredge No. 5.

water would gravitate to the Lower Baiune station and repeat the process. Although the destruction of a section of water race by a landslip delayed progress, the Upper Baiune Power Station began operating in September 1940.

BGD's performance through the 1930s should be viewed in the context of its need to develop and maintain a complex mining operation in an area which had been visited by few white men until the mid-1920s and lacked infrastructure of any kind. It was very much a 'greenfields' operation—if one can so describe the dense jungle which then covered the Bulolo flats. Today, it would be described as a 'cutting edge' venture—never before had so many large dredges been sectionalised, flown in to a remote location and reassembled. Nor had aviation been used to provide on-going support on such a scale. With each dredge requiring about 25% of its weight in parts and grease annually, the logistical challenges were demanding and the price of failure high.

The problems and challenges BGD faced were formidable, and these were addressed and overcome without any tangible support from the Administration.

BGD constructed and maintained all power stations, roads, bridges and aerodromes, and all facilities in Bulolo and Bulwa such as hospitals and a school. The Administration's sole interest in BGD's steadily expanding operations was the revenue they generated in royalties, import duties and a range of ancillary fees and charges. Between 1932 and 1942, BGD contributed nearly 25% of its total revenue.[12]

The significance of BGD's achievements was reflected in a constant stream of visitors throughout the 1930s, including the Australian Governor-General, Lord Gowrie, Federal Ministers, mining experts from around the world and aviation enthusiasts. The Bulolo story (and that of the Morobe goldfields) was also a constant source of articles in international mining and aviation journals and in Australian newspapers.[13]

That it succeeded so spectacularly was due to the quality of its directors and managers and, in particular, their risk and financial management skills. Placer and BGD had common directors, all but one of whom were highly experienced mining engineers. In the 1930s, company directors often acted in an executive capacity, and while Charles Banks was clearly first among equals, each director was personally involved in different aspects of BGD's operations.

Governor-General, Lord Gowrie, at Bulwa, 1937. L to R: Dredgemaster, Sir Walter McNicoll (Administrator), Lady Gowrie, Lord Gowrie, L.V. Waterhouse, L.J. Joubert (General Manager). Others on right unidentified.

Given the difficulty of communicating between Bulolo and Vancouver, where Banks was located, general oversight of the Bulolo operations was left in the hands of Les Waterhouse in Sydney. Important issues were, however, still referred to Banks by cable. Day to day operations at Bulolo were handled by T.D. Harris, with Waterhouse visiting the field regularly. It was a very flexible line of command, involving considerable delegation of responsibility and mutual trust.

BGD's success was critically dependent on three things: the uninterrupted flow of materials and electric power, the ability to fix promptly anything that went wrong, and the quality of its labour force. The whole focus of directors and management was on managing the risks associated with these.

The decision to fly in everything rather than construct a road had been predicated on Mustar's conviction that the risk of losing a plane was low. However, leaving nothing to chance, BGD pursued a strategy designed to minimise the risk of a crash and disruption to its operations if one were to occur.

Considerable quantities of spare under-carriages, parts, wheels and tyres were carried as insurance. Though only light servicing was required every 200 hours, Charles Banks observed that *complete overhauls have always been made as the extra cost and time incurred is more than offset by removing as far as possible, the chance of engine failure from mechanical cause*.[15] In 1934, when BGD acquired a third G31, Mustar wrote to the Controller of Civil Aviation that *It is not our intention to put this machine into immediate service but to keep it as a standby in case of emergency*.[16] BGD's careful management of aviation risk meant that nothing was ever lost and there was rarely a delay in getting any parts needed.

Wherever possible, dredge and power station parts and machinery were standardised so that the loss of a critical part wouldn't interfere with operations. Thus, when No. 1 dredge was being constructed, all parts for No. 2 were already at Lae and could have been substituted for any that were lost. Risk management considerations also underpinned BGD's decision to make No. 7 dredge a duplicate of No. 5.

Given the remote location, self-sufficiency was vital. A second and then a third power station were built to guarantee a reliable supply of electricity, while BGD's own sawmill produced the enormous quantity of timber required.[17] Dredge machinery was kept well lubricated at all times, but inevitably wear and tear caused problems. Lost dredging time was lost money. To minimise stoppages, BGD maintained the most advanced machinery shop in New Guinea, with an oxygen-making plant and boiler making, welding and electrical annexes able to carry out all engineering repairs and maintenance. This usually occurred when the dredges stopped every 10 days or so for the gold to be 'cleaned up'.

The attention BGD directors paid to financial management was equally precise. From their initial decision to purchase two G31s rather than construct a road, they took every opportunity to accelerate revenue streams while containing costs. Making No. 7 dredge a duplicate of No. 5 meant savings in design costs and securing revenue a year earlier. Cheap hydro-electric power and the spreading of overheads over an increasing number of dredges also lowered costs.

Lord Gowrie visited Bulolo in August 1937, where he was presented with a poem by the dredge hands.[14] This, and his reply, were published in the *Adelaide News* on 31 August 1937:

We regret that your job, a representin' of the king
Doesn't let you get to know us as you should,
But believe us when we say, that we'd like to shake your wing,
And have a spot, friend, with you if you would.

We're just a bunch of dredge hands;
Just a rough-neck Aussie crew
And receptions and the like ain't quite our style.
But we're glad you came along, pal,
And we hope you liked it too,
and will look us up again, once in a while.
                              Yours—the dredge hands

To this Lord Gowrie replied:

I never thought that men so tough
Could write such lilting graceful stuff.
With perfect rhythm, perfect rhyme—
How did you ever spare the time?

You say your status ain't so hot;
Well, there I disagree a lot.
For I maintain that men like you
Are good as any man—that's true.

I've seen your dredges and your gold;
I've walked in heat and flown in cold;
And friendliness on every hand
Has made us say your country's grand.
                              —Gowrie

BGD's offices, Bulolo.

Planning in 1931 had been based on working costs of 15 cents per cubic yard; in practice, they were kept to between 8 and 9 cents throughout the 1930s.[18] This enabled smaller alluvial deposits, such as those worked by No. 6 dredge, to be profitable.

BGD also contained costs by concentrating on doing what it did best—mining. Wherever possible, it outsourced other activities which it considered could be done better and/or more cheaply by others. Thus it used private recruiters to recruit labourers, Guinea Airways to fly its G31s and the postal service to deliver its gold safely to Australia.[19] Les Waterhouse became a director of Guinea Airways, but this in no way deterred BGD from driving down the management fees it paid.

Operational efficiency was a byword. As the dredges were widely dispersed, a network of roads was carved out of the jungle, bridges constructed and vehicles flown in so that supplies, spares and men could be moved quickly between different camps and dredges, as required.

Building construction activities were substantial and never ending. In 1932/33, more than 50 buildings were constructed at Bulolo and Bulwa to meet a wide range of needs.[20] It was hardly surprising that, after his visit to Bulolo in October 1934, the new Administrator, Walter McNicoll, observed,

Bulolo is an amazing place. Less than four years ago, impenetrable jungle; today a well planned and well established township … A more striking example of careful and skilful planning and successful execution can hardly be imagined.[21]

Critical to BGD's success was its ability to build and retain an experienced workforce. In March 1932, there were about 125 Europeans and 380 New Guinean labourers at Bulolo. Numbers grew steadily as more dredges were constructed, reaching a peak of 330 and 1,525 respectively in 1939/40. About one third of Europeans had their families with them.

Pay was tax free, and after two years' service, employees received eight weeks holiday pay and their return fare to Sydney. Tom Lega, who came to Bulolo as an 18 year old dredge hand in 1940 said that *when they were due to go back, employees had to report to the Sydney office. Those whose work had been unsatisfactory were given their DCB (don't come back) notice.*[22] Unlike Australia, where the workforce was highly unionised, there were no unions at Bulolo. Some workers objected to the unilateral determination of working conditions by the company and the lack of employment security.[23] However, BGD never experienced a strike, and efforts to enforce compulsory unionism in 1941 came to nothing when BGD employees opposed a draft award—apparently fearing that it would fix conditions inferior to those they already enjoyed.[24]

Recognising the difficulties of maintaining a large, stable workforce in an isolated tropical community, BGD provided excellent living conditions for white employees and their families.

In mid-1932, one of the first women at Bulolo, Kath Honeysett, recorded her impressions in letters to her family. She was overwhelmed by the novelty of living in a place that *has sprung up out of the virgin bush* — where the primitive co-existed with the modern. The early houses had rough limbong floors and thatched kunai roofs harbouring rats and diverse insect life (including particularly large spiders), but also cedar furniture, electric lights and power, electric irons and fans.[25] *The whole system is unique to me — it is so self-contained. The climate, the scenery, the strange unexplored nature of the country and natives, the fantastic setting of the dredge and circling planes makes Bulolo ... an exciting adventure.*[26]

In August 1932, BGD installed a refrigeration plant at Bulolo, and fresh fish, meat, fruit and butter — most of it from Australia — replaced tinned food. Smaller refrigerators were later installed at Bulwa and other camps. As well as locally grown vegetables, married employees could purchase fresh eggs from the company's poultry farm. While there was no hotel, the company store sold Fosters beer to employees, a dozen

Bulwa from the air, 1935–36. Dredge No. 3 is at top right and No. 4 at bottom. Road at left leads to Baiune Power Station.

bottles of which fitted neatly into a Crosley icyball, a primitive refrigeration unit in each house.

The quality of housing soon improved. Unmarried employees were accommodated three to a house, each with their own bedroom, and ate in the company mess. Married men lived in two bedroom houses. Arthur Ives recalled:

> You couldn't wish for a better house. The furniture was absolutely perfect. They bought the best of everything—cutlery, crockery, all that. Electric light, no charge for power or rent. They gave us a big icebox and ice was delivered every day. They came round every day with fresh vegetables. All that was free![27]

A well equipped hospital was also provided.

Initially there was little recreational infrastructure and people entertained themselves as best they could. Bulolo was home to many beautiful butterflies. Arthur John recalled that

> It was always a source of wonder to see Peter Mirovitch, a rigger of Herculean physique, setting off with his butterfly net on Sunday mornings. The first reaction was that Pete had 'gone tropo', but he persisted and others joined him.[28]

Others went bush walking, canoeing on dredge ponds or even prospecting.

As Bulolo grew, so did the range of recreational facilities provided by BGD, and by the late 1930s they would have done justice to a fair size town in Australia. A picture theatre showed films on Wednesday and Saturday nights, and by 1942, Bulolo and Bulwa between them could boast four recreation halls with billiard tables, table tennis, a lending library and reading room, four tennis courts with lighting for night tennis, three swimming pools fed by natural springs, a six rink bowling green, nine and six hole golf courses, a 600 yard rifle range and a concrete cricket pitch. BGD also supported employee involvement in sporting competitions, flying teams around the district. In 1939, the patron of Bulolo Golf Club, Les Waterhouse, donated the Waterhouse Cup for annual competition between golf clubs of the Morobe District.

It was hardly surprising that, as Healy later concluded, *The coherence and camaraderie of the community were a prime attraction, and many men, despite their two year contracts, came to regard Bulolo as home.*[29]

Nor did BGD neglect its indentured labourers. Most came from villages in the Sepik district and were recruited for two or three years, usually as general

Bulolo township, 1937-38. Barracks and married quarters, and night tennis court. Huts in distance belong to BGD labourers.

labourers for which they were paid 6 shillings per month. They were used to unload planes, to clear jungle ahead of the dredges and as assistants to the many different tradesmen at Bulolo, telephone switchboard operators, messengers, mess waiters, labourers, personal servants, cooks and houseboys. BGD realised at the outset that, allowing for normal turnover, it would need many labourers, and that it would be more successful in attracting them if they returned to their villages happy that BGD had treated them well. As Healy put it:

> BGD aimed to create a contented community of indentured workers. Extensive recreational facilities were provided, sports teams were given fields and equipment, and to some extent native workers were encouraged to plant their own plots of ground. These things represented an attempt to retain elements of the familiar village atmosphere, and to blend them with those of a wider community. Housing reflected a similar approach: BGD rejected the large, impersonal barracks typical of plantation compounds, and built a number of small huts holding two to four workers each. Instead of a communal mess, rations were issued individually, so that the natives were free to do their own cooking in little groups of friends and wantoks.[30]

The huts were located within compounds, which had electricity, running water and showers and a septic tank sewerage system.[31] Close by were gardens containing kaukau, taro, corn, paw paws and bananas. There was also a trade store, where goods could be purchased and which distributed food rations and clothing.

BGD paid particular attention to the health of its labourers. They invariably arrived from their villages in a fairly debilitated condition. Within a short time, however, good food and exercise filled out their physique. They had access to a high standard of medical services, Bulolo having the best equipped hospital in the Territory. As a result, their mortality rate was considerably less than elsewhere on the goldfields.[32] It is hardly surprising that there was never a shortage of villagers from the Sepik and elsewhere lining up to work at Bulolo.

If not for the sensitive and insightful way it addressed the many risks and challenges it faced throughout the pre-war period, the BGD story would have had a very different outcome. One has to look no further than New Guinea Goldfields for some idea of how things may have turned out.

Bulwa, 1935–36.

CHAPTER 10
THE EBB AND FLOW OF FORTUNES

The discovery of gold, even in apparently rich concentrations,
was no guarantee of financial success.

Geological and topographical conditions posed many technical challenges. Mining techniques were also critically dependent on water, of which there was often too little or too much. Such factors, together with high transport costs, meant that deposits that would have been very profitable in Australia were often unviable in New Guinea.

Ultimately, it was a company's organisational abilities and discipline in managing risk as much as the gold in the ground that determined its success. Mining companies had to adapt flexibly to the conditions, and some were very innovative in doing so. Several small companies established efficiently run and profitable mining. For others success was more elusive.

If BGD's experience was a case study in how to succeed when mining in a remote location, the experience of some other companies — and New Guinea Goldfields (NGG) in particular — provided the 'how not to do it' case with equal clarity.

By the early 1930s, Placer Development and NGG controlled much of the field — Placer the lower Bulolo valley, NGG Edie Creek and much of the area around Wau. Many other leases pegged during the earlier flurry of company flotations were soon abandoned as being unworkable, unpayable or both.

With NGG's efforts focused on testing its leases and BGD's first dredge yet to commence operations, gold production at this time was almost at a standstill. Day Dawn mine was an exception; though a small operation, it was producing good gold from the rich veins on its property, known locally as 'the jeweller's shop'. Tributers had been working NGG's alluvial leases at Edie and Koranga Creeks and on the Bulolo, but these expired in February 1932 and were not renewed. A few miners worked their own leases at Edie Creek, and while some were beginning to look further afield, the cost of maintaining supplies limited prospecting by individual miners. On occasion, this was resolved by miners sharing the cost of small prospecting parties.

The cost of airfreight discouraged all but the most optimistic and persistent, and those with deep pockets. In December 1930, the Mining Warden observed:

> The cost of introducing the necessary heavy mining plant by aeroplane transportation is economically prohibitive, and is crippling the development of this very promising field. Until direct road communication (and a consequent reduction in transport charges) between the coast and the goldfields is an accomplished fact, this field can never develop along the lines it obviously should. Expenditure which should be devoted to mining development is being eaten up in transportation costs.

This theme was taken up by others during 1931, the Manager of Day Dawn claiming that the cost of airfreighting machinery to Wau exceeded its purchase price.[1]

But the seeds of a revival were sown in September 1931, when Great Britain abandoned the Gold Standard.[2] The flight to gold that followed saw its price rise gradually from £3/17 shillings and 10½ pence sterling an ounce to £6/10 shillings by the end of 1933. The USA abandoned the Gold Standard in April 1933 and in January 1934 devalued the dollar against gold by 40%, raising the price to $US35 per ounce. Competition was also driving down the cost of airfreight. From more than 1 shilling per pound in the late 1920s, it fell to 6 pence in 1931 and 4 pence in 1933, making it economic to use more sophisticated equipment to work areas previously regarded as unpayable.

These developments set the stage for a resurgence in activity. The rising gold price, in particular, led to a fresh surge of aspiring miners from Australia and a second wave of company flotations on Australian stock exchanges. Investors' memories being short, these again included several of dubious intent, leading the Warden to complain that the promoters of 'wild cat' mining companies were undermining genuine enterprise.[3]

Despite the dramatic improvement in the economics of gold mining, for NGG the 1930s were a decade of disappointment. Its issued capital was nearly £4.5 million, much of it in shares issued to acquire leases. Not only did it pay far too much for these, but it had left them to be worked by their owners for 12 to 18 months after taking options over them.

The scale of NGG's expenditure and testing in the early 1930s created great expectations, but delivered little value for its shareholders. Much of the money spent freely to establish the necessary infrastructure was wasted—such as the survey of the light railway from the coast, the ill-fated Handley Page and the flood-prone aerodrome at Salamaua.

With its £1 shares languishing below 5 shillings late in 1931 and the Depression weighing heavily on world stock markets, there was no scope for NGG to raise additional equity. Its major shareholder, the UK-based Mining Trust Ltd, which had been spun off by Ellyou, held an option over 500,000 £1 shares, but was unable to raise the funds to exercise this.

NGG, with shrinking financial reserves, faced the challenge of achieving production on a scale large enough to provide a satisfactory return on its huge capital from leases that were not only widely scattered but posed diverse mining challenges. It was soon evident that its grand vision did not incorporate a plan to integrate its many leases and work them cost effectively.

Given its capital constraint, NGG might have been expected to use its alluvial leases to generate the cash flow required to develop its more complex ore bodies—much as Levien had sought to do with Kaili 4 a few years earlier. That it did so at all, however, was only at the Administration's insistence. And rather than develop the infrastructure to support alluvial mining on a sustained basis, it delegated these operations to tributers, so as to continue devoting all its energies to testing its leases, particularly the perceived jewel in the NGG crown, the Edie Creek lodes.

In 1931, NGG discovered a 100,000 ton ore body at Golden Ridges, about three miles from Wau, on the lower slopes of Mt. Kaindi. It was close to the surface and so amenable to open cut operations. NGG's approach to developing the mine was, however, typical of its poor decision making. Rather than construct a small pilot plant and fine tune processes to local conditions, it imported a full scale plant from America and began operating in August 1932. NGG's intention was to dry the ore by heating it, and then place it in vats where cyanide would leach out the gold, which

Golden Ridges mill.

NGG's Edie No. 4 shaft and mill.

was associated with clay and manganese oxides. However, when heated, the clay formed a cement-like aggregate, greatly reducing gold recovery. Within a year, the process had been replaced by direct leaching of the ore. The vats used for this were made of heavy duty steel, although corrugated iron vats would have been adequate and certainly much cheaper to fly to the field.

Meanwhile, NGG's efforts to develop an underground mine at Edie Creek were beset with problems. Several shafts were sunk and drilling identified three major vein systems. However, considerable water—up to 3,000 gallons an hour—was encountered at depth. Initially, in the absence of electrical power, this was extracted using compressed air pumps. These were inefficient and costly, and progress was slow. The shafts were lined with timber which, being softwood, had to be constantly replaced in the damp conditions. In 1934, the 350 foot deep No. 3 shaft caved in and was abandoned.

Rather than emulate BGD and construct a hydroelectric power station, NGG erected a wood-burning steam power plant at Kunai Creek, near Golden Ridges, with a high tension power line linking it to Edie Creek. However, lack of forward planning meant that power was not available until June 1932, considerably delaying mine development. The power station consumed large quantities of softwood, and soon proved uneconomic. In 1934, NGG decided to acquire power from BGD's

Baiune power station, and by early 1935 it finally had a cost-effective and reliable source of power.

By late 1934, after several years of testing, NGG estimated that its reserves at Edie Creek amounted to 156,000 tons, averaging half an ounce of gold per ton—enough for four years operations. It decided to install a mill capable of treating 100 tons of ore a day, and this began operating in January 1936—nearly six years after the first shafts were sunk.

The production delays and litany of costly decisions attracted increasing criticism in the Australian press, which contrasted the vastly different fortunes of NGG and BGD shareholders. Late in 1933, NGG shares were selling for 6 shillings and 8 pence compared with £5/9 shillings and 6 pence for BGD shares.[4] The widely read *Pacific Islands Monthly* was increasingly strident in its criticism of NGG's refusal to work its leases. In 1934, it was content to refer to the *comparative paralysis* that characterised NGG's operations, but by 1939 NGG was *the black beast which sits upon the neck of Wau ... [a] stupid, blundering, mismanaged and monopolistic concern ...* [5]

From 1932 to 1934, NGG averaged an annual return of less than 3% on its issued capital of £4.5 million. This under-performance was the more striking given the rising gold price and lower freight rates, and largely reflected its obsession with testing and developing the Edie Creek underground mine.

Late in 1934, with its share price languishing at 6 shillings and 3 pence compared with BGD's £9, an Englishman, J.P. Blaikie Webster, was appointed Chairman of NGG. In April 1935, he announced a reduction of 75% in the value of its issued capital. While this was intended to clear the decks, net profit actually fell in each of the next four years, and in 1938 NGG achieved a return of only 4.5% on its reduced capital.

Blaikie Webster approached challenges in the Ellyou tradition. He was a man who, after his resignation three years later, *Pacific Islands Monthly* described as *active and shrewd; but he tried to apply Napoleonic methods to Australian and New Guinea institutions, and he found himself opposed at many points by people who instinctively resist dictatorships.*[6] Rather than address operational issues, Webster's strategy was to attack anyone who could be blamed for NGG's misfortunes, his two main targets being Guinea Airways and the Administration.

From the outset, NGG had aggressively sought to induce Guinea Airways to lower its airfreight rates. Webster intensified this campaign, tearing up contracts, bullying local managers[7] and generally outmanoeuvring the Guinea Airways Board. Criticism of its performance made NGG acutely sensitive to Guinea Airways' generous dividends, which Webster attributed to the fact that it was *not subject to the same punitive taxation as my company, which has to pay the Administration a total contribution equalling one-third of our profits.*[8] Guinea Airways dominated aviation in New Guinea, most other planes being small and unreliable. NGG was therefore dependent on its fleet, and in particular its single large Junkers G31. By giving a share of NGG's business to other operators at lower rates, however, Webster astutely used this as a lever on Guinea Airways, forcing its freight rate down from an average of 3.66 pence per pound in December 1933 to a little more than 2 pence in early 1936.

NGG had had various disagreements with the Administration prior to Blaikie Webster's arrival. These related to the proposed light railway in 1929, NGG's reluctance to work its leases in 1929/30, the 10% duty on mining machinery imports introduced in July 1930, and the Administration's refusal to complete the road between Wau and Edie Creek in 1930/31.[9] But relations nevertheless remained generally harmonious.

Under pressure over NGG's poor performance, however, Webster repeatedly and publicly attacked the Administration over its refusal to build a road from Salamaua to Wau, to introduce a tax on profits in lieu of the 5% gold royalty, or to ease restrictions on labourers operating machinery.

On the last two of these issues, Webster had legitimate concerns, but frustration at the Administration's inflexibility led him to overplay his hand. Thus, at NGG's Annual Meeting in February 1936: *It is demanded that the system of imposing a royalty on gold be abandoned and that a system of taxing profits be substituted.*[10]

However valid his argument against a flat tax on revenue which applied only to gold producers and made no allowance for production costs, Webster's arrogance and NGG's long record of poor and costly decisions did little to encourage a positive response. Administrator McNicoll haughtily rejected NGG's demand on the grounds that *a system of taxation of net profits would reduce any contribution by this company to our revenue to a minimum.*[11]

The issue of using indentured labourers to operate machinery first arose during a strike by winding engine drivers[12] in November 1935, when NGG sought to use lorry drivers to operate winches. Webster claimed that indigenous labourers in South Africa, Rhodesia or India commonly performed work that in New Guinea was performed exclusively by Europeans:

> I feel the time has come, not only because of the very high cost to us of the importation into the Territory of labour, but also because these natives are showing a high degree of competency, when the Company should be permitted … to use natives in any kind of work in the industry, where we find them competent, under European supervision.[13]

Webster's proposal to break the strike using labourers was rejected by the Mining Inspector, who was *not prepared to allow natives to operate machinery in or about mines or works.*[14] This response seemed to imply a new and more restrictive policy, as NGG was already using labourers to operate a range of machinery. The Administrator also rejected Webster's rather pointed request that NGG be permitted to engage 24 experienced Papuans as instructors.

By now, Webster and the Administrator were in open conflict, with Webster requesting that the Government establish an enquiry into the Administration's attitude on the employment of New Guineans, taxation and a raft of other issues. He threatened that, if it did not do so, he would take the matter up with the Permanent Mandates Commission (which monitored Australia's performance under the League of Nations Mandate). The Government called his bluff, though in June 1936 the Administration quietly relented on the use of machinery by New Guineans. The Mines and

Works Regulation Ordinance was amended to permit uncertificated drivers to operate any winding engine or machinery other than to raise or lower men in a shaft or when a shaft was being sunk, as well as other machinery unless prohibited by the Administrator.[15]

This barely mollified Webster, who remained aggrieved at the lack of movement on the tax and road issues, and inability to use New Guineans to operate winding engines without restriction. At NGG's Annual Meeting in February 1937, he claimed these made it impossible to mine a grade of ore that would have been highly profitable elsewhere. He then threatened

> to restrict production until the advent of more normal conditions … rather than undertake the development and treatment of additional ore, which under present conditions, would provide contributions to the Administration, but leave no return for shareholders.[16]

The following month, Blaikie Webster resigned suddenly and returned to England. The new Chairman was a marked (and for the Administration, welcome) change—a quietly spoken, diminutive American, Julius Kruttschnitt, the former General Manager and now Chairman of Mount Isa Mines.

While Kruttschnitt worked hard to improve relations with the Administration, he was less successful in turning around NGG's mining fortunes. At Edie Creek, the poor quality timber used in shoring operations made it uneconomical to progress shafts and tunnels far in advance of production, and thus to estimate ore reserves with any degree of precision.

In 1936/37, the Edie Creek mine yielded 15,245 ounces of gold and nearly 30,000 ounces of silver. Thereafter, as poorer grade ore was crushed, production declined gradually to 10,000 ounces of gold and 57,000 ounces of silver in 1939/40.

Despite early teething problems, Golden Ridges proved to be NGG's most productive mine in the pre-war period, its 140,000 ounces of gold far outstripping the 68,000 ounces recovered from NGG's Edie Creek underground operations. In 1938, its ore finally exhausted, the mill was modified to treat harder ore transported by an aerial ropeway from a new underground mine at nearby Upper Ridges.

In June 1940, all 25 Italians employed in NGG's mining operations were interned, seriously dislocating production at Edie Creek. Golden and Upper Ridges were also affected. NGG hurriedly recruited a number of Australians to replace them, only to find they included many industrial activists. In March 1941, underground

workers at Upper Ridges went on strike for higher pay and shorter hours; miners at Edie Creek went out in sympathy a few days later.

The Territory had no provision for compulsory arbitration, and while the Administrator tried to mediate, he was unsuccessful.[17] The strike dragged on for several months, bringing NGG's mining operations to a halt. Some men gradually returned to work, though a small hard core remained on strike. Gold production by the Edie Creek mill was nevertheless minimal thereafter, and mining at Upper Ridges was permanently suspended in October 1941.

As NGG's fortunes ebbed and those of BGD flowed, so did those of other companies. While some of those floated as a consequence of the rising gold price lacked real substance, eight smaller companies made their mark through the 1930s, with varying success.[18] Their experience provides a perspective on the different types of mining and techniques used, and the way they handled the challenges that confronted them.

At Edie Creek, **Day Dawn's** success proved all too brief. In November 1932, a second mill was added to the one that had commenced milling in May 1931. But Day Dawn made the classic mistake of working only the rich ore and had no reserves to fall back on once this had been extracted. It ceased operating in June 1935, having produced nearly 23,000 ounces of gold.

Day Dawn South (New Guinea) N.L. was formed in 1933 to work a three foot wide reef on the southern fall of Mt. Kaindi, an hour's walk from Edie Creek, in the hope that it would develop into something larger. It didn't. The company folded in 1936 after producing a mere 3,177 ounces of gold.

Two sister companies were formed in 1935 with great ambitions—**Upper Watut Gold Alluvials** (UWGA) and **Irowat Gold Alluvials** (IGA). The former's leases on the Upper Watut were estimated to contain more than 2 million cubic yards of alluvial gravel, valued at 3 shillings and 7 pence per yard. A massive water race was constructed to bring water to the workings from Slate Creek. Sluicing began in August 1936. However, values proved to be one third of those expected and costs far higher due to the unforeseen presence of boulders. The project quickly proved uneconomic and UWGA ceased operating.

IGA's experience also reflected inadequate prior testing. Its leases, at the junction of Iroa Creek and the

Geoffrey Baskett took a job driving tractors for UWGA, and later described the race.[19] A weir across Slate Creek diverted a steady stream of water into a massive concrete water race, 6 feet across and deep, built on a 12 feet wide bench cut into the mountain side. It was four miles long, passing through two tunnels lined with concrete pipes and across a timber viaduct 80 feet high and 200 feet long. At its end, the race was 400 feet above the mine site. The water was then delivered under great pressure through 3 inch nozzles. These were directed at the gold-bearing alluvial gravel lining the river banks, dislodging massive quantities of soil and gravel, which then ran through long sluice boxes.

Baskett's job entailed unusual risks. On one occasion, he was given a revolver. *'What on earth is this for?' I asked. 'Well,' was the reply, 'some of the Kukukuku tribesmen in this area have been shooting up the European owner of a trade store near here ... The boss thinks they might have a shot at other Europeans, and as you will be working in their bush area today, he wants you to take this along with you.'* [20]

Watut, were estimated to contain 1 million cubic yards of gravel with a value of 3 shillings and 9 pence per yard. Water was bought from 2½ miles upstream via an earthen race and six sections of fluming 500 feet long carrying water over gullies on precarious timber trestles. Opened with great ceremony by the Administrator in May 1936, values proved to be a quarter of those expected; within a year IGA was in liquidation.

Bulolo Gold Deposits held productive leases in the Wau and Koranga area. While conducting some sluicing operations with modest success, it eventually decided that it could do better by selling them to BGD (which constructed dredge No. 6 to work them) and NGG.

The remaining three companies used hydraulic monitors and/or elevators[21] fed by long water races, the gold being recovered by sluicing. They demonstrated how modestly capitalised but well run companies could be profitable despite the high costs of operating in such a remote locality.

Using a three mile long race to deliver water under pressure, **Sandy Creek Gold Sluicing** worked Sandy and Poverty Creeks, near Wau, from late 1936. Draining the Kuper Range, they yielded gold of similar high quality to Black Cat gold, averaging up to 3 shillings and 9 pence a yard. Costs were rigidly controlled, with

production using hydraulic elevators being gradually scaled up to exceed 200,000 cubic yards a year. From 1937 to 1940, Sandy Creek Gold's average return on capital of 13.5% far outstripped that of NGG.

Koranga Gold Sluicing (KGS) was formed in 1931 to work terraces at the head of Koranga Creek with hydraulic monitors (or nozzles), the gold being recovered in sluice boxes 30 feet long. However, the area was prone both to sudden flooding and water shortages and gold production was regularly disrupted. Scars on the hillsides around Wau today bear witness to the solution: a 5 mile long water race constructed by NGG to bring water a considerable distance to both companies' leases. In the late 1930s, NGG also constructed a 2.8 mile long race from the Kulolo River to the old Kaili 4 leases — ironically along the route condemned by Jensen to the Guinea Gold Board a decade earlier.

Sunshine Gold Development was responsible for the longest water race on the field, downstream from Bulwa near the Watut-Snake junction. Whereas KGS worked exposed terraces with monitors, Sunshine Gold's gravels were at depths of up to 75 feet, requiring hydraulic elevators and thus considerable water pressure. In the first half of 1936, a race was constructed to the mine from the headwaters of Baiune creek. It was a remarkable engineering feat, being 12½ miles long, 4 feet 6 inches wide and 5 feet deep.

After the procrastination and drama of the late 1920s, the issue of a road from the coast died in the early 1930s as airfreight rates declined. In 1934, Administrator Griffiths reprised the idea — not only to assist the gold industry, but also to encourage the development of agricultural and timber industries. However, his proposal attracted little support and the issue faded with his departure later in the year.

In 1936, Blaikie Webster resurrected the proposal. By this time many miners were being forced to work poorer ground and the belief took hold that road transport would be cheaper than air, enabling lower grade deposits to be worked and the life of the field to be prolonged. Air freight cost £15 to £20 per ton, compared with £88 in 1929, but proponents convinced themselves that the cost by road would be as low as £5 per ton, despite the obviously high costs of road construction and maintenance.

Finally, in 1938, the Commonwealth Government agreed to guarantee the repayment of a loan not

Enterprise of New Guinea Gold and Petroleum N.L. The company had developed an ore body of 285,000 tons at the back of Edie Creek assaying 7 pennyweights per ton. This was uneconomic even at the low airfreight rates prevailing, and the road at least offered the possibility of lower costs.

In the end, with the Administration's indecisiveness and the growing threat of a Pacific War, any decision to proceed was put on hold for the duration.

Other than Western Australia, the Morobe goldfields were the richest gold producing area in Australasia during the 1930s.[22] Between 1931/32 and 1941/42, they produced about 2,056,000 fine ounces. BGD produced 1,297,000 ounces[23] (or 63%) and NGG about 400,000 ounces (19.5%).[24] Of the remaining 17.5%, individual miners appear to have accounted for more than three quarters and smaller companies the remainder.

For the whole period 1924–42, gold production on the Morobe goldfield amounted to 2.3 million ounces.[25] 56.8% was obtained by dredging, 33.7% by other forms of alluvial mining and 9.5% by lode mining.[26]

BGD not only produced three times as much gold as NGG during the pre-war period but did so at lower cost, its profit of £6/12 shillings per ounce of gold produced far outstripping NGG's £2/12 shillings.

It is easy to portray BGD as a methodical, efficient, risk-averse operator and NGG as arrogant, stumbling and inept. While there is some truth in each description, their relative performance also reflected other factors. Whereas BGD's operations were homogeneous, NGG's involved underground and open-cut mining and the working of alluvial river gravels. Each posed distinctive challenges, impairing NGG's ability to achieve economies of scale. Its underground mining operations, in particular, were inherently more expensive to develop and experienced major operational problems. NGG's gold bullion was also of poorer quality, with a higher silver content. Finally, its productivity was affected by the fact that its Edie Creek operations were in a much colder, wetter and more uncomfortable climate than the benign conditions of the lower Bulolo Valley.

Nevertheless, NGG did benefit from a much higher gold price and lower air freight rates than it could ever have foreseen at the outset. As others showed, size was less important than a good understanding and effective management of financial and operational risk. In the end, its failure to manage risk was NGG's undoing.

Water race bridging a gully, Kulolo.

exceeding £150,000 to be raised from New Guinea residents and used to finance construction of a road. Repayments and interest were to be met by a toll. The focus of public debate then shifted to which of four alternative routes the road should take from Salamaua to Wau. The miners wanted a direct route, whereas the Administrator favoured one via the Markham and Wampit valleys, as being of greater value in opening up the interior. Debate raged back and forth through 1939–41, with surveyors and engineers clearly daunted at the challenges they faced.

NGG faded into the background, the role of advocate being taken by a former Mining Warden, Harold Taylour, now General Manager of the grandly-named

PART 4
A HIGHWAY IN THE SKY: THE ROLE OF AVIATION

Junkers G31 'Paul'. The plane's wingspan was 96'8" and its length 58'10".

CHAPTER 11
GOLDEN AIRWAYS

The extraordinary nature of Levien's vision for aviation must be seen in context. At the time, Australian aviation was still in its infancy.

Keith and Ross Smith had won £10,000 offered by the Australian Government in 1919 for being the first to fly between England and Australia, their twin engine plane completing the distance in 29 days. In 1928, Charles Kingsford Smith and Charles Ulm (in the *Southern Cross*) were the first to fly between the United States and Australia.

But such spectacular feats were not matched by progress in civil aviation. By the end of 1926, aeroplanes had flown only a total of about 40 tons of cargo in Australia.

Before 1927, the only planes to fly in Papua or New Guinea were seaplanes—one in 1922 by Andrew Lang, a member of an exploration party organised by Frank Hurley, and an RAAF plane undertaking a defence survey in 1926. Vast stretches of mountainous jungle meant there was little flat ground for airstrips, while the tiny European population and uninviting economic prospects provided no reason to believe there would be much demand for air transport in future.

Against such a background, Levien's belief that aviation could be used to unlock the potential of the goldfields, which he articulated as early as 1925, was remarkable.[1] Not only was the terrain inhospitable, but there was no precedent for using planes in this way anywhere in the world. It was hardly surprising that Guinea Gold, with limited capital and directors who had no aviation experience, should hesitate embracing Levien's vision in the latter part of 1926.

By this time much of the preparatory work for an aerial service between the coast and the goldfield had been undertaken by an aspiring aviator, Nobby Clark, including applying for 30 acres for a landing ground at Little Wau Creek. Levien tried to persuade Guinea Gold to back Clark's operation, but nothing came of this as he didn't have a plane.

Nor did Ray Parer, who despite having little money, had formed the Bulolo Goldfields Aeroplane Service barely two months after the rush to Edie Creek had

begun. Parer was a small man, 5 feet 2 inches in height, but a larger than life character. He had competed in the England to Australia air race, together with a Scotsman John McIntosh, in a former single engine World War I bomber, a (De Havilland) DH9.[2] In November 1926, Parer put a deposit on another former bomber, a DH4, and started looking for a financial backer to conclude the deal.

On 30 December 1926, two entrepreneurs, H.S. Holdgate and P.D. McKenzie, approached Guinea Gold looking to establish an aerial service in New Guinea.[3] They had an option over a DH37 from the Civil Aviation Branch of the Department of Defence, but lacked the funds to complete the transaction. Finally giving in to Levien's pressure, the Board agreed to take over its purchase and on 8 January 1927, Guinea Gold acquired the plane for £2,000.

The Board then arranged with Levien to establish aerodromes at Lae and at Wau, selected a flying instructor at Essendon Aerodrome, A.E. (Pard) Mustar, as the pilot and appointed as Chief Engineer A.W.D. (Mull) Mullins, an aircraft engineer with the Civil Aviation Branch.

The DH37 left Sydney in crates on the *Melusia* on 1 February 1927 for Rabaul, arriving safely despite anxious moments in a typhoon. The next few weeks were taken up assembling and test flying the aircraft and making an aerodrome at Rabaul so it could take off.

Finally, on 30 March 1927, Mustar and Mullins took off on a 540 mile flight in the little biplane from Rabaul to Lae, much of it over open sea. Mustar's diary recorded: *Engine developed an intermittent miss, so did our hearts. Crossed Dampier Straits, saw millions of sharks in our minds; engine took great delight in missing more frequently.*[4] Their destination was a 50 by 300 yard paddock carved out of the jungle on the water's edge, not far from the mouth of the Markham River. However, as they approached, Mustar thought it was like a miniature tennis court. Strips of red cloth showed soft patches to be avoided and white strips marked stumps bordering the aerodrome. It was with immense relief that Mustar landed 5 hours and 20 minutes after leaving Rabaul, with half an hour's petrol in reserve.

Levien was not present for Mustar's arrival, being tied up in Salamaua dealing with a malicious prosecution initiated by an Administration official over the death of a labourer.[5] That night, however, when he and Mustar got together for the first time, they quickly established a strong rapport. Mustar later recalled,

> I was immensely impressed with this man whose gaze penetrated your innermost mind. He had an amazing grasp of many subjects, a quick talker, but a keen and interested listener. Despite his hard living, his actions were full of consideration. He was vital. There was something very human about him and I soon felt that in him I would find a real friend.[6]

Mustar himself was a thoughtful man, not shy of expressing his opinion. Described as 'sturdy, snappy and wiry',[7] at 5 foot 6 inches he was the same height as Levien. He had served at Gallipoli from the landing to the evacuation, then transferred to the Australian Flying Corps, flying with Ross Smith as an observer/gunner in Palestine, where he won the Distinguished Flying Cross. He later qualified as a pilot and worked as an RAAF instructor. Not only did his vision of how aviation might benefit the goldfields coincide with Levien's, but he also had the technical knowledge to convince others.

After a delay of two weeks, word arrived from Wau that the aerodrome was ready. On 17 April, without any maps and confined to the narrow layer between the jungle and towering cloud formations, Mustar searched for Wau without success. As he did so, he flew up valleys at whose extremities the mountains disappeared into clouds, forcing a hasty retreat. The next day, on his third attempt, Mustar flew inland via Salamaua with Mullins and a miner to guide him; after a short flight, he finally located Wau.

The aerodrome was on the side of a hill. To estimate its gradient, Mustar flew across the top end at about 50 feet, the altimeter registering just over 4,000 feet.[8] Similar action at the bottom suggested the altitude there was 3,500 feet. A smoke signal indicated wind direction, but as the plane had no brakes, Mustar had little choice but to land uphill.

With the pilot occupying the last of three tandem seats, landing the DH37 uphill was particularly difficult.

If he got the angle of approach wrong he would have no second chance. After finding himself flying directly at the ground at one point, Mustar managed to get the plane down with a thump and found he had to taxi at nearly full throttle to reach the top of the aerodrome, where he turned the plane side on to avoid rolling backwards down the slope. On his return flight, he flew down the Bulolo Valley, across Snake River and on through a gap in the mountain range into the open spaces of the Markham Valley.

Two months later, an article by Mustar was published, entitled 'The World's Worst Aerodrome'. He described the Wau airstrip as

> absolutely unique. On the lower side of a mountain, triangular in shape, about 800 yards long, 75 [wide] at the top and 400 at the bottom. Very high trees all round. From the timber at the lower end, for a distance of 200 yards, it is flat and soft. Then it starts off with a slope of 4°, for the next 400 yards. Next comes a piece 50 yards long, with a slope of about 2°. The balance is 4°—perhaps more … To make this drome a bit more interesting there is a small watercourse that cuts the top end in two, longitudinally, for 200 yards.[9]

The air service from Lae to Wau began the next day, with six 100 pound bags of rice. Making two or three

Pard Mustar.

Guinea Gold's DH37. The first plane to operate in New Guinea.

trips a day, five days a week, Mustar carried 12 tons of cargo and 84 passengers in the first three months—60% of this to meet Guinea Gold's own needs. The cost per passenger was initially £33/6 shillings and 8 pence inwards and £10 outwards, with freight at 1 shilling and 6 pence per pound. While the DH37 carried up to 650 pounds, Mustar was initially more comfortable with a limit of 500 pounds, due to the altitude and slope of Wau aerodrome.[10]

In contrast, Ray Parer's efforts to get his aerial service off the ground were continually dogged by a lack of finance and poor organisation, both of which were to characterise his operations in the years ahead. After various mishaps, both financial and aeronautical, Parer finally arrived in Lae with his DH4 on 23 June 1927. His arrival brought the companionship of another pilot for Mustar, and the knowledge that if one were forced to land, the chance of being found and surviving was much greater.

In September 1927, a third aircraft arrived on the field: a DH60 Moth acquired by the Morobe Trading Company, established by a group of miners, including Harry Darby and Hector Wales, who had opened a pub in Wau for which regular and plentiful supplies were needed. Guinea Gold also acquired a DH9, which arrived in October.

All four planes were fabric-covered single engine plywood biplanes, designed neither for freight nor New Guinea's climate. The glue that held them together deteriorated quickly in the high humidity, so crude hangars were constructed out of local timber, held together with vines and thatched with sacsac leaves.

Operating at such a remote location was a daunting experience. Lae had no natural harbour and wharf construction was impractical as the seabed dropped away rapidly from the shore. Ships therefore anchored 150 yards offshore where they were exposed to strong winds and often had difficulty holding anchor. For some time, Burns Philp ships would only discharge cargo 18 miles down the coast at Salamaua. Passengers and all freight were then trans-shipped by pinnace to Lae—a five hour trip.

In the absence of a wharf, the pinnace was run onto a small beach used by villagers to land their canoes, and cargo was lifted ashore. Forty four gallon drums of petrol for the planes were dumped overboard close to shore, manoeuvred in to the beach, and then rolled 300 to 400 yards to the aerodrome. Every month or so for the first four years, thousands of gallons of petrol were handled in this way. On arrival, new planes were often floated to the beach on whaleboats lashed together and lifted up onto dry land, where wheels were attached.

The DH37, DH9, DH4 and DH60 Moth could only carry ¾ ton between them, or a total of six passengers — not enough to satisfy the rapidly growing demand. Nevertheless, at the end of 1927, they had the field to themselves, although Parer had another two small planes on the way.

While Levien's obsession with air transport was driven by his vision for the lower Bulolo leases, he quickly realised that it would be highly profitable in its own right.

Ray Parer's DH4 and hangar at Lae.

Mustar brought with him to New Guinea information on a new German plane, the Junkers W34, which had a payload of 2,000 pounds, three times that of the DH37 and 20 miles per hour faster. It would not require a hangar as its aluminium alloy construction was impervious to humidity. Levien needed no convincing and a month after Mustar's arrival, he cabled Guinea Gold that a second plane was needed, one that would carry 2,000 pounds weight. He pointed out that not only was there more business than the DH37 could handle, but if it broke down or crashed, it would be some time before a replacement arrived.

The Board didn't share Levien's sense of urgency. Guinea Gold had received legal advice shortly after acquiring the DH37 that, as a No Liability Company, it could only undertake aviation and other activities such as store-keeping in connection with its mining activities. This was confirmed shortly after Levien's request for another plane, when Guinea Gold's application for a case and bottle licence in Wau was rejected.

Over the next few months, the Board showed no interest in acquiring a new plane or incorporating a new company to conduct more broadly based activities. It did, however, agree to the appointment of a second pilot, Alan Cross, as Mustar was becoming debilitated by recurring attacks of malaria, making it difficult for him to maintain a regular service. Cross arrived at Lae in early July 1927.

Nevertheless, the Board was gradually worn down by Levien's and Mustar's persistent advocacy, not to mention the impressive financial returns Mustar was able to demonstrate. In August it finally relented, agreeing to send Mustar to Europe to test fly and take delivery of a W34. It also agreed to acquire a DH9 as back up for the DH37 until the W34 arrived. The following month, it invited Levien to submit a proposal for a new company to take over the aerial service from Guinea Gold.

By this time, Coldham's testing of the GG South leases was showing very promising results, and Levien and Mustar believed that, if it were possible to construct a dredge in which no part weighed more than 1,500 pounds, the W34 would enable an early start on dredging. At the Board's request, Mustar visited a dredge expert, who advised that, while this was possible, a dredge in which the heaviest single piece weighed 3 to 4 tons was likely to be more efficient. Mustar decided that while in Europe he would explore whether there was a plane that could carry items of this size.

In October, the Board accepted Levien's proposal for a new company, and on 4 November 1927, Guinea Airways Limited (GAL) was registered in Adelaide. Issued capital was 20,000 £1 shares, of which 10,100 were held by Guinea Gold. Levien agreed to underwrite the 9,900 shares offered to Guinea Gold shareholders (7,500) and members of staff (2,400), and was appointed a Director. On 1 December, Guinea Airways formally took over the air operations of Guinea Gold, with Mustar as General Manager.

Mustar arrived in Europe in December 1927 to test fly the Junkers W34, for which a firm order had been placed in October at a landed cost of around £8,000. He was delighted with the plane and its performance. Its cargo compartment was twice as wide as the DH37's, and its capacity more than three times as great. A unique approach to loading freight meant it could also handle individual items of up to 1,000 pounds, with loading and unloading taking only ten minutes. A crane could lower tackle through a circular manhole 30 inches in diameter in the top of the fuselage above a hatch in the rear end of the cabin floor. Items positioned under the plane could then be lifted up through the hatch and repositioned in the cargo compartment. The W34 could cruise fully loaded at 100 miles per hour. Its fuel capacity of only 70 gallons posed no problems as it would only be making short trips.

Before leaving for Australia by sea with the W34, Mustar enquired whether there was a plane capable of handling larger items. He was shown drawings of a new three engine passenger aircraft, the G31, which Junkers's design staff believed would be able to lift three tons, with loading through a hatch on top of the fuselage. Mustar now believed he had the answer to Levien's prayers.

Levien's apprehension about GAL's reliance on the DH37 was borne out early in January 1928 when its engine failed approaching Wau. It was severely damaged and never flew again in New Guinea. Worse was to follow in March, when GAL's DH9 crashed near Wau, and was written off.

Levien promptly bought the Morobe Trading Company's DH60 Moth, just to keep GAL in the air. However, its salvation was the arrival of Mustar with the W34. On 14 April 1928, a year after his first flight to Wau, Mustar flew in a ton of cargo and two passengers. Over the next 4½ months, the W34 carried over 400 passengers and 295 tons of freight,[11] generating revenue of nearly £29,500 from freight and £1,500 from passengers[12] — nearly four times its capital cost. In this period the W34 carried more than three times the total freight carried in 1928 by all planes in Australia.

In May 1928, and again in June, Mustar requested a second W34. Not only did demand justify this, but Mustar wanted to ensure GAL could continue operating if the W34 were to crash. The Board concurred, and a new W34 was ordered, arriving in Melbourne in November 1928. The first W34 had been freighted to Rabaul, assembled and then flown to Lae. This time it was decided to substitute floats for the wheels and fly it to New Guinea as a seaplane. The plane touched down

W34 No. 3 being landed at Lae, 1929. Once ashore, the floats were replaced with wheels.

regularly as it flew up the east coast of Australia; its fuel tanks had a range of only 350 miles and it needed to refuel itself from drums carried in the cargo compartment. Mustar made the trip without any problems over six days, arriving in Lae on 20 December. The plane was beached, the floats removed, undercarriage and wheels attached, and the plane was ready to enhance GAL's profitability.

Levien had returned to Australia in April 1928, still a Director of GAL and active in supporting Mustar's plans to expand the company's operations. In January 1929, he returned to New Guinea as Guinea Gold's agent, following Jensen's departure to work for Ellyou. Within two months, malaria finally forced Mustar to resign, Alan Cross becoming General Manager of Guinea Airways' operations—though under Levien's oversight. Mustar took up a position in Melbourne with the Vacuum Oil Company, though the GAL Board persuaded him to accept a retainer as an adviser.

Levien threw himself into his work with his usual enthusiasm, reorganising GAL's operations and arranging for goods arriving in crates by ship to be repacked in sacks so they could be delivered more cheaply by air to Wau. In March 1929, he reported that *the Company has secured an excellent name for packing and delivery of goods and this has been mainly instrumental in keeping the machines running so fully loaded.*[13] He continually badgered the Board to increase the number of W34s. Within a month of a third W34 being ordered in June, he was pushing for a fourth, which was duly ordered in October.

The third W34 began operating in December 1929, and together the three W34s transported 232 tons of freight in two months—compared with 236 tons by all planes in Australia in eight years to November 1929. GAL had been highly profitable in the year ending February 1929, carrying 434 tons (at an average price of £99 per ton) and 869 passengers. The additional W34s further boosted profitability in the year ending February 1930, 949 tons being carried (at an average price of £77 per ton) and 2,047 passengers. Levien's foresight and persistence had produced another gold mine.

Success did, however, have its downside. GAL's profitability and high dividends generated considerable resentment among miners because of the impact of freight charges on their costs. In 1930, air freight added 2 shillings and 3 pence to a bottle of beer that cost 1 shilling and 6 pence at Salamaua; a pound of rice increased from 6 pence to 1 shilling and 3 pence per

Ray Parer.

pound. The cost of a boiler imported by Day Dawn mine in 1931 was £875 landed at Salamaua; GAL then charged £1,512 to transport it to Wau. Whenever they could, miners would therefore use Parer or one of GAL's other competitors.

The ability of other operators to make serious inroads into GAL's business in the early years was limited, however, by their lack of capital. Planes arriving on the field were often second hand, and all were small and slow. They included several more DH9s and a Bristol fighter—planes designed for bombing and reconnaissance, not freight and passengers. Many were ill suited to the difficult flying conditions and by June 1930, 14 of the 29 planes that had arrived since April 1927 had crashed, including GAL's first W34 in March 1930. As spare parts were at a premium, these wrecks were frequently cannibalised to keep others in the air. On one occasion, Ray Parer used parts from two DH9s to build a new plane, known affectionately thereafter as his DH18.

After three years of strong demand, air cargo volumes eased in the first half of 1930. Mining activity was subdued as NGG concentrated on testing rather than working its leases. This, and the unsettling impact of the world Depression, led the smaller aviation enterprises to cut their rates from 9 pence to 7 pence and ultimately, in 1931, to 6 pence per pound. While none of the six planes operated by four different groups offered serious competition to GAL's W34s, major clients such as Burns Philp and NGG took advantage of their rate cuts to drive down the rate GAL charged them. Ironically, lower rates impaired the ability of the smaller operators to generate the profits that in time might have enabled them to acquire larger and better aircraft capable of mounting a serious challenge to GAL.

Ray Parer was potentially an effective competitor, his quiet, unassuming manner and casual approach to both finance and flying endearing him to all the miners. He was always willing to extend credit to those down on their luck despite his own invariably stretched finances, and to bend the rules to meet their needs. If a miner wanted long, wide planks for a sluice box that wouldn't fit in his DH9, he delivered them strapped to the outside of the fuselage. 'Battling Parer' was held in such high regard that when a plane he had just acquired crashed, miners contributed sufficient money to enable him to buy a new one.

However, solvency was always a day to day proposition, bad luck and poor financial management preventing him from capitalising on the massive goodwill he enjoyed. He rarely had enough money for proper maintenance and spare parts, much less enough for planes with the capacity to challenge GAL. Years later, Parer admitted that he hated routine and office work of any description.[14] Parer lived for flying; making money was for others.

There were two routes from Lae to Wau. The less direct one followed the valleys, and was more subject to cloud. But pilots had the comfort of knowing that, with several emergency landing grounds scattered along the route, they had a good chance of surviving if their engine failed. Alan Cross remarked how much better his engine ran after the emergency landing grounds were established.[15]

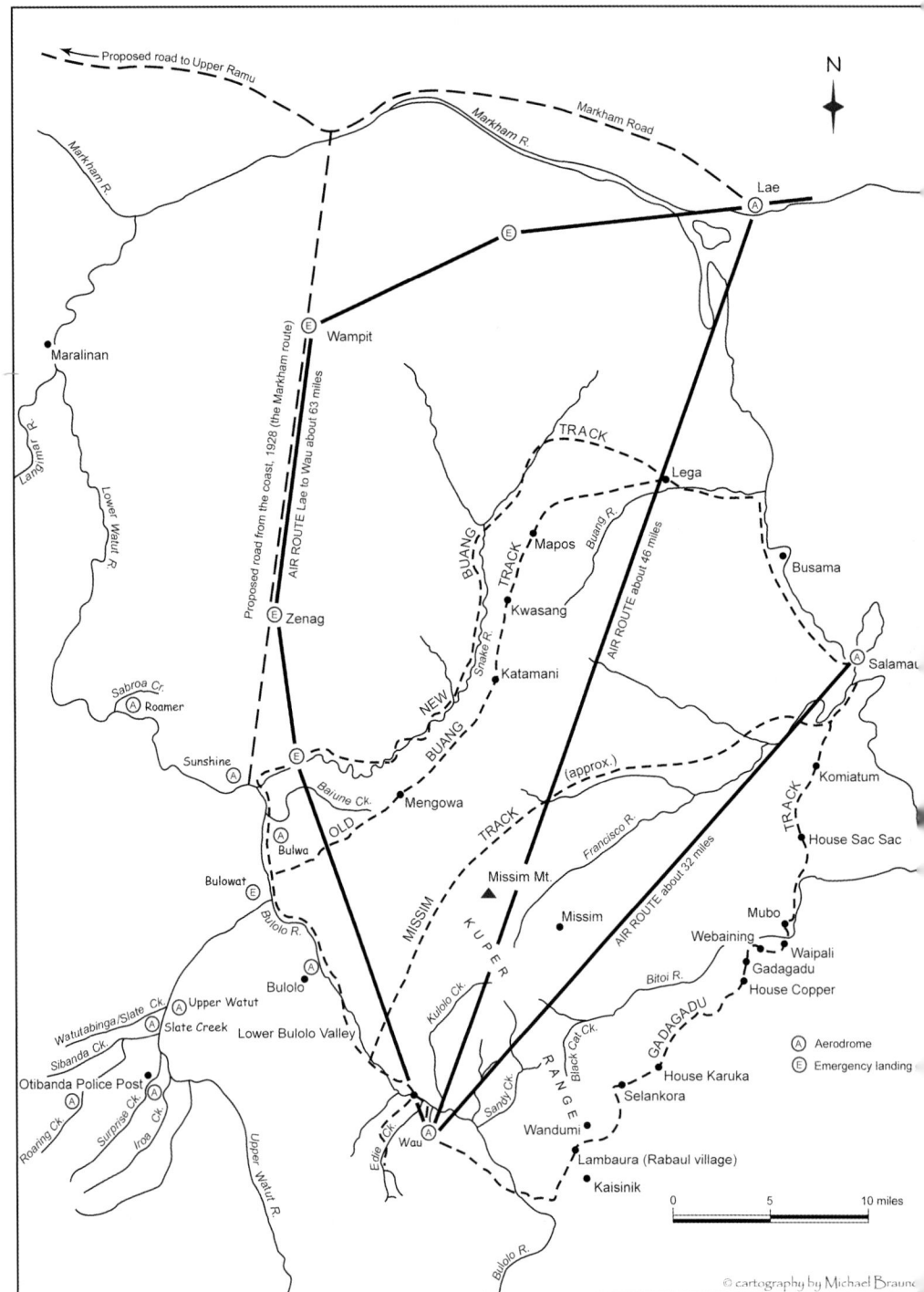

Air routes to, and aerodromes on the field.

112

The more direct route involved climbing to 7,000 feet or more, a height often beyond the capabilities of early planes. As this was over mountainous country, there were also no landing grounds. For many years, pilots carried emergency rations and a pistol, the latter in the belief that villagers along the route were hostile and perhaps even cannibals.

However many trips pilots made, flying light, single

Les Trist.

engine biplanes in the often turbulent conditions was never simply routine. GAL's Ian Grabowsky painted a vivid picture:

> To get caught in a down draught in some steep-sided valley was a terrifying experience. To feel the aircraft sinking—despite using maximum power and rate of climb—to see the jungle mountain sides coming closer and closer and to realise one was being trapped in an area too narrow in which to turn, was frightening.[16]

A cardinal rule from the beginning was 'no see, no fly', as clouds often had 'hard centres'. However, the greatest safety factor was probably the slow speed of the aircraft, which meant that although crashes were not infrequent, fatalities were.

In 1928, a DH Moth returning from Wau ran out of petrol on the final approach to Lae aerodrome.[17] It plunged into the rainforest nearby, coming to rest high up in the canopy, balanced precariously in branches at least 100 feet from the ground. Rescuers arrived and sent villagers up the tree with ropes. These were fastened to a branch and the pilot and his passenger slid down, followed shortly afterwards by the Moth itself, a tangled wreck of broken fuselage, wings and bracing wires.

Two pilots who were not so fortunate were inseparable mates, Frank Drayton and Les Trist. They had been Flight Sergeants with the RAAF, and came to New Guinea as pilots with Airgold. When this short-lived enterprise collapsed, they flew for themselves and then for GAL. Drayton and Trist were experienced

Les Trist on an Emergency Landing Ground in the Buang area.

pilot-engineers, and their easy-going approach to life made them popular throughout the goldfields. Trist died in May 1931 when, in foggy conditions, his W34 No. 4 crashed into the side of a mountain on a flight from Lae to Bulolo. Despite an intensive search, the crash site could not be located, only being discovered near the Wampit Gap in August after villagers brought Trist's head into Lae in a bag. Breaching the 'no see, no fly' rule had cost him his life. Drayton died on Boxing Day 1932, his DH60 Moth crashing at the bottom of Wau aerodrome when his engine cut out.

On several occasions, Ray Parer narrowly avoided crashes. He was renowned for replacing a fractured fuel line with a length of bamboo, and for tying bits of his planes together with clothesline and bootlaces. His easygoing attitude to repairs extended to refuelling. Once when flying the Wau-Port Moresby route across some of the wildest country in New Guinea, he had to land on a beach when his petrol ran out, and another time he landed in Port Moresby but with insufficient petrol to taxi to the hangar. In 1932, his engine cut out at about 2,000 feet and he reached Salamaua aerodrome with 20 yards to spare. In his report to the Controller of Civil Aviation, the District Officer drily noted that Parer

> informed me that although he reached the Salamaua aerodrome safely, it was only by a matter of 20 yds or so … upon examination he found all petrol tanks were dry … I am led to believe that this is not the first time a machine belonging to this company has run out of petrol whilst in flight.[18]

Not that crashing worried Parer unduly. When the engine on his Fokker F111 failed on take off at Salamaua, the plane crashed into trees at the end of the aerodrome. Another pilot, Lionel Shoppee, reported *The cargo manager and myself got to the aircraft through a mangrove swamp towards Salamaua and found Ray sitting on a bag of rice smoking a cigarette.*[19]

For miners, flying was greatly preferable to the rigours of the tracks between the coast and the field. Travelling time was reduced from six to eight days to 30 to 35 minutes. The small planes enabled a scaling up of activity on the field even before the arrival of the first W34. The DH37 could carry as much cargo in a week as 150 or more carriers in a fortnight. Many carriers were thus released to work on claims and leases, dramatically increasing productivity. In December 1927, the Mining Warden noted *It is surprising the difference* [planes] *have made to the transport question … very few carrying lines are now employed on the road …*

With the arrival of the first W34 in April 1928, freight volumes increased appreciably. For the first time bulky and heavy items could be transported by air, giving miners access to more sophisticated machinery and equipment. Day Dawn was the first company to use the W34, flying in around 100 tons of machinery, much of it in sections for reassembly on the field; the largest individual piece weighed 1,000 pounds. With the growing number of planes using its aerodrome, Wau was by now becoming the focal point for the goldfields, a hub from which prospecting and mining developments radiated in many different directions.

Aviation had a significant impact on the lives of Europeans and their labourers. More reliable and regular food and other supplies made it easier for them to move out and prospect new areas. The greater availability of fresh food and medicines reduced the incidence of conditions such as beriberi, while dysentery on the track and in villages nearby also declined appreciably. Men who were very sick could now be flown to Lae and transported to Salamaua hospital on the pinnace; and after the Salamaua aerodrome was opened in May 1929, emergency cases could be flown there directly.[20]

The level of activity built steadily as more planes arrived; in January 1929, there were up to 24 arrivals a day in Wau when the weather was fine. In October 1930, *Pacific Islands Monthly* was able to report

> It is now possible for residents of Edie Creek, where NGG has its headquarters, to leave their homes early in the morning, walk to Wau (12 miles), catch a plane to Salamaua, transact business there for two hours, fly back to Wau and return to Edie Creek before dark.

By late 1930, the frontier days of aviation were coming to an end. As freight rates fell, more ground became payable, and planes made it easier for miners to realise the field's potential. Through its impact on food supplies, health and ease of movement, aviation in these first few years did much to raise the standard of living of miners and built a sense of community. But this was just the beginning; the next few years were to see a massive expansion of air transport to levels beyond any in the world up to that time.

CHAPTER 12
WORLD AVIATION RECORDS

Levien's vision for aviation was matched only by the spectacular way in which it was realised.

Throughout the 1930s, New Guinea led the world in air freight, creating many records and attracting observers from far and wide. Many with knowledge of and experience in aviation or mining were astounded by what they saw. An international mining engineer who visited the field in 1932 observed: *My outstanding impression is one of amazement at the efficiency and adequacy of the service, completely overshadowing any analogous accomplishment I have seen or known of in any other part of the world.*[1] New Guinea's aviation record was also an endless source of fascination to a wider Australian audience, with regular reports and articles in the newspapers.

Reliance on aviation was due to the absence of any economic alternative transport from the coast or around the field, and to strong demand, reflecting the richness of the goldfields, a rising gold price and thus an enhanced capacity to pay. Although it was 27 years since the Wright brothers' first powered flight, commercial aviation in 1930 was still in its infancy. In showing how aviation could be used to shift large quantities of machinery and supplies quickly and efficiently, New Guinea's experience contributed to a paradigm shift in large scale air transportation elsewhere in the world.

Up to 1942, aeroplanes in New Guinea flew 104,000 tons of freight—dramatically outstripping Australia, whose planes flew a mere 5,000 tons.[2] Between 1931 and 1938, they flew more than half as much freight as all aeroplanes in the five other largest airfreight-carrying countries combined—Canada, Germany, the USA, UK and France, and in no year did freight carried by any other country's planes exceed that of New Guinea.[3]

New Guinea also claimed records for the world's busiest airports.[4] Based on the weight of cargo moved, Lae was said to have been the busiest, Bulolo second, Wau third and Salamaua fourth. In numbers of departures and arrivals, Wau was first, Salamaua second, Lae third and Bulolo fourth.

Lae aerodrome, 1931–32. Note the three 3 engine Junkers G31s, two single engine W34s and, in the foreground, two fox moths.

Wau aerodrome, 1932. Supplies for Golden Ridges are being unloaded from Guinea Airways' Junkers G31 into dray pulled by oxen. Mining Warden's office is behind. In the centre is Les Holden's DH 61 biplane 'Canberra' and on the left the tail of Ray Parer's Junkers W33, 'Lady Lettie', is being swung round prior to taking off downhill. Mt Kaindi is in background.

The main single source of freight was BGD, as materials for eight dredges and three power stations, vehicles of all shapes and sizes, cranes, boilers, oxy-welding plant, sawmilling equipment, refrigerators and everything required to sustain two rapidly growing townships was flown in. Freight volumes were further underpinned by the huge quantities of grease required to lubricate the dredges and new parts to replace those which were worn.[5]

In May 1930, BGD ordered two Junkers G31s, each costing £32,000, and a third in August 1933.[6] Between the first G31 flight to Bulolo in March 1931 and their destruction in January 1942, the three planes flew 14,000 trips over 1.4 million miles, carrying nearly 40,000 tons to support BGD's dredging operations, and around 7,000 passengers. As one writer later noted,

> The breakthrough was not just a matter of shattering freight records, although every one of them was demolished time and time again; it involved learning how to do things with aeroplanes that had never been attempted before, of achieving high standards of efficiency and safety under great difficulties.[7]

Much of the credit was due to BGD's attention to risk management.[8] But in no small degree, BGD's aviation success was due to the efforts of Pard Mustar. Not only was the selection of the G31 due to his persuasive advocacy, but he also worked tirelessly to ensure the planes' successful operation and the maintenance of a co-operative relationship between GAL and BGD. If the vision was Levien's, it was Mustar's technical and operational skills that enabled it to be realised. Mustar worked for both GAL and BGD on several occasions over a nine year period, at times battling the debilitating effects of malaria, which forced him to return to Australia; but even there, he would act as an adviser to one company and then the other. When, in 1936, he resigned as GAL's General Manager in Lae for the last time, he had done more than any other person to build the largest and most efficient airfreight operation in the world.

The G31 was one of the largest planes of its day, although the cockpit was open to the elements and the engines started by hand-cranking. Designed to carry 15 passengers, the G31s that flew in New Guinea were all modified by cutting a hatch in the roof over the centre of gravity. Large items were loaded through this hatch directly onto the floor which was strengthened by the strong wing section which ran underneath. Smaller items could be loaded through a side door. Their aluminium construction meant BGD was saved the heavy cost of constructing hangars.

The cargo compartment was spacious,[9] accommodating a normal payload of around 5,800 pounds. Each plane was powered by three American Pratt and Whitney 'Hornet' A2 525 horse power engines, chosen because of their reliability, simple design and excellent power-to-weight ratio.[10]

The first of the G31s, VH-UOU, arrived in Lae by ship in eight crates on 31 December 1930. As there was no wharf suitable for large ships, the crates were unloaded onto lighters 150 yards offshore, and towed by pinnace to a small jetty about ¾ mile from the aerodrome. There was some initial anxiety when the ship, the *Temeraire*, lost its anchor. Thereafter, the crates were unloaded as the ship sailed slowly back and forth.

Belching smoke, the locomotive steam crane raced back and forth along the short jetty loading the crates onto several flat top trucks which it then towed to the aerodrome; the wings were carried by dozens of labourers along the adjoining track.

Assembly was simplified by self-aligned male-female joints for different sections of the wings and fuselage, and within three months the plane was ready to begin flying. Its first flight to Bulolo was on 31 March, four years and one day after Mustar had arrived in Lae in his DH37. The second G31, VH-UOV, arrived in Lae by ship on 12 February 1931, was assembled in the same way, and made its first flight to Bulolo on 6 May.

The size of loads and frequency of flights steadily increased as the crane operators became more experienced in loading the aircraft. Before long the two planes were flying up to 30 trips a week between Lae and Bulolo, and 350 tons per month.

The frequency of their round trips soon led to the two planes being christened *Peter* and *Paul*, after the children's nursery rhyme:

> Two little black birds sitting on a wall
> One named Peter, one named Paul
> Fly away Peter, fly away Paul,
> Come back Peter, come back Paul.

VH-UOV was christened *Peter* and VH-UOU *Paul*.

The first car on the field. Dr Ian Dickson's Austin being loaded at Lae, 1931.

Junkers G31 'Paul'.

By 4 January 1932, each plane had done 500 trips and the 2,500 tons required for construction of dredge No. 1 and the power house had been transported to Bulolo. The key to this performance was rapid turnaround. In December 1929, Mustar had estimated that each round trip Lae-Bulolo-Lae would take 1¾ hours, including 15 minutes at each end for loading and unloading. This time was often bettered, with four round trips a day by each plane common and five under ideal weather conditions. In May 1932, Grabowsky flew a record six round trips in one day, lifting 14.6 tons.

That the planes could be loaded quickly and without damage to the aluminium fuselage was due to careful planning and execution. All cargo was laid out in sequence next to the railway according to priorities determined in Bulolo. The steam locomotive crane then loaded it.

The crane's operators, under Ossie Priebe, were highly skilled in determining the quickest way to load items of every conceivable shape and size through the top hatch. This skill was developed using a full scale wood model of the G31 fuselage set up on stumps next to the railway line, with the height and angle of the hatch and floor the same as that of the G31.[11] Practice with hundreds of different shapes, sizes and weights enabled Priebe to study an item and, within a minute, determine how it should best be loaded and positioned within the aircraft. Its job done, the model was then cut up and used for firewood in the mess kitchen.

The dredge piece which had caused Griffin greatest concern at the December 1929 conference, the upper tumbler shaft, weighed 6,950 pounds. GAL's General Manager, Alan Cross, safely flew it in to Bulolo on 27 November 1931 in good flying weather, though with only 60 minutes' fuel on board for the 45 minute trip. It was later claimed to be *by far the heaviest piece of freight ever put aboard an aeroplane up to that time*.[12]

During the wet season, heavy rain and cloud often curtailed flying. Thus in August–September 1931, only 91 trips were possible, compared with an average of 30 a week at other times. A sense of urgency was therefore the norm, so as to ensure that bad weather didn't hold up construction.

Once the pattern was established, BGD's airfreight operations continued with few interruptions throughout the pre-war period. In April 1933, *Peter* and *Paul* each flew their 1000th flight, and in the year to 30 June, the two of them flew 1,112 trips, carrying 3,063 tons. This was more than all planes in the UK and France combined in that year, and only 20% less than all planes in the USA.

BGD's third G31, later known as *Pat*, was an older plane and cost about half the price of the first two. But as it was only intended as insurance against disruption if *Peter* or *Paul* were to crash, its age wasn't considered a problem. BGD's foresight was soon vindicated when, in May 1934, *Paul* crashed at Lae, after petrol drums shifted on take off, affecting the plane's balance.

The plane stalled at 50 to 60 feet and side slipped into the ground, causing considerable damage, though no injuries. It was 18 months before *Paul* resumed flying, during which time *Pat* shared the load with *Peter*.[13]

The pilots were under no illusions about the significance of their record-breaking activities, and pushed themselves and their planes to the limit. In November 1933, *Peter* and *Paul* made 180 trips, carrying 503 tons of cargo to Bulwa and Bulolo. This stood as the record until October 1936, when they carried 587 tons in 206 trips.[14]

While their maximum permitted payload was around 7,000 pounds, the planes operated with a safety margin, loads usually being limited to between 5,400 and 5,800 pounds. At times, however, items exceeded 7,000 pounds. The heaviest were upper tumbler shafts for the two largest dredges, Nos. 5 and 7, each weighing 7,765 pounds. This required the permission of the Controller of Civil Aviation in Australia, which he reluctantly gave, so long as each was carried on a G31 belonging to GAL (as it had a lower empty weight than the BGD G31s), manned by a pilot but no engineer, and carrying only enough oil and petrol for a one way trip.

Model G31 fuselage.

On another occasion, Bert Heath carried a stator for the Upper Baiune Power station weighing 7,986 pounds, including three bags of rice in the tail to balance the aircraft. He later recalled:

> Nobody told the Department of Civil Aviation about the 3 bags of rice, but it wasn't a dangerous load. We just cut down on petrol. We had enough to get in with perfect weather conditions with about 10 minutes to spare.[15]

Loading 'Paul' with a 5,600 pound boiler at Lae.

Upper tumbler shaft, No. 5 dredge.

GAL's performance was without parallel. Flying a variety of planes, including its own G31 as well as BGD's, it flew more than 60,000 flights over nearly 6 million miles, transporting 73,730 tons or 70% of all air freight in New Guinea in the pre-war period and 106,214 or 76% of all passengers. It was highly profitable; up to 1936 it paid dividends amounting to £128,000 on paid up capital of £75,000.

However, these figures masked many problems. New Guinea aviation in the 1930s was vibrantly competitive, for which GAL largely had itself to blame. Its hands-on but out-of-touch Adelaide-based Board repeatedly failed to translate its 'first mover advantage' into an impregnable competitive position.[17] Excluding 'captive' BGD business, its share of all other airfreight was 51% over the whole period, though rather less in later years. But this was much less profitable than it might have been, due to a dramatic fall in freight rates which, by 1938, were less than 20% of their 1929 levels.

The Board had no eyes for anything other than containing costs and trying to maintain freight rates so as to maximise short term profitability. In contrast, Levien saw high quality service and maximising freight volumes at reasonable rates as the key to longer-lasting profitable operations.[18]

Levien's frustrations with the rest of the GAL Board were never ending. In January 1930, he unsuccessfully pressured them to establish a trading store and freezers at Salamaua, Lae and Wau, to create additional traffic for its aircraft. Several months later, he badgered them into buying a G31, believing that its lower operating costs would enable GAL to lower the freight rate paid by NGG to a level others couldn't match and so reduce the threat of future competition. In July, the Board agreed to buy the G31, but declined to meet NGG on rates.

Nevertheless, Levien's faith in the role and importance of air transport remained unshaken. In November 1931, a couple of months before he died, he gave 300 GAL shares to each of the pilots flying G31s to Bulolo. His confidence reflected the extraordinary volumes being flown. The month before, GAL's planes had carried 580 tons of freight, nearly six times the quantity flown in Australia in the previous year. In 1931, planes in New Guinea carried 2,987 tons of freight. By comparison air services in the USA carried 514 tons, the UK 649 tons, Canada 1,059 tons, France 1,508 tons and Germany 2,175 tons.

Thanks to Mustar's efforts, and the professionalism of GAL's pilots and engineers, BGD had little cause for complaint. This is not to say there weren't strains at times, usually when BGD sought to reduce the management fee paid to GAL. Les Waterhouse joined the GAL Board in September 1932 *to assist in furthering the smooth running of affairs between the two companies,*[16] and he adroitly managed a potentially difficult conflict of interest situation to secure progressively lower management fees for BGD. By 1938, the original fee of £5 per ton had fallen to £1.

In 1932, Ray Parer embarked on a rate war with GAL. His two earlier efforts to establish aerial services had folded, and he now operated Pacific Aerial Transport (PAT), with which his brother Kevin was also a pilot. He was enthusiastically joined by Les Holden, who had formed Holden's Air Transport Services (HATS) on his arrival in New Guinea in June 1931.

A dashing airman who had won the Military Cross in World War I, Holden was one of a fortunate few to have survived an attack by Baron von Richthofen. He flew a large DH61 biplane, *Canberra*, in which he had located Charles Kingsford Smith and Charles Ulm in 1929 in the Kimberleys, after they disappeared while flying to England. Holden was described as *a courageous but modest man with a sunny temperament and whimsical humour*.[19] His decision to provide a regular service to remote airstrips was enthusiastically received by miners, and he established a popular weekend shuttle service between Bulolo and Wau, as there was still no road between the two townships. His contribution to New Guinea aviation was shortlived, however, as he was killed in a plane crash in Australia in September 1932.

By the end of the year, rates had fallen to about half their 1929 level of around £88 per ton. Doggedly determined that pricing should be decided in Adelaide, GAL was feeling the pinch. Despite its dominant market position and larger aircraft, it was a pricetaker: whenever smaller, undercapitalised operators with inferior planes cut their rates, GAL followed.

Worse was to come. In January 1933, W.R. Carpenter, with stores in Salamaua and Wau, began its own air service with two DH83 Fox Moths. This had an immediate impact. Mustar reported that in February,

> Carpenters' activities affected our turnover because NGG, Day Dawn, Koranga Gold Sluicing and other large consumers of rice, boys' meat and biscuits find it more economical to buy at Wau stores.[20]

In June, the GAL Board noted,

> Carpenters are now quoting our clients hardware ex their Wau store and the sale of 1 ton of galvanised iron was made to the Day Dawn Co. Normally this would have been purchased on the beach and carried by us.[21]

The wisdom of Levien's 1930 plea for GAL to establish a trading store and freezers at Wau must now have been a cause for reflection by the Board, which was finally forced to give Mustar, as its general manager on the ground, discretion to negotiate prices. GAL's loss of business was compounded when it was forced to lower freight rates paid by Burns Philp to enable it to compete with Carpenters.

The only ray of sunlight for GAL throughout this period was its decision to establish a service between Port Moresby and Wau in March 1932. After the *Montoro* and *Macdhui* began making regular six weekly visits, a service commenced with Orm Denny flying a Junkers F13. The service was so popular and profitable that a W34, modified to carry eight passengers, was also put on the route later in the year.

In June 1933, 21 planes were flying between the coast and the field, owned by GAL (ten), HATS (five), PAT (four) and Carpenter (two) — a position that was little changed a year later. After Holden's death, HATS was floated on the stock exchange. It had built a strong following among miners, who took up many shares.

In May 1934, GAL tried to regain the ascendancy by acquiring 51% of HATS in a secret deal. However, its efforts were thwarted when another distinguished World War I flyer, one of HATS' pilots, Eric Stephens, started out on his own a couple of months later. Despite lacking capital and suitable planes, he maintained a viable operation by concentrating on good service to miners.

Rates continued their downward spiral, reaching an average of £28 per ton in 1935. Believing that rationalisation was the key to reasonable freight charges, GAL lobbied for a merger of all existing airlines. In December 1935, the Government agreed in principle, to enable a 'safe and efficient' aviation service to be maintained with the regulation of fares, freight rates and frequency of services.[22]

The announcement was met with a howl of opposition. The mining community directed particular hostility towards GAL, as the architect of the proposal. Letters poured into the Government pointing out the outstanding safety and efficiency record of planes in New Guinea under a competitive system.

In the face of such concerted opposition, the proposal was quickly shelved.

Nevertheless, rationalisation did occur. In 1936, GAL finally acquired the rest of HATS, while Carpenters and PAT merged to form Mandated Airlines. Together with Stephens Aviation, these companies dominated aviation in New Guinea through to the War. But this was no cosy oligopoly; competition remained vigorous, with rates falling further to £16 to £17 per ton, where they finally stabilised.

As evident from the ill-conceived merger proposal, the Government had little idea of what role it should play in relation to aviation in New Guinea. It ostensibly controlled aviation under the *Air Navigation Act 1920*. But although the level of activity in New Guinea was much greater than in Australia, the Department of Civil Aviation for a long time declined to station an officer there or exercise any effective oversight. Aerodromes proliferated that wouldn't have passed muster down south and aircraft unsuited to the conditions were often used, contributing to frequent crashes.

Self-preservation was the main regulator, though at times even this was a dubious constraint. It wasn't just Ray Parer who had a cavalier approach to flying. Bunny Hammond later recalled

> I flew the Waco to get urgent cargo in for weeks with fabric splitting on each trip and, with a 6 inch roll of sticking plaster from BGD, stuck together the splits every time on landing at Bulolo.[23]

Not surprisingly, by the end of 1933, there had been 19 crashes, with 17 planes written off. Finally, a permanent officer, Max Allen, was appointed in 1934. One of his first acts was to seek the Department's permission to ignore Australian standards or aviation in New Guinea would have ceased.[24]

The Administration was even less interested. Though responsible for maintaining aerodromes, it did little more than cut the grass. Salamaua aerodrome was a particular problem. It was leased to NGG, which claimed to have spent £16,000 establishing it in 1929. The Francisco River frequently flooded, forcing planes to land and take off in water. The wheel ruts, when dry, created a corrugated surface that was particularly hard on undercarriages. In 1934, NGG refused an official request to put the aerodrome in good order, arguing — not unreasonably — that as aeroplanes of all companies used it, the Administration should be responsible for maintenance. Early in 1935, the Administration resumed the aerodrome, though it was some time before users noticed any improvement.

The situation was little better at Lae. Although GAL didn't have a lease over the aerodrome, and it was used by most other aviation companies, as the main user GAL had little choice but to maintain it. It continually pressed the Administration to accept responsibility for maintenance. Finally, in January 1934, the Secretary, Department of Defence, advised the Prime Minister's Department that

This Department feels that there is a good deal of justification for Mr Wells' suggestion that a reasonable proportion of Administration funds should be expended in the preparation and maintenance of landing grounds. There is no question that aviation has made possible the development of the very rich gold mining districts in the Territory and it is only reasonable that a proportion of the revenue from this source should be applied to supporting and developing this very essential form of transport.[25]

Administrator Griffiths limply acknowledged that they were perhaps not doing all they should, defending the lack of action on airfields, of which there were now 35, as being due to the need to construct a road from the coast to the goldfields.[26]

Nor, despite the obvious transport and communication difficulties in New Guinea, did the Commonwealth Government provide any support for aviation. In late 1928, Ray Parer's Morlae Airlines sought a Government subsidy of £12,000 over three years to provide two flights a month between Lae or Wau and Port Moresby, meeting the *Morinda* on its inward and outward voyage and taking mail and passengers each way. This would have halved the time mail took between Australia and the field and given visitors two weeks there before returning on the same ship. Although aviation companies were extensively subsidised in Australia, the Government refused Parer's request, and it was not until March 1932 that GAL started a regular, unsubsidised service between Port Moresby and Wau.

Mail deliveries were another source of contention. Flights between Lae and Port Moresby were not allowed to carry mail for Australia; this could only be sent by ship via Salamaua. From September 1932, the Government finally permitted mail to be flown to Port Moresby for the ship to Australia. But it was another five months before it permitted mail from Australia to be offloaded in Port Moresby and flown to the field.

In July 1934, and with much publicity, Charles Ulm and Scotty Allen in the *Faith in Australia* flew the first official airmail flight from Australia to New Guinea. However, despite the huge volume of mail it carried and the high level of passenger traffic by ship, the Government saw no need for a regular air service between Australia, Port Moresby and the goldfields. It was another four years before a subsidised service, passing through Salamaua, was inaugurated by Mandated Airlines.

One small incident said much about the Administration's attitude to air transport. The *Faith in Australia* carried a commemorative airmail letter from the Minister for Territories to the Administrator. However, it couldn't be delivered by air as Rabaul still didn't have an aerodrome, and so it was held in Lae awaiting delivery by the next available ship. The lack of an aerodrome in Rabaul at a time when world airfreight records were being set regularly on the New Guinea mainland was symptomatic of the Administration's resistance to change. Successive Administrators and officials clung to the old ways, preferring to travel by schooner. It was not until the Australia-New Guinea service began in May 1938 that there was a regular air link between Rabaul and the mainland.

If the Government and Administration were slow to recognise and support New Guinea's aviation achievements, the pilots themselves embraced the challenges.

Bulolo was BGD's centre of operations, but Wau was the hub of the field. Planes were constantly arriving from the coast and leaving for the network of small aerodromes established to meet the needs of miners. By 1933, there were up to 70 landings and takeoffs per day at Wau. While GAL flew mainly to and from Lae, for the many smaller planes the main route was Salamaua-Wau.

Salamaua aerodrome was close in under the mountains; planes took off over the sea, circling the isthmus to gain height before heading inland.[27] Passing over a village, gardens and isolated huts, planes soon reached the Landslide, a fresh scar on the shoulder of a mountain at 5,000 feet. Turning into the Bitoi Gorge and still climbing, planes passed over Black Cat Ridge at 6,000 feet, through a gap in the Kuper Range and then made a gradual descent to Wau. All in about 20 minutes.

But it was rarely so easy. Swirling cloud and rain often lessened visibility as planes threaded their way through valleys, gorges and gaps, increasing the risk of flying into a 'stuffed cloud'. Few had sufficient power to climb out of any trouble they encountered, and there were no emergency landing grounds below. Pilot skill, and at times luck, were the key to survival.

While there were many crashes, only four pilots died—Les Trist and Frank Drayton in 1931 and 1932 respectively, and two others. In 1935, Col Ferguson, one of W.R. Carpenter's Fox Moth pilots, died when he was trapped by bad weather, failed to find the Bitoi Gap and crashed. Ron Doyle and his two passengers were killed in 1940 when he misjudged the slope of Wau aerodrome. Approaching at too steep an angle, he tried to pull out but lacked the power to do so.

In the absence of ground-to-air radio communication, there were two forms of improvised 'ground control' at Wau. Smoke from a fire was used to indicate wind strength and direction—as at Lae, Salamaua and Bulolo. But the other feature was unique. Only one plane could land or take off at a time, and the steep slope and location at the base of Mt. Kaindi meant that an aeroplane was committed once it began its take off or final approach. To regulate activity, a board with large horizontal louvres was suspended between two posts at the top of the aerodrome, green on one side and white on the other.[28] When the side facing down the aerodrome was green, an aircraft was cleared to land; when it was white, a plane was taking off, and the incoming pilot was required to delay his approach until the board clicked over.

And there were other risks. Arthur Affleck recalled an occasion when he saw a fight between two groups of villagers. To get a good view, he flew on a course that brought him quite close to the action:

> As though all the combatants were actuated by a mastermind, they ceased their battle, looked up at me, and then loosed a cloud of arrows at me. In spite of the fact that I was out of range, I got such a fright I never afterwards allowed my curiosity to entice me anywhere near a hilltop village … I learned, later, that most New Guinea pilots of those days had been through a similar experience.[29]

Pilots revelled in carrying unusual cargo and the incidents they often generated—the goats that progressively ate the fabric-covered Moth they were flying in, the large boar on the rear seat whose struggling ceased only when its hind legs pierced the fuselage, the 550 pound bull and 490 pound cow which travelled at 6 pence per pound, the surveyor working on the Wau-Salamaua road who received his rations by parachute on Tuesdays and Fridays—only two eggs lost.

For the first time in the world, horses were airfreighted: three Suffolk Punch medium draft horses flown in a G31 to Wau in September 1933, followed by several race horses for the first Wau Racing Club meeting in 1934. Nothing was impossible. If an item didn't fit in the plane, it was attached to the outside. A 30 hundredweight truck for NGG arrived in Wau with much of its chassis protruding through the rear door.

Falling passenger rates did much to engender a sense of the goldfields as a single community. Residents of one township thought nothing of flying to a dance in another, while sporting teams travelled back and forth as regular competition developed in cricket, tennis, billiards and snooker. Even inbound tourism developed. Passengers arriving by ship in Salamaua could fly for the day to Wau and Bulolo to see the sights, rejoining the ship at Lae.

Notwithstanding the risks, pilots often competed in setting new records. Ray Parer held the record—63—for the most solo flights in a month between Lae and Wau. Bunny Hammond recalled that

Johnny Jukes and I had a duel to see who could fly the most trips in a day from Salamaua to Wau and we tied at 11 full loads each, the last one in the semi-dark and the usual race over the Gap … The boys entered into the spirit of the thing and raced the cargo into the planes almost before they came to rest.[30]

This 1933 record was decisively beaten in 1936 when Dick Allen flew 15 round trips in his DH50A biplane, carrying 9 tons of rice.

It was an exhilarating time. But for pilots it was more than matched by the experience of meeting the needs of scattered miners whose tiny airstrips were perched precariously on hillsides throughout the goldfields.

Wau aerodrome, 1936. The large plane is a De Havilland 84 Dragon.

Part 5
The New Guinean Experience

Singsing, Bulolo aerodrome. Note dredge tailings in the background.

CHAPTER 13
EARLY ENCOUNTERS: THE EUROPEAN PERSPECTIVE

The Morobe goldfields were surrounded by different tribal groups, living in hamlets or villages and pursuing a traditional way of life.

Kaiwa men.

The Gadagadu track ran through the territory of two of these, the Kaiwa and the Biangai.[1] The first section passed through or near the Kaiwa villages of Komiatum, Mubo, Waipali, Webaining and Gadagadu. The boundary was at 'House Copper', after which the track passed through or near the Biangai villages of Selankora, Wandumi, Lambaura (often misnamed Rabaul village) and Kaisinik. The tribes were small—with fewer than 900 Kaiwa and 700 Biangai.[2]

The old Buang track ran through territory inhabited solely by the Buang people, of whom there were around 8,600 in the 1930s, in the area stretching from Lega, near the coast, through to Mengowa, close to the northern end of the Bulolo valley.

Between the Buang to the north and the Kaiwa and Biangai to the south were the Hote, Yamap and Missim. A track through Missim territory was rarely used by Europeans and so these tribes had less direct contact with miners.

The Bulolo valley itself was uninhabited.[3] The upper reaches—around what was later to become Wau—were predominantly covered with long kunai grass. This gave way to heavy timber in the gorge downstream, which in turn opened out onto the densely timbered lower Bulolo valley. The anthropologist John Burton has suggested that the name 'Bulolo' was derived from 'Piololo' or 'Biololo', probably given to the area by the Kaiwa.[4]

The territory west of the Bulolo River and Edie Creek was the domain of the

Biangai village, upper Bulolo valley.

Kukukuku, a number of tribes sharing a common culture and inhabiting about 6,000 square miles in Papua, Morobe and the eastern New Guinea highlands. By the 1920s, the Kukukuku were well known in Papua for their fierce resistance to all intruders on their territory. Between 1910 and 1920, Papuan prospectors and government officials had been attacked 17 times by Kukukuku inhabiting the watershed of the Tiveri and Tauri Rivers, close to the border with New Guinea.[5]

Contact with Lutheran missionaries before World War I meant that most villagers on the coastal side of the Bulolo valley were well disposed to the first prospectors and miners moving through their territory in the early 1920s. These miners treated villagers well. While the tenuous nature of supply lines made good relations essential if they were to obtain carriers and acquire food for their labourers, their goodwill was clearly also based on respect for them and their culture.

One miner who was exemplary in this regard was a German, Hellmuth Baum. He had been a plantation owner and in 1914 he disappeared into the jungle rather than surrender to the Australians.[6] He lived among the Buang during the war, out of reach of Australian patrols, prospecting for gold and occasionally visiting Lutheran missionaries on the coast for supplies. He became very close to the Buang people, helping them when sick and in fights against their enemies.

After the war, Baum continued prospecting and mining, roaming the area barefoot, hatless and usually unarmed. Mick Leahy described him as *a stocky, trim-looking man, dressed from head to foot in immaculate white … His hair was cropped close about a round pink face, a strong and kindly face …*[7] In supporting a request for fair treatment in connection with the expropriation of his plantation, Frank Anstey described Baum in 1927

> as the Livingstone of New Guinea. He is a pathfinder. An explorer. An unarmed fearless wanderer among hostile tribes. The miners of New Guinea are nine tenths returned soldiers … There is not one of them that does not admire Baum for his courage, his courtesy, his generosity, and never ending kindnesses.[8]

Baum was widely respected for his nature, but also for his knowledge of the ways of the bush and his treatment of villagers. Uniquely, he sought to bridge the cultural gap between Europeans and villagers, arguing that white men must look at things from the villagers' point of view. In the bush, he lived by a strong moral code, never taking anything without payment but also never allowing a theft to go unpunished. For miners such as Mick Leahy, he was a role model without peer.

Villagers encountering the early miners were quick to appreciate the trade goods, particularly steel axes, knives and plane blades, they could obtain by carrying and by selling them kaukau and other local food. Buang gardens were very productive, and later an important source of food for miners throughout the field.

As miners' efforts before 1926 were concentrated on the Namie/Koranga Creek area and the Bulolo River, they were able to prospect and mine without major interference from the Kukukuku, whose villages were mainly on the western side of the Watut River.

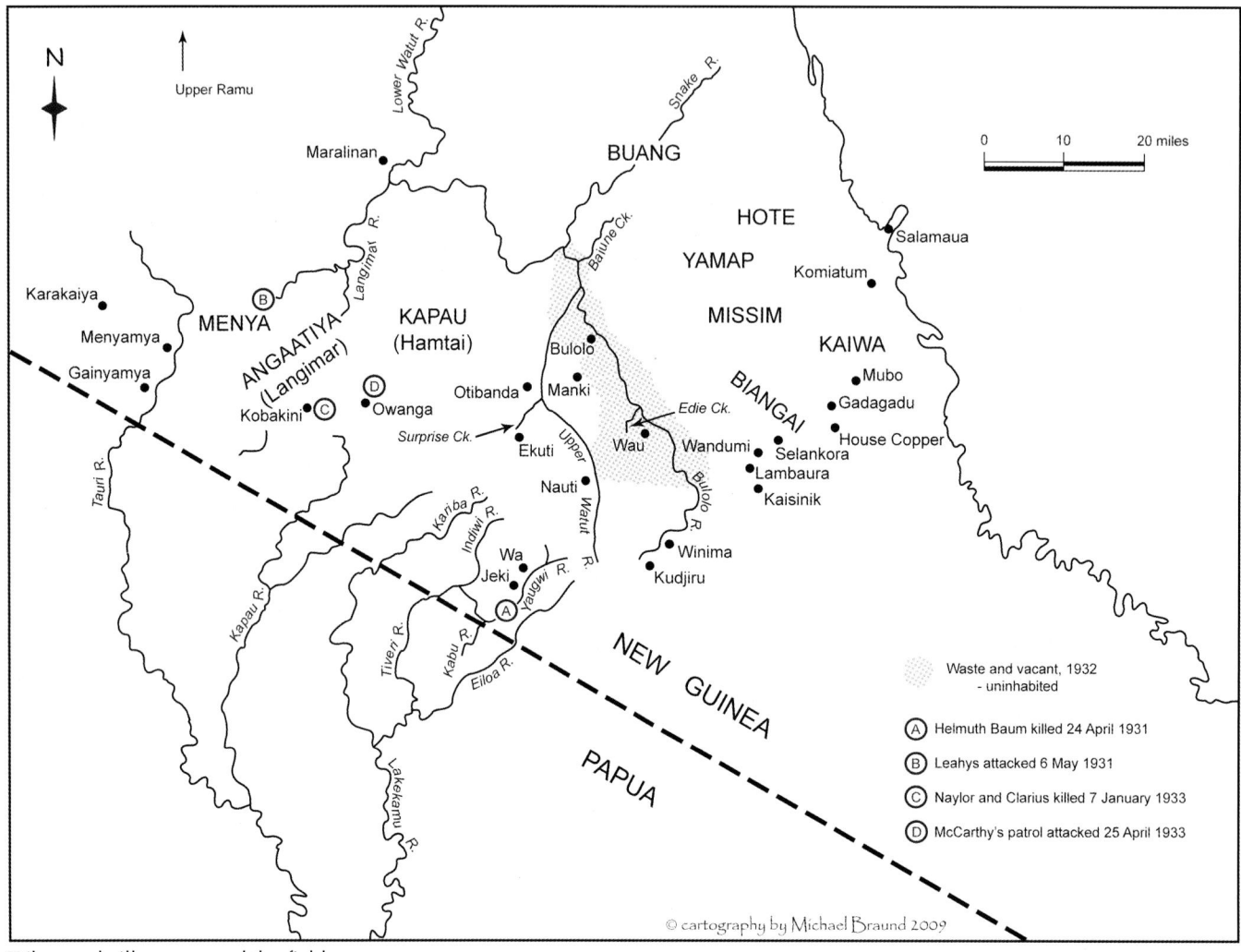

N

Upper Ramu

Lower Watut R.

Snake R.

Maralinan

BUANG

HOTE

YAMAP

Salamaua

Komiatum

0   10   20 miles

Karakaiya

MENYA

Langimar R.

KAPAU
(Hamtai)

Bulolo

MISSIM

KAIWA

Menyamya

ANGAATIYA
(Langimar)

Baiune Ck.

Mubo

Gainyamya

Owanga

Otibanda

Manki

Edie Ck.

BIANGAI

Gadagadu

House Copper

Kobakini

Surprise Ck.

Ekuti

Upper Watut R.

Wau

Wandumi

Selankora

Lambaura

Tauri R.

Nauti

Kaisinik

Kariba R.

Bulolo R.

Indiwi R.

Wa

Winima

Jeki

Yaugwi R.

Kudjiru

Kapau R.

Tiveri R.

Kabu R.

Elloa R.

NEW GUINEA

PAPUA

Lakekamu R.

Waste and vacant, 1932
- uninhabited

Ⓐ Helmuth Baum killed 24 April 1931

Ⓑ Leahys attacked 6 May 1931

Ⓒ Naylor and Clarius killed 7 January 1933

Ⓓ McCarthy's patrol attacked 25 April 1933

© cartography by Michael Braund 2009

Tribes and villages around the field.

In the late 1920s, Edie Creek was the focal point of most prospecting and mining. At more than 7,000 feet, it was too high for habitation by villagers and so there was little or no contact between the new wave of miners and the Kukukuku. Although there was some prospecting along the Upper Watut River and its tributaries, there was little incentive for most miners to explore further afield until NGG exercised its options in 1929 over much of Edie Creek and nearby areas.

The Administration nevertheless recognised the potential for trouble. In his evidence to the 1927 Royal Commission, the Government Anthropologist, E.W.P. Chinnery[9] noted *My experience was that natives are always up in arms whenever white men broke into new country; there were always big tragedies. That was my experience at Yodda.*[10] However, the fact that miners in the Bulolo valley and at Edie Creek were encountering no problems seems to have lulled the Administration into a false sense of security.

The Administration classified territory throughout New Guinea into categories according to the degree of control or influence it exerted over the inhabitants. An area was said to be 'under control' if an unarmed policeman could proceed to a village and arrest an offender without danger from the inhabitants and a complete census had been taken. It was 'under influence' if it had been patrolled and a census taken, though this may not have included all inhabitants, and where villagers would visit the District Officer for advice or for the settlement of disputes. It was 'under partial influence' if patrols had established friendly relations with villagers, whose population had been estimated. An area had been 'penetrated' where it had been visited but friendly relations had not been established with villagers. All other areas were uncontrolled. [11]

Extending control was time consuming. A patrol would usually comprise one or two white patrol officers, or *kiaps*, several New Guinean police[12] and a larger number of carriers, who carried food, tents and equipment for the whole party. An initial patrol into new territory was usually intended as a flag-waving exercise, designed to secure the friendship of villagers it encountered, though also discouraging warfare which was usually endemic. If all went well and the patrol was not attacked, subsequent patrols would take a census and begin the process of extending influence.

However, as people were often scattered in hamlets over a wide area rather than concentrated in large villages, even a lengthy patrol might contact relatively small numbers of villagers. As well, many of them—and particularly the women and children—would frequently disappear on the arrival of a patrol, and it might take several visits before they became sufficiently accustomed to the visitors to respond in a way that might be deemed 'friendly'.

If extending control was difficult, maintaining it was no easier. As patrols were infrequent, their ongoing influence over village activities and conditions was limited. In contrast to African colonies of European powers, there were no obvious chiefs who might be persuaded to act as representatives of the Administration. It therefore adopted the pre-war German practice of appointing local officials to act

as its representatives. Once a village was considered friendly, a man would be appointed as a *luluai*,[13] with responsibility for resolving minor village disputes and undertaking local works such as maintaining tracks in good condition and ensuring the maintenance of good village hygiene. He was assisted by a *tultul*,[14] usually chosen because of his ability to speak pidgin English and thus act as an interpreter.

In the mid-1920s, about one third of the Morobe District was (somewhat optimistically) deemed to be 'under control'—including the coastal fringe and the area between the coast and the Bulolo valley.

In 1926, the goldfields were nevertheless proclaimed an Uncontrolled Area, entry to which required a special permit. This enabled the Administration to require miners to have typhoid injections and post a bond to ensure that it would not have to bear the cost of repatriating to Australia any who later became destitute. Despite Chinnery's views, there was no restriction on the movement or behaviour of miners or their carriers and labourers toward any villagers they might encounter.

It didn't take long after the rush began in September 1926 before problems began to develop, and from an unexpected quarter. As the demand for carriers quickly

Patrol Officer L.G. Vial conducting a Buang village census.

outstripped the capacity of the Kaiwa and Biangai, carriers and labourers were recruited from elsewhere, mainly New Britain and coastal areas on the mainland.

Before long, carriers making their way back to the coast were stealing kaukau, yams and sugar cane from Biangai and Kaiwa gardens, and cutting down their betel nut and pandanus trees. When Biangai women tried selling kaukau by the side of the track, carriers would often take it but refuse to pay unless a white man was present.

Even where Europeans did accompany carriers on their return journey, many of the 'new chums' couldn't speak pidgin English and were thus unable to exercise effective control. Other Europeans contributed to the growing problem. Some supplied carriers returning to the coast with very little food, believing that hunger would discourage idling; the quicker they reached Salamaua, the sooner they would return to the field with fresh supplies of food. On several occasions, Europeans even added directly to the mayhem, shooting villagers' pigs. The impact on the Biangai and Kaiwa of more than 1,000 carriers passing back and forth through their territory each month, became an increasing problem.

In November 1926, some villagers asked a visiting kiap to hold court and compensate them for garden robberies by carriers. They said they had asked Oakley (the acting Mining Warden) three times, but he had done nothing.[15] Nor did this latest plea for help produce any action. Assistant District Officer Sam Appleby later reported that

> at last the women of Wandumi village went to the house set apart solely for the use of the adult males of the village. Here they abused the men, calling them cowards, saying, 'You are not men, you are only women; if you were men, you would not allow the carriers to treat us as they are doing; you allow them to rob us and our children of the fruits of our labour.' Stripping themselves naked, they threw their pul-puls (grass skirts) into the men's house, saying at the same time, 'You are not men, you are only women; here are our pul-puls, wear them.'[16]

Appleby continued,

> Several days after the above incident, which occurred early in December 1926, two men of Wandumi village, Yanduik (whose betel nut trees had been cut down and whose wife and sister had each lost a pig) and his full brother Kauwi, together with a half-brother from Duari

Police on patrol with Buang men as observers, Snake River.

village (of the Winima area) set out from Wandumi village towards the Biololo River where they waylaid and killed two carriers who were returning to Salamaua from the goldfield.

When word reached Salamaua, a patrol officer was sent to investigate. Unable to locate the murderers, he followed normal practice of arresting anyone in the general vicinity. He managed to induce 30 men from Lambaura village to come to Webaining on the pretext of building a rest house. However, when he tried to proceed with them to the coast, 17 escaped, including the tultul of Selankora village.

On 10 January 1927, three more carriers were killed between Wandumi village and Wau and their bodies thrown into the Bulolo River. This raised the ire of the Edie Creek miners. As the historian, Ian Willis, noted,

> most of the miners were concerned for quite practical reasons: they knew that successful mining operations entirely depended on the continued movement of carrier lines between the goldfields and the coast. If the carriers became so frightened that they deserted or refused to engage for carrying work, the goldfields would have to shut down, as there could at that stage

be no mining without the supply lines provided by the carriers.[17]

The Mining Warden at Edie Creek, J.D. McLean, had arrived on the field less than a fortnight earlier. Always a man of clear conviction, he didn't let his lack of local experience discourage him from direct action. In his highly colourful report on the events that followed, he claimed that official action was required as *the miners were going to organise a force to deal with the natives under Anzac rules*.[18] To build his case, he claimed that

> Previous to my arrival on the field, much inconvenience had been caused to miners ... owing to the depredations of these natives and many carriers who had been reported as deserters were reasonably suspected to have been murdered by the natives.

Further, while offering no evidence, he claimed that the tultul who had escaped in December had *resumed his previous malpractices and made himself the terror of the road*.

McLean radioed Rabaul for authority to lead a patrol against the villagers. The Deputy Administrator gave him approval to form a 'special expedition' of five Europeans and 20 New Guinean police to arrest the ringleaders and restore order, while emphasising

Entrance to a Biangai village.

that reprisals would not be countenanced. McLean set out on 12 January with eight Europeans and 20 police, including a number of 'special constables' chosen from labourers on the field. All were apparently issued with rifles or shotguns. In writing of the event, which she had no hesitation describing as a punitive expedition, Doris Booth said she was grieved to record that one of the 'special constables', her head 'boy' Usendran, *looked upon the adventure rather from the sporting angle than from that of justice.*[19]

Over the next three days, McLean burnt Lambaura village, on the pretext that it *was so indescribably filthy and infested as to be a serious menace to the health of the natives.*[20] Frustrated by his inability to engage with the Biangai, who had decamped onto the surrounding hills from where they shouted their defiance, he also destroyed their gardens. At one point, as several police were trying to outflank the Biangai, McLean reported that they saw

> a number of carriers run screaming along the track pursued by the natives who were armed with spears and bows and arrows. The police boys intervened in the nick of time and the natives, baulked of their prey, showed fight.

Two Biangai were shot and their bodies carried to Kaisinik by the others. Another was shot in a separate encounter.

Again without offering any evidence, McLean identified Kaisinik as having been a 'hotbed of rebellion' for some time and, when it refused to surrender the tultul and other 'murderers', he ordered the police to attack. McLean claimed four men were killed in the ensuing melée; the tultul escaped but was shot in a gorge some distance from the village.[21] Kaisinik was then burnt to the ground, and the party returned to Edie Creek, believing justice had been delivered.

Monica Panga was four or five years old when these events occurred. In Kaisinik in March 2001 she told the author

> The carriers had been stealing food from our gardens, killing our pigs and raping our women, and so they killed some of them. When white men attacked us, we fought back … There were four or five high fences around the village. However, a policeman got in through a gap in the fence and arrested three people and the rest ran away. My mother also ran away with me. The fighting began early in the morning and lasted all day. The village, houses and fences were burnt.

Assistant District Officer Appleby arrived on 17 January to find the whole area in a state of ferment. Palisades enclosing villages were being strengthened and there was evidence from different villages that

> although their gardens had not been interfered with, they were willing to throw in their lot with the Kaisinik and Lambaura (Rabaul) people who, after the fight at Kaisinik, appear to have adopted guerrilla tactics.[22]

To keep supply lines with the coast open, Appleby used police to escort carriers in both directions through the danger zone under cover of darkness. Over the next month, he used his experience and calm manner (not to mention 100 police) to restore order. Finally, in late February, Lambaura villagers surrendered Yanduik and his half-brother Yawa as a condition of being allowed to return to their old village site and gardens.

Appleby concluded that three men were killed and one wounded during McLean's expedition. As well, an old woman was found dead in her house and a young woman was missing, assumed dead. While fewer than the total of eight dead claimed by McLean, to these must be added seven captured by the patrol officer in December 1926, whom Surveyor Sheldon said died in the dysentery epidemic in Salamaua.

As the drama unfolded, the Australian press ran a series of lurid stories. McLean's description of the Biangai being 'baulked of their prey', was reinterpreted by *The Daily Guardian* so that his expedition *actually saw carriers run screaming before the flesh-eaters.*[23] There was no evidence that the Biangai ate any of the carriers they killed, and McLean was the only official ever to claim this. Nevertheless, in evidence to the Royal Commission in April 1927, Doris Booth suggested that all five carriers had been killed and eaten, and the title of her book *Mountains, Gold and Cannibals* only entrenched the Australian public's view of the dangers of gold mining in New Guinea.

The character assassination of the Biangai was taken to its ultimate conclusion in the 1930s by Ion Idriess's description of the Biangai as having

> strangely dead, fish-like eyes, but with a baleful glare—a remarkable characteristic of the real cannibal's eyes.

He helpfully assured readers that

> tribes who only occasionally eat a man, perhaps from necessity at initiation rites, have quite different eyes.[24]

The stories were too much for Shark-Eye Park, by this time living in Sydney. In response to a newspaper report that 500 villagers had assembled at Rabaul village and offered armed resistance to a government party,

Park wrote to the Minister for Home and Territories:

> I should like to state I was about the first white man to come in contact with these natives and I know them all well. The statement of 500 to me seems to be absurd. Unless they had outside help, the most they could muster up would be about 70. I should also like to state these same natives have had to suffer a lot through having their gardens molested and their property stolen.[25]

A small, poignant but ultimately futile attempt to bring some balance to the Government's understanding of the situation.

The 'Kaisinik Killings' might have been avoided with a little foresight by the Administration. When trouble did occur, McLean's aggressive response may well have been influenced by that of a similar force at Nakanai on New Britain in November 1926, when 18 villagers were killed, and by the Administrator's resolve on the need for prompt action when trouble occurred.

Defending the approach of the Nakanai expedition, but doubtless with Kaisinik also in mind, Wisdom wrote to the Minister in February:

> Our policy is, and always has been, against wanton aggression and punitive measures ... [but] to prohibit aggressive action would absolutely prevent any effective dealing with natives where the murderers are being shielded by native villages.

Warming to his theme, he continued

> If these people were to become imbued with the idea that they could treat the white man with contempt, and resist the arrest of murderers, our task in New Guinea would be impossible without much bloodshed. Opposition must be broken down when met and failure to do so will inevitably bring about much greater bloodshed later.[26]

This philosophy raised a moral dilemma: how aggressively should one seek to break down opposition when initially encountered, so as to avoid later bloodshed? Several incidents over the next few years were to demonstrate vividly the downside of this dilemma, with the New Guinea experience at sharp variance to the more benign approach adopted in Papua.

However, for the moment, with Kaisinik out of the way, the Administration did at least focus on reducing the potential for further problems. It amended conditions under the Uncontrolled Areas Ordinance so as to prohibit anyone, European or New Guinean, entering a village except in an emergency, making camp within a quarter of a mile of a village or hamlet, or calling on villagers to act as carriers or provide them with food.

While overdue, these conditions—and Appleby's efforts following McLean's punitive expedition—did stabilise the situation, and it was not long before the growing availability of air transport and opening up of a new and easier Buang route contributed to a decline in the number of carriers using the Gadagadu track.

———

By mid-1929, miners were starting to prospect beyond Edie Creek, and the risks alluded to by Chinnery two years earlier began to intensify as more Europeans came in contact with the Kukukuku.

Prior to this, while Government patrols and miners had clashed intermittently with the Kukukuku in Papua, patrols on the New Guinea side had only made fleeting contact, though on each occasion they received a hostile reception.[27] The first major patrol into Kukukuku territory did not occur until 1930 when the patrol officer Alan Roberts visited the Upper Watut.[28] He was accompanied by Hellmuth Baum who had established a semi-permanent camp at Otibanda on Surprise Creek, some time before, forging close relationships with the local Kukukuku by treating them as equals. Descendants of the luluai at Ekua village, Wauqui Dipato, told the anthropologist John Burton that, unlike other miners, 'Masta Bom' 'sat down at table' with him.[29]

The Kukukuku today number about 70,000 people speaking 12 different languages. There were three main groups in the Morobe District, living in an arc from south of the Watut River to the north-west and stretching south and west into Papua.[30] The largest group were the Kapau, whose eastern boundary was the Watut. To the north-west were the Angaatiya or Langimar people, who previously had also occupied an area close to the Watut, but been driven out early in the 20th century, as the Kapau expanded from the west. A small number of Langimar had survived and moved further east, to the Bulolo-Watut divide, where they were known to miners and patrol officers as the Manki people. The third group, the Menya, lived further to the west.

In Papua, the name 'Kukukuku' was given to these people by Motuan traders on the southern Papuan coast, and later adopted by white men; it was first used officially in British New Guinea (Papua) in 1900.[31] The Kukukuku never saw themselves as a socio-political

Kukukuku men, Menyamya, standing outside a barrier (*banis*).

entity, fighting as vigorously amongst themselves as with others. They do, however, form a broad linguistic and cultural group. Their family of languages is unrelated to the Melanesian languages spoken by coastal people. But their common appearance was evocative of their shared culture.

The Kukukuku were short, typically no more than five feet tall, wiry and strong. Their hair was short except for a tuft of a few inches on the crown of the head to which a bark cape, or *mal*, was tied, extending to below the knees. It could be drawn around them as protection against the rain and cold, but also as camouflage. Men and women wore a sporran of up to 12 strings of grass, the men also wearing many narrow bands of woven yellow orchid fibre around the waist and over one shoulder. Men had pierced noses, through which a small piece of bamboo or bone was typically worn, and often wore two cassowary thigh bones, extending from the hips to the front of the waist where they joined. Their bows and arrows were always at hand, with a club usually secreted under their *mal*, ready for immediate use should the need arise.

Their distinctive appearance and intensely hostile nature created an aura which for Europeans was fascinating and deeply unsettling. Nevertheless, initial contact in the late 1920s between miners and the Kukukuku in the Surprise Creek area appears to have passed without major conflict. Items were occasionally stolen from miners' camps, but if this led to conflict,

it was not officially reported. With the nearest patrol officers located many days distant at Salamaua, it is likely that if theft did occur, the usually well armed miners took matters into their own hands. The fact that Europeans and their labourers were unable to speak the Kapau language would have done little to foster the peaceful resolution of difficult situations.

In October 1930, the District Officer, Eric Feldt, wrote that

> there does not appear to be any special need for protection as far as prospectors etc. are concerned [and] … I do not propose to expend any further effort to bring the Upper Watut natives under control as the effort is far too great compared to the results achieved … [32]

Two incidents within a fortnight in April-May 1931 were to shatter any illusion the Administration may have had that peaceful coexistence could be sustained between miners and the Kukukuku.

On 23 March, Hellmuth Baum left Surprise Creek with 15 Buang carriers on a prospecting expedition towards the Papuan border to the south. It was to have been his last such trip before a visit to Germany, which he had not seen since before the War. A few days earlier, a Papuan patrol officer, Jack Hides, arrived at Baum's camp and warned him that he had encountered many hostile villagers in the area through which Baum intended to travel, and that he should take a large party.[33]

On 27 April, several of Baum's carriers returned exhausted to Surprise Creek with news that Baum and several others had been murdered three days earlier in Kapau territory in the headwaters of the Tiveri River. Another miner, Michael Angelo, was the last European to see Baum alive, and the first to hear of his death. He recounted the story 30 years later:

> About a month after he had left my camp, three of his boys staggered in late one afternoon. Well, they were skeletons, that's all I can say. They couldn't talk or communicate, so I let them rest for some hours and then I got the story. Hellmuth Baum and party were attacked in the very early morning. (Some natives) brought sweet potatoes to trade and Hellmuth kept his axes, knives, etc. under his bunk. He bought some kai and leaned down to get an axe or something and as he was doing so he was smashed to the ground and his head half chopped off with a disc club, and then it was on for young and old.[34]

Seven carriers were also killed and several others badly wounded.

Within two weeks, there was a further attack—on brothers Mick and Paddy Leahy prospecting the headwaters of the Langimar River to the north-west. Just before daylight on 6 May, Mick Leahy was awoken by one of the carriers yelling, *Masta, Masta, kanaka killim me fella*.[35] He barely made it out of bed before being felled by a stone pineapple club to the side of the head. Paddy received arrow wounds in his left arm and right shoulder, and two carriers were wounded. Nevertheless, they beat off their attackers, five of whom died in the fight, and made their way with great difficulty down the Langimar River until they reached the Watut, where they encountered a patrol officer.

The timing of these incidents was coincidental, involving two different groups—the Kapau and Angaatiya—and many miles apart. However, they marked a turning point in the Administration's attitude towards the Kukukuku. It now realised that firmer action was necessary to avoid further incidents.

Mick and Paddy Leahy prospecting, head of Tauri River, March–April 1931.

CHAPTER 14

'PACIFICATION' OF THE KUKUKUKU

In killing Baum, the Kukukuku could not have picked anyone whose death would be more likely to arouse anger within the European community.

Typical of responses was that of the normally reserved Bank of New South Wales manager, Harry Johns, in a letter to his parents:

> A kindly old soul, inoffensive and generous to a degree in his treatment and care of the natives, [Baum] had lived in these parts for most of his life. These swine crept into his camp in the early hours and 'bashed' his brains out with a pineapple stone club … and then hacked him to pieces … The District Officer, with 16 police boys has gone out with the hopes and blessings of every white man that every native in that part will cease to exist.[1]

There was no doubt in the mind of every European that Baum was innocent of any actions that might have caused the attack. Most shared the view of Lutheran Missionary, Rev. Johannes Flierl, that

> the motive prompting them to their dark deed apparently was avarice, the strong desire to get more of the knives and tomahawks of the white man as he could give them for their foodstuffs.[2]

Baum was widely mourned. A later writer, Robin Radford, observed that

> He was the romantic ideal of the frontier prospector— tough, humane, and a survivor—and it was not just the loss of a friend, but the revelation of even his vulnerability amongst the mountain people that shocked the white community.[3]

Baum's murder was a seminal event, the Administration now realising that if Baum could not travel safely in Kukukuku country, no-one could. Occasional patrols from Salamaua were clearly insufficient to protect prospectors breaking into new country and, for that matter, miners working on the Upper Watut and its tributaries.

The Administration could have prevented attacks on prospectors by prohibiting entry to areas where these might occur, but its need for revenue precluded that, and so its priorities shifted from spreading the benefits of civilisation[4] to protecting gold prospectors

and miners. Restrictions on entering uncontrolled areas were tightened after Baum's murder, but they were less concerned with avoiding conflict with the Kukukuku than with tilting the balance if this should occur, by requiring larger parties and more firearms.

The Administration's 'pacification' policy now took on a harder edge, with large, well armed patrols arresting villagers believed to be responsible for attacks on Europeans, and the ruthless suppression of any resistance. Given the volatile and aggressive nature of the Kukukuku, violent conflict was inevitable.

District Officer Eric Feldt and Patrol Officer Ted Sansom set out on 7 May 1931 for Yaugwi River, where Baum had been murdered; the party included Baum's cook as a guide, 21 police and nearly 40 carriers.[5] Travelling about three miles a day in unceasing rain through sparsely populated country, they arrived at Baum's camp on 15 May. In his first three days there, Feldt saw no villagers at all. Years later, Feldt wrote

> It was my duty to arrest the murderers and bring them to trial; but the prospects of doing either did not look very bright … Even if caught, they could not be tried, as no one could speak any language they understood.[6]

With their food running out, Feldt's luck changed when seven villagers visited the camp. Baum's cook identified one of them as one of Baum's assailants, and Feldt promptly arrested them all. On the return trip, one escaped when the party was carefully negotiating its way along a heavily timbered razorback ridge. But Feldt succeeded in getting the others back to Bulolo, from where they were flown to Lae and then taken by pinnace to Salamaua.[7]

Wanting to send a strong message to the Kukukuku, the Administration did not let matters rest.

In November 1931, Assistant District Officer Nick Penglase and Patrol Officer Mark Pitt conducted a patrol into what became known as 'Baum country' to apprehend more of Baum's killers. Not surprisingly, given the previous arrests, they were attacked by

Baum's 'murderers', May 1931.

villagers, eight of whom were killed. After several days scouting, they located a village west of the Yaugwi River.[8] On 23 November, Pitt set out for it, accompanied by ten police. Later in the day, he returned to camp with a single prisoner and a young boy. Unusually, the patrol diary provides no explanation as to how the two were captured, the nature of any fighting or how many (if any) were killed. The prisoner and boy just appear back at camp, where the former was said to have died of 'natural causes' or perhaps 'sheer fright' at 4 am the following day.[9] The boy, whom Penglase claimed had been 'abandoned by his people', was taken back to Otibanda to be taught pidgin.

Still the Administration was not satisfied. The previous two patrols had been hampered by an inability to obtain supplies as there were few villages en route. In January 1932, after aerial reconnaissance, a new patrol was sent out, led by Penglase and Sansom, with 18 police, nine long-sentence prisoners, and 65 carriers—this time with the intention of approaching the Yaugwi River area from the south. An airstrip was established at Kudjiru to enable supplies to be flown in from Wau. Biangai carriers then guided the party to the area, following a track used in the past when fighting the Kukukuku.

Early in March, Penglase and Sansom captured eight prisoners over a three day period in the general vicinity of where Baum was murdered. The official patrol report is again vague about events surrounding their capture, but notes that

> The prisoners are from the villages of Wa and Jeki, which were implicated in the Baum murder; but to what extent they were actually involved will not be definitely ascertained until the interpreter returns from Finschhafen.[10]

Several accounts up to 70 years apart suggest that each of the Penglase patrol reports tells considerably less than the whole story.

In December 1933, Cadet Patrol Officer John Black was a member of a patrol returning the eight prisoners arrested by Penglase and Sansom. With him was a young boy, Mokera, whom he used as an interpreter. In his personal diary, Black noted on 8 December,

> Came to [Mokera's] place Hauwernatuwe. It was all desolate and going back to bush. Not a soul lives there now. Men, women and children were killed by Messrs Feldt [sic] and Penglase and police party early in 1932 [sic]. Baum was killed a short distance away on the river … Mokera says he was caught hiding in the bush and crying after everyone else was killed.[11]

There is little doubt that Mokera was the boy Peng-lase took back to Otibanda in November 1931 to learn pidgin. Black was wrong about Feldt's involvement and the date, but as he didn't arrive in New Guinea until June 1933, this is understandable.[12] Black saw the remains of the village and clearly believed Mokera's account of what had happened there. Its credibility is only strengthened by the silence in Penglase's report about the events of 23 November 1931.

The facts surrounding the capture of eight prisoners from Wa and Jeki on Penglase's second patrol were similarly glossed over in his report. Two separate accounts suggest that another massacre may have occurred. Penglase told the miner Roy Struben of events on the Kudjiru patrol, which Struben later described as a 'punitive expedition' on which 'a number of natives were shot down'.[13] These deaths are not mentioned in Penglase's report, although it is unlikely that eight prisoners would have been taken in three separate encounters over three days without fierce fighting. While Struben didn't suggest that women and children were killed, if they were it is unlikely that Penglase would have told him.

In 2003, Bawa Yandoapo, a member of the Titama clan, told the author that his people

> killed a miner called Bop and threw him in the water. Then a kiap came from Otibanda and killed plenty of people. They went to the village of Yaki [Jeki] and killed everyone. Nobody was left there afterwards.[14]

Such punitive measures—or, more accurately, reprisals—were expressly prohibited by the Administration.[15] On Feldt's patrol and Penglase's two patrols there was no attempt to mount an objective investigation of who was responsible for murdering Baum. With patrol officers, police and carriers all unable to understand the Kapau language, it was inevitably a question of guilt by association. Violence and the practice of arresting anyone near where a murder occurred were predictable consequences of Administrator Wisdom's determination not to show any weakness in dealing with villagers, together with frustration at the inability of successive patrols to identify and arrest the individuals responsible for Baum's murder.

The Administration now decided to establish base camps or patrol posts in areas where contact was likely between miners and villagers, with a patrol officer and small police detachment in each. The first was established in January 1932 at Otibanda, on Baum's old camp site, after miners in the Surprise Creek area complained about increasingly frequent thefts by Kukukuku.

Over the next few years, Otibanda—with its adjacent Surprise Creek airstrip—became the key frontier outpost on the fringes of Kukukuku territory. From it, patrol officers monitored working and living conditions in nearby miners' camps, worked to develop closer relationships with villagers in the surrounding area, and sought to ensure that any Europeans travelling into uncontrolled areas complied with requirements under the Uncontrolled Areas Ordinance. It was also a base for patrols to more remote areas.

In October 1932, inter-tribal fighting and growing conflict between miners and the Kukukuku led the Administration to form a special unit comprising Penglase and three patrol officers (Sansom, Pitt and McCarthy) with responsibility for bringing villagers of the Watut watershed under control. This resulted in more frequent patrols west of the Watut River, but had no positive effect on relations with the Kukukuku.

On 29 December 1932, two prospectors slipped out of Otibanda into uncontrolled territory without permits and without notifying Patrol Officer Pitt. Bill Naylor was a thin, experienced miner of about 35 years of age, Emile Clarius fair haired and nuggety, and still in his 20s. With them were nine carriers, one fewer than required under the Ordinance. On 8 January 1933, one of the carriers reappeared in Otibanda, reporting that the party had been attacked, with many deaths.

Several days later, District Officer Townsend and Penglase arrived at the scene of the attack, near the village of Kobakini to the west of Otibanda on the headwaters of the Kapau River. They found the bodies of Naylor and Clarius, each of whom had evidently been clubbed to death while prospecting; Naylor also had seven arrows in his back. Three carriers were dead and another two were later found to have died on their way back to Otibanda. No villagers were to be seen, but a sweep of Kobakini revealed several items belonging to Naylor and Clarius. After searching unsuccessfully for villagers for two days, Townsend and Penglase finally encountered some who appeared to be preparing an ambush. In the ensuing fight, three villagers were shot dead and two wounded. A second patrol sent out three weeks later returned after several weeks without seeing any villagers.

On 17 March, Keith McCarthy left Maralinan on a patrol to explore the upper reaches of the Langimar River, to determine the site for a base camp and aerodrome. As he travelled, McCarthy tested the streams for gold, with some success. The patrol then began its return to Otibanda, reaching Kobakini on 22 April, approaching it from the north-west. The villagers they encountered in the area kept their distance, but the following day several were lured into McCarthy's camp with knives and trade goods. At his signal, ten men were seized by police and carriers. Three of them died in the struggle and two escaped. The patrol was two to three days out from Otibanda, and broke camp immediately to return there with the five remaining prisoners.

As they progressed, McCarthy was aware that they were being shadowed, although no-one was seen. At times one or other of the prisoners would call out, sometimes provoking a response from the surrounding bush. On 25 April, the patrol was working its way down the side of a mountain in the vicinity of the village of Owanga. The path was narrow and slippery, with heavy undergrowth on each side. The first McCarthy knew that there were hostile villagers nearby was when he received an arrow in the stomach. In a letter to his brother, Laurie, he said it

> entered the left side of the navel and went in about 6 inches—I doubled up and fumbled for my revolver when I got another in the right thigh—high up. It went right through the leg but I only discovered it sticking out when everything was over ... I thought I was a goner for a bit—as I spat some blood out and couldn't bear to let anyone touch the arrow in my belly—but one police boy got up behind me and grasping me round the shoulders—Boko stepped in and with a smart tug pulled the beastly thing out.[16]

Charging the attackers in the bamboo, Corporal Anis was hit by three arrows, but not before he had bayoneted one of the Kukukuku and shot another. The attackers were shooting arrows at other police, whose responses were hampered by the ropes tying them to the prisoners. However, Corporal Anis's actions gave them time to get organised and they began firing back. McCarthy noted in his official report:

> I saw the man who had evidently shot me, he was only about five yards away and was coming nearer as he fitted another arrow; when he was near, Boko and Constable Boganau fired together and killed him. All was confusion for a few minutes but our attackers failed against the now steady fire of the police. Another

Plaque on Corporal Anis's grave, Salamaua.

attacker was killed about fifteen yards from me and then they broke and quickly disappeared into the heavy timber.[17]

The conflict resulted in the death of seven of the 30 or so attackers, with six police, a servant and McCarthy injured. The patrol struggled in to Otibanda early the next day. McCarthy and Corporal Anis were flown out to Salamaua soon afterwards. McCarthy made a full recovery, but Anis died four weeks later. In an unusual gesture, McCarthy acknowledged Anis's bravery by erecting a plaque over his grave.

Meanwhile, the Administration was establishing other base camps from which patrol officers could more easily monitor and protect miners. In September 1932, one such camp was established on the Ramu plateau in the eastern highlands north of the main Morobe goldfield, at what is now Kainantu, an area that was attracting a small but growing number of prospectors.[18]

There were 20,000 villagers in the vicinity of the Ramu Valley. Though generally more peaceable than the Kukukuku, they were equally attracted by the miners' possessions, and particularly their axes and knives. Echoing his comments to the 1927 Royal Commission, Chinnery (now Director, Department of District Services and Native Affairs) wrote to Acting Administrator Griffiths on 10 January 1933, foreshadowing further trouble in the goldfields area, especially in the Upper Ramu field. It follows inevitably that where prospectors are pushing forward in scattered units into uncontrolled country inhabited by hostile natives, conflicts mutually deadly may occur at any time.[19]

The following month a further base camp was established at Purari, near the Bena Bena airstrip, after a small goldfield discovered by the Leahy brothers was proclaimed in December 1932.

Chinnery's concern was understandable, given the miners' attitude towards stealing, their willingness to use firearms, and the much larger number of inhabitants in the Ramu area than on the Upper Watut. Miners were unwilling to let villagers get away with even minor thefts. Thus, Jack O'Neill once refused to pay for some kaukau because villagers with whom he was trading stole an empty meat tin. He suggested that *Everyone, including patrol officers, recognised this was necessary for survival in an area where there could be so many stacked up against so few.*[20]

Violence was often only narrowly avoided. In 1933, John Peadon was prospecting in the Upper Ramu area when villagers stole two axes and a knife.

> [I] decided to teach them a lesson—camped in good defensive position and sent for chief and told him through an interpreter that if the axes and knife did not come back I would come out and shoot them up—replied derisively that if I wanted a fight I can have it—fired a few shots over their heads and ordered boys to fire a few volleys with shot guns at a distance of about 150 yards—stayed in camp all day—late in the afternoon the two axes returned [and the knife the next day].[21]

A year later Lea Ashton on the Purari wrote to Jack O'Neill:

> We are expecting [Patrol Officers] Nurton and Mulligan out any day, and have hopes that they will convince these bastards out here that bows and arrows are not as good as rifles, an opinion they have. As a last resort, we may ourselves have to change their minds (which fact we communicated to Nurton) ... [22]

By 1933, with gold mining now spread out over a wide area, the District field staff were under enormous pressure. In his 10 January letter, Chinnery's frustration is evident:

> The truth must be faced that we have not at present sufficient field staff in the district services satisfactorily to cope with emergencies. As a matter of fact, we require 15 new appointments (cadets) ... to bring it to the strength of 1929.

This plea elicited a small increase in cadet patrol officers, although officials in Rabaul remained insensitive to the pressures on district staff on the mainland. Indicative of their rather different priorities was the memo issued by Acting Administrator Griffiths to District Officers on 6 June 1933:

> It has been decided that claims for boot allowance (£3 per annum) must show the approximate number of miles covered by patrol during the year for which the boot allowance is claimed.[23]

In June 1933, Assistant District Officer Ian Mack became the first European fatality on the Ramu field when he was shot with an arrow when trying to make an arrest.[24] He had been sent to Ramu Post three months earlier with instructions to get the upper hand in the area as quickly as possible. The arrow severed an artery and he died in Salamaua Hospital shortly afterwards.

⸺

While a serious effort was made to locate those who killed Naylor and Clarius, patrol officers felt that the two miners had brought misfortune on themselves by entering such dangerous and unknown territory ill-prepared and without a permit. The attack on McCarthy was another matter and it generated a violent response, one clearly endorsed by senior officers, who were being pressured to bring the area under control but had insufficient staff to achieve this using traditional patrols.

The word 'treachery' was used frequently by Administration officials to describe the behaviour of the Kukukuku. It is nevertheless surprising that Chinnery, an anthropologist, should have been among the most vocal in this regard—though doubtless he was expressing what others were thinking. He observed that

> The savage is extremely cunning and patient. He is a past-master in the arts of disarming suspicion and simulating friendship. Treachery is one of his most effective weapons in ordinary native warfare. The majority of Europeans who have lost their lives in New Guinea, owe it to lack of caution. They have been lulled into a false sense of security and then treacherously slain ... [25]

The most charitable interpretation one can put on such sentiments is that they were designed to make it easier to justify to others, including the Permanent Mandates Commission, the vigorous nature of their response to Kukukuku aggression.

Twenty-one year old Cadet Patrol Officer John Black had been in Salamaua barely a week when he recorded in his diary on 4 July 1933 that *POs Sansom and Bird are going out to pick a fight from Surprise Creek and give the Kuku-kuku a chance to learn definitely the power of the Government. This the DO* [District Officer] *told us tonight.* And on 1 August: *Patrol Officer Bird came in today from the new Slate Creek Police Post where they have an open season with the local kukus. They are the crowd that went McCarthy and POs Sansom and Bird have been ordered to clean them up. They have killed nine to date.*[26]

The official version, if more circumspect, was no less clear:

> Though Mr Sansom's objective was in restoring settled conditions and extending Administration influence, he had definite instructions to adopt drastic measures if the slightest hostility was shown, as it was realised that no risk would be taken against natives who had already successfully adopted the offensive. He had recourse to shooting on several occasions but the circumstances justified such action and this … achieved the desired result as the natives have been friendly for some time …[27]

Teaching the Kukukuku a lesson in the headwaters of Slate Creek and the Kapau River was one thing, but they were also widely dispersed to the north, west and south. Base camps and Uncontrolled Area permits would not prevent another tragedy if prospectors moved into this area in larger numbers. In February 1933, Chinnery expressed his opposition to *the wanderings of ill-equipped and inexperienced prospectors into hostile country. It is extremely dangerous for the miners and their native labourers, … dislocates important district Administrative work and runs the Government into endless expense …* His solution was to invite miners to prospect the area under the escort of a special patrol, noting that *if reputable prospectors fail to find payable gold in these areas, other miners will probably not want to enter them.*[28]

In his patrol in March-April 1933, McCarthy had found signs of gold in the Langimar and Tauri River watersheds. While this had not been publicly disclosed, the Administration knew that several prospectors were anxious to visit the area. It therefore adopted Chinnery's suggestion and formed a patrol to accompany several prospectors who would re-examine the area to see whether gold was present in commercial quantities. The patrol was the largest in the goldfields area between the wars, and was marked by intermittent fierce conflict with the Kukukuku.

The first stage involved establishing a base camp and aerodrome at Menyamya, on the upper reaches of the Tauri River due west of Otibanda and less than ten miles from the border with Papua. McCarthy was chosen to lead the patrol, supported by Cadet Patrol Officer John Black and surveyor Jack Ballam. The patrol comprised 25 police, 59 carriers from the Waria and three personal servants. Jack Lewis and Jack Lorenz, representing the Edie Creek Progress Association,[29] and Tom Yeomans

Menyamya expedition members, September 1933. Rear, l. to r. Jack Ballam (surveyor), Peter Jensen (BGD), Jack Lewis (Edie Creek Progress Association), Tom Yeomans (BGD), John Black; Front: Jack Lorenz (Edie Creek Progress Association) and Keith McCarthy.

Police Parade at Menyamya.

Preparing for patrol, Menyamya.

Menyamya camp, September 1933. Aerodrome is next to huts.

and Peter Jensen of Bulolo Gold Dredging joined at Menyamya.

The patrol left Otibanda on 7 August 1933. The trip was uneventful, and on 20 August it reached river flats at the junction of two tributaries of the Tauri among rolling grass-covered hills. Over the next fortnight, a landing ground was cleared so a plane could land on 3 September, as had been arranged previously.

While this was happening, McCarthy and Black patrolled the surrounding countryside. The villagers had never seen Europeans and were frightened by mirrors, mouth organs and matches. They were willing to trade some food for wood plane blades, knives and small cowrie shells, though on more than one occasion when they didn't bring in enough food to trade, Black went out and took food from their gardens. Although he left payment, his actions invariably produced a volley of arrows.

On 12 September, when investigating the death of a carrier who had passed through the base camp with another miner a few days earlier, McCarthy and Black were subjected to a shower of arrows from 30 or 40 men near Gainyamya. McCarthy:

> We were in a dangerous position, for they were aiming at us from a point above us. Our party then rushed the hill. The natives stood their ground and, after wounding one man with my revolver, I narrowly escaped being hit by his arrow. I took one side of the hill, as I wanted to clear the heavy undergrowth of lurking men, and

Black took the other. Black received a nasty wound on the left side of the head, very near his eye. The arrow entered his head and, striking the skull, splintered. It bled very much … We stayed on the knoll for an hour and all that time were subjected to arrow fire. We were lucky not to suffer further casualties for we were being fired at from the undergrowth and our enemies were unseen. It was now 3.30 p.m. and time for getting back to the camp … The natives fought every yard of the way, attacking our rearguard without cessation. They suffered several casualties from our rifle fire but this did not deter them.[30]

The next day Tom Yeomans recorded in his diary:

> A few Kanakas in with kau-kau from the village that shot J. Black. They are quite happy and jovial about it & talked about the fight & said 7 were killed. Police boys recognised some who were fighting & if we had not been there would have carried on the fight. They wanted to shoot a couple.[31]

Over the next five weeks, patrols went out from Menyamya in different directions with the miners prospecting the streams for gold. It soon became clear that it was not present in economically viable quantities. McCarthy therefore decided to abandon Menyamya as a base camp.

In a broader sense, however, the patrol was a success. As Chinnery had prophesied, the fact that well respected prospectors had been unsuccessful was sufficient to discourage others from moving out into this area.

McCarthy and friends, Menyamya.

Trading kaukau, Menyamya.

By eliminating from miners' expectations most of the large area inland from the Watut River, the Administration succeeded with this one patrol in defusing the potential for future conflict between miners and the Kukukuku.

To be on the safe side, the Administration imposed additional requirements on prospectors wanting to enter the area. They were required to post a substantial bond towards the cost of sending out a patrol if they got into difficulties, and to be better armed and travel in larger numbers. In March 1934, one miner was told that to obtain a permit to the Upper Langimar area, he would require a line of 15 to 20 carriers and a minimum of ten serviceable firearms.[32] Finally, in 1935, the Administration decided to prohibit entry until the area was under sufficient Government control.[33]

On the Upper Watut as well as on the Ramu/Purari, patrol officers distributed seeds of European vegetables to villagers living near miners' camps, encouraging them to grow food they could trade as a way of developing mutual acceptance and confidence. However, each side remained wary of the other. In 1934, Daphne Murcutt had recently arrived in New Guinea as a new bride:

> I had only been at Upper Watut [5 miles below the Otibanda Post] a few months when one day my kelpie dog was barking ferociously ... Looking out I saw about 50 or so kukukuku viewing the house from about 30 yards away ... I had been told about the kukukukus. They were the most feared, vicious and bloodthirsty tribe in New Guinea. In 1931 and 1933 they had murdered four men a few miles from our house ... I took the loaded rifle from behind the door, and with trembling hands took the chance and fired a shot high above their heads. They turned and fled so very quietly and quickly, there was not a sound.[34]

A benefit of arresting villagers in more remote areas was the exposure this gave them to the white men's world and ways, and even some knowledge of pidgin English. When they returned to their villages, stories of their experiences usually resulted in less hostility towards Europeans.

While the frequency of thefts by villagers from miners' camps kept patrol officers busy on tributaries of the Upper Watut as well as on the Upper Ramu and Purari, only rarely did this result in serious conflict. When it did, it could escalate rapidly. In February 1934, the miner Bernard McGrath was killed on the Upper Ramu. Frustrated with continual thieving, he had taken matters into his own hands, arresting a village chief and shooting two villagers. The villagers, who had previously been friendly, promptly killed him. Cadet Patrol Officer Tom Aitchison went to investigate and was himself attacked; returning fire killed three villagers. District Officer Ted Taylor then arrived and tried to arrest several men from the attacker's village. In intermittent fighting over five hours, at least 19 villagers were killed and 17 wounded.[35]

Jim Sinclair, former District Commissioner turned historian, has observed that

> Compared with Papua, New Guinea was a violent territory ... Much blood was shed; patrol officers, police, and a number of prospectors and recruiters fell to spears and arrows ... many other attacks were beaten off, and it will never be known how many New Guinea tribesmen were killed by rifle fire.[36]

Bunny Hammond's DH50, with interested bystanders, Menyamya.

In the main, patrol officers did a remarkable job in the 1930s protecting gold prospectors and miners and, indeed, protecting villagers against the intolerance of miners. While miners undoubtedly took the law into their own hands at times, such incidents went unreported. Years later, Michael Angelo told Ian Grabowsky that he had shot a few kukukuku: *They look better with a few perforations.*[37]

Many deaths occurred on or around the goldfields when patrols and miners were attacked; these might reasonably be explained away as the 'fortunes of war'. However, stories of reprisals live in the shadows of the official accounts. While not officially admitted or sanctioned, retribution involving whole communities did occur. Such incidents can be explained — though not justified — as a reaction by district staff to interpretation difficulties and the impracticality of applying the principle of individual responsibility for attacks in the face of group hostility. It is reasonable to assume that the perpetrators took their cue from Administrator Wisdom's emphatic philosophy that *Opposition must be broken down now when met and failure to do so will inevitably bring about much greater bloodshed later.*

Was 'pacification' of the Kukukuku a success? If the measure is the extent to which they were brought under 'control', the answer is no. Jim Sinclair noted that *By the outbreak of war, a degree of control had been established around the fringes of the Kukukuku country, but the interior remained completely uncontrolled.*[38]

Given the cost of drawing labour from the Sepik and Madang Districts, some in the Administration had initially hoped that the large Kukukuku population in the Tauri-Langimar area might provide a reservoir of lower cost labour.[39] However, control was never extended sufficiently for this to happen. From late 1933, the Manki sometimes worked as carriers on Administration patrols, as did villagers from Kobakini in 1937, while some did occasional labouring work for miners. Apart from such isolated instances, trading food remained the limit of Kukukuku interaction with Europeans before the War.

But in view of the potential for conflict between miners and the Kukukuku — and villagers on the Ramu and Purari — the Administration was doubtless satisfied that its goals had been broadly achieved. There are no recorded instances of attacks on miners after the death of Bernard McGrath, possibly reflecting the large number of deaths which followed the dramatic intervention by patrol officers after such incidents.

Did this end therefore justify the means? Can Administrator Wisdom's view be held to have been right?

While the death of villagers in conflicts with patrol officers may have led to fewer deaths subsequently, from a humanitarian viewpoint the Administration's approach was morally indefensible. One cannot help but reflect on the extent to which its need for revenue from gold mining — due to the Australian Government's insistence that it be self-sufficient financially — compromised its responsibility under the League of Nations Mandate to promote the material and moral well-being and social progress of the inhabitants of New Guinea through more peaceful means and at a more measured pace.

CHAPTER 15
EARLY ENCOUNTERS: THE NEW GUINEAN PERSPECTIVE

Europeans interpreted their interactions with villagers in terms of their own values.[1]

If the Kukukuku didn't react to something in the way Europeans might have reacted, they were considered unpredictable. If they didn't fight according to European 'rules', they were treacherous. When they kept attacking despite being shot, they were brave. The reality was rather more complex.

If Europeans relied on their own values to interpret their experiences, it is hardly surprising that the same should be true of villagers. The arrival of white men was a singularly dramatic event for all isolated communities.

To understand the reaction of tribes living close to the goldfields to the first Europeans they encountered, one needs to understand their relationship with the environment, their beliefs and values, their social and political organisation and the circumstances of the encounters.[2]

The Kapau lived in isolated hamlets, typically comprising an extended family group of 15 to 25 people occupying between two and six houses. A hamlet was usually located on a steep ridge or spur and protected by a palisade of bamboo stakes. More heavily fortified hamlets were surrounded by rings of closely planted trees or pitpit. The defensive position of hamlets and their palisades reflected the precarious nature of everyday existence—the constant threat of raids, when men, women and children might all be killed. Biangai settlements were also built on ridges and surrounded

Barricaded Biaru village, 1924. The Biaru people lived to the south of the Biangai; their villages are believed to have been similar to pre-contact Biangai villages in layout and construction.

Bubu (Upper Waria)
River women and
children, 1924.

by bamboo palisades. They were larger than Kapau hamlets, but appear never to have numbered more than 60 to 80 people.

Consistent with the tendency of their cousins on the Langimar to live in villages of 40 to 50 houses, all 130 or so Manki lived in a larger village on the Bulolo-Watut divide. Menya settlements comprised hamlets, though these appear to have been located near each other. McCarthy estimated that the Menyamya community numbered about 2,000 people.

While Europeans tended to identify Kapau villages as comprising a group of several hamlets, it is less clear that the occupants saw themselves as belonging to such an entity, even though there may have been close family links between the hamlets. The anthropologist Beatrice Blackwood, who lived among the Kapau (and Manki) in 1936-37, noted that each small Kapau hamlet was *usually separated from its nearest neighbour by a descent of perhaps 1,500 feet, an inconvenient ford, and a climb of as much or more on the other side …*[3] The people practised shifting cultivation, so their gardens were typically at some distance from the hamlet, often involving travel over difficult country.

Before the arrival of Europeans, the Kukukuku were largely self-sufficient. Little trading occurred, even between adjacent people, and none between the Kapau and people on the other side of the Bulolo valley closer to the coast, such as the Biangai and Buang, who were their traditional enemies. Kukukuku languages were unrelated to those of the Biangai and Buang and as relations between them were confined to conflict, they had no basis for developing an understanding of each others' languages.

As with villagers throughout New Guinea, the lives of the Kukukuku, Biangai and Buang were dominated by the spirit world and sorcery. Good fortune and misfortune could be explained by the activities of spirit beings or sorcerers. Although people's view of the spirit world differed between areas, it was generally accepted that there were spirits of the dead and spirits of non-human origin. Either could be benevolent or malevolent. Shamans — where they existed — might seek to propitiate spirits and harness their powers for the good of the community, whether in peace or war.[4]

The rugged topography, multiplicity of languages and dialects, and the risk of being killed if they travelled beyond the narrow confines of the area in which they lived and had their gardens meant villagers often had little understanding of what existed beyond their territorial boundaries. These factors, together with the unknown dangers of sorcery and the spirit world, fostered a deep suspicion of strangers.

Unlike villagers in other areas of New Guinea, where reciprocal obligations were central to the economic and social framework, the Kukukuku were strongly individualistic, temperamental and aggressive. There was little co-operative activity beyond the hamlet, with the exception of warfare and possibly male initiation.

The Kukukuku and Biangai did not have hereditary chiefs, or 'big men' such as existed in the highlands. Fight leaders were the most important men. James Saro, a Kapau, told the author in 2001 that each clan had a fight leader and the Kapau today still regard clan membership as important. However, the anthropologist John Burton sees little evidence that group activity was organised along clan lines.[5] Nevertheless, the Kapau seem to have had little difficulty organising sufficient men to confront European trespassers on their territory and such co-operation seems to have extended over quite some distance, commonly involving groups of 30 to 50, but sometimes many more.

———

The arrival of Europeans was incomprehensible to the Kukukuku. Linguistically isolated from coastal tribes and frequently from each other, they often appear to have had no forewarning of the arrival of patrol officers and prospectors. Their sudden appearance raised two issues: who were these intruders and what should be done about them? Inevitably, the starting point in answering each question was their own belief systems and values.

A common reaction throughout New Guinea to the unexpected and certainly unwelcome appearance of white men was that they were the spirits of dead ancestors, another that they were spirits of unknown origin, possibly from the sky, and that their carriers were dead ancestors. The anthropologist, R.F. Salisbury, recorded that the Siane people of the Eastern Highlands believed Europeans to be spirits who had returned from the dead and had an intimate relationship with valuables, a view strengthened by their lavishness in giving highly prized items such as salt and axes in exchange for things of little value, such as food.[6] Another possibility, if the strangers came from the direction of one's known enemies, was that they were malevolent spirits sent by them.

Initial reactions ranged from curiosity to fear. On his 1933 trip to the upper reaches of the Langimar, McCarthy reported that the villagers were puzzled by his clothing and shoes, thinking they were part of his body.[7] The anthropologist E.L. Schieffelin reported a similar reaction to a 1935 patrol in the southern highlands in Papua, where the footprints of patrol officers' boots *seemed to indicate a being that had had its toes cut off. Moreover the corrugations printed from the boot soles suggested the marks of a skeletal foot – a creature that walked along on exposed bones ...*[8] The hair of Europeans was of particular fascination; pieces were often sought—and given—and carefully wrapped in leaves and taken away.

Guyo Saweo, a Kapau of the Nauti clan, who as a small boy saw the first white men enter the Bulolo valley, told the author in 2003 that when his people first saw Europeans,

> we thought they were the spirits of people who had died—our ancestors. When we saw the colour of their skin, we were frightened, as we thought they were bad spirits. The first white men stayed for some time and gave us salt, knives, axes and matches. However, when they came too close we ran away, so they couldn't get too close to us.

While trading was largely an alien concept to the Kukukuku, most were attracted to the knives, salt and shells offered by the white intruders in exchange for food.[9] But in early contact situations, women and children were typically kept well away from the strangers, and trade items offered that were unknown—such as matches and mirrors—often seemed to instil great apprehension.

Aeroplanes were a particular source of fear and wonder. James Saro told the author that

> When the Watut people first saw a plane they were very scared, throwing themselves on the ground. They couldn't work out where it had come from or where it might go when it took off—perhaps straight up into the sky. When they saw the first plane land and white men emerge from it, they thought the plane was a mother giving birth to white men. They inspected the underneath of the plane, but couldn't see anything like breasts, just round things.

A widely held belief was that a plane was some kind of bird. At Menyamya the noise of its engine terrified the villagers, and when it passed over their heads, they cowered in the grass, holding their ears and shivering. Once they overcame their fear, they gingerly inspected the plane, depositing several bilums of kaukau in front of it so it could eat.[10]

Their fear frequently took the form of great animation and excitability. Some Europeans interpreted this as hostility, although those who were more experienced recognised it as nervousness.[11] Silence and inaction could mean the same, although this was more likely to be interpreted by Europeans as acceptance of their presence and, if accompanied by trading, even as friendship.

Whatever conclusion they came to about who white men were, they still had to decide what to do about them.

The Kukukuku's reputation for unpredictability developed because of the frequency with which they would trade with the white intruders one day and attack them the next.[12] Or they might seem friendly but later shoot arrows into a camp for no apparent reason. Patrol Officer Ian Downs observed that villagers near Kobakini base camp in 1937 *used to amuse themselves turning our camp into a pin cushion for their arrows in dawn raids. They would return to sell us food later in the same day.*[13]

Such responses were, in fact, perfectly logical, given a single underlying premise: strangers were enemies. As one observer noted when writing about contact situations in the highlands:

> Usually, the visitors were prepared for barter, and the locals prepared for war. There was no question of mutual need ... The New Guineans did not need or want their visitors; for them, the initial hostility and attack as well as subsequent attempts to kill the strangers and seize their property were sanctioned by the traditional reality that strangers were in fact enemies.[14]

This assessment is equally true of the Kukukuku.

What Europeans described as unpredictable behaviour may have been little more than confusion or even competing views within a group as to the best strategy to get rid of the intruders; if one strategy didn't work, try another. However, as Europeans had no knowledge of their beliefs or culture and no ability to communicate with them — at least in the earlier years — they could often only guess at what was happening.

Charles Rowley suggested that the outcome of a situation involving frightened warriors with a tradition of treacherous attack

> depends a great deal on how determined village leaders are, how far they have understood their helplessness against the firearms of police, the kind of rumour which has preceded the visit, the effectiveness of explanations often translated from pidgin through one or more vernaculars, memories of other experiences, religious beliefs and the like.[15]

Such factors underline the complexity of the contact experience and the difficulty of predicting and interpreting villagers' responses.

Whether or not Europeans were perceived as spirits, the instinct of villagers encountering them was to attack. They didn't need a specific reason. Contemporary descriptions of Kukukuku behaviour suggest they had much in common with the Nembi in the southern highlands, whom the anthropologist Crittenden described as being

> contemptuous of the weak and quick to take advantage where they perceived vulnerability. They were continually testing the situation and were ready to act on any show of uncertainty with confrontation. Further, The Nembi were probably much more uncertain and frightened than they let on but they were also dealing with the situation as they normally dealt with situations of danger and uncertainty in their lives: by projecting an arrogant attitude and testing and provoking the opposition at every point to locate its vulnerability.[16]

A visit by the Kukukuku to a camp to trade was an opportunity to size up the strengths and weaknesses of the intruders. If Europeans viewed this as a sign of friendship, then perhaps they were simply misreading the situation. Similarly, firing arrows into a camp could be testing its defences or, at other times, a warning. Depending on the response, an attack might follow. There were many reports of patrols being shadowed by noisy groups of Kukukuku, whirring their bull roarers, shouting and letting off the occasional arrow, but keeping their distance. Such harassment may have been intended to test or deter patrols as it was rarely followed by attacks. When these came, as McCarthy found out near Owanga, they were usually ambushes.

Nevertheless, at times there was a catalyst for an attack: it might be a patrol passing through a village or taking food from a garden, even where payment was left. Both were regarded as confrontational behaviour inviting a hostile response.[17]

One particular catalyst, embedded firmly in Kukukuku values, was that of payback. It has been suggested that *the Kukukuku are not particular about making some kind of accurate selection for a payback. Anyone will do, so long as he or she is in some remote way connected to the killer.*[18] The reason for Hellmuth Baum's murder in 1931 was a mystery to his contemporaries, the most widely accepted explanation being that it was due to avarice. However, James Saro told the author that a Kapau fight leader, Kuwaweto Yayau, had been killed by a European and that Baum's death was payback for this.[19]

Payback was also involved in the death of Naylor and Clarius. In 1932, several women were murdered by villagers from Kudushu and Gumi, north-west of

Otibanda. A patrol subsequently arrested several men from the immediate area and took them to Salamaua. The notion of 'arrest' was unknown to the Kukukuku who naturally thought they'd been taken away and killed. One of those arrested, Iapangu, told McCarthy: *A man came to my village Owanga, and reminded us that some of our men had been taken away in the past, and had never returned. He then cried out that we should kill the two Europeans.*[20] Owanga villagers were related to those from Kudushu and Gumi, so that when Naylor and Clarius entered the area, the principle of payback determined their fate.

Other more spontaneous attacks were dictated by the circumstances and individuals involved. Thus, encounters with a group of young warriors were more likely to result in a hostile reaction than if older and wiser heads were present.

Another strategy appears to have involved recourse to sorcery. The belief that white men were spirits appears at times to have been reflected in the activities of shamans. On 4 October 1933, an exploratory expedition from Menyamya base camp arrived at the large village of Karakaiya. The villagers were taken by surprise and amid general commotion, pelted the 'invaders' with arrows. This reaction was hardly surprising as the sudden appearance of five white men, 13 police and 34 carriers could only have been taken as a threat by people of a generally suspicious nature.

After the party withdrew a short distance and put a light rope around where they camped to mark the boundary, McCarthy reported that

> An old man suddenly left the Karakaiya men and slowly came towards us. He was old and feeble … Two pieces of short bamboo were held in his hands and he advanced towards us swaying and muttering … He laid the two pieces of bamboo within ten yards of us and then slowly went back. I advanced and carefully put two large knives near the bamboo … After an hour the old man came forward with a small pig and I tried to give him an axe. He would not look at the steel but eagerly accepted a gold lip shell. My first two knives were returned—a man bringing them back held by a vine, so that the knives would not come into contact with his skin.[21]

A little time later, another man suddenly emerged.

> His face and body were completely covered with heavy mud and he wore a head-dress of leaves which completely covered his face. He came out to us in a crouching and jerky dance and two other men who

followed his movements carried 3 or 4 poles each, about 12 feet in length, on which were tied bunches of sugar cane. With mutterings and many turns he placed a dozen or so pit pit stalks in line with our rope. The ceremony was evidently enacted to prevent us from entering the village.

McCarthy concluded that so long as they didn't do so, they wouldn't be attacked, and this proved to be the case.

The strategy of using shamans (if that's what they were) no doubt seemed to Karakaiya villagers particularly effective, as the patrol stayed out of the village, left the next day and didn't come back.

Europeans noted several phases through which villagers seemed to pass after the initial contact. Mick Leahy, whose arrival on the Upper Ramu caused great confusion among villagers, observed:

> On your first trip into new country, unless you take the natives by surprise, they will probably be too much in awe of you to turn hostile. On your second trip they will begin to size you up more closely, to lose their fear of you, and to consider how desirable are all those steel axes and shining baubles in your packs. On your third trip, look out![22]

Resistance to intruders was so entrenched in the culture of New Guinean villagers, that any delay in attacking them is likely to have had less to do with peaceful intentions than with taking time to assess their weaknesses, or perhaps substituting an initial non-violent strategy with a more overtly aggressive one.

Dealing with what they perceived as unpredictable behaviour, where one group might be welcoming and the next hostile, or the same group friendly one moment and antagonistic the next, was a strain for patrol officers and others travelling through uncontrolled areas. On leaving one camp in 1933, where McCarthy felt he had made friends with the locals and had left gifts of steel and salt, he saw the Kukukuku set fire to their shelters:

> Arrows were shot in our direction to help us on our way. The same old jeers of contempt followed the arrows and I wondered if anyone would ever be able to make friends with such an unpredictable people.[23]

Four years later, the answer was no clearer. After 40 arrows were shot into Kobakini base camp by villagers who had hitherto been 'friendly', Patrol Officer Milligan observed:

> I am at a loss, at the moment, to explain their attitude, and can only offer as a reason, either their love of

fighting and difficult temperament or as just one of those things likely to happen in dealing with such suspicious, warlike, treacherous people.[24]

The notion that the Kukukuku were inherently treacherous was deeply entrenched amongst district staff, and was of course shared by miners. Baum, Naylor and Clarius were all considered to have been 'treacherously' attacked by villagers with whom they had been trading or who had accompanied them as they walked on the day or so before the attack. However, from the Kukukuku perspective, if the 'enemy' gives you a break, by letting you travel with him or engage in trade, so you can assess his strengths, it is hardly treacherous simply because he doesn't realise what you are doing.

Their approach to fighting reinforced the perception of treachery among Europeans. Ambushes were preferred, with cover provided by the natural vegetation or rain and heavy mist. In some cases, a party or individuals were enticed by offers of food or other apparently friendly behaviour into a position where they could be attacked. Invariably, such attacks involved a shower of arrows designed to maim, followed by clubs at close quarters. Equally acceptable was an attack at dawn, though their fear of evil spirits discouraged night time attacks.

All tribal groups in the goldfields area used footspears—sharp bamboo needle-like slivers 12 to 18 inches long set in a hole about two feet deep and lightly covered with sticks and earth, often just below a natural step down on the track. The weight of a man stepping on the cover would drive the stake right through his foot. These might be placed at a place where a distracted party could be ambushed or simply embedded on a track to deter strangers.

However unappealing their mode of warfare may have been to Europeans, these fighting techniques were a natural response to the conditions. Within the limitations of their technology, their military tactics were similar to what later became known as guerrilla warfare in jungle conditions, with footspears conceptually little different from landmines.

Arguably, in fact, the Kukukuku displayed considerable integrity. Giving warnings seems to have been very much part of their culture. They were expert bowmen and so when arrows were fired close to patrols or miners or into the track ahead, rather than directly at them, this was a clear warning not to proceed further. In the Kobakini area, John Black recorded on 14 August

1933: *Yesterday the road was fastened by kanakas with a small branch of a sapling and two broken arrows, the former a sign of warning, the latter a sign of peace.*[25] Both were common signals, broken arrows and an offering of sugar cane or bananas also being used to indicate that they wanted to stop fighting.

While McCarthy's party was patrolling out in the Menyamya area in September-October 1933, there were several occasions when Kukukuku tried to lead Europeans away from their villages—not the actions of people bent on treachery. Tom Yeomans recorded on 10 September that about four villagers *came up to our line & did all they could to stop us going on, illustrating by signs we would be speared or clubbed, crying they would fall down in front of me, blocking up the pathway.*[26]

⟋

The respect Europeans such as McCarthy and other patrol officers had for the bravery of the Kukukuku was doubtless well founded. But 'bravery' may also have reflected other factors. To demonstrate the power of their guns and thus discourage hostility, it was common practice for patrol officers and prospectors to line up several shields one behind the other and shoot one or more bullets through them. Despite such demonstrations of firepower that villagers couldn't hope to match, there were many deaths in combat situations as they persisted in fighting patrols with weapons that were clearly inferior. Europeans attributed this to their courage and determination to protect their way of life against the invaders.

There may be a further explanation.[27] A clue lies in a statement to the author by Monica Panga at Kaisinik in 2001, when she said that, during the attack on Kaisinik in 1927,

> a man was wounded by a bullet in the upper arm and could not understand how this happened. We did not understand guns and thought our spears and arrows were more powerful than anything that the white men and police had.

It is not known how prevalent this perception was, but it suggests that even among villagers with some years of experience with Europeans, there was little appreciation of the true nature of guns.[28]

This is not as surprising as it may seem. An arrow is a visible projectile. When a rifle is fired, however, no projectile is evident—just a loud noise and perhaps a man killed or injured. Thus in early encounters, rifles may have been viewed as a form of magic.

If fight leaders did indeed clean evil spirits away before a fight, as James Saro suggested to the author, it is reasonable to assume that they sought to convince fighting men of their ability to protect them.[29] Certainly, this would explain why attacks continued at times, despite deaths and injuries and in the face of greatly superior weapons. And to the extent that a dozen rifle shots might result in only one man killed or injured, fight leaders would perhaps have been able to argue that their 'cleansing' activities worked most of the time.

———

Stealing was endemic on the goldfields. Miners' camps were the main target, but parties moving through inhabited territory were usually joined by villagers from nearby hamlets who would often accompany them for considerable distances, and an unguarded moment would see the disappearance of knives or other items. An imaginative variant—a form of arbitrage—was to steal kaukau from some miners' gardens and sell it to others who didn't grow their own food.

Given the material imbalance between their respective cultures, it is hardly surprising that the Kukukuku and other New Guineans would covet the possessions of Europeans. The Upper Watut today freely acknowledge that stealing occurred, and that some of their men were killed when doing so, but it is also possible that villagers were often the convenient scapegoats for thefts by miners' own labourers.

———

Despite the hysteria about cannibalism at the time of the Kaisinik killings in 1927, this was never an issue on the goldfields. The Biangai, Kapau, Angaatiya and Menya all practised cannibalism, though not on a large scale and never involving Europeans.

Each tribe had its 'specialty'. The Biangai collected heads and long bones as trophies. The Angaatiya (including the Manki) ate the whole body (though thighs and arms were said to make the best eating). The Menya and Kapau were more selective. Guyo Saweo told the author:

> Cannibalism never happened where other clans were involved, only tribal enemies such as the Biangai. However, the whole body wasn't eaten, only the muscles in the right arm and left leg. These were only

eaten by young men, to gain strength, and old men whose muscles had wasted. Not by middle aged men, or by women and children.[30]

While patrol officers spent much time trying to stop cannibalism, to miners it wasn't an issue. Jack O'Neill dryly observed,

> It was generally accepted that [the Kukukuku] were, like so many New Guinea native tribes, cannibals, but I had never heard any evidence of their putting white men on the menu though they had killed a few; I found that native people were distrustful of strange food.[31]

However, desertions of indentured labourers were common, and as they were often located by Europeans trying to make their way back to their villages, often many days travel away, it is possible that some may have been caught by villagers while stealing from their gardens. Retribution would have been quick, effective and final though whether they were eaten is unknown. Certainly, patrol officers thought it likely. In November 1934, Patrol Officer Ken Bridge, a quiet, humorous, sandy-haired Scot stationed at Otibanda, wrote to Jack O'Neill who was mining nearby:

> Ten minutes ago I received some information from G. Engle who reported a line of thirty Madang and other natives loaded up with gear, passing over the head of Surprise Creek and saying they were on their way to Ramu. This of course means they will provide meals for the Slate Creekers and I have sent the rest of my available police, medical orderlies, cooks, etc. to Slate Creek to intercept the bastards.[32]

———

While cannibalism played no part in the goldfields story after 1927, the concern Europeans initially had about this epitomised the gulf between their culture and that of villagers living close to the goldfields. While Hellmuth Baum had argued that white men must look at things from the villagers' viewpoint, they simply didn't have a good enough grasp of their culture to do so. As a result, they were usually well wide of the mark in their assessments of the reasons for the behaviour they were witnessing. Given their premise that villagers were unpredictable and treacherous, while villagers believed that all strangers were enemies, it is perhaps surprising that more early contact situations didn't end in tragedy.

CHAPTER 16

'IF THE NATIVE
IS TO BE UPLIFTED ...'

Indigenous labour was pivotal to the success of the goldfield, and this was provided by a highly organised indentured labour system.

Initially, villagers living close to the tracks in from the coast carried supplies for Europeans travelling to the field. But when the 1926 rush required far greater numbers to work as carriers and labourers, a labour system already existed which enabled them to be recruited from elsewhere.

Labourers had long been recruited to work on plantations and in Government labour lines. At this stage of New Guinea's development, a free labour system, where people volunteered to work for payment, was impractical. The concept of paid work was unknown and villages were usually a long way from where labour was needed. Travelling through unknown territory was dangerous and there was no organised or reliable transport. Nor was there any way of matching the supply of labour with demand. Too many labourers looking for work would create major social problems close to urban centres, too few would have adverse economic consequences.

An indentured labour system had been developed by the Germans, and this was maintained by Australian military and then civil administrations. Labourers were recruited from villages in areas previously opened up to European influence and transported, often over long distances, to where they were needed. They signed contracts, at first for one or two years, but in the 1930s more commonly for three, during which they were indentured to specific employers. In June 1922, nearly 27,000 labourers were employed in this way, of whom more than 20,000 were working on copra plantations.

Only where villages were close to where labour was needed did anything like a free labour market develop, involving the use of day labour. Local villagers were employed extensively in Lae and Salamaua. However, there were no villages close to Edie Creek and those near Wau and Bulolo were small or (in the case of the Kukukuku) not under Administration 'control'. Thus most labourers were recruited from areas where the population was relatively large but there were few employment opportunities.

The Administration faced the formidable challenge of motivating young men to leave their villages voluntarily and for extended periods to work in remote and unfamiliar locations. Its solution was simple and effective: it imposed an annual head tax of 10 shillings on each man of working age in areas under complete or partial Government control, but exempted labourers.[1] Very few villages had any way of raising money and so relied on labourers returning at the end of their contracts with enough money to pay the tax.

———

The League of Nations Mandate required Australia to *promote to the utmost the material and moral well-being and the social progress of the inhabitants of the territory*, though it didn't define what this meant or how it should be achieved. From an early stage, however, the Permanent Mandates Commission expressed concern that Australia's duty to raise the level of civilisation among New Guinea's indigenous inhabitants should not become subservient to the Territory's economic exploitation.[2]

On the other hand, Administrator Wisdom saw social and economic progress as intertwined, proclaiming in 1921 that *If the native is to be uplifted, it must be done in conjunction with the progress of the country, and progress is only possible with abundance of native labour.*[3] Making a virtue out of necessity, the Administration presented the indentured labour system as a benign substitute for warfare, the latter being prohibited in areas under Government control. In doing so, it adopted the philosophy of the Lieutenant Governor of Papua, Hubert Murray: *to substitute the activity of labour for that of fighting and to transform the tribe of disappointed warriors into a race of more or less industrious workmen.*[4]

The Administrator nevertheless saw progress occurring within the framework of the traditional village and its subsistence economy. Young men would leave their villages for up to two years to work on plantations, the goldfields or elsewhere and then return for good, to be replaced by others. In this way, they would contribute to the country's economic progress and be introduced to civilisation, returning to their village wiser in the ways of the white man.

The reality was not so simple.

⸺

Sensitive to excesses which had occurred under the Germans, the Administration regulated each stage of employment from recruitment to repatriation. Once tribal fighting had ceased in an area, labour recruiters were permitted to begin recruiting. While there were always a few professional recruiters working for employers on a commission basis,[5] most were employers seeking labour for their own operations; between 400 and 500 licences were issued annually for this purpose.

Jack O'Neill observed that recruiters *walked a razor's edge with 'one foot in the grave and the other in jail'.*[6] Not infrequently, recruiters moving into newly opened areas were attacked and had to fight their way out of trouble. In more settled areas, they depended on village headmen or officials to help them secure new recruits and, before 1932, could pay them up to £1 for each recruit. When it became evident that young men were, in effect, being sold to recruiters whether or not they wanted to be recruited, the Administration prohibited such payments and the involvement of village officials in recruiting.

Illegal recruiting activities—including threats of imprisoning villagers if recruits were not forthcoming—were common at the time of the 1926 gold rush when carriers and labourers were particularly difficult to obtain.[7] While there were instances of abuse during the years that followed,[8] most recruiters wanted 'repeat business' and usually dealt fairly with villagers so as to maintain their trust and goodwill.

Once a villager agreed to 'make paper' (sign a contract), he was given a present of trade goods—often a knife or tomahawk—and with other recruits he then travelled with the recruiter to the nearest District Office. Here, after a medical examination, the District Officer or one of his staff sought to ensure, through an interpreter, that recruits had not been coerced and understood the nature of the contract they were to sign.[9] This included details of the nature and place of work, his wages and that he was bound to his employer for the term of his contract. Once they had signed, recruits were sent—usually by the next available ship—to the nearest port to their intended workplace. In the case of the goldfields, this was Salamaua.

⸺

While labourers employed on plantations always greatly outnumbered those in mining, most of the increase in the labour force was associated with the goldfields. In 1925/26, before the gold rush, there were 23,400 indentured labourers in New Guinea. By 1937/38, there were nearly 42,000, half of whom were labourers on plantations—little more than in the early 1920s.[10] Most of the growth occurred in mining (from 1,900 in 1930/31 to 7,200 in 1940/41) and supporting activities—domestic service, shipping, commerce and industry. Labourers in the Morobe District accounted for only 5% of the New Guinea total in 1926, but more than one third a decade later.

Whereas villagers on New Britain and New Ireland who otherwise lacked access to the cash economy tended to work on plantations, those from the Markham Valley and elsewhere in the Morobe District naturally gravitated towards the goldfields. But as the growth of mining outstripped the District's capacity to provide the labour needed, many labourers were recruited elsewhere, particularly in the Madang and Sepik Districts. In 1926, there were no Sepik labourers on the Morobe goldfields, but by the late 1930s they accounted for nearly 30% of the total.

The reason was summed up by Richard Curtain:

> The Sepik River and its numerous tributaries provided a unique opportunity for labour recruiters by making possible deep penetration into an unproductive but densely populated interior. The main river is navigable for at least a thousand kilometres for vessels up to 200 tons. The lack of alternative cash-earning opportunities meant a readily available workforce once initial resistance had been overcome and the relative attractiveness of work conditions on the Bulolo goldfields had become known in the mid-1930s.[11]

⸺

Recruiting and repatriating labourers was costly,[12] and it was some time before new recruits became productive. In his 1929 report to Placer Development on the Bulolo leases, the mining engineer Louis Decoto observed:

> The raw native recruit is usually in very poor physical condition, and it requires good food for a period of from three to six months to build him up so that he can do a fair day's work.[13]

In 1931, the Mining Warden further noted:

> As mining work generally calls for experience and a considerable amount of skill, a 'boy' is just becoming useful when, at the end of his two years period of indenture, he has … to be discharged.[14]

These views were widely held and, in 1932, led to the maximum period of indenture being extended from two to three years.

Pressure from mining companies to build a more permanent and experienced workforce and the reluctance of many labourers to return to their villages often resulted in exemptions to the requirement that they be repatriated as soon as their contracts expired. Increasingly, they were permitted to make new contracts, with the result that many were absent from their villages for up to six years.[15]

Finally, in 1935, the Administration formally accepted what had become general practice and allowed employers to renew labourers' contracts for up to a further three years.[16] If a labourer had already been under contract for 4½ of the previous five years, he was to be sent back to his village for three months before the new contract commenced. The District Officer could waive this requirement, and often did when labourers didn't wish to go home. As the Administration itself noted: *A large number of natives who have been in constant employment, especially with one employer, no longer have any sympathy or connection with village life …* [17]

Through most of the 1930s, between 40% and 45% of BGD's time-expired labourers re-engaged each year. Given the high regard in which labourers held BGD, this was probably a greater proportion than for the field as a whole, but re-engagement was still common.[18] Thus inexorably and inevitably the ties between labourers and their villages loosened as the labour system evolved.

In its efforts to ensure that labourers were not exploited, the Administration specified employment conditions in great detail: clothing, food rations and cooking arrangements, housing, beds, medical services, working conditions and, of course, wages.

The minimum wage for labourers was initially set at 5 shillings per month, half that paid in Papua. Defending this, the 1921/22 Annual Report said this *may seem small, but it must be remembered that the wants of the native are few, and that he might not make wise use of a larger wage.*[19] Later, labourers renewing their contracts received 6 shillings, while the wage for those engaged in mining and carrying was set at 10 shillings per month. Labourers engaged in general labouring for mining companies such as BGD were not considered to be engaged in mining, and were paid 6 shillings per month. As labourers couldn't easily change employer, there was no scope for them to parley their increasing skills and experience for higher wages.[20]

Half a labourer's pay was deferred until his contract expired, to ensure that he could return home with trade goods and the money to help his village meet its head tax obligations. To guarantee payment of this deferred amount and the expense of repatriation, employers were required to lodge a surety with the District Officer when the contract was signed.[21]

From the employer's perspective, labourers were not cheap, with wages only a small part of their cost. Apart from the costs of recruiting and repatriation, employers had to provide clothing, blankets, food and tobacco, as well as meet medical costs and Government charges. In his survey of the labour system in New Guinea, Decker estimated that in the late 1930s the annual cost for employers was £33/16 shillings per labourer, though on the goldfields the costs of flying in labourers and provisions increased this to as much as £70 per year.[22]

While the price of gold had risen to around £8 per ounce by the mid-1930s, miners with teams of ten or more labourers would still not have found it easy to make a living, particularly as they were increasingly working old and poorer ground.

Although a labourer could be transferred between employers, he was otherwise bound to the one for whom he was recruited for the duration of his contract. Bert Weston recalled:

> Native labourers of any kind were a saleable and negotiable asset and although it was generally and conveniently referred to as a 'transfer of indenture' the boy himself had little say, or no say, in the transaction and the terms 'buying' and 'selling' were in everyday

Labourers working a sluice box.

use. I personally have 'bought' a good cookboy for $80 and sold mining and plantation labour for $30 and $20 per head respectively, which was the going rate.[23]

The relationship between labourer and employer was often a difficult one, and penal provisions could determine how this played out. These were inflexible and rarely delivered an outcome that was satisfactory to anyone.

Labourers might not live up to an employer's expectations, whether through a lack of understanding, laziness or obstinacy. Employers were not, however, permitted to apply corporal punishment, withhold wages or confine labourers. The only direct action permitted was to withhold their weekly ration of tobacco. But various 'offences against discipline' in the Native Labour Ordinance were used to control recalcitrant labourers. If they failed to show reasonable diligence in their work, refused to perform work allotted to them or disobeyed any reasonable order of an employer, they could be reported to the District Officer and fined £1 or imprisoned for up to a month. Decker reported that between 1930-31 and 1936-37, an average of 374 labourers a year were convicted for disobeying their employers' orders and neglecting their duties.[24]

Employers generally ignored the prohibition on corporal punishment, because of the inconvenience of going to Court for minor offences and as they believed

many labourers regarded a spell in jail as being as good as a holiday.[25] Lucy Mair wryly noted: *Striking with the hand … or kicking is regarded by many as the normal way of emphasising a point to a native.*[26] District officials usually turned a blind eye, though they were quick to investigate and punish serious assaults.

A more significant issue was desertion. Any labourer who was absent from his place of employment without permission for more than four days was deemed to be a deserter, for which the penalty was three months' jail. Patrol Officer Ian Downs later recalled:

> Our most unpleasant duty was the apprehension of deserters from distant labour contracts. There was no such thing as a reasonable excuse. Deserters had to be taken into custody and transported back to their place of employment … [27]

In the two years following the 1926 rush, more than 13% of the Morobe District's labour force deserted — one third of all deserters nationally, although the District's share of the national labour force was only 10–11%.[28] This primarily reflected illegal recruiting practices and the fear of working at Edie Creek once stories circulated about the many deaths there from dysentery and pneumonia. While there was some improvement thereafter, in the next few years between 5% and 8% of the District's labour force deserted annually—still well above the national average of 3% in the period 1933 to 1935.

Desertions on such a scale were a clear sign that the labour system was not working effectively or equitably, particularly as labourers were usually employed far from their villages and had no local support base. Getting home across unfamiliar territory carried very real risks.

The 1933/34 Annual Report concluded that desertions reflected the high level of recruiting of labourers who were unused to working conditions and deserted shortly after entering their contracts. But it noted many other reasons given by labourers themselves. The most common was dissatisfaction with an employer or conditions of employment, though other factors included difficulties adapting to a new and ordered environment compared with the freedom of village life, the attractions of village life during leave between contracts or transport difficulties preventing their return to work, the death of a labourer whose spirit was believed to remain in the vicinity, an epidemic or fear of sickness and unsettled living and working conditions when employed by prospectors who were frequently on the move.

Whatever the catalyst for individual desertions, the fact that the Administration wasted little time opening newly pacified areas to recruiters undoubtedly created the pre-conditions for later problems. These were compounded by the new recruits' lack of understanding of contracts and what they entailed. In 1941, a Commission of Inquiry into Native Labour expressed the view that labourers signing on for the first time often had no idea of the obligations involved in a contract – a telling observation after two decades of operation of an indentured labour system in which the binding of a labourer to his employer was a critical, and enforceable, element.[29]

As with any new job, new recruits took time to settle in. While some employers had unreasonable expectations, the majority recognised that new labourers had to contend with many changes. Most had never travelled far from their village, could not speak pidgin and were expected to do work unlike anything they had ever encountered. But they learnt quickly. As the Mining Warden noted in 1931:

> The newly recruited native raw from his village takes a

good deal of breaking in before he is of much use for mining, but under efficient supervision adapts himself readily enough to his work.[30]

Indeed, their adaptability at times brought grudging—if patronising—acknowledgement. Taylour and Morley remarked:

> In cases where natives have been specially trained, they have shown quite a surprising capacity, for a primitive race, for the assimilation of useful knowledge.[31]

More astute was Jack O'Neill, who observed:

> Sometimes we are inclined to confuse intelligence with knowledge and experience ... In assessing their quality it would be pertinent to appreciate how useless we would be if thrust into their environment.[32]

Labourers were used primarily for heavy labour, whether landing supplies from ships, carrying, working sluice boxes or clearing jungle, a role that persisted right through the pre-war period. Increasingly, however, Europeans realised their potential to do a wide range of semi-skilled work. The extent to which New Guineans adapted to such work led the Mining Warden to observe, in 1933:

> On construction and mining work, firing steam boilers, attending machinery etc. the native responds very well, and it is doubtful whether he will in future be satisfied with the primitive life of his village.[33]

It was only a matter of time before the increasing skills of New Guineans brought them into conflict with white workers. In 1935, when European winding engine drivers went on strike in the Edie Creek mine,[34] NGG sought to replace them with New Guinean lorry drivers and other semi-skilled workers familiar with operating machinery. This promptly resulted in a strike among all NGG's European employees.

The Administration openly deplored the strike action, fearing the lessons New Guineans might learn from a show of organised resistance to authority. Its fears were not groundless; in 1929 the whole New Guinean labour force in Rabaul had quietly organised a strike in support of higher wages, without Europeans becoming aware of what was planned. But neither was the Administration interested in encouraging a skilled indigenous labour force, which would put up-ward pressure on wages and discourage more men from returning to their villages at the end of their contracts.[35]

The Administration eventually agreed to permit uncertificated drivers to operate winding machinery,

Labourers carrying poles.

mining often involved cutting into steep, unstable, jungle-covered terraces. Explosives were used extensively. Flash floods, landslips and falling trees or rocks were common. Rockfalls occurred underground when softwood beams and supports rotted in the damp conditions.

Accidents were often attributed to occupational risk or carelessness, as distinct from negligence. But the distinction was a fine one. A casual approach to safety appears to have been endemic. Supervision was often limited, or left to inexperienced Europeans. Labourers new to the field had a minimal grasp of pidgin English, the *lingua franca* for all instructions, increasing the risk of accidents that would be later explained away as being due to carelessness. It is easy to see accidents such as that involving a labourer who tamped an explosive charge with a crowbar as falling into this category, or another where a labourer was electrocuted when he touched high tension wires.

In 1935, the Mining Warden expressed concern about the widespread nature of unsafe alluvial mining practices.[38] Nevertheless, up to this time, there was often no Inspector of Mines on the field, and a Mines and Works Regulation Ordinance did not come into effect until 1936.

It is ironic that the Administration should put so much effort into the health and welfare of indentured labourers but, at least until 1936, do little to ensure the safety of their working conditions. It is unclear whether this reflected a rational use of limited resources—there being far fewer deaths from accident than from pneumonia and dysentery—or whether the Administration was unable to attract inspectors with the necessary technical qualifications. Certainly, after 1936, supervision of mining activities appears to have become more rigorous, and prosecutions of employers more frequent. Thus, in 1937, BGD was censured for allowing labourers to paint a building housing a transformer without adequate supervision.

However, the Administration saw no need for employers to compensate the families of labourers who died as the result of accidents. In a memo to the District Officer, Salamaua, in October 1936, the Mining Warden noted that, while the Mining and Works Regulation Ordinance provided for compensation where accidents reflected negligence by an employer, most accidents reflected occupational risk or negligence by the labourer. He proposed a fund, to be contributed to by employers, to provide compensation other than where accidents

except where this involved raising or lowering men in a shaft. The latter exclusion was justified, at least in the eyes of the Inspector of Mines, as

> The natives have not yet been educated to an appreciation of the value of human life and they are also liable to fail at times of emergency, and hence are not used in positions involving responsibility for the lives of either white men or natives.[36]

By 1937 New Guineans were operating a wide range of electric motors and other machinery, and the Administrator claimed that all mining and milling was being done by natives under white supervision.[37]

Accidents involving death and injury were common. Mining was inherently dangerous, the more so given the difficult terrain on the Morobe goldfields. Alluvial were due to gross negligence by a labourer. No action was ever taken to implement this.

In 1940, Decker claimed that, while the 1912 Employer's Liability Law of Papua, which applied in New Guinea, provided for a labourer or his family to receive the equivalent of three years' pay in the event of total disability or death, there were no recorded cases of compensation being paid.[39] However, the 1941 Commission stated that of 21 fatalities on the goldfields between July 1936 and March 1940 compensation of between £5 and £60 was paid in 11 cases.[40] Not that compensation was ever paid to the families of hundreds of labourers who died of pneumonia or dysentery.

In administering the labour system, the Administration's main priority was to ensure a flow of labour sufficient to meet the mining industry's needs. Insofar as it was concerned about the impact of recruitment on village life, its focus was solely on population numbers. A village was usually closed to recruiting if women of child-bearing age exceeded adult males by 5%. From the mid-1930s, the absence of 25% of adult males was the catalyst for village closures.[41] In each case, the decision was left to local District officials. Village closures were frequent, though usually for short periods. In the Sepik area between 1928 and 1939, 350 villages were closed for twelve months, with 40 closed at least twice. However, this policy was unevenly administered, and the 25% figure appears often to have been exceeded.[42]

The tension between ensuring adequate labour for the goldfields (and elsewhere) and preserving traditional village life intensified in the late 1930s. Progress was slow in extending control and so opening up new areas for recruitment, while many villages which traditionally provided labourers were periodically closed because of over-recruitment. When this happened, labourers from those villages were required to return home when their contracts expired. As labour became more difficult to obtain, the issue of village closures became a growing source of frustration for employers, who not unnaturally argued that those who wished to work should be able to do so.[43]

The proportion of labourers renewing their contracts also declined steadily — BGD reported that 45% of time-expired labourers re-signed in 1937, but by 1940 this had fallen to 30%. Desertion remained a problem.

Nevertheless, the indentured labour system was effective in meeting the needs of employers on the goldfields through most of the inter-war period. For such an administratively complex system involving the movement of so many labourers from their villages to workplaces and back again, this was no small achievement.

If the system worked reasonably well for employers, what about the labourers themselves? Was it, as the Lieutenant Governor of Papua, Sir Hubert Murray, concluded, 'really rather like slavery'?[44]

Labourers transporting newly-landed goods. Boat day, Salamaua.

CHAPTER 17

THE SHADOW BATTALION –
THE INDENTURED LABOURERS'
EXPERIENCE

Europeans had little doubt that the indentured labour system was good for New Guineans individually and, to the extent that they considered its impact on villages, had few adverse consequences collectively.

As late as 1941, the Native Labour Commission concluded that the balance between the sexes was not a problem, as there were about 26,000 more adult males than females. It opined:

> These surplus males are a sort of shadow battalion whose energies were absorbed in tribal warfare prior to the establishment of ordered government, and who in the changed conditions of today find a ready outlet in the labour system.[1]

This benign view contrasted sharply with Sir Hubert Murray's.

What was the truth? The high rates of desertion and the high levels of contract renewals suggest quite different answers.

In the early years, the head tax was undoubtedly the main motivation for villagers to volunteer to 'make paper' – though it is doubtful whether they saw the head tax in quite the light suggested in the 1937/38 Annual Report: … *those from whom it is collected regard it in the nature of an institution symbolic of their participation in the affairs of the Territory.*[2] Villagers avoided the tax by becoming labourers and returned with money to enable others to pay it.

Having been introduced to the cash economy, villagers soon discovered the wide range of goods they could obtain. Recruiters promoted this new materialism by handing out axes, tomahawks and knives, as did time-expired labourers returning with trade goods. One such man was Hawaina, from the Sepik District. Returning after working in Rabaul, he was met in Wewak by people from his village, Marambanja, and another nearby, Ambukanja.

[They] carried my cargo back over the mountains. The next morning they all gathered at my village so I opened my box and gave out knives, lap laps, matches, salt and other things to each of my relatives. The axes in particular were much prized because stone axes were still being used at this time.[3]

Richard Curtain (who interviewed Hawaina) added that

> Wants soon began to expand so that clothing, nails, razors, mirrors and trade store tobacco were soon considered necessities.[4]

As more labourers returned with money, trade goods and stories of their experiences, the spirit of adventure took hold. The anthropologist Ian Hogbin, writing about Busama village, noted:

> Many young men also sought employment as an escape from boredom. The Lutheran Mission disapproves of dancing and bodily decoration, and the result was an early ban on the old festivals which were the focal points of village life, giving it zest and flavour. The eternal round of work with only prayer meetings to relieve the monotony was felt by the high-spirited youngsters to be too dull. 'Back here there's only toil and church,' one of them who had not long completed a contract remarked to me in disgust. 'But in the labour compound we had our dances after knocking-off time. We painted our faces, put on ornaments, played the hand-drum, and enjoyed ourselves.'[5]

For the many thousands of labourers who found their way to the goldfields during the years 1926 to 1941, their experience couldn't have been more different from the life they'd left behind. New recruits typically arrived at their destination under-nourished and apprehensive, unable to understand pidgin or the languages spoken by labourers from elsewhere in New Guinea. Most were young men, some as young as 14, who were either unmarried or had left their wives behind. The sociologist, S.W. Reed, recorded that of 1,060 labourers employed by NGG in March 1937, only 35 were accompanied by their wives. At Bulolo, there were 30 with wives among 1,231 labourers.[6]

Work usually involved heavy manual labour, and was often monotonous. The larger employers formed labour lines of 30-40, all engaged in the same kind of work under the direction of a European overseer. Individual miners usually had a 'boss boy' to keep their labourers working, particularly when they were absent.

Kokomo, of Emul village in the East Sepik District, later described his experience working for NGG, including at Edie Creek. After cutting copra at Suain for two years,

> I finished and came back with my brother. Then we walked to Maprik and went to Salamaua to work the gold. We worked with shovels, picks, crowbar and explosives. We had water too and broke down the hills. We broke the rocks and later it went into the machines and was crushed and separated. Some worked outside with the water guns. Shot down the hills. I worked under the ground in the hole. It went down and down. Number one level the passages went this way and that. We had special hats, boots and trousers. No. 1, 2, 3, 4, 5, 6. No. 6 had a big pump pumping the water out. This water went into a tank and was used to wash the gold. Many men died in this hole. White men too. Men who were careful were alright. Those who were careless were killed or injured. It was hard work and we worried about getting killed, but it was good money. After two years you could go if you were frightened. But you had to finish the contract.[7]

Gotokwa Bengo was about 18 when he went to work for BGD. He left his village in the Keram River area in the Sepik when he heard that young men were wanted to work on the goldfields, and was taught to operate a pump, near Wau.

> In the morning, the bell would be rung at about 6 am and we would get up and set off for work, in that very cold climate. When I touched the water, it was just like ice. At about 12 noon, the bell would go again and we would come back to our quarters for lunch and then go back to work at 1 pm. The work finished at 6 pm

and we returned to our quarters to meet our friends. Every working day was the same. The weekends were the most exciting times, when we went to see inter-tribal soccer games, or went down to Salamaua to do our shopping.[8]

Night work was permitted in mining after 1928 where approved by the District Officer. While this decision was criticised by the Permanent Mandates Commission, Albert Kaluah's informants confirmed that most labourers liked working at nights, as hot tea and biscuits were provided. Conditions were also not as strict as during day work. They were allowed to roast kaukau, taro and yams on fires, which they used to warm themselves and light their tobacco.[9]

The Administration was initially quite lax in regulating working conditions, leading Assistant District Officer Harry Downing to complain in 1931 of the large number of desertions, at times whole lines, due to excessive working hours:

> As the officer directly responsible for the enforcement of law, and the general welfare of natives on the goldfields, I am finding it increasingly difficult to keep some employers to what constitutes a fair day's or week's work.[10]

Downing noted that there was no limit on the number of hours per week worked by a mining labourer, no restrictions on overtime and no provision for rest periods such as weekends. His complaint prompted action and strict rules were imposed thereafter on the length and frequency of shifts, rest periods and meals to be given before, during and after shifts.[11]

While slapping or kicking labourers for minor misdemeanours was not uncommon, most were well treated by their employers. This was as much about self-interest as fair-mindedness. Labourers treated badly were likely to desert or, at best, not renew their contracts. As experienced workers were usually more efficient than new recruits, the greater the turnover, the less productive the mining.

For larger employers, a good reputation was the key to maintaining a stable workforce. BGD was particularly successful in this regard, paying careful attention to labourers' accommodation, eating arrangements, medical care and spare time activities. Labourers felt they were well treated, and respected the fairness of the Native Labour Superintendent at Bulolo, a tall Englishman, Ted Knight, who was responsible for

NGG labourers in raincoats, Edie Creek 1936.

organising labour for all jobs, arranging housing and food and exercising discipline when necessary.

Reed observed that *there was universal agreement among the Sepik natives that 'Bulolo' was a fine place to work.*[12] As a result, many were happy to renew their contracts, while new recruits were relatively easy to obtain.

NGG was less highly regarded, due in part to its less flexible approach to meeting labourers' needs, but also to the discomfort and dangers of underground mining and the higher incidence of dysentery and pneumonia at Edie Creek. The many deaths from disease contributed to a view among labourers that unfriendly supernatural forces were at large on Mt. Kaindi.

Some labourers preferred working for individual miners, such as Jack O'Neill, as conditions were less regimented, the range of work more varied and relationships more personal. Not that this was always the case: Hank Nelson reported that Bishop Mambu of the Lutheran Church was 15 in 1938 when he was flown to Wau to work in the hotel, but the lawlessness of the town frightened him.[13] He then went to work on the Watut where he carried stones, dammed creeks, dug races, directed the hoses while sluicing, and amalgamated gold. But there was no sense of

camaraderie with his employer. Mambu was given food, a bush house to sleep in, instructions and a cuff when he was slow to act or learn.

In the absence of alternative or cheaper sources of power, indentured labourers were 'it', whether this involved cutting down trees or using a foot pedal to drive a dentist's drill in isolated mining camps. Carriers were always needed to transport supplies to remote locations, while teams of labourers employed by individual miners and the smaller companies worked and re-worked old ground, pouring it through sluice boxes, yard by yard. BGD's labourers cleared the aerodrome at Bulolo, built the water race to the power station, carved new roads out of the jungle and built bridges. And when the dredges began operating, they cleared the jungle ahead of the dredges, dug 'deadmen' holes to anchor dredge hawsers, and ditches to bring water to the dredge pond. In Lae and Salamaua, large teams of labourers unloaded every ship, manhandling everything onto lighters or whaleboats and from these onto the shore.

Increasingly, however, many undertook a wide range of semi-skilled activities. In Lae, they not only

NGG's labour barracks, Edie Creek, 1936.

cleaned the aircraft, but also kept the flying wires clean and greased against corrosion, helped with refuelling and removed carbon from aircraft engine piston heads. In Bulolo, they were assistants to tradesmen: fitters and turners, electricians, carpenters and motor mechanics. Here and elsewhere they operated pumps, boilers, generators and other machinery and drove trucks.

Village life did not prepare labourers well for their experiences on the field. Working in unfamiliar situations, many lacked the insight needed to avoid danger, a deficiency compounded by a limited knowledge of pidgin English. The Mining Warden's report for 1938/39 provides a representative picture. Of 54 accidents that year, seven were fatal—all labourers. Three were killed in landslips—one when an abandoned alluvial face of about 12 feet of clay overburden collapsed, another when a race was being cut through a 15 foot bank, causing it to give way, and a third when a face of alluvial wash slipped when being cleared of overburden. One labourer was killed by a falling tree when clearing a landslide that had blocked a water race, and another when a hydraulic elevator collapsed. The other two men were drowned in a flash flood following heavy rain upstream. Injuries included fingers crushed by rolling stones, and legs broken by landslips or falling timber, and flying debris when blasting.

Labourers in or near townships usually lived in compounds and were subject to a strict curfew. Accommodation was often in barracks with corrugated iron roofs and cement floors. These may have met the Administration's standards, but were about as far from village housing as you could get. In NGG's barracks, built on this model, 20 to 30 labourers slept in double tiers of bunks, and shared toilets and three fireplaces.

Not surprisingly, labourers preferred huts constructed with native materials. BGD gave them what they wanted, creating a way of life similar to that in their villages. In the main compound at Bulolo and in smaller ones near their power stations and dredges, labourers lived in huts each holding two to four workers. Married couples lived in a separate compound, two couples to each house. Electric lights, shower baths, toilets and recreational facilities were provided. Labourers working for individual miners or the smaller companies also lived in huts, though conditions were generally more basic.

Harry Downing noted:

BGD's housing for labourers, Bulolo.

garden. Sepiks, Madang, Manus, Aitape, Biangais, all have their own patch of ground where they grow their own sugar cane, bananas, kaukau and paw paws ...[16]

Paradoxically, while most labourers were in excellent physical condition after they had been on the field for some time, there was a high mortality rate from disease. From 1933 to 1940, more than 1,200 labourers in the Morobe District died from pneumonia or dysentery, an average of 150 a year. Accidents rarely caused more than ten deaths a year. There were several deaths every year from tuberculosis, but none from beriberi once labourers' diets improved in the early 1930s, nor from typhoid, against which all labourers were vaccinated. The mortality rate of labourers in the Morobe District during the 1930s averaged 2.8%, or twice that elsewhere in the Territory—though after 1935/36, it fell to a rate more in line with that in other areas.

The death rate at Edie Creek was particularly high. Frequent dysentery epidemics were blamed on poor sanitary habits, while the relatively cold, damp conditions and NGG's policy of concentrating labourers in barracks encouraged the spread of infectious disease.

Despite the mortality rate, the Administration took little or no preventative action. Apart from ensuring that new recruits were fit for work and that employers had large enough medical facilities, it left things to employers to manage. Inspections to ensure the adequacy of medical facilities were fairly sporadic. NGG had a small hospital, but its medical facilities were far inferior to BGD's. It was therefore hardly surprising that its mortality rates were significantly higher—4.3% among its labourers in 1935 compared with 1.8% for BGD.

Labourers certainly benefitted from Bulolo's more temperate climate, while BGD's practice of housing them in small huts also contributed to better health. But the main factor, and one that carried great weight among labourers, was the high quality of medical care that BGD provided. It maintained a well equipped

Very few complaints are ever received against employers for insufficiently feeding their labourers or improperly housing them. In this respect few employers really conform to the letter of the law, but most observe the spirit of it—if only in order to get a fair return from their labourers.[14]

Omas began working for NGG immediately after World War II when conditions had changed little. He crisply observed to the author in 2001 that *A benefit of working for the company was that we were fed well. We learned to have lunch.*

NGG issued each labourer with a daily food ration that was cooked in a communal kitchen. In contrast, BGD issued food to each labourer once a week so they could do their own cooking and eat with their wantoks. Gotokwa Bengo recalled:

Every Friday we got rations, which consisted of five pounds of rice, one pound of navy biscuits, three sticks of tobacco, one pound of tobacco, one bar of soap, one bottle of kerosene, two tins of fish, three tins of meat, one roll of newspaper and half a pound of salt.[15]

All large employers maintained vegetable gardens so as to reduce food costs. At Cliffside, in 1932, apart from numerous fruit trees and European vegetables, 60 acres were planted with kaukau, yielding four or five tons to the acre. In 1940, NGG's gardens at Wau produced 840 tons of kaukau. Labourers were often encouraged to grow some of their food to give them an activity that would keep them interested and occupied when not working. Most of BGD's labourers had their own small garden plots. Sarah Chinnery noted in 1933 that, at Cliffside,

Large areas of hillside have been cleared to make gardens for the natives. Each wantok group is given a hospital, with separate wards for men and women, an operating theatre, isolation ward and skin clinic. Every foreman also had a portable first aid kit, and dressing stations were maintained close to labour lines.

Provided labourers survived epidemics and occasional accidents, the combination of good food, exercise and prompt treatment of injuries and skin problems meant they returned to their villages far healthier and more robust than when they left.

———

The assembly of hundreds of young men in compounds without access to women inevitably resulted in what the Administration coyly described as 'a number of intricate problems'.[17] 'Acts of indecency' were prohibited and punishable with six months' imprisonment, but despite this, and much moral posturing, the Administration's efforts to discourage homosexuality were a failure. Ian Hogbin observed that

> men of more mature years made a practice of taking a youth of sixteen or seventeen as a lover. He was first attracted by gifts of tobacco, sweets and gaily coloured clothing and then seduced. Resistance was countered with the threat of sorcery, of which many are still in deadly fear.[18]

Not that the youths were necessarily unwilling participants. Chairing a Mission Conference in 1927, where the problem was discussed, Administrator Wisdom disdainfully observed: *I believe in some cases it is usual to give the passive party, usually a monkey [boy], a lap lap as payment. One monkey's box was opened and 40 lap laps were found in it.*[19]

Given the potential for their labour lines to be seriously disrupted by any prosecutions, employers usually ignored what was happening. Although the Administration sought to encourage more married labourers to bring their wives after 1936, few did. Many Administration officers believed that controlled prostitution was the only solution, but were under no illusions that this would ever be officially sanctioned.[20]

With so many labourers living close to goldfields townships, the unease of Europeans about their sexual urges and activities was accentuated during the 1930s by the arrival of increasing numbers of white women. While there were few sexual assaults, the fear of these contributed to growing racist sentiments in the late 1930s.

———

Village discipline was replaced in labour compounds by a more liberal and attractive lifestyle. The supply of alcohol to New Guineans was prohibited under the Mandate, and anyone found in possession could be fined heavily. While it was still consumed, alcohol did not pose a major social problem.

In contrast, the prohibition on gambling was regularly flouted. The game 'Lucky', similar to poker, was played relentlessly in compounds all over the goldfields. Ian Hogbin remarked:

> The chief pastime for the hours of idleness was gambling. I have known of labourers who collected several pounds after a single night of the card game 'Lucky' and others who were not only penniless but had mortgaged their earnings for some months ahead.[21]

Saturday afternoons, when most labourers were off work, provided the main opportunity for socialising. Their inability to write and thus communicate with their families made visiting wantoks of special importance. Reed noted:

> On Saturday afternoons the roads in the vicinity of Wau are dotted with groups of native workers ... on their way to other camps where friends and wantoks may be found. They frequently walk for miles to visit relatives and friends in other lines, and to gossip, sing, reminisce and lay plans for the future.[22]

There was also some socialising with women in villages—labourers from around Wau with the Biangai and around Bulolo with the Buang, while on the coast labourers at Lae visited Butibum village nearby and those at Salamaua visited Logui village. Over time, some inter-marriage occurred.

Soccer, or 'kikbal', was the main recreational sport on Saturday afternoons and Sundays, often attracting large numbers of spectators. Fields were provided by employers such as BGD or the Administration, though any reasonably flat surface would do. Any number could play, the size of the goal posts didn't matter and there were no rules and no referee.

At times, a challenge match ('kikros') would be held to settle a dispute between labourers from different areas—most commonly those from the Sepik and the Markham between whom there was considerable ill-feeling. Such games often degenerated into a full scale fight, involving sticks, iron bolts, safety razor blades and other weapons carefully concealed beforehand. On these occasions, labour overseers or police were called on to restore the peace. The distinction between tribal warfare and sport was indeed a fine one.

The origins of the hostility between labourers from the Sepik and Markham Districts were unknown, at least to Europeans, but feelings ran deep. Reed noted that on the goldfields, where both were well represented, these led to bloody brawls and even homicides. As a result, *employers have had to adjust to this traditional feud by putting workers from these districts in separate lines, and by housing them at a considerable distance from one other.*[23]

Singsings were the other major recreational activity.[24] With labourers coming from all over the Territory, it was inevitable that traditional singsings would became become a further focus of competition between districts. Some were informal and spontaneous, others were held on special occasions as when dredge No. 1 was launched. The biggest were on Christmas Day in Bulolo, Wau and Salamaua, with participants dressed in the elaborate costumes and headdresses characteristic of their home areas.

Bulolo singsings were held on the airstrip, with BGD's encouragement. Tom Lega, who worked his way up from dredge hand to dredge master, later recalled,

> Groups from Madang, the Sepik, Salamaua, Lae, Finschhafen, Ramu and the Tolai from Rabaul would dance to kundu drums for hours. Those from the Sepik and Rabaul were the best. The dancing would go on from early morning till well into the night, each group in a circle about 30 feet in diameter. By the end there

was not a blade of grass. They were rewarded with a bag of rice and some cans of meat.[25]

Large singsings were also held in Wau and Salamaua at Easter.

Less appealing to Europeans were the Sio singsings, which began to be held weekly late in 1938 around Wau. Not only were they said to reduce efficiency due to the exhaustion of participants, but 'depravity' was said to occur between those attending.[26] Administrator McNicoll denied they contained any objectionable features and believed that suppressing the dances would be unwise *as they fill a void in the monotonous existence of the labourer and give him an emotional outlet.*[27] Nevertheless, he bowed to political pressure and early in 1940 labourers were forbidden from participating in a singsing between 11 pm and sunrise without the consent of their employers or District Officer.

The requirement that labourers return to their villages when their contracts expired did much to discourage detribalisation and thus the development of an urban underclass. Nevertheless, an increasing number of labourers gradually lost any connection with their villages, drifting between employers.

The 1941 Commission expressed concern that detribalisation was leading some labourers to become

Preparing for singsing, Bulolo aerodrome.

The journey home was exciting. A European passenger on a small inter-island ship described the scene at Salamaua:

> While we leaned over the deck-rail yarning, hundreds of natives were crowding noisily aboard, filling the well-decks and covering the hatches. Each hung grimly onto his new trade box, in which was packed the treasure of lavalavas, tobacco, mouth organs, knives and such things … they were taking back to their villages after two or three years of labour …[32]

Not all made it home safely. Henry Eekhoff who ran a trade store at Lae, recalled that, around 1930: *Finished time boys were often killed and their boxes and possessions stolen. Later, police boys used to escort parties of finished timers along the Markham Road.*[33] A decade later, things hadn't improved. Two members of the 1941 Commission described the repatriation process as most unsatisfactory:

> It is hard to see how the average employer who acts with the best intentions and often pays an exorbitant sum for a fare, can be blamed if the native is badly accommodated, robbed by sophisticated natives en route and reaches home some weeks later with half or all of his effects stolen.[34]

To minimise the risk of theft, District Officers could forward deferred wages to the station nearest the labourer's home to be paid there, but this rarely happened. In effect, the Administration took the view that its responsibility ended once labourers had been paid off.

prey to anti-social practices, creating a criminal element[28]:

> The impudent native is met with more often than ten years ago, but he is by no means numerous, is usually found in towns … [where] supervision outside working hours is difficult … [Some of] the more sophisticated labourers … who have been allowed to remain many years in a European environment exert a bad influence upon the other labourers.[29]

Elsewhere, cases were cited of mercury being put in milk left for Europeans, of insolence and 'brazen arrogance', and 'peeping Tom' activity.[30]

For most labourers, their goldfields experience ended with repatriation to their villages. Their first stop was Salamaua, where they were given a medical check and paid their deferred wages. Bert Weston recalled:

> Scouts from local Chinese trade stores would be hovering in the background and would hurry the cashed-up victims to their stores, give them a sumptuous meal of bully beef and rice prior to the big selling spree, [after] which the customer would head for his home village carrying a small bokis containing bush knives, lap-laps, beads, talcum powder, a torch (useless when the batteries expired) and other oddments as presents for his family.[31]

The notion that work introduced New Guineans to civilisation was espoused by the new civil Administration as early as 1922,[35] though no effort was ever made to articulate what this might mean in practice. In fact, this 'introduction' proved to be highly disruptive, unleashing fundamental changes in traditional society.

The Commission of Inquiry into Native Labour concluded in its 1941 Report that the indentured labour system had a greater impact on the life of New Guineans than any other aspect of the European 'cultural invasion'. It particularly identified its effect on marriage, the division of labour, initiation to manhood, control by elders (including a lessening of the force of tribal sanctions) and the village economy. The strength of this conclusion stands in contrast to the Administration's apparent indifference to what was happening. Although ostensibly committed to preserving village life, it made little effort to help villages adjust to pressures rising from the indentured labour system.

The impact on villages was far greater than could be inferred from an imbalance in the ratio of the sexes. It was also more subtle. The use of steel tools to clear ground for new gardens meant that, notionally, men could be released to work as labourers without affecting agricultural productivity.[36] However, the anthropologist Ian Hogbin observed that …

> it occasionally happens that, while the proportion of absentees from the district as a whole is reasonable, individual kinship groups are handicapped. The houses cannot then be repaired or rebuilt, the gardens shrink in size, and the old folk, women and children may be inadequately provided for.[37]

It also changed the division of labour between the sexes, with women having to undertake heavier work. The Lutheran missionary, Rev. G. Pilhofer, claimed in 1938 that the need to do much heavier work was affecting the health of the female population, with a heavy increase in mortality among girls at the age of puberty.[38]

Ceremonial life was also affected, as many of the leaders had left to work as labourers, while those who remained were preoccupied maintaining the gardens. The pervasive influence on village communal life in the five villages close to Lae was later noted by Ian Willis:

> At one time the central building in every village was the 'lum' or men's club house … where the men spent much of their spare time discussing and planning village business. The 'lum' had been the focus of most village activities, but once the town sprang up, the 'lum' and all its traditional practices—feasting, the performance of rituals, the production of artefacts and artwork, singing, dancing and the telling of old legends—became less important. The men returned home tired out every day and no longer had time to spend in the 'lum' working on village affairs.[39]

Of course, the labour system was not the only source of change. The activities of the Missions and the Administration's prohibition of warfare each changed village society in important ways. But the new cash economy, of which the labour system was a key part, was perhaps the single greatest source of disruption to traditional values, affecting every aspect of village society and economy.

The Administration may have seen the labour system as introducing villagers to civilisation, but in practice, labourers acquired little knowledge that was useful in a village context. Hogbin and Wedgwood concluded that *the information they obtain about Western culture is vague in the extreme and usually inaccurate, the tasks carried out in no way enrich their outlook, and the elementary hygiene picked up is quickly forgotten.*[40] Writing later, Heather Radi concluded that a labourer, confined to the compound and restricted to unskilled labour,

> observed only the fringe activities of that civilisation which he was expected to emulate. The Administration's paternalism shielded the native, but by denying him initiative it made it more difficult for him to come to terms with what lay beyond that shield.[41]

Certainly, a returned labourer was able to use various European tools, and was now familiar with different food, clothing, housing and a wider world. But any skills he had acquired, such as the ability to operate machinery and even his knowledge of Melanesian pidgin, were of little use in the village. The changes which occurred came less from the practical information he acquired than from the change to his values.

Returning labourers often created much disharmony in the village. Arrogant and unco-operative behaviour seems to have been commonplace, although this usually settled down fairly quickly. However, the pressure for change to traditional ways did not abate.

Whereas village life was based on co-operative behaviour and community responsibilities, returned labourers had learned to be independent. They understood that there were alternatives to the traditional way of doing things, which led them to question many aspects of village life and to challenge their elders' viewpoints at every turn. Nor was village harmony helped by the fact that, although economic power traditionally rested with elders, the latter were now dependent on the young men's earnings to acquire a rapidly expanding range of trade goods as 'wants' became 'needs'.

The process of change accelerated as the stories of returning labourers and the trade goods they brought back excited the next generation of young men, who volunteered to 'make paper' themselves at the first opportunity. And slowly but gradually, by destabilising traditional village society and creating needs and expectations that were not easily filled, the ground was being laid for the emergence of cargo cults in the post war period.

Part 6

Life and Death on the Goldfields

Edie Creek, 1929. The business centre and Government Reserve, with the Amalgamated Wireless Company's offices in the right corner, hospital and dispensary on the left, old Warden's mess in the centre, Court House and police quarters in the background.

CHAPTER 18
THE 1920s:
ISOLATION AND MATESHIP

Most of those who joined the early rush in 1926 soon disappeared when the promised riches didn't materialise.

But there were many who stayed or arrived later for whom gold was the excuse rather than the reason. For these men—and they were mostly men—New Guinea was as much an 'escape from' as a 'search for'. Not surprisingly, fortunes were often as easily lost at poker as won on the field.

Doubtless many shared Hellmuth Baum's view that the unpredictability of gold mining and challenges of jungle life were infinitely preferable to what passed as civilisation, *so monotonously organised into safe and careful little patterns*.[1] Not for them the steady job and regular pay cheque, but the rough and ready camaraderie of like-minded men. Problems with the law or families gave others good reason to head for the Territory and start a new life.

And there were those for whom isolation itself was the attraction. At the Salamaua Hotel, Alice Innes recalled one such man, Ned Coakley, who told her that

> when the first plane brought in women he would pack his swag and put his dog on the leash and go over the ranges far beyond. 'For women and goats, missis, do be both curses no miner be wantin' ... faith the pair of them be disruptive influences around a camp, and I mean no thoughts against you, you're a good bushwoman!'[2]

Whatever their motives, those who found their way to New Guinea in the late 1920s had extraordinarily diverse backgrounds. The first Manager of the Bank of New South Wales in Salamaua, Harry Johns, spent his first Christmas dinner in Wau in 1929 in the company of men

> from all parts of the world and of every occupation—a mining director, member of the Melbourne Hunt Club, an ex-Baptist clergyman—now in the furniture trade, an aviator, surveyor, English Lord, banker, one time champion boxer of Australia and NZ, men with military rank and decorations, some with their tens of

thousands, others with nothing—but all friends and only known by their Christian names.[3]

While they came from many countries, most miners were Australians or British. Many had come to New Guinea to take over or work on plantations expropriated from the Germans. As returned servicemen were permitted to acquire these plantations on highly favourable terms, 90% of New Guinea's white male population in 1926 comprised men who had served with the Australian or British forces in the Great War. For many ex-servicemen, gold mining had much greater appeal than routine plantation work, and their shared experience in war provided a core around which strong bonds of mateship were forged in the early years on the field.

These bonds also reflected two central shared elements of their existence: the many challenges they faced, and their isolation from Australia and the world. The belief that 'we're all in this together', with mutual assistance the key to survival, was particularly strong in the early years. Thus, Shark-Eye Park, with his chooks and established garden, didn't hesitate to help the Booths when their supplies ran short. In turn Doris Booth, when asked by the Royal Commission whether it was common for miners to seek to purchase green vegetables from her, responded *Yes, I gave what I could spare, but I would not sell them*.[4] Taking advantage of another's misfortunes was not consistent with the spirit of the field. Miners would lend food and equipment to others in dire straits, even when the recipient's capacity to repay was doubtful, for tomorrow they might need help themselves.

⁓

The men and few women attracted to the goldfields were practical and resilient. The country was difficult and dangerous to travel; they endured isolation, privation and disease. Death was always close at hand. Such adversity reinforced bonds between miners — and others on the field — and was reflected in levels of trust and honesty unheard of on other goldfields.

The pilot, Alan Cross, observed: *Everyone is so lackadaisical about gold in New Guinea. You go into miners' huts to have a wash and find the basin full of gold or maybe there is a biscuit tin of it on the floor.*[5]

Bert Weston was the Lae agent for an aviation company:

> A miner would come down [to Wau] from Edie Creek with perhaps 500 ounces of gold in a tea tin. The fellow would drop his gold, perhaps on the pilot's seat or anywhere, and go and get sozzled. He'd think no more about it … But when the plane arrived at Lae the next morning, I'd have a look, and I might find half a dozen lots of gold—in one pound tea tins, tobacco tins, with the lids secured with a strip of sticking plaster, and some very carefully sewn up in little canvas parcels. I'd throw the gold in a box under my bed until the launch came across from Salamaua … I'd just put it into a wheelbarrow, and tell the boy to take it down to the beach and put it on the launch. I've had as much as three thousand ounces under my bed, labelled in the most casual way. Two lots came down once from a chap in white woollen socks, just tied up at the top. Written on one sock in indelible pencil was 'BP from Scotty'. There was never any instance of it being lost. It all got there by divers means, passed on from hand to hand, everybody trusted everybody else.[6]

As a bank manager, for whom security was of paramount importance, Harry Johns was incredulous at the lack of it:

> The crowd here have no equal for generosity and honesty … not one ounce of gold has been stolen … I was sitting on the hotel verandah [in Salamaua] talking to an old prospector who asked me if I want to see a few bits of gold, to which I agreed. He directed [me] to his room—door wide open—and I found £2,000 worth in string-tied unsealed canvas bags under his bed. Touch the other fellow's gold! It would no more be done than the GG would attack his soup with a knife.[7]

While gold stealing was non-existent, there were some who took advantage of others' trust and generosity. Errol Flynn spent two periods in New Guinea before leaving for Hollywood, leaving behind many less than flattering stories. Flynn arrived in October 1927, and spent the next two years drifting from job to job, mostly on plantations, but also finding his way to Wau where he briefly worked receiving cargo for Guinea Airways. With what one biographer described as *his footloose charm and easy morals,*[8] his approach to life was the antithesis of others in that small community where most Europeans worked hard and supported each other — even if his boxing ability was a source of respect.

By early 1933, Flynn was back in New Guinea. His efforts recruiting in the Finschhafen area and gold mining at Edie Creek were unsuccessful; when Keith McCarthy saw him in Salamaua soon afterwards he was broke. McCarthy recalled: *To keep going he had borrowed from many of the generous miners, and owed money everywhere.*[9] Years later, when he was famous and wealthy, several wrote enquiring if he might like to settle his debts. Flynn's standard response was to send a large autographed picture of himself — but no money. One creditor was the dentist Eric Weine. Flynn's first major film, Captain Blood, was eventually shown in Wau. As the credits rolled, it was finally too much for Weine, who roared *And teeth by Weine, and not bloody well paid for yet either!*[10]

⌒

In the early years, there was little communication with or news from south (as Australia was universally referred to). There were no organised mail services. Letters might take months to be delivered, passed from hand to hand; even radiograms could take weeks. The occasional newspaper found its way onto the field, was read avidly and passed on — the main source of news about events in Australia or elsewhere. For miners at remote locations, visitors broke the monotony and were always welcome. They brought the latest Australian and world news, and local gossip. There was always a cup of tea for visitors, or something harder.

Until the first wireless transmitter began operating at Edie Creek in November 1926, runners carried messages to Salamaua and thence by canoe to Morobe, a journey of up to ten days, and the same back again. The transmitter was a welcome link with the outside world, though transmission hours were severely limited by atmospheric interference. It transmitted only to Morobe, so messages were re-transmitted to Rabaul and a third time if Australia was the destination. Errors in transmission or poor communication links meant that messages were often corrupted en route.

Over the next few years, communications gradually improved. The Administration installed a radio

The Kunai pub and NGG store, Wau, January 1929.

transmitter at Salamaua in August 1927—nearly a year after the transfer of the District Office from Morobe. A year later, a more powerful transmitter was installed at Edie Creek, capable of transmitting directly to Rabaul, reducing the time for messages to and from Australia. With the advent of local airmail in 1928, mail deliveries became more frequent and reliable. However, it was not until the mid-1930s that short wave radio enabled miners to keep more directly in touch with world events.

Miners often worked in pairs. Not only did this provide companionship and greater security, but they could take turns to visit Wau for provisions and to catch up with their mates. Wau provided welcome respite from the rigours of working and living in the bitterly cold, wet conditions of Edie Creek or Black Cat Creek. The miner Jack O'Neill later described Wau, with its grassy slopes and mild temperatures as *a paradise after a long spell in the jungle*.[11]

And the pub in Wau was an obvious magnet for weary miners fresh from the bush. In late 1927, the two most successful miners at Edie Creek, Harry Darby and Hector Wales, were part of a syndicate that established the Kunai Pub, so called because it was built of bush materials and thatched with kunai grass. Darby and Wales were said to be its best customers.[12]

No money changed hands when drinking as the manager, C.C. Holleris, was often out prospecting. Instead he undertook a stocktake at the end of each month to calculate how much had been consumed, allocating the cost more or less equally between those who had visited the pub, irrespective of who had drunk what. His successor 'refined' the practice so that people were charged each month on the basis of their capacity to pay. One man who pointed out that he hadn't been in town and therefore couldn't have drunk what he'd been charged for, received a friendly reply that *if you had been here, that's what you would have drunk*.[13]

Supply lines being rather tenuous, the pub would occasionally run out of beer. On such occasions, men would wait expectantly for a plane, and when it was spotted, take bets on whether it was bringing new supplies. If it did, there was rarely a shortage of men to carry them back up the hill.

New Guinea was a far from healthy place and mining a distinctly risky occupation. In pre-aviation days if a man injured himself or fell seriously ill it could take many days to get him to the nearest medical assistant, in Morobe. Thus, when George Arnold became very ill with dysentery in 1925, he was carried out to the coast on a stretcher. He survived. Some didn't. More than a few died in accidents. From 1927, however, chances of survival improved with the opening of a small hospital at Wau, and planes to fly the worst cases to Lae and thence by boat to Salamaua where there was a doctor.

Typhoid was virtually non-existent, due to the Administration's policy of vaccinating all new arrivals. Nor was dysentery a major problem among Europeans. Dengue fever was common, however, and everyone on the goldfields had malaria at one time or another. This was usually contracted at the coast; being above 3,000 feet, Edie Creek and Wau were largely free of anopheles

Wau hospital, January 1929.

mosquitoes. In severe, untreated cases, malaria could develop rapidly into blackwater fever. Death was not infrequent where harsh living conditions had lowered miners' resistance. As former miner Joe Bourke bluntly observed: *Often the pall bearer of today became the corpse of tomorrow.*[14]

Salamaua's beauty belied its growing reputation as an unhealthy place. This was due in part to nearby swamps which were fertile breeding grounds for mosquitoes. However, as it was the location of the District's main hospital, many deaths probably had their cause elsewhere on the field.

In the early days, burials were at a small cemetery round Bayern Bay towards the Francisco River, next to the track used by miners on their way inland. Years later, Alice Innes reflected on one such occasion:

> When the little hand cart went up and down the isthmus, it carried cases of beer, it carried mining shovels and tinned food, but so often, in those days, carried a rough home made coffin. Once it was being slowly pushed past the little temporary hotel bar, and all hands stood respectfully to attention as the small procession passed, but the coffin slid off, right at the bar door. 'Well, you wouldn't expect Teddie to pass a pub', said one of the mourners and they gravely spilt a glass of whisky on the packing case coffin and all hands drank a last toast to a fine mate.[15]

In July 1928, the manager of the Kunai Pub at Wau, C.C. Holleris, died of blackwater fever. Alice Innes recalled,

> I think I shall never forget that funeral. Life was so intense then that one dare not lose one's grip, so his

many mates carried armfuls of swamp lilies and a bottle of crème de menthe, and Norman Neal tried to remember the burial service. There must have been a touch of hysteria amongst us. There had been death after death in so short a time. Poor old Mac, in his Chinese silk dressing gown, went to sprinkle the roughly made coffin with the liqueur and, as the grave was dug in sand, he slid into the grave. 'Hang on, Holleris', he said. 'I can't come till I feed my coons.'[16]

With the risk of death ever present, it is hardly surprising that miners' humour was black and sardonic. Sep Underwood recalled the funeral in Salamaua of 'Simmo', who had also died of blackwater fever:

> The marker for Simmo's grave was a simple wooden cross made from a condensed milk case, and whether by design or accident, the bar of the cross was made from the section of the case which carried the words 'Stow away from boilers' ... A week after Simmo was buried the waves from a violent storm washed out his grave, which was on the beach just above normal high water mark, and broke up the coffin. When the storm subsided all that could be seen of Simmo was one of his hands protruding from the sand ... The story goes that his chief mourner put an empty glass in the hand and filled it with Simmo's favourite tipple.[17]

By comparison with other goldfields, on the Morobe field the number of Europeans was very small in the late 1920s. At first, there were no concentrations of people that could reasonably be described as townships, just the constant movement of miners and their teams of labourers and a handful of people in strategic locations, all enduring primitive living conditions.

Salamaua was an improbable gateway to the goldfield—a narrow, sandy, tree-covered isthmus that, by the end of 1926, was bisected by a single roughly-formed road. With sweeping bays on either side, and a backdrop of towering mountains, many were later to describe it as one of the most beautiful places in New Guinea. But few of the early miners had time to appreciate their surroundings.

Its shallow harbour meant ships had to stand some distance offshore, with people and supplies being transferred to whaleboats or lighters which were in turn unloaded onto a rubble beach or simple jetties. The late 1920s foreshore was a collection of hastily assembled structures built with whatever materials were to hand; corrugated iron roofs perched on roughly hewn local timber frames coexisted with even more crudely constructed buildings with earth floors and roofs of sacsac leaves. Stretching round what was otherwise a picturesque bay on the southern side was a motley collection of sheds, tents and humpies briefly occupied by miners passing through.

In 1926, the most imposing building was Burleigh Gorman's two storey boarding house. Built using available bush materials, it was prone to sway in the breeze, but was 'home' to as many as 40 aspiring miners at a time. The upper floor, reached by ladder, was their bedroom, their beds no more than blankets thrown on the pit-sawn plank floorboards. A year later, this was replaced with a more permanent structure boasting a corrugated iron roof.

Gorman's amiable nature endeared him to new-comers, as he dispensed advice about their stores and equipment and checked them before they left for Edie Creek. He became a vital cog in their supply line, packing their carriers with fresh provisions every few weeks, looking after their gold and sending orders to Rabaul.

Each ship brought more miners, recruiters and officials, and a fresh burst of feverish activity, as all kinds of equipment and provisions from whaleboats were landed on the beach or jetty. Here labourers *swarming like white ants in a broken post* (to use one observer's curiously inappropriate aphorism)[18] sorted, claimed, disputed and ultimately carried them away; and all the time, there was the shouting, cursing, and haranguing of Europeans trying to maintain a semblance of control.

Burleigh Gorman's Boarding House and store, Salamaua, November 1926.

Grabowsky recalled: *The arrival of a ship from south was always, and for many years, a great event at these lonely outposts. Local residents … spent much of the ship's stay on board.*[19] In the years before freezers were installed ashore, each ship was a floating pub offering cold beer and fresh food—a welcome break from the tinned variety. Harry Johns recorded that, with the arrival of a ship, *all is activity for a few days. Officials put on a tie for the occasion and return to the low neck shirt the day the boat leaves.* Afterwards, *the inevitable reaction and the town sinks back to its former lethargy.*[20]

Gradually Salamaua began to take on a more permanent appearance. In 1928, there were 16 to 18 white residents, mostly catering to the needs of miners on the field or passing through. The Salamaua Trading Company had bought out Burleigh Gorman, and under the management of Allen Innes and then his wife Alice, erected a new 16 room hotel facing Bayern Bay, with wide verandahs open to the prevailing sea breezes and protected from the tropical sun by a large *Calophyllum* tree. The building with the corrugated iron roof became the bar and billiard room, a discreet distance from the accommodation. This came to be a home-away-from-home for miners down from 'on top' (as Wau and Edie Creek were known). It was the domain of Bill Cameron, ex-juggler, barman and entertainer, one with a waspish sense of humour. His speciality was a 'millionaire's shandy'—champagne and stout.

Successful miners arriving in town would often shout the bar, and Cameron soon converted this into a

Miners' storehouses, Salamaua, c.1928.

Salamaua waterfront, 1929.

Salamaua Hotel, 1929.

competition by allocating to each 'shouter' a purlin on the underside of the roof, along which a row of nails protruded. Whenever they paid for a shout, a young boy would climb up and stick the champagne corks thus liberated onto the nails, to general acclamation. The race to be the first to complete their purlin became the talk of the field; Harry Darby eventually won, with the runner up Hector Wales.

With his Eldorado lease living up to its name, Harry Darby was a firm believer in the adage 'you can't take it with you' and pursued a somewhat frenzied lifestyle. When in Salamaua, he was said to hire a plane to fly to Wau each day, as he liked the way the Kunai Pub made bacon and eggs; at Edie Creek, he would sometimes walk from shack to shack offering an ounce of gold for an egg. But Darby was equally renowned for his

Salamaua from Parsee Point, c.1929.

Bill Cameron's Billiard Saloon, Salamaua June 1929 (Cameron holding cue left of centre).

Wau township and landing ground, January 1929. The cluster of buildings bottom right are The Kunai Pub and NGG Store, shown earlier in this chapter. The saddle in the mountain range is the 'Bitoi Gap' through which planes flew to and from Salamaua.

largess, and not only in the bar, Harry Johns noting that *He was generous to a degree and the mark for all the bots in the community.*[21]

Hotel Bulolo, Wau.

Late in 1929, Darby left on an extended overseas trip, having first given £10,000 to the Brighton Babies Home in Victoria for the construction of a new wing. In early July 1931, at the age of 31, he committed suicide by swallowing strychnine at a fashionable seaside resort near Bombay, India. His final message, delivered later to the orphanage, was *Passing over tonight; thanks for all you've done for me. Cheerio. Harry.*[22] No reason was given, but Harry Johns speculated that *Towards the last, aided by the usual bottle of brandy a day, he wearied of life which could give him nothing beyond what he could buy.*[23]

Salamaua experienced a dramatic upsurge in activity in 1929 as NGG began developing the infrastructure for its future operations. Within three years, the resident European population had trebled. By late 1931, in addition to the Hotel, Salamaua boasted a hospital, District Office, post office, police station, customs office, a branch of the Bank of New South Wales, general stores operated by Burns Philp and W.R. Carpenter, and residences, trade stores and cargo sheds.

Wau — Late in 1928, there were still only a handful of white residents in Wau, living close to their lifeblood: the Kunai Pub and the aerodrome. However, during 1929 more permanent structures replaced the scattered handful of thatched roof houses, hangars and sheds as NGG poured resources into establishing its presence on the field. The number of Europeans rose steadily, and with this the first stirrings of social life. In September 1929, 12 women and 100 men attended a dance at Wau, many flying in from Lae and Salamaua for the occasion.

Shortly afterwards, financial difficulties saw the Kunai Pub quietly disappear, to be replaced early in 1930 by a new hotel, the Hotel Bulolo. Located up the hill a little from the aerodrome, it had a commanding view across the wide, grassy valley towards the Bitoi Gap, the dip in the Kuper Range through which planes

came from Salamaua. Inevitably, it soon became the focal point for miners, pilots, recruiters and officials — anyone passing through Wau.

Accommodation was fairly basic, the men's rooms lacking doors. Those leaving the bar late often found their bed already occupied. John Cooke, who worked as a barman at the hotel in 1931, recalled:

> With the arrival of the *Macdhui* at Salamaua a limited number of blocks of ice from the ship's freezer were flown up with the freezer goods bartered for tropical fruits for the ship's dining saloon. Otherwise, Wau's temperate climate and cool nights kept the beer in the cellar at a pleasant drinking temperature.[24]

The bar was rowdy and open to all hours, with billiards and high stakes poker an attraction for many. But the owner and manager, Flora Stewart, or 'Ma' as she was known to most, ran the Hotel with a firm hand and a sense of humour. 'Ma' was a tall, outgoing woman whose resilience and resourcefulness were forged through her Scottish ancestry and years of confronting life's challenges.

A former miner, Roy Struben, later recalled that brawls and fights were common, with miners who were great mates when sober, frequently coming to blows when drunk.[25] 'Ma' Stewart sent anyone wishing to fight outside to resolve their differences in the light of hurricane lamps, with the enthusiastic support of many of the drinkers. One inveterate fighter was the dentist Eric Weine, *a very large Australian, ex-Anzac, with a jutting jaw, who loved a scrap and was not fussy who he fought with, large or small.*[26] When one of his many

Lae, c. 1931-32. Note railway line linking the aerodrome with the jetty on the southern side of Voco Point. Also, three G31s, two W34s and two Fox Moths. This is an aerial view of scene on page 115.

opponents lost both the fight and his dentures, Weine, in true goldfields spirit, made him another set free of charge.

By 1931, the Mining Warden's office and associated activities had been transferred from Edie Creek, and Wau was developing rapidly as the administrative and commercial centre of the goldfields. In contrast to Edie Creek, which was nearly 4,000 feet higher, its climate provided comfortable living and working conditions. With the opening of Burns Philp and W.R. Carpenter stores selling a wide range of items and freezer goods and bread being available from NGG's bakery, miners no longer needed to order all their supplies from Salamaua.

Lae — In August 1928, the white resident population of Lae was 25 to 30, mostly pilots, engineers, and others associated with the growing air operations. Lae had few natural attractions. The heat and humidity were oppressive and malaria was rife. Most houses were built of local materials, offering adequate protection from the frequent heavy rainfall, but not the thriving insect life and reptiles they attracted. Henry Eekhoff, who ran a small trade store, claimed that local villagers called his place 'house snake'.[27] The only place of refuge, day or night, was under the mosquito net. Little or no fresh food was grown in the early years, forcing residents to rely solely on tinned food, much to their disgust. Mustar railed: *there was the constant dampness of clothes, mattresses and pillows. But I think worst of all, the food ... everything ... was encased in tins. Tinned flour, tinned milk, tinned butter, jam, fruit, meat, etc.*[28]

Until 1929, when Salamaua's aerodrome was constructed, visitors to the field had to travel by sea between Salamaua and Lae and then fly from Lae to Wau — and the reverse when leaving. However, with no shops, hotel or other sources of entertainment, there was no reason for travellers to stop in Lae. For several years it remained a lonely outpost of mostly single men, with little to relieve the monotony. The one saving grace was a weekly trip on the Guinea Airways pinnace to Salamaua for shopping or medical or dental treatment. And if this could be arranged to coincide with the arrival of a ship, cold beer and a meal of fresh food, so much the better.

As ships only called at Salamaua every six weeks at this time and rarely stayed more than one night, getting mail and replying to it quickly was were essential. This was manageable for locals, but until the Salamaua aerodrome opened, more difficult for Lae residents. They relied on the pinnace making a trip across from Salamaua before nightfall on the day the ship arrived. The following morning letters in reply were flown over to Salamaua and dropped onto the isthmus from the air — wrapped in oiled paper in case the pilot missed.

Edie Creek — By August 1928, the scattered tents which initially predominated were giving way to more permanent structures. There was plenty of timber for building, but very little roofing material. Bark and canvas proved moderately effective until the establishment of a saw milling plant enabled the construction of weatherboard buildings with timber roofs and floors. Not that everyone could afford such luxuries. One house, known locally as 'Haus Tin Biskit', was constructed of saplings to which flattened biscuit tins were attached. Each had previously held 25 pounds of biscuits and when flattened out covered several square feet. In other cases, rice bags attached to a frame of saplings were covered with mud which, when dry, provided a protective covering.

In the early years, the main everyday concerns were getting dry firewood to ward off the bitter night cold, and a reasonable variety of food. Wood supply was usually resolved by drying damp firewood above a fire that was kept going 24 hours a day. However, food supplies were monotonous and unreliable. The nearest village where vegetables might be obtained, Kaisinik, was several hours walk away. Mustar's dislike of tinned food was shared by the miners. Bert Weston recalled:

> Rice was the main food for the natives, tinned meat for the miners. The classic thing to do was to pull all the labels off so you didn't know what you were getting each day. You might be having tinned tripe or you might be having sausages.[29]

With BGD and NGG rapidly expanding their workforces, the European population associated with the goldfields climbed from about 150 in 1928 to around 500 in 1931. Where two years earlier there had been dense jungle, Bulolo had a European population of 124, most living in roughly constructed temporary housing, compared with 130 at Wau and 103 at Edie Creek. On the coast, Salamaua's population was 60 and Lae's 50. Other Europeans were scattered along the Bulolo and Watut Rivers, and in the Black Cat Creek/Bitoi area.

While living conditions were still fairly basic, by the early 1930s the rough frontier character of the field in its formative years was changing. In part, this was due to the growing number of company employees with their different needs and aspirations, and an influx of wives and girlfriends. But the growth in aviation, installation of freezer and chilling plants, improved radio communications and more frequent visits by ships also contributed to a greater variety and more reliable flow of food and other supplies, to better health and a reduced feeling of isolation.

The 'new' goldfields society that emerged during the 1930s was to be uniquely different from any other in Australian history.

CHAPTER 19
SMALL MINERS, SMALL PLANES AND SMALL 'DROMES

In 1932, after a couple of bleak years, the tide began to turn, and with it the fortunes of small miners.

The rising gold price and lower airfreight costs enabled miners to make a living from ground that had become unpayable, and encouraged prospecting further afield. Miners started arriving in larger numbers. Whereas those in 1926 were mainly Australians and English, many of the new arrivals were from other countries. While Australians still predominated, the South African Roy Struben encountered miners of at least 20 nationalities.[1]

But even with a higher gold price, the gravels often yielded poor returns, and by the mid-1930s, miners were widely scattered. What alluvial gold they found was generally in small pockets. Thus, in November 1935, within a few days of gold being discovered in the Wampit Valley, about 50 miners arrived, along with a few hundred labourers. A battler, Bill Babbington, who made the discovery, recovered 180 ounces from his claim in a few weeks, but that was the extent of it.

Some miners worked the terraces at upper Edie Creek using small pumps, others re-treated the tailings from previous workings, their activities intermittently disrupted by the usual problems—too much water or too little.

One of the most ambitious, an American, Albert Schrater, held rich leases at upper Edie Creek and set out to construct a race to bring water from the

Doris Booth, her sister-in-law Eileen Wilde and labourers at Cliffside.

George Clark, Spider and Jack O'Neill on the Lower Watut.

Upper Watut 16 miles away. Starting in 1937, he had completed benching for the whole race through rugged, inhospitable country when he died suddenly in December 1939. Schrater's race was never completed, but the base he constructed was later widened and used as a road by the Australian Army during the War.

Tex Thomas, who as President of the Morobe District Miners' Association in 1926 had led the attack on the Administration's approval of the Big Six leases, settled down with his family in 1932 at the junction of Edie Creek and the Bulolo. He constructed a power plant, water races and sawmill, using electric winches to move the many large boulders that made the creek here difficult to work. Nearby, Doris Booth continued to work Cliffside, assisted by five Europeans and 200 labourers. Her permanency was reflected in a tennis court and a 60 acre garden planted with kaukau, numerous fruit trees and vegetable and flower gardens.

But such miners were the exception. Most were constantly looking for new ground, ever hopeful. Some considered exploring the area west of the Upper Watut, but the murders of Hellmuth Baum, and then Naylor and Clarius by the Kukukuku and attacks on Government patrols made the risk-reward proposition particularly unattractive. Finally, in 1933, their curiosity was extinguished when prospectors from BGD and the Edie Creek Progress Association, escorted by Patrol Officers McCarthy and Black, concluded that gold was not present in payable quantities.

Other miners moved down the Watut, below its junction with the Snake River. The Lower Watut was rugged, malaria-ridden country with few foot tracks, the river winding through a narrow, rock-walled gorge, with occasional flats and terraces. This far downstream from the gold's source, yields were low. Nevertheless, by the mid-30s, there were 35 miners at work here, though as Jack O'Neill noted:

> The water in the river was too thick to drink and just too thin to shovel, fed as it was by the sluicing, hydraulicing and dredging from Edie Creek, Bulolo, the Watut and all points in between.[2]

Some prospectors moved north to the Upper Ramu, where a little gold had been found in 1930, and to the headwaters of the Purari River. However, no rich finds were made—one of the more significant providing a living for ten men for about three months. Others tried the Upper Waria again, with little more success than their predecessors. It was a difficult time, their only reward a way of life that satisfied some deep-seated, inexplicable, longing.

Working conditions were often difficult. After torrential rain upstream, a creek might rise six feet very rapidly, washing away one's workings, causing landslips and generally creating havoc. And always there was the risk of serious accidents. Deaths from falling timber, landslips, drowning and dynamite explosions were not uncommon—and not only among labourers. In 1932, George Clark wrote to Jack O'Neill:

> Poor old Frank Trimble is dead. A tree fell on him near his camp at Little Wau and pinned him against a big rock. He lay there for two hours and some boys pulled him out. He lived for three hours and asked everyone to shoot him. Broken back, hip, ribs, an awful mess.[3]

Miners often faced a long walk to the nearest aerodrome for supplies. In April 1933, George Clark bemoaned: *The drome is three days away, and my boys lose five days when I send them up for cargo.*[4] It was, therefore, hardly surprising that as miners moved out to increasingly remote locations, small landing grounds began to appear—usually little more than narrow, uneven strips of hillside from which kunai grass or jungle had been cleared. With no civil aviation authority to tell them what they could or couldn't do, miners only had to convince pilots that their 'drome was safe, and their problems were over. A 'drome meant regular mail and supplies, greatly improving the productivity of their labourers, and making ground payable that otherwise was marginal at best.

Even with higher gold prices and greater productivity, however, most found it difficult to make ends meet. The number of individual miners on the field was fairly stationary between 1933 and 1937, at around 220. Nearly three quarters were making less than £1,000 a year, and most considerably less.

Debt and hope were constant companions. George Clark wrote to Jack O'Neill in March 1933:

> At present I only owe £140 to WRC, that's all, £12 to BPs, but with a box team of 9 or 10, I can fix that up in three months.

In August 1935, however, things were no better:

> Well Jack, I have no worries now other than my debts. Do you think we'll ever be out of it? Ain't it a bastard to be like this; yet it is nothing if we could get a bit of good ground.

The stores and airlines were usually prepared to tide miners over, though the latter attributed their financial woes to their luck and suppliers in equal measure, and reserved crisp epithets for the latter: Burns Philp (BP = Bloody Pirates), W.R. Carpenter (WRC = Would Rob Christ) and Guinea Airways (GA = God Almighty).

Some miners down on their luck would drift into other work for a while to restore their finances, usually with one of the mining companies, but as soon as they were on their feet again it would be back to prospecting. Others, including several pilots, threw in their jobs to go prospecting. Within a year or two most were back flying.

Living conditions were often rough, though they did improve a little in time. Jack O'Neill's accommodation at Edie Creek in 1931 comprised a canvas tent fly for a roof with walls that were saplings laced together with bush vines. Unless oiled, the roof became a sheet of mildew within a couple of months and leaked like blotting paper. By 1934, Daphne Murcutt on the Upper Watut could boast a house of rough-sawn creosoted timber and a galvanised iron roof, but with upturned boxes for chairs and no refrigeration.[5] By 1939, Jeanette Leahy at Surprise Creek had a kerosene refrigerator and a short wave radio, even if the latter was hooked up to fume-generating batteries kept under the verandah to avoid the smell.[6]

Those on the move or living in more remote camps didn't enjoy such luxuries and were more exposed to the local wildlife. Death adders and scorpions were common, rats and leeches more so. George Clark, on the Lower Watut, complained that

> every conceivable bloody pest is here. I know of 14 different species of ants, and each species has an army of 15 million. A tilly lamp at night is out of the question, beetles and moths in millions. But the most troublesome of all are the little black bees; life is almost unbearable with them.[7]

Jack O'Neill:

> These bees do not bite or sting; they don't need to. Their habit is to crawl all over you in countless thousands, attracted by your sweat, and they go everywhere to find it.[8]

While it was generally too high for malarial mosquitoes, except on the Lower Watut, a number of miners died from scrub typhus, contracted from tiny bush mites.[9] The first reported incidence was in the mid-1930s and though relatively few were affected, it had a high mortality rate. The other endemic problem was tropical ulcers, a scratch or insect bite leading to what Jack O'Neill described as *that horrid, fleshy volcano,*[10] up to two inches in diameter, which could take up to three months to heal.

Alice Innes

Flora ('Ma') Stewart

In the early days, mining was concentrated in relatively small areas, such as Edie Creek. Thus, while the field was far from urban centres, miners had ample interaction with each other. However, by the mid-1930s, miners were more spread out, often working ground that was little better than marginal for one European and a small team of labourers, and so unable to sustain a partnership. While some of them persuaded women from down south to share their life on the field, in 1935-36, more than four in five remained unmarried. Their day to day existence was therefore often more solitary than among miners a few years earlier. George Clark's experience highlights the isolation some had to endure. In October 1933, he wrote to Jack O'Neill from the Lower Watut: *Am eagerly looking forward to a break at Xmas in Salamaua. Bernie Parer and Erickson are the only two chaps I've seen since March.*[11]

Sometimes other miners broke the loneliness as they moved up and down river, on their way to or from the nearest 'drome. Every visit was an excuse for a cup of tea, lunch or, even better, some overnight company. Pilots also brought news of the outside world. Small things made life more bearable—the gramophone, a soda siphon, books and periodicals that were read avidly and passed on. And later, for a fortunate few, the static of short-wave wireless sets broke the silence, enabling cricket enthusiasts to transport themselves to England for the 1938 Ashes tests.

Dogs were always good company as well as a deterrent to intruders. George Clark's greyhound-chow cross, Spider, was one of many who accompanied their owners everywhere, on foot and on planes.

Isolation and shared hardships contributed to a breaking down of barriers between miners and their labourers. The harsh assessments of some Europeans in the early years often gave way to a greater appreciation of labourers' capabilities and more concern for their welfare. In June 1936, Jack O'Neill returned to the Lower Watut after a visit to Wau:

> I had been away for ten working days. Bulwa, the boss boy, had some very large balls of amalgam for me, which weighed forty ounces eleven pennyweights. That was the equivalent of more than 20 ounces of gold, the best result I had had since I started work on the river. When I saw the place the boys had been working, I was amazed; I had never even considered working there ... When left to their own resources good lads like mine hunted for good ground; with responsibility they developed amazingly ... [12]

Coping with the difficult conditions required optimism that things would get better and resilience when they did not. The key to the latter was an unwillingness by miners to take anything too seriously, even life itself. Ion Idriess recounted the story of Ernie Bowden, ill with blackwater fever, being carried on a stretcher past the pub in Salamaua:

> He weakly waved to the crowd and croaked out wanting to know the odds of his recovery. 'Thirty-three to one against!' they shouted back. He took the odds to three fivers—and collected. [13]

Neither did George Clark express much empathy when he wrote to Jack O'Neill in 1936:

> Ned Shields is running Bill's place, but yesterday he was bitten by a scorpion in the instep. It was in his

boot. Last night he was nearly mad with pain so I went over but could do nothing for him only tell him what terrible things they are, but he was in a better position to tell me that. Don't know how he is this morning, might be dead.[14]

Miners continued their casual approach to security in the 1930s, keeping gold wherever was convenient rather than safe. When an account needed to be settled they would put it in a tobacco or biscuit tin and give it to a pilot to pass to BPs or the Bank in Salamaua—no receipts were expected or issued.

If trust was one aspect of their philosophical outlook, so was generosity. At Salamaua, the Manager of the Bank of New South Wales, Harry Johns, wrote to his parents in 1930, *I acquired a further specimen today. 'First out of the bag's yours, Banker', says the miner and upends a bag with about 300 oz of nuggets. The one I drew was worth over £10 and is about 60% gold.*[15] Miners often presented John Cooke with gold specimens during his days as barman at the Hotel Bulolo. He recorded that when an Irish miner drowned trying to cross the Watut River in flood, Harry O'Kane donated a large dark yellow Black Cat nugget to be raffled to raise money to send the miner's wife and child back to Ireland.[16]

The principal escape from the monotony of everyday life was a visit to Wau or perhaps to Salamaua. But once there, miners were largely denied the pleasure of the intimate company of white women. Unlike on goldfields overseas, there were no gambling saloons or dance halls, nor the various excesses traditionally associated with them. To prevent the emergence of prostitution and other activities that may have disrupted the harmony of the field, single women were not permitted to travel there unless they had family members or specific employment.

There were, however, three women to whom miners could— and did—turn for emotional support as well as practical assistance. In Salamaua, drawing on her training and experience as a nurse[17], Alice Innes helped many miners who arrived down from 'on

top' suffering from malnutrition and various tropical illnesses. She was a kindly, compassionate person who, despite running a hotel that grew steadily larger over the years, always found time to listen to lonely miners as they talked about their womenfolk—their mothers, wives, sisters and girlfriends—offering advice where this was wanted.

Despite her 'no nonsense' disposition, 'Ma' Stewart in Wau was also generous and caring, rarely turning away someone in need. Her daughter, Flora Bowman, recalled that she would often help miners through periods of financial difficulty, as well as the wives and children of miners who, through ill fortune or ill-treatment, were destitute.[18] At times, when she was dressed in her long evening gown for dinner, miners would ask her to dress their injuries or cut their hair so they could go to a dance. From time to time, women would write to her from Australia or elsewhere enquiring about their men, of whom they'd heard nothing for years. She would confront the miners concerned in the bar, stand over them until they wrote a letter and then mail it herself.

'Mum' (Alice) Bowring arrived at Edie Creek late in 1932 as cook and house-keeper to the NGG mess, but within a year started a mess and boarding house of her own, providing regular meals to as many as 40 miners. Like Alice Innes, she had nursing experience and treated their ailments while listening to their troubles and concerns.[19] But it was as much for her *joie de vivre*

Alice ('Mum') Bowring

as her practical help that miners warmed to her. Jim Sinclair recalled that she

> had the gentle appearance of one's favourite grandmother, but a kind face, a twinkling eye, fat rosy cheeks and a vast bosom were but a camouflage for a character of Rabelaisian dimensions … She had a wild, deep belly-laugh, called her native labourers 'bloody coons' … Yet her labourers loved her and boasted to their fellows of the hard time she gave them, although they were fat and sleek from her good food and careful attention to their welfare. [20]

A more restrained Alice Bowring later wrote: *The miners were very grateful for small kindnesses and my house was always a place to come and sit by the fire for a cup of tea and a yarn. This seems to mean a lot to men a long way from home …* [21]

Visits to Wau were a way of restoring the body as well as the soul. The dentist Alan McKay occasionally flew to outlying 'dromes, though treatment in Wau was infinitely preferable. Grabowsky recalled later that his travelling equipment *always included a one native foot powered pedal drill. Oh how this could hurt when the power supply became tired or disinterested and the drill groaned in short jerks.*[22]

Unhealthy working and living conditions contributed to various ailments, particularly tropical ulcers. Miners experimented and improvised with different concoctions to treat these, but inevitably occasional visits to Wau were required for medical treatment. The increasing number of 'dromes meant that what previously would have required several days' walk to the nearest one became a short trip; and in the event of an emergency, Wau was only a few minutes away by plane.

Having sorted out their dental and medical problems and had a haircut, it was off to the Hotel Bulolo to meet their mates and drown their sorrows. As in gold mining towns everywhere, this sometimes got out of hand. When a miner was on a bender for too long, the District Officer would prohibit the sale of liquor to him or lock him up. George Clark wrote in 1935:

> Chas Erickson is in town. His account for 7 days is £560—some going what. ___ sold him a horse for £160—bloody shame, and he don't know anything about it yet. He is buying champagne for everyone, even for breakfast. 20 tins of cigarettes in an hour for the women. He was arrested yesterday, but only for his own benefit.[23]

By 1932, small mining camps dotted creeks and rivers all over the Morobe District. Wau was the key distribution point for their supplies, all cargo being shifted from the coast as quickly as possible in case bad weather there delayed much needed supplies. The establishment of commercial freezers in Wau meant that even perishables could be stored for considerable periods.

In the absence of roads, small Moth aircraft were soon flying supplies and passengers to the rapidly increasing number of 'dromes being established by miners. In September 1933, the Bank of New South Wales noted that the 24th aerodrome had just been opened,[24] and by June 1935, there were about 50—each the hub of a small European community, and up to 1,500 labourers in total.[25] Daily flights were common to many of these 'dromes.

The level of aviation activity was increasingly hectic: in March 1936, *Pacific Islands Monthly* reported:

> At times 20 or more planes can be seen landing at Wau within short intervals of one another, on their way to and from the mining camps that lie scattered far away in the distant ranges. Like a flock of birds they alight and fly off to all points of the compass …

Bunny Hammond later recalled,

> At stand down in the evening (at Wau), my Ford '50' would be taxied up to the fence of my house ready for morning take-off at 6 am, to arrive at Salamaua and wake up the staff by flying over Innes' Hotel at 6.30 am, when Jack Devaney would race out to the strip in the red truck and organise loading for either Wau, Bulolo or Ramu. Then about 9 am, I would pop into the Waco or Avian for the 'milk run', loaded with packages, parcels and mail for the hairy strips of Sunshine, Upper Watut and the 1 in 8 steep Surprise Creek, Roamer in the narrow gully, Maralinan and sometimes Kaiapit, then back to Wau for morning tea and resume the Salamaua run.[26]

With the landing grounds often only a few minutes apart, it was common for Moths to make 30 take-offs and landings in a day.[27] The range of items carried was diverse. Bunny Hammond:

> You know the types of cargo, gelignite, rice, etc. and … detonators sent by unscrupulous miners in boot boxes marked as a pair of boots. Of course, the small cargo on the top aerodromes was false teeth from Eric Weine, bottles of whisky, panama hats, wooden toilet boxes made to measure for clients, urgent medicines and, of course, tools, generators, batteries—all wanted urgently.[28]

Cargo that didn't fit in a plane, such as planks for sluice boxes and pipes for sluicing, was simply strapped to its side.

The most important deliveries were fresh food. Suddenly, tinned food—the staple of those living several days' walk from a 'drome—was replaced with fresh meat, bread, butter, vegetables and fruit. Deliveries were irregular at first, so that when they heard a plane, miners would send in two or three of their labourers on the off-chance that their supplies were on it. GAL made things easier when it painted the 'kai kai balus' silver and its registration numbers red, though only when it was flying long red and white streamers was it carrying perishable food.

At Surprise Creek, several small structures were constructed at the top of the aerodrome from any materials to hand. The pilot had a key to the padlock of each, and collected outgoing mail and orders, replacing them with incoming mail and supplies, before locking it again. The miner or his labourers would arrive later and complete the cycle.

Holden's Air Transport created goodwill among the scattered mining fraternity by sending a plane to small 'dromes every day, whether or not they had cargo. Gradually deliveries became more predictable, with planes visiting each 'drome on Saturday mornings with freezer food.

For some isolated miners, deliveries were often to the door … more or less. A small plane delivered mail to the Murcutts every three weeks. Glen Murcutt, later a renowned architect but a small child at the time, remembered …

> you'd hear in the distance the plane coming, and the excitement! … Because of the air currents you couldn't direct where the plane was going to drop the stuff off, and … the plane went on two or three very tight banks and all of a sudden out of the aircraft was this canvas bag with a big tail on the end of it, a red tail, so all you had to do was look for the tail. There were food parcels in it as well, and the food parcels were all stitched up in hessian.[29]

Moths were also increasingly used as aerial taxis, running a shuttle service back and forth between the miners' aerodromes and Wau, and enabling miners to attend dances, pictures, sporting events and, in 1933–34, the Wau races.

Moth plane on the turntable at Surprise Creek aerodrome.

The 'dromes themselves were narrow, uneven or steep, and often all three, and a daily challenge to even the most experienced pilots. One of the earliest, established in 1931, was the 300 yard long strip at Surprise Creek, adjoining the Administration's base camp at Otibanda.[30] A pilot approached the airstrip over an 80 foot deep river gorge and between two spurs, landing the plane in the hollow of a saucer, about 30 yards wide. The bottom lip of the saucer had been cut away to make landing easier, while the upper lip—the 'drome itself—had a slope of about one in eight. Having descended between the spurs, the pilot had to change immediately to a climb, so his plane was almost parallel with the rising ground. Once the wheels touched, he opened the throttle wide to taxi to the top of the 'drome.

The slope was so steep that a level turning area had been constructed to stop planes running backwards downhill and to enable them to be turned for take-off. District Officer Townsend described the takeoff procedure:

> Natives pull back on the struts on both wings, and the pilot puts his wheel brakes hard on. The engine is then revved up fully, and at a sign from the pilot, who then takes off his brakes, the strut of the wing lying uphill is released. The machine swings at once, owing to the drag on the one wing, and at once bolts downhill. At the gap, the machine is lifted off the ground and swings over the ravine, thus gaining 80 feet in height.[31]

Even more dramatic was Roamer 'drome, on the Lower Watut between Snake River and Maralinan.[32] George Clark constructed (for want of a better word) this 440 by 50 yard airstrip in 1933. Once a plane began its approach, there was no turning back. This involved a descent over the Watut River between two lightly timbered mountain ranges rising 2,000–3,000 feet on either side, to within 100 feet of the water, at which point the pilot was effectively flying in a narrow gorge. He followed the winding river course until, 100 yards from the strip, the pilot was confronted with a sheer rock wall, necessitating a 90° right turn, at which point

the airstrip came into view. He then immediately closed the throttle prior to landing. If he overshot, a steep cliff face was guaranteed to bring his landing to an abrupt halt.

Other 'dromes such as the Upper Watut, Roaring Creek and Slate Creek were more accessible—but not much. They typically involved dodging ridges or hills while coping with varying wind strengths, cross winds and down draughts, and then landing on short, uneven surfaces where there was little room for error.

In many respects, and certainly when it came to risk-taking, pilots were kindred spirits of the miners, and most did not baulk at flying to these new 'dromes. When the Civil Aviation Controller, Max Allen, was finally appointed in 1934, he considered closing down several of them for safety reasons. To do so would have had major repercussions. While some were used by only a handful of miners, they might employ up to 300 labourers, who were dependent on air deliveries for their food and tobacco. As well, labourers were always leaving and new recruits arriving, with planes their only practical form of transport.

Allen's solution was to prohibit passenger traffic into and out of some 'dromes, such as Roamer, except in the case of sickness, and to limit planes to a full inward load but only half a load out. In a bizarre interpretation of the rules, the prohibition did not apply to labourers, who were classed as 'cargo' and carried at so much per pound. With regulations only as good as the minds focused on getting round them, Bunny Hammond observed: *Every time I went in* [to Roamer] *there was a miner very sick (?) with a stack of picks, shovels and sometimes an anvil to bring out, and possibly his boy on his knee.*[33] Allen eventually came to realise the futility of his restrictions; by September 1936, although nothing had changed, Roamer had been declared safe again for passenger traffic.

It is a tribute to their skill rather than any regulations that, while there were occasional minor accidents, no pilots lost their lives flying in or out of these improvised 'dromes.

CHAPTER 20
THE 1930s: TOWNSHIP LIFE—
A SLIGHTLY MANIC EXISTENCE

The 1930s saw the rapid transformation of the Morobe goldfields from a frontier society to one with all the trappings of modern civilisation.

The 1942 Pacific Islands Yearbook reported that the Morobe plateau had been converted

> from a tropical wilderness into a place enjoying all the amenities of European civilisation. A series of townships … are linked up by motor roads. They have electric light and power, radio stations, schools, cinemas, racecourses, cold stores; and, above all, they have regular supplies of fresh meat and vegetables delivered frozen by aeroplanes.

Margaret Dovey (Whitlam), visiting her former school friend Jeanette Leahy in late 1940, wrote home from Wau, obviously surprised by what she encountered:

> Jeanette and I went to church in the morning—very High Church … Had Christmas dinner last night at the pub prefaced by two cocktail parties … Everyone was very merry—I had oyster cocktail, iced asparagus, cutlets, peas, turkey with guava jelly, plum pudding, brandy sauce, masses of nuts, chocolates, fruit, crystallised fruit and coffee.[1]

A far cry from the tinned food staples of the pioneers a decade earlier.

Between 1931 and 1938, the European population of the Morobe District increased from around 500 to 1,800. This growth was mainly due to an influx of company employees and their families, and as a result,

the proportion who were individual miners fell from about one third to less than one tenth of all Europeans.

From 233 in 1931, the European population of Wau (including Edie Creek) quadrupled to around 1,000 in 1938, overtaking that of the capital, Rabaul. There were

Salamaua from the air, c. 1933.

189

400 at Bulolo and Bulwa, 140 at Salamaua and 100 at Lae, with the rest at various remote mining camps. Collectively, they represented 40% of the European population of New Guinea—more than twice the percentage of seven years earlier.

Inevitably, this growth and change in composition of the population led to a transformation in goldfield society.

To the casual observer in 1941, Wau was a quintessential Australian country town. It had two hotels, two churches, a masonic hall, school, hospital, post office, two banks, four stores, a bakery, doctor, two dentists and three solicitors, a chemist, laundry, hairdresser, tailor, bootmaker, dressmaker and a taxi service. The Savoy Café and hotels offered dine-in meals, while the milk bar doubled as the newsagent. Neither were cultural and sporting activities neglected. The Wau Dramatic Society put on regular productions at Hoile's Picture Theatre, the Regent Theatre showed the latest films and at the Wau Club patrons danced to music played by the Bulolo Orchestra. The public swimming pool, tennis courts and golf course were well patronised, gymkhanas were held at the racecourse, and cricket and football were played regularly at the sports ground.

Rows of attractive bungalows lined well-formed roads, used by as many as 65 cars and named after Levien, Park, Royal, Sloane, Darby and other early pioneers. Many were connected to the local telephone system and relied on electricity from BGD's Baiune Power Station, 28 miles away. Taking advantage of the temperate climate, residents took pride in their gardens. As early as 1931, an observer noted

> One of the most interesting features of Wau at present is the beautiful gardens almost every home possesses. Masses of dahlias, roses of choicest varieties, pansies, snaps, etc., bloom profusely in almost every garden [with] most home gardens producing fine English potatoes, lettuce, peas, cabbage, etc.[2]

When it came to services, food and lifestyle, Wau residents lacked very little.

Wau in the late 1930s. Scar on hillside is a water race. Road to Edie Creek can be seen climbing Mt Kaindi in background.

Main street, Salamaua, c. 1934.

Further down the valley, Bulolo and Bulwa residents were similarly well off, their comforts provided by a single benevolent employer, BGD.[3] Edie Creek residents—the majority of whom were (by 1941) NGG employees and their families—used Wau's facilities. Writing in *Pacific Islands Monthly* in 1940, 'IMEB' commented on the improved conditions at Edie Creek:

> In 1933 we slept on home-made, canvas beds and brought a few yards of cretonne to dress up packing cases for furniture, and to disguise our rough wooden-shuttered windows. Now there are spring mattresses, cane furniture and glass windows and NGG employees have electric light [and] kettles, toasters and irons. Some ... even have telephones.[4]

Salamaua remained the Administrative centre and main port for the Morobe District throughout the pre-War period despite the growing claims of Lae. A visitor in 1935 reported

> In the broad bay itself are small craft of all descriptions, while the waterfront is broken by a succession of jetties and stores of the various trading and air companies. While there still remains occasional evidence of the primitive conditions of the early days at Salamaua, in the few humpies of bag and tin that straggle along the roadway outside the town, today it is a settlement of spacious offices, large general stores, a bank, wireless station, hospital and tennis courts; with European residential bungalows wherever space allows.[5]

The rapidly growing transient population led the Salamaua Hotel to expand its accommodation capacity progressively from 16 in 1927 to 180 by 1936. The township soon outgrew the isthmus, with most residential housing after 1934 being at Kela on the north-western side of the harbour. Here and on the isthmus, bungalows were set in colourful gardens of frangipani, bougainvillea, hibiscus, zinnias, marigolds and gerberas, with masses of orchids clinging to tree trunks.

The growth of Lae's aviation activities was not matched by its development. Despite the limited supply of land at Salamaua, the Administration and commercial businesses preferred its more pleasant climate and surrounds to Lae's high rainfall and oppressive humidity. Lae remained largely dominated by Guinea Airways, whose recreation club provided most of the amenities. However, the town was given a lift when the two storey Hotel Cecil opened in 1936. Despite Lae's small population, its Progress Association sought to foster community pride by planting trees and maintaining the few roads.

Each township, small as it was, had its own distinctive personality, reflecting its location, climate and the activities of the people who lived and worked there. But at the same time, each saw itself as part of a homogeneous entity, in its own way contributing to the success of the goldfields.

The speed with which the settlements were established was remarkable given the absence of any infrastructure in 1930 and, other than planes, of any transport links capable of conveying the materials to establish it. And these townships needed to support not just 1,800 Europeans, but as many as 10,000 New Guinean labourers. It was an extraordinary logistical achievement.

An aircraft designer who visited Wau in 1937 wrote:

> It is a wonderful experience to walk around the little township of Wau realising that every person one meets, all the produce in the shops, the cars, horses, lorries, pianos, furniture, corrugated iron, beer and dynamite, have all been flown up from the coast in large or small freight aeroplanes.[6]

It was even more remarkable when one realises that

every single item delivered to the field in the pre-War period had first to be unloaded from ships standing offshore onto whaleboats or lighters and then rowed, towed or floated ashore. Only then could they be flown to the field.

Collectively, the European inhabitants of all townships numbered no more than an average Australian country town, and superficially their lifestyle was similar. But several aspects of their existence made their life very different indeed.

———

Initially, there was no way of storing perishable food so most of it came in tins, including butter—universally condemned as 'axle grease'. This began to change when freezers or cool stores arrived in Salamaua and Wau late in 1929. Limited supplies of fresh meat became available in 1930, when 40 sheep were flown in and some cattle, goats and horses were driven in along the new Buang track. Within three years, there were freezers at Bulolo and Lae, each with a capacity of up to 10 tons.

The impact on morale was immediate. At Bulolo, Kath Honeysett wrote in July 1932 with excited anticipation: *By the next boat come refrigerator supplies. Think of it—real butter once more … Then there will be eggs, meat, fish and fruit.*[7] Three months later, Dorothy Waterhouse, in Bulolo to launch the second dredge, observed

> When the food supplies arrive by air they are placed in cool storage rooms … In one is placed all meat for the settlement, in another, butter eggs and cheese, and another contains fresh fruit and vegetables. The housewives get their provisions daily from these cooling chambers.[8]

Few houses had kerosene refrigerators; most made do with coolgardie safes, with the fortunate ones having an 'icy ball' to keep food cool.[9] Frozen food was flown in daily to replenish the freezers, so these arrangements were more than adequate.

Increasingly, imports from Australia were supplemented by locally grown food. A dairy just outside Wau supplied fresh milk daily, while Hunter and Clem Kirke's market garden and orchard were a prolific source of fruit and vegetables. Villages nearby also supplied fresh vegetables. The Buang people were excellent gardeners, growing yams, kaukau, potatoes, corn and European vegetables such as tomatoes, cabbages, carrots, onions and radishes. Even coffee was grown locally, and was of exceptional quality.

If there was a major drawback, it was the cost of imported supplies. In 1930, with airfreight 8 pence per pound, a bottle of beer that was 1 shilling and 6 pence at Salamaua was 3 shillings and 9 pence in Wau. A 50 pound bag of rice that cost 15 shillings in Rabaul, was £3/15 shillings in Wau. While airfreight rates fell to around 2 pence per pound in the late 1930s, a ton of flour that could be purchased for £9/15 shillings in Salamaua in 1936 was still £33/1 shilling and 8 pence in Wau. It was estimated that in 1940 Wau's cost of living was 100% higher than in Australian mining towns.[10] Even locally grown produce was expensive, because of the high cost of fuel for generators and cars. BGD employees were more fortunate than most: the company's store sold them a range of supplies, including groceries, at prices no higher than in Rabaul.

———

The Administration played only a limited role in providing basic services—hospitals, power, roads, aerodromes and communications. Its unwillingness to build or maintain the infrastructure necessary to support the goldfields, despite the range of fees, taxes and import duties it levied, was a constant source of resentment.

The Morobe District was a far from healthy place. Coastal residents had to contend not only with malaria and its particularly unpleasant cousin, blackwater fever, but also with dengue fever. Bob Iredale, an early Lae resident, claimed to have had malaria 25 times and dengue fever three times in three years.[11] At higher altitudes, malaria was less common, though Europeans everywhere shared the ritual of passing the quinine at dinner.

Medical facilities were generally good, Europeans having access to a doctor and hospital at Bulolo, Wau and Salamaua. The two dentists in Wau were the pugilistic Eric Weine and the somewhat unreliable Syd Barker, who was known to stop working on someone's teeth and dash off on hearing news of a strike.[12]

Communications between Wau (to which the Edie Creek transmitter was transferred in 1932) and the coast were largely confined to radiograms throughout the 1930s, the difficult terrain making installation of fixed lines impractical. BGD established a radio-telephone link between Bulolo and Lae in 1933, but reliable voice communication between Lae, Salamaua, Bulolo and Wau only became possible in 1939 when an advanced radio-telephone system was installed, with a single handset

Building the road from Wau to Edie Creek.

in each township and two in Lae. Communication with Rabaul and Australia was confined to radiograms—a radio-telephone service installed between Rabaul and Sydney in 1937 was not extended to the mainland.

The feeling of isolation eased when improvements in short wave radio reception in the mid-1930s meant goldfields residents could listen in to overseas broadcasts. At first, reception was confined to radio operators picking up the news transmitted from Sydney to ships at sea, and producing daily news sheets. But short wave sets soon began to appear, and by 1936 Wau residents were able to listen to a full description of the Melbourne Cup. In June 1938, *The Rabaul Times* reported that people were sitting up all night listening to the test cricket in England.

Road links between the townships—or the lack of them—were a source of on-going tension between residents and the Administration.[13] Three sections were necessary to link the extremities of the field: Edie Creek to Wau (13 miles), Wau to BGD's power house at the opening of the lower Bulolo valley (12 miles) and the

power house to Bulwa and Baiune (16 miles). Within two years of beginning operations, BGD had constructed the last of these roads, and thereafter maintained it without any assistance from the Administration. The story of the other two sections was as tortuous as the roads themselves.

While Edie Creek was the administrative centre of the field until 1932, the Administration made no effort to construct a road to it from Wau. In 1927, NGG cut an initial track up the side of Mt. Kaindi, a rise of 3,500 feet over difficult terrain. The following year, the Administration agreed to share the cost of converting this into a mule track; it would construct the upper half and NGG the lower half.

An official report in 1931 was scathing:

Both halves were started according to the arrangement but the Administration defaulted when portion had been completed and the Company had to complete the work itself ... After being completed there was the upkeep to be arranged as washaways were frequent, but although the road was used by everybody— employees of companies, prospectors, mule teams, tradesmen, businessmen and government officials—

the Administration refused to maintain it although [previously] agreeing to keep half in repair. There is no doubt that the way to Edie Creek would still be a bush track had it depended on the Administration.[14]

NGG did its best to maintain the narrow mule track, but the movement of supplies along it was difficult and time-consuming. An enterprising young Australian, Fred Deckert, finally took matters into his own hands, using parts from a range of vehicles and a shortened chassis to construct a lorry that could use the track. In April 1933, Deckert began carrying loads of up to ¾ ton between Wau and Edie Creek. Deckert's 'Bitza' soon became the talk of the goldfields, providing passengers with what the new Administrator, Walter McNicoll, called *a thrilling drive probably unequalled anywhere in the world*[15] and what another described as *a unique if somewhat terrifying experience*.[16]

The track negotiated a narrow 'bench', often only four feet wide and with 14 hairpin bends, most of which had gradients of one in three. Alistair Grabowsky, who briefly operated in competition with Deckert, later recalled they were so sharp that to navigate a bend, a truck had to 'back and fill' up to four times with several men on the bonnet and front bumper bar or hanging on lifelines out the side to keep its wheels on the ground. Chains were used to improve traction and so prevent the truck sliding over the edge and somersaulting to the creek bed 600 to 1,000 feet below.[17] When Deckert's chains broke, as happened often, he repaired them with wire recycled from a beer carton.

When the outside edge of the road collapsed—a not infrequent occurrence—repairs involved cutting two Y-shaped pieces of timber and driving these into the ground at either end of the section concerned. A strong pole was laid in the V part of the Y, parallel to the edge of the road. Timber and saplings were then laid on the pole and the adjacent road, forming a platform, which was covered with earth. The truck was then free to proceed.

Construction did not begin on a full width road between Wau and Edie Creek until April 1934, when the Administration finally agreed to meet the cost. Private contractors built a new section, designed to bypass the most difficult part of the old track, and this opened for motor vehicle traffic on 26 April 1935. While landslides intermittently cut the road in the years that followed, the ability of ordinary rather than specially modified vehicles to use it lowered costs and improved access to Wau for Edie Creek residents.

A road between Wau and Bulolo, the two main townships on the goldfields, was also a long time coming, and for most of the 30s, though the distance was short, direct access between the two townships was only possible by air or on foot. Until 1933, there was only a rough foot track through the long gorge, the river being crossed at one point by a suspension bridge made of fencing wire and bamboo, and in other places by enormous logs deposited by the river when in flood. Gradually, sections of the track were converted into a mule track and then into one that cars could navigate, using a temporary wooden bridge to cross Koranga Creek near its junction with the Bulolo. By October 1936, the road was still ¾ mile short of the BGD power house. This final stretch, and a bridge across the river at this point, were not completed until late 1938. No sooner had this happened than the Koranga bridge was washed away in a flood. Although a new bridge was hastily constructed, the road was rarely fully

The Levien trophy.

Wau races.

functional, with landslips frequently isolating Wau and Bulolo from each other for short periods.

Although the shipping service between Australia and New Guinea became more regular and, from 1932, an air service linked Wau and Port Moresby, the goldfields retained their feeling of isolation. Being able to 'listen in' to events overseas on short wave radio but to communicate with Australia only with difficulty accentuated the sense of separation; but it also fostered a sense of unity. So did the shared difficulties of everyday life—the rugged, inaccessible topography, the ever-present risk of malaria and other tropical diseases, the disruption caused by rain and floods, the lack of roads and the high cost of living. Residents responded by looking inward, forging a community that was strong and vibrant.

Anzac Day was a singular unifying force, in much the same way as in Australian country towns. A sub-branch of the Returned Sailors' and Soldiers' Imperial League of Australia was formed in 1934, and within six months more than 10% of the European population were members. A visitor reported that, in April 1935, 200 ex-servicemen, representing nearly every allied nation, fighting arm and rank, flew in to Wau for Anzac Day from all over the goldfields.[18] This became an annual event, with a parade and memorial service followed by sporting activities and a dance in the evening.

Sport was the other main unifying force, competition often having a tribal intensity. The first inter-town sporting contest was between Lae and Salamaua in October 1930, when the Lae Sports Club flew to Sala-maua for a weekend of snooker, tennis and cricket.[19] Early the following year, with the goldfields at last beginning to realise the potential of which he'd dreamed, Cecil Levien offered a trophy for sport among the Morobe townships. In doing so, he provided a gentle reminder to Europeans who would contest the trophy of who was responsible for their opportunity to do so. The trophy was a small bronze statue of a New Guinean carrier, carrying a pack, and called 'The Real Pioneer'.

The Levien Trophy was for competition between Wau, Salamaua, Lae and Bulolo (and in some years Edie Creek) in tennis, billiards, snooker and cricket, points being awarded for each.[20] Initially, the Trophy was contested over the Easter long weekend. But from 1935, matches were held over a series of weekends leading up to Easter, when the two leading teams contested the final. Guinea Airways flew teams, and often many of their supporters, to the different venues at no cost. Barracking was vigorous, as was the partying before and afterwards, and a dance was usually held in conjunction with the matches. Reporting on the 1939 final, *The Rabaul Times* observed on 21 April, *This is the greatest sporting competition in the Morobe District and has done much to bring together many people who in the ordinary walk of life might never meet.*

Other competitive sports that provided a reason for travel between centres included horse racing (at Wau), swimming and yachting (at Salamaua), and golf (at Wau and Bulolo). One Sunday in 1934, 40 people flew from Wau to Salamaua just to watch the yachting.

The Morobe Turf Club was formed in 1933 and held its first race meet at Wau on Boxing Day, a six event program with the Morobe Gold Cup as its feature race. Local horses competed with others flown in by G31 in specially constructed horse boxes—the first time in the world horses had been flown to a race meeting. A two day meeting was held at Easter 1934, with several horses being walked in beforehand along the Buang track. Whether this was ideal preparation or because of its breeding, a horse owned by 'Ma' Stewart won five races over the two days. After one more meeting, racing ceased, only resuming in 1940 with several picnic race meetings and gymkhanas.

The development of golf courses from the mid-1930s, requiring as they did a considerable investment of time and money, conveyed an increasing sense of permanency about the goldfields townships; more and more people were viewing them as 'home'. Near Golden

Buffalo Ball, December 1939.

Ridges in 1936 NGG opened a six hole course, followed soon after by the formation of the Wau Golf Club with a six hole course that gradually expanded to 12 holes by 1940. BGD opened a six hole course at Bulolo in 1938, and this was progressively lengthened to nine holes. Bulwa also had a nine hole course which, as at Bulolo, was constructed on and around the aerodrome.

Golf club membership grew rapidly, and the clubs assumed a pivotal role in the social life of their communities. In 1939, BGD's Sydney-based Director, Les Waterhouse, formalised the growing enthusiasm, donating the Waterhouse Cup for competition between Wau, Edie Creek, Bulolo and Bulwa.[21] This was vigorously contested over several months each year, the final being held between the two leading teams.

Competitive sport between the townships not only unified the goldfields, but reflected a desire among residents to make a 'normal' life for themselves—to recreate their Australian life in New Guinea. This was also reflected in other social activity.

As in Australia at the time, dances were popular, and people would fly in for them from all over the goldfields. In Wau, they were held monthly at the Wau Club, on Anzac Day and in association with many sporting events. More formal balls were also organised, sometimes annually, by the Buffaloes Masonic Lodge, the Race Club, the Women's Guild, the New Guinea Mining Association, the Red Cross—even the Australian Labor Party (Wau Branch). There was a Bachelor and Spinster's Ball, Returned Soldiers' Ball and a New Year's Eve Ball. Many were attended by up to 200 people, or one in nine of the District's adult European population.

On such occasions, Wau's dress shops and ladies' hairdressers were well patronised. In 1938, *The Rabaul Times* noted (8 April),

> It is hard to realise at these functions that we are ostensibly living in a 'mining town' when one looks around at the assembly of good looking and stylishly dressed ladies who grace the dance floor; it almost reminds one of Romano's. And be it remembered that we have a floor which would not be out of place in many capital city cabarets.

Dances were also a feature in other townships. No excuse was overlooked: to celebrate the arrival of two new planes, the opening of a new store or hotel or to farewell those departing by ship. In Salamaua, W.R.

Carpenter hosted the annual Christmas Eve Ball and its rival, Burns Philp, the New Year's Eve Ball. The Bulolo Orchestra, domiciled in Wau, was kept busy flying between engagements.

In Bulolo, BGD hosted a dance whenever it was asked. Arthur Ives recalled,

> You could invite anyone you wanted from outside, you had to put them up because there were no facilities, but the company would supply the planes, fly them in from Lae and Salamaua, from Wau … and Bulwa, all free. The company put on supper, a sit-down one, about midnight. Roast pork, apple sauce, peas, potatoes, you name it. It cost us 15 shillings a couple to go to the dance, including the supper and the grog. We had a regular band for the music … After the Saturday night dance the company would fly them all back home.[22]

The intensity of sporting competition, with teams and their vanguard of supporters flying back and forth, and the frequency with which many residents flew from one township to another for a specific event—a dance, a party or a dinner, despite the cost of doing so, suggest a slightly manic existence. Together with farewell parties and welcome home parties, life at times seemed one long round of social activity, culminating in Christmas and Easter, the peak times for intra-goldfields travel. The restless ebb and flow of people between townships was quite unlike anything in Australia. Although the District's European population was fewer than 1,700 in 1936, planes flew 16,559 passengers in that year, or nearly one quarter the number of passenger flights in Australia with its population of nearly seven million.

Goldfields humour retained its edginess despite the changed make of its population. In the period leading up to October 1936, patients in Wau hospital were flattered by the number of callers enquiring about their health. They were less impressed when they realised they were among the favourites in the matmat (or cemetery) double being run by a local bookie.[23] To win, a punter had to choose the winner of the Melbourne Cup and someone who had died by Cup Day.

In Bulolo, Cyril Aultrier, a staid Englishman, was upset that his bitch was attracting the unwelcome attention of a number of dogs and fashioned a tin shield to discourage their attentions. Within a few days all the male dogs in town were running round with tin openers attached to their collars.[24]

If goldfield residents were seeking to replicate life in Australia, it was their privileged lifestyle that enabled

Waco 10T biplane. Pilot, Tom O'Dea, with passengers (left) Jack Mitchell (BGD Accountant) and Jack Wood (Bank of NSW, Salamaua).

"All dressed up ..."

them to do it with such unbridled enthusiasm.[25] Women, in particular, usually had a lot more time on their hands than their counterparts in Australia. Ione Hoile, the first European child born in Wau, later recalled

> In large households there is usually one 'boy' for cookery, one for laundry, one for house cleaning and one for messages and gardening ... This leaves plenty of time for tennis, golf, swimming, cards and visiting the club.[26]

And visiting friends in other centres.[27]

The ratio of women to men changed steadily from about one woman for every five men in the early 1930s, to nearly one for two. By September 1941, the European population in the Morobe District was estimated to comprise 828 men, 373 women and 229 children.[28] Not all women were the wives of men working on the field; some were employed by the Administration and companies as typists, stenographers and book keepers, while others worked as barmaids, dressmakers, hairdressers, nurses and house keepers. There were also the wives of Lutheran missionaries at Finschhaffen.

Apart from Alice Innes, 'Ma' Stewart and 'Mum' Bowring, two other women stood out from the rest in bringing 'life' to the goldfields—though in utterly different ways: Connie Hoile and Tiger Lil. Connie Hoile was the driving force behind the Wau Dramatic Society. Each year between 1935 and 1941, she directed several productions as well as a Christmas pantomime involving most of Wau's school children in the picture theatre built by her husband, the sawmiller and former miner Jim Hoile. A highly energetic and talented person, Connie also made the costumes and painted the sets. The well-attended productions contributed greatly to Wau's sense of community.

Tiger Lil was a tall, good-looking blonde who worked the goldfields in her own unique way, accumulating a series of lovers and not a little of their gold.[29]

While most women dressed simply, she always made sure she was the centre of attention. Roy Struben recalled that

> Lil didn't see why she should conform to the majority, and she would appear among the shirt-sleeved clientele on the hotel verandah in marvellous evening gowns, or stroll down the dusty street of Salamaua attired as for a royal garden party.[30]

Bunny Hammond recalled that, at the Wau races in 1933, *Tiger Lil was done up to kill and was the social centre of the visitors at the race course.*[31]

Nevertheless, she could be very intimidating, physically and verbally. She didn't hesitate to put men in their place with a well aimed punch or a withering comment.[32]

Tiger Lil was a source of endless fascination to the men and irritation to the women. When one man was seen dancing a lot with her at a Wau Club dance, Assistant District Officer Black noted that

> All the prim and proper damsels of the town vowed they'd wipe him off their dancing list in future.[33]

Jan Roberts claimed that

> many a ... husband ducked for the exit when Tiger Lil entered the room because she had something over nearly every man who had ever set foot on the goldfields. One wife remembers that 'she had no inhibitions about calling out across crowded rooms and causing untold embarrassment to her old friends'.[34]

The Morobe goldfield needed women like Alice Innes, Flora Stewart, Alice Bowring, Connie Hoile and Tiger Lil, and they were happy to oblige, each in their own distinctive way, enriching those on the field greatly with their zest for life.

But however exhilarating life was for Europeans, it was not without its darker side.

CHAPTER 21
RACE RELATIONS ON THE GOLDFIELDS

In 1940, there were over 12,000 indentured labourers in the Morobe District, the majority on or around the goldfields.

There were also about 1,600 Europeans and as many as 200 Chinese. Administrative regulation enforced racial segregation in New Guinea in a way that was conceptually little different from apartheid in South Africa, and the factors which gave rise to it were much the same.[1] The Administration's policies and, indeed, European attitudes ensured that each group lived a very different existence with little social interaction between them.

From the outset, the vastly disproportionate numbers of New Guineans and Europeans led the Administration to pursue policies designed to establish a social order in which Europeans were both superior and set apart from the country's indigenous inhabitants. A 1923 prohibition on New Guineans wearing European clothes signified their inferior status and so discouraged the forming of relationships between Europeans and New Guineans. Many other rules followed, firmly entrenching racial segregation.

Administrator Wisdom doubtless had in mind preserving the social order when he wrote in 1930 that

> It is not desirable nor should white miners desire, that men should work cheek by jowl with natives.[2]

As E.P. Wolfers noted,

> An Australian who spent too much time with, rather than over, New Guineans was thought to imperil the entire structure of territorial society ... [3]

If they didn't know any better, casual readers of *The Rabaul Times* and *Pacific Islands Monthly* during the 1930s may have concluded that Europeans were the only people on the goldfields. New Guineans and Chinese were rarely mentioned. Only in the late 1930s did they appear more often in reports—usually in a negative light. And yet without New Guinean labour, and to a lesser extent the activities of the Chinese, everyday life would have been much harsher for Europeans and the potential of the goldfields would never have been realised.

At Bulolo, as Healy noted in his monograph, rigid divisions existed between Europeans and New Guineans.[4] Living areas and amenities were separate, and contemporary attitudes and differences in background and culture made meaningful interaction difficult. Neither was there any inter-racial job mobility which might have reduced barriers. BGD's facilities for its labourers were excellent—but separate.

The same comment was broadly true of other townships.[5] NGG's labourers at Edie Creek lived in their own compound, sleeping and eating together and having little or no interaction with Europeans outside working hours. In Wau, Lae and Salamaua labourers working for company employers typically lived in barracks and compounds located at various points around town. Labourers worked under European supervision, but spent the rest of their time with their wantoks and other New Guineans.

Household servants usually lived in their own quarters behind the houses of their employers. Their interaction with Europeans was naturally far greater than labourers', though often still circumscribed by rules that limited social intimacy. Thus, many (though by no means all) Europeans did not permit their servants to look a white woman in the eye, and they were expected to address all Europeans respectfully and stand up when spoken to.

Underpinning the Native Administration Regulations, which governed what New Guineans could and couldn't do, was the principle of the 'white prestige'—the presumed intellectual and moral superiority of Europeans. Keith McCarthy, who had little time for the concept (or evidently for the Administrator's views on the subject), suggested 'white prestige' was less apparent on the goldfields than elsewhere, at least in the early 1930s, which he attributed to the fact that *The miner worked side by side with his native worker*.[6] He doubtless had men such as Jack O'Neill in mind who, working with small teams of labourers in remote locations, grew to respect their abilities and treated them well.

However, many of the new arrivals thereafter happily embraced the idea of 'white prestige', Reed observing that they seemed to take it much more seriously than older residents.[7] It followed that many Europeans believed there was little point wasting money educating New Guineans. Thus in 1929, when the Administration proposed sending seven students to Australia for higher education, strong and apparently widespread objections by European residents led to the scheme being abandoned.[8]

Writing in *The Rabaul Times*, Wau correspondents doubtless reflected the views of many when reporting situations where New Guinean behaviour confronted their sense of propriety. In 1938, one commented that footpaths had been installed in Wau,

> but they are being used by all the natives in town! I think the same rule should apply here as does in Rabaul (and in native countries generally) in that natives should walk close to the side of the road and leave the footpaths to the white population.[9]

Fourteen months later, he (or she) reported somewhat despondently,

> After the construction of footpaths some time ago, natives, including prisoners from the Gaol, took complete possession of them to the exclusion of the white population. The authorities then reserved the footpaths for white people. However, they haven't been maintained and now both whites and natives walk once more on the roads.[10]

In 1939, another correspondent complained of the crowds of New Guineans using the sheds at the Wau Recreation Reserve on weekends when there was no cricket match. *This raises the vexed question: 'Is this Reserve a European Reserve or a Native Reserve? … If reserved for both, then I consider it against all the best traditions of Colonial occupation.*[11]

Such expressions of dissatisfaction reflected a growing concern among many that New Guineans were becoming more contemptuous of authority, whether officials or employers, contributing to a breaking down of existing social structures where each race had its

place. 'White prestige' and the clearly defined separation of the races in everyday life were under threat.

In the 1920s, the shock of the different lifestyle to which new labourers were exposed and the short duration of their indenture meant they usually behaved as Europeans expected them to. Over time, however, an increasing number were on contracts that had been extended, sometimes indefinitely, and as townships grew, many lost contact with their villages and became long term residents. This coincided with the arrival, from about 1935, of more labourers from New Britain and New Ireland, who had long been exposed to European ways and were less inclined to live within their rules. Convictions for drinking, breaking and entering and discipline offences increased.

As concerns grew about abberant New Guinean behaviour, real or imagined, the Native Administration Regulations progressively narrowed the range of activities deemed to be acceptable. By the late 1930s, not only were drinking alcohol, carrying weapons and gambling prohibited, so were being absent from their place of residence between 9 pm and 6 am without reasonable excuse, playing any game in any street in any town, beating drums, singing or dancing in any town after 9 pm, or taking part in any singsing between 11 pm and sunrise. As August Kituai later sadly observed, some of these restrictions helped reduce criminal activities but most simply undermined initiative and took away labourers' self-respect and dignity.[12]

In 1937, Assistant District Officer J.R. Black expressed concern at the spread of 'undisciplined sophistication' among indentured society in the Morobe District. He suggested, as contributing factors, labourers' lack of access to New Guinean women, which was responsible for widespread perversion (i.e. homosexuality), and

> the acquisition of European outlook and with it the desire for white women. Newspaper cuttings of European women in various stages of undress pasted up in indentured labour quarters bears mute but nevertheless strident witness to this unexpressed desire.[13]

Latent fear about possible sexual attacks was fuelled in the 1930s by the increasing number of European women and the disproportionate number of New Guinean labourers and servants. Women arriving in New Guinea were cautioned to be careful in their dress and the way they behaved to avoid creating any problems with their servants, most of whom were men.

The downside, as Nelson later noted, was that *the largely unwritten laws about avoiding sexual excitement and how best to deal with servants stopped many white women from ever knowing Papua New Guineans as ordinary people.*[14]

In fact, sexual assaults on white women appear to have been few in number.[15] But the fear of what might happen generated increasing alarm. The Administration responded with a new criminal offence: *entering or being in a dwelling house with intent to indecently insult a female inmate,* for which about 15 New Guineans a year were convicted between 1935 and 1940.[16] In 1937, a public meeting in Rabaul called attention to *the alarming increase of crimes by natives against European women,*[17] and Reed recorded that

> 'Boy-proof' sleeping rooms, enclosed by heavy chicken wire, were being installed … at government expense, in all houses where European women resided. The fact is, however, that almost all the attacks have taken place in the large towns. White women who live constantly among masses of natives in the outstations cannot understand why those in large European settlements should feel in any danger.[18]

The only violent attack on a European woman on the goldfields occurred as late as 22 June 1941 when the 28 year old Jean Wilson was murdered with an axe. Before she died, she claimed to have been attacked by a native. The murder is noteworthy not for its outcome[19] —the case was never solved—but for the intensity of the previously repressed anger it unleashed towards New Guineans generally.

Remarks by the Anglican Minister, the Rev. V.H. Sherwin, at her funeral service provide an insight to the mood of the Wau community:

> This tragedy is the worst of its kind we've experienced. It marks the logical sequence of a series of offences that have steadily grown from a pianissimo of cheek, arrogance, passive resistance and policy of calculated irritation to a growing tempo of revolt, and exploitation of circumstances in order to gain opportunities for criminal indulgence … Who is to blame? … Progress has been knocking on the door of Central Administration for a long time, and found no response but snores from within. The growing problems of this Territory are becoming too big for the mental capacity of those in authority in Rabaul to adequately deal with.[20]

The following month, a public meeting in Wau formed the Morobe Citizens Association, which adopted a series of recommendations to be forwarded to Rabaul: any native reported not wearing his lavalava in a manner to adequately cover the lower part of the body will be dealt with; the curfew to be amended to 8 pm; natives should not have inappropriate pictures of European women in their possession; and natives convicted of sex offences against white women should be branded on the forehead.[21]

In August 1941, A.J. Bretag, a member of the Legislative Council and owner of the weekly newspaper, *The Morobe News,* made a scathing attack in the Council: Not only were labourers less amenable to discipline, but there were also more frequent displays of open insolence and of women being 'interfered' with, cases where mercury had been placed in milk (his own) and phenyl in the food of other Europeans, 'peeping Tom' behaviour and a general disregard for law and order. He continued:

> In searching natives' boxes in a number of cases, they were found to contain some most intimate feminine garments, either stolen by the possessors or carelessly discarded by the owners … I cannot escape the observation that the customary modesty and delicacy as exercised by our womenfolk in a more civilised community is not sufficient in a country where lascivious attentions are continually being directed against them by the animal instincts of perverted savages … [22]

It is hard to gauge what the outcome might have been of this crescendo of racial hatred had the War not intervened a few months later. However, the fact that most European women entrusted their children to their servants, [23] who were usually New Guinean men, doesn't suggest widespread insecurity about 'native' behaviour. The extent to which the responses to Jean Wilson's murder were born of fear and misplaced male chauvinism, or simply provided a catalyst for expression of latent racial bigotry, remains an open question.

European-Chinese relations involved quite different issues. Chinese immigration had been freely encouraged by the German Administration before World War I, and Chinese residents outnumbered Europeans in the early years of the Australian military and then civil administrations. In October 1923, there were 1,347 Chinese in the Territory, mostly in Rabaul, 67 Japanese and 900 Europeans.[24] Some were traders, store keepers and hotel keepers, but most were artisans—carpenters, plumbers, mechanics, lorry drivers, cooks, bakers, tailors, hairdressers and laundrymen. Rabaul had a thriving Chinatown.

This posed problems for the civil Administration, given the well-entrenched policy in Australia that was designed to exclude Asians—the White Australia Policy. From the outset, Administrator Wisdom made his feelings clear on the subject. In 1923, the Secretary, Department of Home and Territories advised his Minister that *The Administrator is of the opinion that we should discriminate against all Asiatics, or, in any case, against Japanese and Chinese.*[25]

And he proceeded to do so. Chinese (and other 'Asiatics') were not allowed to live on or own land in the European areas of towns, hold long term leases, acquire plantations, possess firearms or engage in recruiting or mining.[26] Neither, of course, were non-resident Chinese allowed to migrate to New Guinea. Permanent Chinese residents who married abroad after 1922 were not permitted to bring their wives and children back to New Guinea.

The Administration employed very few Chinese, even in junior positions—despite the difficulty of attracting staff from Australia.[27] This self-imposed constraint contributed to the Administration's ineffectiveness and finally, in 1935, the Legislative Council unanimously agreed it was *in favour of the employment of natives and of Asiatics born in the Territory, in subordinate positions in the Public Service of the Territory.*[28] It was recognised that there was

a supply of young, efficient, locally-born Asiatics sufficient to fill a considerable number of the subordinate routine positions in the Service … where the official does not exercise any discretion, where he has nothing whatsoever to do with policy.

However, the real attraction was that they could be paid a third as much as Australians and the funds thus released used to attract suitable Australians to more senior positions.

Nevertheless, two years later little seems to have changed, with non-official Council members again debating that the White Australia Policy should be less rigidly enforced in New Guinea than in Australia, with lower grades in the Administration being filled by Asiatics.[29]

The history of Chinese involvement with gold mining in Australia had been a troubled one in the 1850s, when Australian miners' resentment towards industrious Chinese ended in violence on the Buckland River in Victoria and Lambing Flat (now Young) in New South Wales. The origins of the White Australia Policy can be traced to these events.[30] And it was not long before there were echoes of those distant conflicts on the Morobe goldfields.

On 30 December 1928, a meeting of the short-lived Bulolo Goldfields Progress Association unanimously resolved *That this Association considers it would be derogatory to the interests of Europeans to allow Asiatics on this field for the purposes of trading, being employed in any capacity or residing.*[31] It argued that as Asiatics were not allowed to hold Miner's Rights, and thus profit from alluvial mining, it was inconsistent that they should be granted business licences on a goldfield entitling them to profit by trading. Other reasons given were the prevalence of gold stealing when they were allowed on a goldfield, the inability of Europeans to compete against them because of their low standard of living, their unscrupulous exploitation of natives when trading, and the dissemination of venereal disease and consumption (tuberculosis) among the native population. Mining Warden McLean was clearly of like mind, replying that *It is not my intention to grant business areas to Asiatics in localities on the Goldfields situated in a favourable position for the carrying on of gold stealing.*[32]

Given such attitudes and restrictions on their activities, far fewer Chinese found their way to the goldfields than lived in Rabaul. By 1941, there were

Chinese cooks and New Guinean mess staff employed by BGD, October 1932.

about 60 Chinese living in Lae, half the number of Europeans. Many had arrived in the early 30s as carpenters, mechanics and gardeners, but as their wages were half (or less) those of Europeans, some opened trade stores to earn extra income. NGG and BGD employed a few Chinese, mainly as cooks—but never in connection with mining activities. There were two Chinese eating houses, both well patronised by Europeans, Ah Mang's in Salamaua and Ah Pang's in Wau. And there were small numbers of Chinese working in the different townships as carpenters, cooks, tailors, hairdressers and as trade store proprietors.

If the discriminatory restrictions under which the Chinese lived and worked affected them, they didn't show it. They kept to themselves, having little to do with Europeans socially, and for all practical purposes were model citizens. Their most visible activity was their trade stores—meeting the needs of labourers on the field and those being repatriated at the end of their indenture.

In Salamaua, from where most goldfields labourers were repatriated, there were a dozen Chinese trade stores in 1933, half of them in town and half in Chinatown, out past Kela. Being prohibited from having shops in European areas, it was common practice for Chinese traders in Salamaua to pay Europeans to be nominal licence holders. The Administration was well aware of this blatant side-stepping of its rules, but did nothing about it.

Europeans were contemptuous of what they regarded as the exploitation of labourers by Chinese trade stores. As early as 1921, Administrator Wisdom argued that to pay New Guineans more was *only to … enrich the Asiatic trader,*[33] while many years later Bert Weston recalled that after labourers had been paid off, *Usually the local Chinese trade store owners would be hovering in the background and would bear off the newly rich to their places of business extortion …* [34]

However, Willis gives another perspective. He cites a local missionary in 1933 who observed that *Chinese store keepers were popular among the villagers because they 'gave their customers consideration' the people were not used to receiving from the Europeans.* His report continued that, by being patient and smiling, the Chinese had *an immense amount of power over the naïve natives.*[35] Willis concluded that *Doubtless the Chinese wanted just as much from the New Guinean as the white man did but he was more subtle in his approach …* [36]

There appears to have been only one instance where the Chinese aroused the ire of Europeans in Wau. From 1937, reports in *The Rabaul Times* indicated growing concern about the operation of Chinese stores in the European residential area. By July 1940, it was claimed that they were spreading everywhere and that

> Wau (was) becoming an unpleasant place for Europeans to walk around in, especially at weekends, owing to the hoards of natives who hang around the stores and commit nuisances all over the place.[37]

The Administration seems finally to have acted in response to these complaints, as in November *The Rabaul Times* reported that the lower end of Wau was being rewired so as to enable a Chinatown to be established.[38] A year later, peace seems to have been restored, and the Mining Warden was able to report that

> The recently established Chinatown at Wau has grown rapidly … It is difficult to perceive how such a large number of Chinese, all plying a similar type of business can profitably carry on … [39]

It is noteworthy that the problem was not seen by Europeans to be the Chinese themselves. Indeed, a letter in *The Rabaul Times* seemed anxious to distance the writer from any suggestion of anti-Chinese sentiment:

> We have no grudge against the Chinese, in fact we realise their many estimable qualities, but it is largely the congregation of natives in the residential area which their stores attract which forms the nuisance.[40]

Although the segregation of Europeans and non-Europeans was largely achieved by administrative regulation, there were no such requirements preventing closer relationships between Chinese and New Guineans. Certainly, enormous cultural differences discouraged the formation of close social ties. But the barriers between the two racial groups were far less rigid than with Europeans and clearly there was social contact, as many Chinese men took New Guinean wives or formed relationships with New Guinea women. No doubt, restrictions on Chinese residents marrying in China and bringing their wives back to New Guinea contributed to this. But the fact that Chinese seem usually to have shown New Guineans greater respect than Europeans did at least provided a basis for greater social intercourse.

CHAPTER 22
THE COMING OF WAR

*New Guinea residents were more sensitive than most Australians
to the deteriorating political situation in Europe during the 1930s,
fearing that, sooner or later, Germany would seek to reclaim its former colony.*

In 1935, German nationals comprised more than 10% of the European population.[1] Although the majority were missionaries, many were far from apolitical. When the German Consul in Sydney, Dr. Hellenthal, visited New Guinea in 1936, he reported that *The Lutheran mission in Finschhafen, over which reigns an excellent national-socialist spirit, had decorated all stations I visited with Swastika flags.*[2] He was greeted by a native band playing Horst Wessel-Lied, the Nazi Party's official anthem, and reported that *all hope naturally for a speedy return of the colony to Germany.*

Such behaviour naturally caused unease among Australians in the Territory.[3] Whatever the desires of Germans located there, however, there is little evidence that the German Government seriously considered reclaiming New Guinea. Although it periodically raised the possibility, this seems to have been more to highlight the 'injustice' of Germany's treatment after World War 1, than to indicate any real intent.[4]

Nevertheless, as tensions rose in Europe, New Guinea residents became more apprehensive, the Bank of New South Wales in Salamaua reporting in April 1939 that *The situation in Europe has had its effect on every class of business and on the people generally.*[5]

———

Two 'domestic' issues were also disturbing the harmony of the goldfields.

In late May-early June 1937, Rabaul was severely damaged in a volcanic eruption. After investigations confirmed that further eruptions were likely, the Government decided to move the capital to the New Guinea mainland, and a committee headed by the former Administrator, Brigadier-General Griffiths, was appointed to advise on the best location. In April 1938, it recommended Lae, with Salamaua as its port and a road connecting the two towns.

The Minister in charge of Territories at this time was former Prime Minister, Billy Hughes. In his inimitable autocratic style, he rejected the Griffiths Committee's views, and in June announced that the Government had instead chosen Salamaua as both port and capital, for good measure adding that a road would be built from there to Wau. While the road proposal was widely welcomed by miners, the decision to make Salamaua the capital attracted howls of derision.

Administrator McNicoll had favoured Salamaua and this doubtless influenced Hughes. But he seems not to have done his homework, as when he visited there in July 1938 with senior officials of the Public Works and Lands Departments, McNicoll realised the shortage of land made Salamaua unsuitable. To reclaim the surrounding swamps would be very costly. This, and the generally hostile reaction, forced the Government to reconsider its decision.

In November 1938, Eric Harrison replaced Hughes, and announced an enquiry into the possibility of combining the administrations of Papua and New Guinea. In the meantime, Salamaua would be the 'temporary capital' of New Guinea with the Departments of Customs and Public Works moving there immediately from Rabaul.

The Committee appointed to undertake the enquiry reported in August 1939. It recommended against amalgamation and reaffirmed that Lae should be the new capital. However, with the outbreak of war in Europe the Government decided the time was not right to transfer the Administration.

Further seismic disturbances in Rabaul in the first half of 1941 and continuing Government indecision amidst a political crisis in Canberra, finally led McNicoll to announce unilaterally that the Administration would move to Lae—and the Government belatedly endorsed this in September 1941. The transfer of some departments began immediately, McNicoll arriving there in late November.

***

In July 1938, the Government enacted legislation guaranteeing repayment of a loan not exceeding £150,000 for the construction of a road between Salamaua and Wau.[6] However, the route it would follow remained undecided. Broadly speaking, the choice was between a direct route to Wau via the Bitoi River (the short route) and one skirting Lae and then via the Markham valley and the Wampit (the long route).

The Administration favoured the latter which, though 118 miles in length, would open agricultural and timber country to the north-west of the Markham Valley. The New Guinea Mining Association pressed vigorously for the short route—a distance of about 49 miles—and in September 1938 the largest public meeting ever held in Wau also voiced its support.

Surveyors and engineers equivocated over which route was the most practical and, indeed, whether any road at all could be constructed for £150,000. Over the next three years, the Administration intermittently announced decisions on the road, and as regularly reversed them. Having been promised a road, the miners were increasingly critical of the Administration's indecisiveness and the interminable delays. But their concerns counted for little; by the end of 1941, the Administration was still no closer to a final decision on the route, much less a start on construction.[7]

***

The outbreak of war in Europe in September 1939 raised the question of New Guinea's defence. The apprehension of the Territory's residents about Germany's intentions was clearly not shared by the Australian Government. Nor were the Japanese seen as an immediate threat. The USA and Australia had been concerned about Japan's expansionary intentions in the Western Pacific since the early days of World War I, and these concerns intensified in the mid-1930s when Japan withdrew from the League of Nations and fortified the Caroline Islands, a former German possession north of New Guinea. Nevertheless, Australia took comfort from Japan's decision not to enter the War on Germany's side in 1939 and deployed most of its forces in Europe.

Australia had observed its obligations under the League of Nations Mandate, which prohibited the establishment of naval bases or military fortifications or the military training of New Guineans other than for internal policing and local defence.[8] Although the Mandate clearly permitted the training of New Guineans to defend the Territory, no effort had been made to do so. New Guinea was completely defenceless against possible future German or Japanese aggression.

Despite this, and notwithstanding its concerns about Japanese expansionism, Australia's response was more symbolic than practical.

On 4 September 1939, the Government authorised the Administrator to form a volunteer defence force, comprising 20 officers and 400 other ranks.[9] To be called the New Guinea Volunteer Rifles, or NGVR, it would be headquartered in Rabaul, with a rifle company and a machine gun platoon at Wau and rifle platoons at Lae and Salamaua. In December, a medical detachment was authorised, to be located at Bulolo. Amidst great enthusiasm, detachments were raised within six weeks at all four goldfields towns. Training was held at weekends and holidays, and over the next six months, whenever there was sufficient ammunition, shooting competitions were held at rifle ranges constructed at Lae, Salamaua, Bulolo, Wau and Edie Creek.

However until the arrival of an AIF battalion (Lark Force), in Rabaul in April 1941, no Australian troops were transferred to New Guinea. Nor was any effort made to train New Guineans to assist in the possible defence of the Territory or to establish fortifications on the mainland that might be used to resist an invader.

***

After the initial flurry of activity, including a number of young men leaving for Australia to enlist, life on the goldfields continued much as normal, although irregular shipping schedules sometimes disrupted mail deliveries and supplies. Occasionally departures south also left the field without a necessary service (whether teacher or bootmaker) or an employer with insufficient employees.

Early in 1940, the death occurred of two of the early miners whose early exploits were commemorated in Wau by streets named after them. Ernie Dover died in January in Wau hospital,[10] a victim of scrub typhus, while in February Shark-Eye Park died in Vancouver, still wealthy from his Koranga Creek discovery. A third pioneer, George Arnold, had died in April 1939. George had spent 46 years as a miner in Papua and then in New Guinea, and been immensely popular throughout the field.[11]

Internment camp, Salamaua, 1941.

The War was far away and although there was some nervousness about the Japanese, goldfield residents went out of their way to maintain a sense of normality. In Salamaua, attendance at the Burns Philp New Year's Eve ball at the end of 1939 was the largest ever. Sporting events continued, the Wau Dramatic Society put on new productions and dances were held regularly in all centres. But the drift of residents back to Australia continued, and by September 1940 the goldfields population had declined by at least 200.

Not all this outflow was voluntary. A number of Germans, most of them missionaries, were interned after the outbreak of war and shipped back to Australia. The goldfields were not greatly affected, but it was a different matter when Italy entered the War on 10 June 1940. The next day, the NGVR rounded up every Italian on the field and interned them at Wau. As they included 25 miners employed at Edie Creek and a smaller number at Golden Ridges, this seriously affected NGG's operations. Elsewhere, a fairly large scale operation on the Upper Watut run by a group of eight to ten Italians, known as the Bulowat syndicate, came to an abrupt halt.

While the NGVR was acting on orders, some found it hard to take this seriously, as the Italians were friends to many. Horrie Harris, with the Bank of New South Wales in Wau, later recalled:

> They were held under guard pending despatch to Australia, and sometimes they would ask their NGVR guard to bring up a case of beer and charge it to their account at the local store. Upon arrival … the guard would often stand his rifle in the corner of the room and help them drink the beer … The Italians wanted to join the NGVR and help us, which to me would have been OK.[12]

On 8 July, the internees were transferred to Salamaua, where they were briefly interned in the European hospital. Many years later, Bob Emery, who was with the NGVR, reflected on the perversity of the situation, where *We were outside in tents and all these 'wops' are in the hospital on the verandah with electric light, playin' concertinas and singin' and havin' a helluva time and we're out in the rain guardin' them.*[13] In late July, together with other internees taken on board in Rabaul, all 42 Salamaua internees were shipped off to Australia.[14]

During 1940, Japan's militarism in south-east Asia, and particularly its invasion of French Indochina in September, contributed to increasing apprehension in political and military circles in Australia.

There had been signs of greater Japanese interest in New Guinea for some time. Bert Weston observed visits in the late 1930s,

> by a number of navy type Japanese sloops which were designated as Fisheries Research craft. They were heavily manned by cadets and these would come ashore in immaculate white uniforms and hung around with a variety of cameras. In a chartered plane they would do a day tour of all goldfield areas snapping pictures from aloft and on the ground. At night powerful searchlights would traverse the Salamaua waterfront from end to end, pausing for a long look at each feature.[15]

Elsewhere in New Guinea, Mary Murray was also concerned. *In 1941 it became noticeable that the ship* [*Carolina Maru*] *was making frequent calls at Territory ports, although on some trips she brought little, if any cargo.* But on each trip it brought 'students', often of mature age, who took an active interest in the wharves, shipping, how many Europeans there were in the vicinity, transport arrangements, the local airfield, and so on.[16] In this way, the Japanese gradually developed a first hand knowledge of New Guinea port facilities and other infrastructure that was to prove useful in 1942.

But for most goldfield residents, the War was still far away. During 1940, there was a frenzy of fund raising for the war effort in Europe. Concerts and fetes, sports carnivals and picnic race meetings were held to raise funds, the main recipients being the Red Cross, the London Relief Fund, the Australian Comforts Fund and the Overseas Ambulance Appeal. By late 1940, inspired by the Battle of Britain, most fund-raising activity was focused on a single objective: the Morobe Spitfire Fund Appeal. The cost of a spitfire plane was £6,250 and, as *Pacific Islands Monthly* recorded in January 1941, *already there is rivalry between the five sections of the Morobe Goldfield as to which can, per capita of population, make the best showing in this contribution to Britain's war effort.*

By May 1941, half the cost of a Spitfire had been remitted to London. Donations flowed in more slowly over the following months, with the balance being raised late in the year in a competition between the 'Queens' of Aviation, Mining, Nursing, Commerce, RSL

and Sport. The final down payment on the 'Morobe Spitfire' was never made, as a month later the Japanese attacked the New Guinea mainland.[17]

By 1941, the early enthusiasm of NGVR members had faded. Tired of waiting for something to happen, many of the younger men had left for Australia to enlist. For those remaining, the endless training and lack of ammunition made it difficult to maintain their commitment, and numbers dwindled. In April 1941, the arrival in Rabaul of Lark Force, the 2/22nd Battalion of the 8th Division AIF, enabled the NGVR headquarters to be transferred to Bulolo under a new Commanding Officer, Major W.M. (Bill) Edwards.[18] He set about restoring numbers and morale, and by December the mainland strength of the NGVR was around 175 – a tiny force of bank tellers, dredge hands, mechanics, farmers and the like who 'soldiered' in their spare time.

Any sense of detachment changed abruptly with the Japanese attack on Pearl Harbour on 7 December 1941. The war was no longer something happening 'over there', though Jeanette Leahy recalled the general feeling that the Japanese would never get past Singapore.[19] And so there was considerable annoyance when, on 12 December, the Government decided that women and children, other than missionaries and nurses who elected to remain, were to be compulsorily evacuated.

Earlier in the year, as a defence precaution, a census had been undertaken of all non-indigenous people in the Morobe District.[20] While some had since departed, the authorities were well prepared and the evacuation proceeded with remarkable efficiency. Women and children in Lae and Salamaua were flown directly to Port Moresby, while Wau was used as a marshalling point for all others on the mainland – women and children being flown in from outlying centres. The first evacuees left on 18 December and by Christmas Day in Wau and Bulolo only men remained. Once in Port Moresby, many were evacuated by ship, while others were flown to Australia.

Altogether, 739 women and 471 children were evacuated from New Guinea. A telling oversight, however, was the omission of all Chinese women and children. Horrie Niall, who was arranging the evacuation later wrote …

> unfortunately no direction was given regarding the Chinese population and they were left behind. Later

Evacuation day, Salamaua, 1941.

on we were able to evacuate the Chinese women and children from Salamaua and Wau, but those at Lae and the other centres had to remain.[21]

With women and children gone, preparations were made for the coming assault. At all centres, slit trenches were constructed in which those remaining could take refuge should the need arise. At Bulolo, the aerodrome was protected by six thick steel cables, hoisted and lowered by winches, and an anti-aircraft pit manned by a Lewis machine gun of World War I vintage. Through all this, the dredges continued working as usual.

Japanese aircraft began bombing Rabaul on 4 January, when 22 Type 96 Mitsubishi bombers, based in Truk, launched a daytime raid. Intermittent attacks followed and then on 20 January Rabaul was attacked by 100 bombers and fighters. The following day, at 11.50 am, Patrol Officer Lloyd Pursehouse in Finschhafen radioed that 60 Japanese aircraft were headed for Lae and Salamaua. Five minutes later, 27 fighters and bombers struck Lae, raking the town with machine gun and cannon fire and then bombing from a low level.

The Administrator, Sir Walter McNicoll, had malaria and was running a high fever. Writing to his son afterwards, he said

I could see the planes through the verandah, three flights of nine each in good formation. My two helpers got me on my feet but the machine gunning started around our ears while we were on the short track to the slit trench. All three got in and spent the hour there. Three bombs fell in garden and vicinity and scattered mud on us but no serious damage to our new GH. All the buildings and planes of Guinea Airways were destroyed and every house was machine gunned ... [22]

The attack lasted 55 minutes. None of the 100 or so Europeans in Lae were injured, but all Guinea Airways' hangars, workshops and stores, the power house and six planes were destroyed. However, the early warning had enabled four planes to get away.

The Japanese strike force had split, with 24 fighters and bombers attacking Salamaua. Passing over the isthmus, the planes directed their attack mainly at the aerodrome. In an attack lasting 40 minutes, four planes were destroyed, along with various workshops and hangars; a few buildings on the isthmus were machine gunned. Les Ross was beginning his landing approach in the Guinea Airways G31, but pulled out when he saw the attackers and flew back to Wau.[23] Less fortunate was Kevin Parer. Sitting in the cockpit of his DH84 Dragon at the seaward end of the aerodrome, he was about to take off when the Japanese fighters swept in behind him over Bayern Bay; he died in a hail of machine gun fire.

Bulolo received a warning of the enemy planes from Lae at 11.59. The air raid alert was sounded, power to the dredges was switched off and the cables across the airstrip were raised to prevent landings. Suddenly Bert Heath appeared in his G31 carrying three tons of Foster's lager. Buster Mills had moved to the weapons pit on the edge of the runway:

> Panic set in as we waved him away while we cleared the obstructions, then after the landing two of our members started replacing them again. Before this could happen, five Japanese zeros arrived hedge hopping with the sound of angry bees. We were now between three large cargo planes or should I say targets and for the next 15 minutes we were treated to a magnificent display of flying as they swept back and forth over our heads. By this time our magazines of World War 1 ammunition had been used up without visible effect and of course the three burning cargo planes no longer needed our protection … As for the beer from Bert Heath's plane, the top layers had burnt from the heat but a good supply of refreshment was still useable from the bottom.[24]

Mingisin, a labourer from the East Sepik, had a different perspective:

> On Saturday we were walking along—then all of a sudden they came and destroyed the planes on the airstrip. We ran in all directions to hide. Some hid in the grass, others hid in the timber shed, while others hid in the bush or in the stone quarry. Some simply laid down in the grass where they were. 'What was it that was shaking the ground everywhere?' we asked. It was the bombs falling.[25]

Three days later, Fred Godden, BGD's General Manager, noted in his diary:

> Charlie Blake arrived here today and had an interesting tale to tell. He had just walked in from Lae … On the day of the attack on Bulolo, he was near the Wampit and saw Bert Heath going in to Bulolo on the last trip of UOV. About a mile behind him, and a good bit higher, were the zeros that attacked Bulolo. They were cruising round and round and keeping behind the Junker, evidently depending on it to guide them in.

'Pat' on Bulolo aerodrome, 21 January 1942.

When they were in a position to see Bulolo, Blake said they veered off and let the Junker land, and then went in and attacked.[26]

Wau escaped on this occasion, as the planes that attacked Bulolo turned east to return to the coast before reaching it. This was fortunate, as there were five planes on the Wau aerodrome, including Guinea Airways' G31 VH-UOW, the only planes remaining on the field.[27] In the three attacks, the popular Kevin Parer was the only person killed. The following day, the Japanese assault on New Guinea began in earnest when 5,000 Japanese troops launched a massive attack on Rabaul, overwhelming the 1,400-strong Lark Force garrison.

Half an hour after the Japanese left Lae, McNicoll, weak from malaria, agreed with Major Jenyns, second in charge of the NGVR, that a state of emergency existed and told him to 'take over' with his soldiers. He also ordered Ted Taylor who, for much of the 1930s, had been District Officer for Morobe, to arrange the evacuation of all men unfit for military service from Lae, Salamaua, and Wau. After a couple of days in secluded bush camps behind both towns, their evacuation began. Most left Lae for Wau on foot, drifting in over several days early in February.[28] The 70 or so in Salamaua split into two groups. One party travelled by canoe down the coast to Buna and were then evacuated by air to Port Moresby; the other struggled on foot for six to seven days over the old trails, much of the time in torrential rain, until they reached Wau.

Not surprisingly, most labourers deserted Lae and Salamaua after the attacks. In Salamaua, Palili, of Mambuk village in the East Sepik, decided to stay with the Australians. But he later recalled:

Some men ran away and headed towards the Sepik. They were very strong and after walking and fighting their way through, they came to Wewak. There the kiap told them to go on to their villages.[29]

Frightened by the bombing of the aerodrome nearby, the people of Logui village moved up into Kaiwa territory in the hills.[30]

Only a handful of NGVR men remained behind. Those in Lae destroyed most of what had survived the Japanese assault, including the steam crane, a fuel dump and surplus stores, before retreating into the jungle. The handful of NGVR men in Salamaua remained there for several days refuelling RAAF aircraft which arrived periodically. However, when an RAAF pilot reported Japanese shipping possibly moving towards the mainland, the military authorities in Port Moresby ordered them to destroy all they could. That evening they threw petrol over the main offices, the stores and the sprawling Salamaua Hotel, burning them to the ground.

Thus by the end of January 1942, virtually nothing remained of the two coastal townships which for so long had been pivotal to the goldfields' success.

At Bulolo and Bulwa, some of the dredges continued working after the attack, before finally ceasing operations on 24 January when all remaining NGVR personnel were mobilised. Jim Huxley, an oiler on No. 8 dredge at Bulwa, recalled the feeling of shock: *In a sudden fleeting moment on 21 January 1942, I went from a full-time dredge hand and part time Army 'hacker' to a full time soldier, serving in Australia's front line.*[31] With the dredges at a standstill, all BGD employees who weren't NGVR members, including Fred Godden, moved to Wau.

By late January, men were streaming in there from all over. Many were flown out to Port Moresby under RAAF escort on whatever planes were available. Before long, however, the hard-pressed RAAF planes were needed elsewhere. Ted Taylor moved the majority of those remaining to an improvised refugee camp at Edie Creek while arrangements were made for them to travel overland to Port Moresby. Eventually, about 250 men in several groups, supported by carriers, made their way on foot through difficult country as far as Bulldog, several days walk south-west of Wau, then by canoe along the Lakekamu River to the Papuan coast, and finally east to Port Moresby by whatever means they could.

So far, Wau had escaped the enemy's attentions. However, on 1 February, nine four-engined Japanese flying boats bombed the top end of the aerodrome. Damage was limited—the Regent picture theatre being the main casualty. Gotokwa Bengo from the East Sepik later recalled:

Early one morning to our surprise, Mr Knight told us that work was now finished and that we could now go home by road. When it was lunch time, we were all getting ready for our walk home. Suddenly we heard planes roaring in the distance and then we saw things falling out of these planes. On reaching the ground, they burst, causing fires and damaging things in their vicinity. Mr Knight quickly warned us that we must move out that night, because the war was coming that way soon. This was the first bombing of Wau.[32]

The second occurred a month later, on 1 March. Coleman O'Loghlen recalled:

> About mid-morning some bombers came over quite high in a formation of three Vs. They made a dummy run, a wide leisurely circle and then their run. They bombed between the two top-to-bottom roads with a mix of high-explosive, anti-personnel and incendiary and with a copybook demonstration of carpet bombing … The central commercial and industrial part of the town was between these roads and was thoroughly worked over.[33]

This time the damage was much greater, with Guinea Airways' offices, shops, the bank, Anglican Church, Masonic Temple, Wau Club, Savoy Café and Wau Hotel all destroyed.

In February 1942, the civilian governments in Papua and New Guinea were suspended, with Brigadier Morris, who commanded the 8th Military District,[34] assuming responsibility. Early in March, he formed the Papuan and the New Guinea Administrative Units. On 21 March, following the Japanese landings at Lae and Salamaua, these were merged to form the Australia New Guinea Administrative Unit, or ANGAU. It comprised members of the two pre-war Administrations and other experienced residents of both Papua and New Guinea, and was responsible for maintaining law and order and medical services in areas not occupied by the Japanese and marshalling the resources of land and people for the war effort.[35]

With few troops available to defend the New Guinea mainland, a 'scorched earth' policy was central to the Army's strategy. However before leaving Bulolo in late January, Godden sought and obtained a commitment from the NGVR Commanding Officer, Major Edwards, that if the situation deteriorated, the dredges would be immobilised rather than destroyed.[36]

Steam crane, Lae, after demolition.

Machine shop, Bulolo, after demolition.

But there was no such commitment regarding other BGD infrastructure, and on 19 February, in response to an order from Port Moresby, Edwards reported:

> From and including Bulolo power house to Upper Baiune Power House have been prepared for demolition being all mechanic shops and plant therein all stores and cranes freezing plants oxygen plants all garages carpenters shops and plant and particularly 11 aeroplane engines ... Key moveable parts are being removed from good deal dredging plant.[37]

On 5 March, during an attack on Bulolo by five Japanese bombers, a bomb landed outside the Machine Shop, setting off the demolition charges there and in nearby buildings. Most of the support facilities for the dredges at Bulolo were completely destroyed.

Three days later, 3,000 Japanese troops landed virtually unopposed at Lae and Salamaua in the pre-dawn darkness. Apparently fearing that the Japanese would advance on Wau, the 8th Military District HQ immediately instructed the NGVR to destroy Wau airfield. At Bulolo, Major Edwards was concerned that the Japanese might attack with airborne troops if the heavy cloud cover lifted, but lost radio contact with his forward observation posts and so was unaware of what was happening at the coast. Having been warned not to leave demolitions until too late, he authorised

destruction of the three power houses, three bridges over the Bulolo River, and BGD's refrigeration plant, derricks, European hospital and stores.

The scale of this destruction caused BGD much angst, Les Waterhouse complaining to the Government that

> the Power Houses and machines in the Machine Shop could have been rendered inoperative by simply removing vital parts and burying them or removing them to some place where they could not possibly be located.[38]

Pressure by Waterhouse eventually secured an acknowledgement from the Army in July that, as certain vital dredge parts had been removed, *This should eliminate any necessity for destruction in the face of direct threat of possession by enemy.*[39] Subsequent events suggest it was perhaps just as well that he obtained this commitment.

For four months after the attacks on Lae, Salamaua and Bulolo, 250 thinly scattered NGVR troops were the only Australian military force in New Guinea. In late May, a new guerrilla group, called Kanga Force and commanded by Lieutenant Colonel Norman Fleay, established its headquarters in Wau. Kanga Force comprised the NGVR and about 450 reinforcements; its role was to harass and destroy enemy personnel.

Fleay was 25 years old with no New Guinea experience or knowledge of tropical conditions. An incident in early August, also raised questions about his judgement.

Asked by Canberra to comment on the demolitions by Major Edwards on 8 March, Fleay said

> It is my opinion that all demolitions were unnecessary and were the result of needless panic by the persons authorising them [and that] the removal of small essential parts would have been all that was necessary.[40]

Although the events concerned had preceded his arrival, Fleay's indictment of Major Edwards' actions was expressed without waiting for a report from him, which he only received a week later.[41] Less than four weeks later, Fleay himself ordered scorched earth activity on an even greater scale, a decision roundly condemned by New Guinea residents for many years afterwards.

In August 1942, knowing they were under observation by Australians, the Japanese at Salamaua engaged in a strategy of deception. Troops were seen moving daily along the coast between Salamaua and Lae, creating the impression that they were building their numbers and planning an assault inland. However, as Jim Huxley later recorded,

> According to young Buang villagers, who had been watching them, the Japs marched their troops out of Salamaua along the coastal tracks in daylight and then took them back to Salamaua by barge at night. They repeated this manoeuvre quite often to give the impression they had many more troops than they had. This information ... was reported to Lieutenant-Colonel Fleay in Wau..[42]

Despite this advice, however, Fleay was convinced that a Japanese attack was imminent and, in the eyes of most of the NGVR troops under his command, he panicked, deciding on a strategic withdrawal. The official War History records the events that followed:

At 3 pm on the 30th (August) Fleay issued instructions for the 'scorching' of the Bulolo valley and withdrawal to Winima and Kudjeru ... As darkness fell, the camp buildings and any others still standing in Wau township were set alight. Equipment, stores, ammunition that could not be carried, blazed in great fires. At Bulolo, Bulwa and Sunshine, the demolition parties worked steadily with petrol and dynamite. The night resounded with explosions and demolition charges were blown on the Wau and other aerodromes, roads were cratered and bridges shattered. By midnight the main body of troops was clear of the smoke and glowing embers that marked Wau.[43] Every house, every building in Wau, Bulolo and Bulwa was systematically destroyed. The devastation was total.

Only the disabled dredges remained.

⸻

And so the cycle of destruction that began with the Japanese attacks on 21 January 1942 was finally completed by the Australian forces. Of the vibrant goldfield towns of the 1930s, nothing but memories remained.

The Japanese never occupied Wau or Bulolo. The furthest point they reached in the Bulolo valley was the foot of Wau aerodrome. Here they were turned back with heavy losses in the Battle for Wau in January-February 1943. Lae and Salamaua remained in enemy hands for 18 months, eventually being recaptured in September 1943.

Of the four Junkers G31s, which more than anything symbolised the extraordinary achievements on the Morobe goldfields in the 1930s, only Guinea Airways' VH-UOW survived—though not for long. It flew to Australia on 30 January 1942 with Guinea Airways staff and their families, and was impressed by the RAAF for use as an air ambulance. However, after an accident on 31 October 1942, it was written off and broken up for parts.

Part 7

Administration of New Guinea between the Wars

Brigadier General E.A. Wisdom, 1923.

Brigadier General T. Griffiths.

Brigadier General (Sir) W.R. McNicoll.

The First Legislative Council in New Guinea.

Left to Right—Back Row: Mr. J. C. Mullaly (planter), Dr. E. T. Brennan (Director of Public Health), Messrs. W. E. Grose (planter), G. G. Hogan (Crown Law Officer), H. H. Page (Government Secretary), A. N. McLennan (Mining Representative), E. W. P. Chinnery (Director of District Services and Native Affairs), B. B. Perriman (Commercial Representative). Front Row: Messrs. N. P. H. Neal (miner), V. A. Pratt (planter), E. P. Holmes (Secretary for Lands), General Griffiths (Administrator), Messrs. R. L. Clark (Commercial Representative), G. H. Murray (Director of Agriculture), H. O. Townsend (Treasurer).

New Guinea Legislative Council, 1933.

CHAPTER 23

HOW COULD SO MUCH GO SO WRONG?

A full history of the administration of New Guinea under the League of Nations Mandate has yet to be written – a challenging task given the destruction of its records by the Japanese between 1942–1943.

However, the key elements are clear, and being pivotal to the country's history at this time, the Morobe goldfields provide a prism through which one can view the Administration's performance.

The critic will point to the lack of economic or social progress in two decades of civilian administration.[1] The economy was dominated by copra production in 1921 and by gold and copra twenty years later; other agricultural development was negligible. In 1940, little more than 40% of the country was deemed to be 'under control', with 30% unpenetrated and thus outside the scope of any administrative activity. Communications were largely non-existent.

Headquartered in Rabaul on New Britain, the Administration allocated resources disproportionately there and on nearby New Ireland although only one fifth of the 'enumerated population' lived there.[2] The Administration's road construction record was deplorable – only 799 miles of roads existed in 1940. Of these, 60% were on New Britain and New Ireland, but only 10% in the Morobe District – the main revenue-generating area. In 1940, there were six government schools with about 500 New Guinean pupils – all but one in New Britain or New Ireland.

The apologist will point to the enormous difficulties – that the indigenous population was widely dispersed over inaccessible country, spoke hundreds of languages and, unlike African colonies, had no hereditary chiefs to whom administrative responsibilities could be delegated. Nevertheless, they will argue, the Administration succeeded in eliminating warfare across large areas, improved the health of many thousands of villagers and, through the indentured labour system, introduced them to European civilisation without significant detribalisation and its attendant social problems.

Neither perspective is particularly satisfactory – not least because both ignore the other 'players': the Australian (Commonwealth) Government and the Permanent Mandates Commission of the League of Nations. Their policies and views exerted powerful pressures on the Administration and had much to do with the outcomes achieved between 1921 and 1942.

In arguing for control over New Guinea at Versailles in 1919, Prime Minister Billy Hughes was concerned only with Australia's security. As Charles Rowley observed, *His was the pessimism of the practical man: there would be other wars, and sovereign control of New Guinea was, he assumed, strategically essential for the next.*[3]

The Territory's development and the welfare of its people mattered little to Hughes. More important was that New Guinea should not become a drain on Australia's resources. And so, with the Mandate secured, the Government made a policy decision that determined the Territory's future, with repercussions through to the present day: it determined that New Guinea should be financially self-supporting. Rowley summed up its philosophy:

> Broadly, the role of the Government here as in colonies elsewhere was to bring the benefits of law and order. In the main, Government expenditure on education, health and agriculture had to be limited to what the colonial economy could afford from its own revenue; as revenue depended on the expansion of the cash economy, conditions favourable to its growth had to be maintained, such as for instance the availability of 'native' labour.[4]

There was a long tradition that colonies should be self-supporting and, indeed, make an economic contribution to their parent. The British Empire had developed on that basis. However, by the early 20th Century, there was growing recognition that the major powers had a responsibility for their colonies' indigenous inhabitants. Germany expended considerable amounts in New Guinea in the years leading up to World War I, providing a subsidy of about £85,000 in the last complete year of the German administration.[5]

The changing philosophy was also reflected in the wording of the Mandate. Article 22 of the League's Covenant stated, as a fundamental principle, that the *well-being and development* of the inhabitants of former colonies such as German New Guinea, form *a sacred trust of civilisation*. Reflecting this, Article 2 of Australia's mandate required it to *promote to the utmost the material and moral well-being and the social progress of the inhabitants of the territory …*[6]

If the Government saw any inconsistency between the 'sacred trust' and its intention to make the Territory financially self-reliant, it appears simply to have ignored it. The *New Guinea Act 1920*, which provided the framework for the Territory's administration, legislated the various obligations required by the Mandate[7] — with the singular exception of Article 2. The Act merely noted that the Minister's annual report to the League's Council needed to include information on the well-being and progress of the native inhabitants.

The Government was far more interested in expropriating German property and businesses, both as reparation for some of its losses in the Great War and the employment opportunities they would provide for returned soldiers. To this end, it established two parallel organisations: the Expropriation Board and the civil Administration. Their respective administrative arrangements clearly reflected the Government's priorities.

The Board's Chairman, W.H. Lucas, who had previously been Island Inspector for Burns Philp, was also 'Technical Adviser to the Commonwealth Government upon all matters appertaining to German New Guinea'. This required him to spend most of his time in Melbourne where, as Charles Rowley noted, he *had direct access to the Prime Minister, and was soon the real power in the Territory.*[8]

In contrast, the New Guinea Act curtailed the Administrator's powers, providing for the Governor-General (in effect, the Minister and his Melbourne-based Department) to make Ordinances, the Administrator only being permitted to make regulations. This division of responsibility ensured that there was little scope for an enlightened, 'pro-native', administration to emerge in New Guinea (as it had under Sir Hubert Murray in Papua), that might hinder its commercial exploitation.

The Government's indifference to the quality of New Guinea's administration was also reflected in the preference it gave to World War I veterans when appointing Administration staff. Many were untrained and unsuited to the challenging conditions, not least the Administrator himself. Chosen for his ability to make decisions 'on the ground', but with no experience in colonial administration, Brigadier-General Wisdom was gruff, strongly opinionated, disinclined to listen to the views of others and singularly status conscious. The White Australia Policy was a further burden, restricting staff positions to natural-born British subjects and so excluding Chinese or New Guineans from any meaningful roles.

So from the outset three elements critical to a successful mandate — adequate finance, appropriate legislative powers and appropriately experienced staff — were all denied to the new Administration.

These deficiencies were compounded by the retention of Rabaul as New Guinea's capital. Although economic progress was increasingly concentrated on the mainland, all senior officers resided in Rabaul through most of the inter-war period. The absence until 1938 of a regular air service between Rabaul and the mainland underlined the Administration's isolation from — and ignorance of — much of the territory it was administering.

The two Administrators who succeeded Wisdom were also Brigadier-Generals.[9] Griffiths was a career army officer who had been the military administrator in New Guinea in 1921 and later the administrator of Nauru. While more accessible than Wisdom, he was also a man of strong convictions and inclined to 'micro-manage' his senior staff accordingly. McNicoll was a school headmaster after his army career in World War I, whose appointment followed a brief stint in politics. A compassionate man, he was cautious and at times indecisive — but the only Administrator with any real affinity with New Guineans. He was knighted in 1937.

As if they needed other impediments, the Administrators had to deal with 16 changes of Minister in twenty years, and 13 different Ministers, including a three year period (1929–1931) when there was no Minister at all. The general lack of public interest in New Guinea meant that Ministers with responsibility for its administration had little influence within successive governments—not that this discouraged them from meddling in the way Administrators discharged their responsibilities.

Mandates granted by the League of Nations required mandatory powers to report annually on measures taken to carry out the obligations they had accepted in respect of the territories they had agreed to administer on behalf of the League. These reports were considered by the Permanent Mandates Commission (PMC) which advised the League's Council on whether their obligations were being observed. However, members of the PMC were unable to visit mandated territories and only met for two three week sessions a year, when they conducted annual examinations of different mandatories. An examination rarely lasted more than a couple of days, and relied on questioning to encourage any policy changes PMC members considered necessary.[10]

While the Commonwealth Government was required to promote the well-being and social progress of the Territory's inhabitants, the League's failure to clarify what this meant in practice enabled the Government to avoid committing itself to any plan for achieving it. As the *New Guinea Act 1920* failed to enshrine this obligation as a principle to guide the Administration, it is unsurprising that the Administration should have lacked a clear vision of how to develop the Territory. Even if it had had one, the Commonwealth's control over the legislative process meant it would inevitably have been hampered in pursuing it.

The absence of any policy framework was a source of on-going concern to the PMC. When in 1925 it sought to draw out the Government's intentions, Sir Joseph Cook responded with several 'heads of policy'.[11] These included:

1. The preservation of native laws and customs so far as they are not repugnant to our sense of morality;
2. The eradication of native diseases and acceptance of responsibility for the medical care and treatment of natives;
3. The protection of the native labourer in his contractual relationships;
4. The inauguration of a system of native agriculture for the cultivation of foodstuffs and economic crops;
5. The inauguration of a system of technical and general education; and
6. The participation of natives to an increasing extent in the Government of the territory.

This was the closest the PMC ever got to eliciting the Government's objectives. As late as 1938, it was still pressing. With the Administration failing to make much progress towards most of these policy objectives, William Rappard pointedly asked

> whether the mandatory Power would not find it useful, not so much for the enlightenment of the Mandates Commission as for the guidance of the New Guinea Administration, to formulate a general policy indicating the objects, both material, social and humanitarian, of its policy towards the Territory—in other words, a philosophy of its colonial administration.[12]

His was no more successful than earlier efforts.

The PMC was particularly concerned about the Commonwealth's lack of financial support for the Territory. It was given an early 'free kick' when the Government appointed an experienced former British colonial official, Colonel Ainsworth, to review the whole system of administration in New Guinea. Ainsworth's 1924 Report was scathing. Noting that *the Commonwealth requires the Territory to find the whole of its expenditure from local revenue*, he concluded that …

> the Territory cannot, from its present resources, provide for an effective administration and at the same time make provision for the many urgent and absolutely necessary requirements, such as roads, communications, and other essential public works.[13]

Ainsworth further noted that … *any tropical country in its early stages of administration stands in need of financial assistance,*[14] and that as the Territory couldn't afford to borrow, assistance must be in the form of grants. *The country, if it is to be worth anything eventually, must grow up as a healthy child, and not be brought up as an anaemic one.*[15]

The Government responded in 1925/26 with the first of several annual £10,000 grants for the welfare of natives.[16] However, the PMC saw them for what they were—a token gesture rather than a serious attempt to boost the level of financial support. In 1930, Lord Lugard suggested that

> in its initial stages, the administration of New Guinea and the surrounding islands must cost a very large sum of money if it were to be effective, more, indeed, than an annual subsidy of £10,000.[17]

But such pleas went unheeded, and in 1931/32 the grants were phased out on the grounds that the Administration's financial position was now strong enough to meet the cost of native welfare programs from its own resources.[18]

While unwilling to concede the principle of financial self-sufficiency, the Government was nevertheless mindful of its international image. Its statements of 'Expenditure on Native Administration and Welfare' in the Territory's Annual Reports exaggerated its commitment by including arbitrarily determined proportions of general expenditure and items that had little to do with native welfare.[19] Information was rarely provided on how these contributed to the well-being and development of New Guineans. The PMC was less than impressed. In 1933, Count de Penha Garcia observed acidly that most of the items in its 1931/32 statement *were generally classified in other parts of the world as expenditure on administration.*[20]

———

There was a darker side to the financial relationship. Australia was required not to exploit the Territory for its own profit.[21] However, there is compelling evidence that it did so through some 'financial engineering' — particularly by creating dubious liabilities, then ensuring that the 'loans' to which they gave rise were repaid as soon as the Territory's finances permitted.

In his 1924 Report, Ainsworth drew attention to a proposed loan of £24,000 at 5% interest to recoup what the Government had paid to the Prize Court for ships captured from the Germans. He described the debt as an unreasonable burden on the Territory,[22] as the ships had been used extensively by the military but had since been of little use to the civil administration. Two were almost useless and a third required considerable repairs. His view was confirmed by the Commonwealth Auditor-General, who concluded that the ships were 'practically worthless'.[23]

Before a consistent reporting method was adopted in 1928/29, several unexplained loan movements added £12,350 to the Territory's debt to the Commonwealth.[24] The PMC, and particularly Rappard — the Commission's public finance expert — were frustrated by, and increasingly suspicious of, the lack of clarity in the Territory's accounts.[25]

The issue came to a head in 1927/28 when an adjustment of £34,516 was made *in respect of stores supplied and services rendered for civil purposes shortly before and after the inception of civil administration on 9th May 1921.*[26] The delay was explained as being due to the difficulty in allocating expenditure between the Administration and the Defence Department. In an attempt to deflect criticism, the Government indicated that the liability need not be repaid immediately and that, temporarily, interest would not be payable on the debt.

Rappard was deeply concerned by this transaction, and at the 1928 Session asked who had stated the case for the Territory in reaching agreement on the amount of the liability. His disquiet was reflected in an unusually direct 'Special Observation' by the Commission at the conclusion of the Session, requesting further information, including about the principles on which the settlement was based.[27] No answer was ever forthcoming.

Excluding the £34,516 'adjustment', the Territory's debt to the Commonwealth reached £61,425 in 1930/31. This was repaid in full by 1933/34, provoking Rappard to observe that

> the financial prosperity of the Administration—not of the territory, which was not particularly prosperous— had served … to improve the financial situation of the Commonwealth.[28]

This was doubtless intended as a sharp rebuke. If so, it was ignored and the £34,516 was progressively repaid between 1936 and 1940 — the Administration borrowing twice from its own Trust Funds to make these repayments. Thus, by 1940 the Territory's debt to the Commonwealth had been completely extinguished.

Coincidentally, the loan for the ships, the unexplained debits in the 1920s and the Department of Defence 'adjustment' together broadly cancelled out the grants the Government had made for native welfare. So taking the inter-war period as a whole, the Government achieved its goal of making the Territory financially self-sufficient.

———

The precise meaning of the well-being and social progress of New Guineans was unclear. Did it mean preserving traditional village society and subsistence economy? If so, was this compatible with 'progress'? Should economic development drive social progress or be secondary to it?

The Government's financial straitjacket and the Administration's narrow revenue base[29] suggested that 'progress' was always going to be limited, and that village society should therefore be preserved. Not only was this the easiest option, but it coincided with the PMC's views — that the economic and social life of native communities should not be endangered.[30] But if the PMC and Administration shared a view as to the desired outcome, they had very different ideas about how this should be achieved.

The PMC became increasingly concerned that the Administration's emphasis on developing the Morobe goldfields was deflecting it from the work of civilisation entrusted to it by the mandate.[31] But for the Administration, it was really not a question of one or the other. Its pro-development stance was about survival. Lacking Commonwealth financial support, there could be no social progress without development and the revenue this generated.

By 1930, Wisdom had realised that gold mining would be the Administration's salvation:

> To my mind it would be wrong for the Government to permit anything to hamper the progress of these [large mining] companies towards the production of gold in a big way, which we all devoutly desire and need.[32]

Throughout the 1930s, the need for revenue was the main factor determining how the Administration allocated its resources. District staff were largely occupied opening up new areas where labour could be recruited, supervising the recruitment and employment of labour and protecting prospectors and miners. The mathematics were simple. As Eric Feldt expressed it:

> If ten men get on the field and average an ounce a day each, the royalty will pay for a Patrol Officer to be stationed there long enough to bring the Ramu and surroundings under control, apart from the possibilities of development into something bigger.[33]

Keith McCarthy expressed a similar view:

> New Guinea was run on a pittance, and there could be no expenditure on new posts unless dividends followed in the shape of gold. Exploration and pacification were simply luxuries that could not be afforded ... [34]

By 1939, more than 41,000 New Guineans—or an estimated 27.8% of adult fit males —were employed as indentured labourers throughout the Territory. The PMC viewed the extended absence of large numbers of young men as a major threat to the continuing existence of villages. Its primary concern was with what it regarded as excessively high levels of recruiting, the length of labourers' contracts and the frequency with which they were permitted to re-engage when their contracts expired. It pressured the Government and Administration to control recruiting levels, favouring as an alternative a 'free labour system', where labourers

could work whenever, wherever and for as long as they liked.[35]

Other aspects of the labour system also caused it concern, including the use of coercion to obtain recruits, high desertion and mortality rates and the adequacy of inspections of living and working conditions.

The Government argued that the indentured labour system contributed to the well-being and social progress of New Guineans:

> From village conditions, which often were insanitary and comfortless, from conditions of life which often provide foods lacking in essential qualities, and from circumstances of superstition and strong liability to horrible diseases, he was removed to conditions in which he found excellent shelter, good food, medical attention and protection against the world.[36]

Other benefits were said to include the educational effect of participating in a cash economy, the acquisition of skills including the use of European tools, greater knowledge about sanitation and personal hygiene and satisfying the urge for excitement among young men which might otherwise be expended in warfare. The use of pidgin English as a lingua franca was also seen by some as contributing to a wider sense of community.[37]

Despite the inflated claims in its annual statements of 'Expenditure on Native Administration and Welfare', little of the Administration's budget directly promoted social progress or economic development at the village level. The anthropologist W.H. Stanner observed that, between 1930 and 1940, administrative salaries and normal departmental contingencies were never below 73% of total expenditure, and in five years, were 80% or more. *This was an aggravation of a weakness common to most colonies. The margins left for social and economic development were trivial.*[38]

However much the Commonwealth's financial stringency was to blame, the Administration's rigidly conservative fiscal policy made things worse. Already burdened by the need to generate sufficient revenue to service and repay Commonwealth loans, the Administration recorded a cumulative surplus (after these payments) every year from 1926/27.[39]

Furthermore, while the Administration borrowed from its trust funds to repay Commonwealth loans, it was unwilling to do so to fund programs that would promote the well-being of New Guineans. These funds accumulated steadily throughout the 1930s and by 1940 amounted to nearly £300,000. Although superannuation comprised more than 50%, the trust funds included £87,687 in seigniorage—profit on the issue of coinage. Rather than being paid into the Territory's revenue and used for the welfare of New Guineans, this profit was paid into a Coinage Trust Fund, and invested in Commonwealth securities.[40]

The Administration's fiscal policy was particularly demoralising for hard-pressed district staff, who were the focal point for discharging Australia's responsibilities under the Mandate.

Their efforts were spread over many activities. They undertook patrols to extend and consolidate Administration influence, and administrative patrols which conducted censuses, collected taxes, settled disputes, investigated complaints and crimes, appointed village officials, inspected villages and roads, undertook medical inspections and gave basic advice on crop growing.[41]

Supervising the operation of the indentured labour system under the Native Labour Ordinance was particularly time-consuming, involving as it did the movement of thousands of labourers each year from their villages to workplaces and back again, and the inspection of their living and working conditions wherever they were employed.[42] And, finally, District staff were responsible for administering everyday life in their Districts—arresting criminals, conducting district courts, acting as coroner, performing marriages and so on.

The Director of District Services and Native Affairs, E.W.P. Chinnery, regularly sought increases in staff numbers, but with little success. His Department's expenditure increased at about two thirds the rate of overall Administration expenditure between 1926/27 and 1939/40, its share falling from 29.5% to 25.4%. In January 1933, Chinnery wrote to Administrator Griffiths warning him that, with 15 fewer field staff than in 1929 and 24 fewer than an independent review had suggested were needed, there were too few to cope with emergencies.[43]

Two years later, when making another case for additional field staff, Chinnery advised the new Administrator, McNicoll, that

> Since the date [January 1933] of that letter, three non-officials and one official have been killed in the uncontrolled areas of the Morobe District, and there has been a regrettable loss of native life owing to the fact

that we have not had the staff to proceed gradually with the work of peaceful penetration and our patrols have been forced by emergencies into hostile encounters, either to protect Europeans or to arrest people for killing and molesting them.[44]

This had some effect, the cadet system which had been suspended in 1930-31 for financial reasons (despite the on-going accumulated surplus), being reinstituted in 1935.

Morale among District staff frequently suffered, particularly under Wisdom and Griffiths—McNicoll showing greater sensitivity to the pressures under which they worked. Thus in 1933, the Morobe District Officer, Ted Taylor, vented his frustration to Chinnery about Griffiths' efforts to reduce staff: *Am disappointed in the Old Man's economy campaign – particularly this District … He will find that he has another surplus at end of year.*[45]

Not only were staff allocations influenced by their revenue-generating possibilities, but there was also constant pressure to contain expenditure. As well as the petty boot allowance requirement (see Chapter 14), J.K. McCarthy noted on a letter from the District Officer reminding him to 'keep a careful record of expenditure incurred': *All these bastards think of is money. The Administration even charged me £30 for medical expenses when I was wounded in the first Menyamya patrol.*[46]

The well-being and development of New Guineans were thus secondary to financial considerations, and despite pressure from the PMC (and to a lesser extent non-official members of the Legislative Council), the Administration made only limited progress in areas where it might have been expected to advance village welfare—health, education and agriculture.

HEALTH—In 1925, Sir Joseph Cook advised the PMC that *the eradication of native diseases and acceptance of responsibility for the medical care and treatment of natives* were one of the main heads of Government policy.

Early efforts were promising, particularly those directed towards the health of labourers. The Director of Public Health from 1924 to 1927, Dr (later Sir) Raphael Cilento, instituted procedures to ensure that labourers were healthy before they signed on, had anti-typhoid vaccinations, balanced diets that built their strength and contributed to the elimination of beriberi, received free medical care from their employers and were healthy when they returned home so that diseases weren't introduced to villages. However, continually frustrated by bureaucratic obstruction, Cilento clashed with Administrator Wisdom and resigned in May 1927, *in final recognition of the futility of my attempting to establish in this Territory an efficient and effective medical service.*[47]

'Native health' accounted for 15% to 17% of Administration expenditure during the 1930s. Despite this, year after year labourers in the Wau-Edie Creek area died in large numbers from pneumonia and dysentery.[48] The preventable nature of these diseases was evident — and thus the Administration's failure highlighted — by the fact that few Europeans contracted or died from either of them. As well, despite the high incidence of tuberculosis among labourers on plantations, the Administration never mounted a campaign to diagnose and treat it.[49]

At the village level, the Administration conducted campaigns against yaws, a chronic disease leading to disfigurement and disability, and hookworm, and established many medical posts staffed with indentured medical orderlies. Patrols undertook medical examinations, treating villagers where practicable for diseases and teaching basic sanitation. However, improvements in village health were difficult to sustain as visits were rarely more than annual. By 1940, there were 4,000 'medical tul tuls' in villages throughout the Territory; but they were poorly trained and supported and appear to have had little lasting impact on village health.

EDUCATION — The 1926/27 Annual Report claimed that

> The aim of the Administration is to provide such educational facilities as will afford all natives of the Territory an opportunity of qualifying themselves to participate in the economic and social life of their own country.[50]

Twelve years later, despite constant probing by the PMC, Valentine Dannevig concluded that *She knew of no territory under mandate in which native education progressed so slowly.*[51] Indeed, outside the Rabaul area, there had been virtually no progress at all. In 1941, very few New Guineans could read and write English. Reed contrasted the situation with that in East Africa *where many more positions are open to natives,* [and] *there is a great incentive to acquiring an education and a passionate desire to master the English language.*[52] While missions often ran village schools, their focus was primarily religious and most mission workers had insufficient knowledge of English to teach it.[53] After 1931/32, Administration expenditure on education never exceeded 2% of total expenditure, and in 1939/40 was 14% less than it had been 17 years earlier.

AGRICULTURE — Sir Joseph Cook's 1925 list of the main heads of government policy also included *the*

inauguration of a system of native agriculture. Again, there was little meaningful progress. A single agricultural school was established near Rabaul to meet the needs of the whole of the Territory, despite widely divergent soil types and climatic conditions. At the village level, agricultural extension efforts appear to have been constrained by lack of staff, and were largely confined to the copra industry, experiments with alternative crop types and encouraging villagers to substitute crop rotation for shifting agriculture — all with little success.

Thus, in terms of the central obligation of the Mandate, the Administration had little positive impact.

The scale of the indentured labour system and diversion of staff and funds to support economic activity may appear to suggest that successive Administrators were constructively pro-development in a broader sense. This was far from the case. Not only did they lack a vision or coherent philosophy for developing the Territory's resources, but they were little interested in establishing infrastructure as a platform for economic development. And far from being the 'captive' of commercial interests, the Administration often had a strained relationship with mining and other enterprises.

Remote from the mainland, the reputation of Rabaul bureaucrats for obstructing rather than facilitating development was an enduring source of frustration. Process was more important than progress. Administrators and their staff clung to the comforts and pace of travelling by ship long after air travel was feasible. Terms such as 'Rabaul inertia', 'lazy lethargy' and 'drugged sleep' were used to describe their responsiveness. District officials had little autonomy, with decisions on minor matters often having to be referred to Rabaul.[54] And when they did exercise their judgement they were often overruled.[55]

As early as 1930, observers viewed the goldfields as a potential catalyst for the development of the Territory's agricultural, timber and pastoral industries. However, Wisdom rejected or ignored advice from officers on the ground about the potential agricultural and pastoral possibilities of the goldfields area, also claiming that gold didn't provide capital for development as it was all exported.[56] Neither did he show any interest in encouraging new private investment by providing infrastructure, such as ports and roads. In 1932, a visiting engineer commented: *This is one of the richest tropical countries in the world. We cannot understand why Australia does not push on with the job of developing it.*[57]

In 1924, Ainsworth had referred to the need for expenditure on roads, communications and other public works. Eight year later, the Bank of New South Wales Manager in Salamaua, Harry Johns, reported to his superiors that

> Unhappily the Administration of this mandate ... has failed to recognise its obligations to the industry and ... whether it be in the matter of road construction, clearing areas for 'dromes, building roads, etc. those requiring these essential works have long since realised they have only themselves to look to to provide the necessary funds and labour.[58]

That the Administration then implied in the Territory's Annual Reports from time to time that it was responsible for what others had achieved was, to the say the least, economical with the truth.[59]

Expenditure on road development fell by one third in the two years to June 1937, leading the PMC to query whether this wasn't paradoxical in a country where the road system was still embryonic? The Australian Representative, Major Furman, bluntly dismissed the PMC's concerns:

> The Commission should leave the Administration to be the best judge in the matter of road extension ... as much as possible was being done. Persons who had not visited the Territory could not appreciate the difficulties of road construction and, more particularly, road maintenance.[60]

So far as the road to the goldfields was concerned, there was a lot of surveying activity, but little to show for it.

Other infrastructure was similarly neglected. The construction of a jetty at Salamaua was considered in 1932 but never undertaken, although with Administration buildings under threat there from the encroaching sea, it did engage in extensive foreshore protection activity in 1936.

Communications were left largely to the mining companies. As late as 1931, although NGG had a telephone line between Edie Creek and Wau, the Administration was using runners. A public telephone system was introduced in Wau in 1935 but the Administration made no effort to establish voice communication between the goldfields and the coast, much less Australia.

Aerodromes were for years a source of tension between the Administration and GAL. Wisdom wanted nothing to do with them, and even after 1933, when the Administration accepted responsibility, Griffiths continued to believe that the operators should make and maintain them. The only significant aerodrome maintenance activity by the Administration was at Salamaua after 1935. Otherwise its efforts were confined to cutting the grass.

Such inactivity, unresponsiveness and lack of vision were also a source of frustration for non-official members of the Legislative Council. A veneer of polite debate was regularly punctuated by interventions about the Administration's antiquated roads policy, the lack of a co-ordinated agricultural policy, the chronic shortage of field staff, the failure of its native affairs policy, the large expenditure on unproductive works and disproportionate expenditure on Public Service salaries and contingencies.

Frustrated at the Administration's failure even to articulate constructive policies, A.N. Mullaly was eventually prompted to observe in 1941:

> For eight years I have listened to questions that have been asked in this Legislative Council for a statement of native policy, agricultural policy, road development policy and financial policy and invariably the reply has been that it is not the policy of the Administration to state its policy—or equivalent words.[61]

The legacy of Australia's administration of New Guinea between the wars was so much less than it might have been. The Commonwealth Government's mandate was to administer the Territory—on behalf of the League of Nations. During the 20 or so years of civil administration, the Government paid lip service to the Mandate, but in practice administered New Guinea as if it had been annexed. It was narrow in its vision, inflexible in its financial constraints and resistant to PMC suggestions as to how its obligations might be discharged more effectively.

The three Administrators were far from ideal choices. Isolated from most of the Territory they were administering and with poor communications, they were for the most part ineffectual. As ex-military men, they readily accepted their orders,[62] despite being fully aware that the limitations these imposed would make it impractical to achieve Australia's obligations under the Mandate.

If the PMC had been given stronger investigative powers and been able to play a stronger advocacy role, perhaps the Australian Government would have adopted a more constructive approach to its responsibilities. The Commission often engaged in vigorous questioning of the Australian representatives, but however terse their questions and observations, a brief annual examination was never going to be sufficient to hold the Commonwealth accountable for its stewardship or to secure major policy changes.

Gold proved to be a mixed blessing. It provided substantial revenue, through royalties and a raft of fees and import duties, enabling the Administration to run a cumulative budget surplus and divert money to the Australian Government. It was also the main contributor to the Territory's massive trade surplus in the 1930s, accounting for 70% of all exports. Copra, which had accounted for 80% or more in the 1920s, was relegated to around 25%.

The changed economic focus from copra to gold and the increased demand for labour contributed to the opening up of the interior of the New Guinea mainland. It should also have provided a platform for the development of a more diverse economic base. In fact, it had the opposite effect, by removing pressure on the Administration to secure the revenue it needed by promoting the large scale development of the Territory's agricultural, pastoral and timber industries.

Perhaps the Administration's most glaring shortcoming, however, was its failure to develop the Territory's social capital. The Commonwealth claimed to have as policy objectives the ability of all New Guineans to participate in the economic and social life of their own country and to control their own destiny (albeit under Australia's supervision). Education was identified as the key to this.[63]

By 1941, however, very few New Guineans were employed for their skills, and where they were, these had usually been acquired while working for mining companies. The Administration's resistance to NGG's efforts to train and use New Guineans as skilled workers[64] underlines just how superficial was its commitment to promote the progress of the Territory's indigenous inhabitants.

The Administration did employ some New Guineans in clerical capacities, while others who had attended the Native Technical School at Rabaul were employed doing clerical work, plumbing, carpentry, painting, cement work, driving motor vehicles and tractors and working as telephone exchange operators, medical orderlies, and linesmen to surveyors. The fact that there were so few employed in such activities simply emphasised the lost opportunity associated with the Administration's failure to extend such education more widely throughout the Territory. Most of those who did gain skills on the goldfields eventually returned to their villages and any benefit was largely lost.

The Administration did nothing to encourage New Guineans to participate in the government of the Territory — one of the 1925 'heads of policy'. While in the early 1930s the PMC was anxious that someone should represent the interests of New Guineans on the Legislative Council, no indigenous person was ever appointed.

⸺

The Administration saw the process of change as incremental: labourers were recruited, exposed to the ways of the white man and returned to their villages, for the most part to continue village life as before. However, its policies unleashed a process of change far greater than it ever realised. It (and the PMC) overlooked the dynamic effects on the economic and social life of villages of extending Administration influence and control, abolishing warfare, introducing a cash economy and the pervasive effect of a labour system which opened the eyes of villagers to new possibilities but did little to satisfy them.

The complex interplay of pressures on these communities is nowhere summed up better than by Patrol Officer Black in February 1936, after a patrol to the Lower Waria:

> These people are not making the progress one would expect, considering the number of years they have been under control. The chief reason is largely one of neglect by the Administration. For some years now it has been impossible for an adequate number of patrols to visit this area, due to the acute shortage of field staff. In view of this it is not surprising that roads, villages and village plantations are sadly neglected and that old inter-village feuds and jealousies are awakening.
>
> One of the chief reasons for this unfortunate state of affairs is that the old laws and the old morality are in progress of rapid disintegration. The sanctions of established custom, the traditions of law and order, are being questioned and often flagrantly ignored by the new generation. These people are now in the throes of the bewildering transition stage between the discarding of the old and the adoption of a new culture, and in the process are not getting the assistance from the European they have a just right to expect.[65]

However Black's was a voice in the wilderness.

Part 8
After the War

Winchroom, No. 5 dredge, 2001.

CHAPTER 24
DECLINE AND RENEWAL

Post-war reconstruction was not simply a question of rebuilding what had been destroyed. The pattern of development was to be very different. War had changed the goldfields forever.

Virtually nothing survived of the four pre-war townships. Heavy allied bombing had devastated Salamaua. In April 1945, Toby Millar recorded that it was

> flattened out of all recognition. There remain only one or two battered bungalows; the skeleton of Guinea Airways office and store; the fly wheel of the pub refrigerator. Bomb craters are everywhere, and the promontory is scored by naval shell explosions … Not a coconut tree remains of all those tall old palms that formed the beautiful avenue along the isthmus; and a lump formed in my throat when I stood beside the remnants of that wonderful old calophyllum tree alongside the hotel. The Japs, in digging a fox hole at its base, had evidently cut its life root and in place of the luxuriant, spreading, shade-giving old warrior only a blackened wreck remains … Salamaua is just a sorry and heart-breaking memory.[1]

At Wau and Bulolo the signs of devastation had been smothered by secondary jungle growth and kunai grass, interspersed with splashes of colour from the crotons, bougainvillea, hibiscus and other tropical flowers planted by pre-war residents.

Lae, on the other hand, was a hive of activity. It had been the focal point of the allied advance and the Army had occupied it since September 1943, constructing several large docks, barracks and other buildings. In 1944, Army engineers completed what the pre-war Administration had been unable to—a road between Labu, on the south side of the mouth of the Markham River, near Lae, and the Bulolo valley. This was now to have a major impact on how the goldfields area developed.

Other than the absence of a link to Salamaua, the road broadly followed the route favoured by the Administration pre-war—via Zenag and linking up with the Bulolo valley at the junction with the Snake River below Baiune. From there, it continued through to Wau—an overall distance of 93 miles. In the early post-war years, the journey was far from easy. To get from Lae to Labu, where the road began, travellers faced a barge trip across a turbulent two mile stretch of water at the mouth of the Markham. It was not until January 1955 that a bridge was finally constructed eight miles upstream.[2] Progress along the road was frequently disrupted by landslides and flooding, and it was not uncommon for a trip to Wau to take up to three days.

The new road and port facilities in Lae were the death knell for Salamaua. Lacking road access and with an overgrown airstrip in an unsuitable location, the township was abandoned. In 1947, the sole European inhabitant was Yorkie Booth, running a trade store for local villagers.

Neither was the road good news for Wau. The largest pre-war concentration of Europeans in New Guinea had developed around, and because of, its aerodrome. With the new road, air transport declined and Wau never regained its former glory.

———

Civil administration was restored in Papua and that part of New Guinea south of the Markham in October 1945, with a single administration for the two territories. The remaining areas of New Guinea were progressively transferred from military control until the whole of it and Papua were under civilian control in June 1946.

A Labor Government in Canberra, with the vituperative Eddie Ward as Minister for External Territories, had new plans in mind for the country's labour market. Initially, it limited labour contracts to a year, but after 1948 abolished the indentured labour system altogether. Non-indigenous employees in New Guinea were also brought under Federal awards. In January 1948, a 40 hour working week was introduced in Australia, and this flowed through to New Guinea. This was soon followed by a 10% increase in the basic (or minimum) wage. These developments significantly reduced labour market flexibility and added substantially to employers' costs.[3]

Early reconstruction efforts were further impeded by

No. 5 dredge after capsizing during the war.

labour unrest on Australian wharves, labour shortages in New Guinea, a critical lack of shipping, unreliable road transport and insufficient aircraft capable of carrying heavy machinery.

Although the Junkers G31s and W34s had all been destroyed, Guinea Airways sought to resume operations in PNG. However, its long and impressive pre-war experience counted for nothing with an Australian Government keen to see its newly acquired airline, Qantas, become the main operator in New Guinea, and it was refused a licence.[4] Qantas also took over the Australia-New Guinea service from W.R. Carpenter.

BGD soon demonstrated its adroit management of difficult circumstances and made good progress while others, including NGG, made little. The first BGD representatives to the field in May 1944 found all the dredges safe except No. 5, which was partly submerged. However, the Army had removed motors, winches, electric cables and transformers from most of the dredges, and what equipment remained had deteriorated from exposure and lack of maintenance.[5]

In March 1946, while awaiting parts from America to recommission the Upper Baiune power station, a generator and transformers from No. 6 dredge were used to restore limited power supplies to Bulolo and particularly to the sawmill and machine shop. Using local timber, BGD made rapid progress in rebuilding the accommodation necessary for its steadily increasing European and New Guinean labour force; by August 1946, this numbered 130 and 370 respectively. The reconstructed Upper Baiune power station commenced operating in November 1946.

BGD also set about preparing to transport the large quantity of materials needed to rehabilitate the dredges. It acquired road building equipment and ex-Army trucks and semi-trailers in Lae and Finschhafen, as well as barges to transport everything from Labu to the Lae side of the Markham. Given the difficulties it faced, progress was remarkable, with four dredges and the Lower Baiune power station back in action during 1947, and another three dredges in 1948. Rehabilitating No. 5 dredge proved more difficult and it did not restart until February 1949. By this time, BGD was employing 350 Europeans and 1,200 New Guineans.

For all BGD's efficiency, however, rising costs and a fixed gold price reduced the area of ground that could be dredged profitably. In December 1947, it foreshadowed that, in the absence of new discoveries, six dredges would be closed down at intervals during the next six or seven years. The 40 hour week intensified cost pressures and over the next three years rising wages significantly reduced margins for all the dredges, accelerating the closure timetable.[6] No. 1 closed down in July 1949 and Nos. 3 and 6 in May 1951.

By this time, BGD was looking to another potential source of revenue—timber. The Bulolo valley was surrounded by plentiful supplies of hoop and klinkii pine and cedar. Many trees were 100 feet to 150 feet in height, with enormous girths and few branches. Their potential exploitation had been an integral part of Levien's vision for the development of the field in the mid-1920s.[7]

Pre-war, it had been impossible to transport commercial quantities of timber to the coast and for the most part it was only used locally. In the 1930s, BGD's sawmill produced cedar for fluming, furniture and even for the construction of a bridge; pine was used primarily for building purposes. Post-war, however, the road to Labu enabled back loading to the coast and the last part of Levien's vision finally fell into place.

In October 1949, the Australian Government announced that timber resources in and around the Bulolo Valley would be developed by a company in which it would have a majority interest; its primary focus would be on the production of plywood veneer. BGD had experience in sawmilling, the necessary infrastructure—particularly hydro-electric power—and was looking for a new opportunity to use its labour force as dredging wound down.

After protracted negotiations, Commonwealth-New Guinea Timbers (CNGT) was incorporated in June 1952, with the Government owning half the shares plus one and BGD the remainder. Drawing on overseas expertise, BGD designed and constructed a plywood factory, which began operating in January 1954. It operated 24 hours a day, five days a week, producing about 1,000 tons of plywood a month. There was a ready export market to the USA due to the high quality pine used in its manufacture. To ensure a continuing supply of timber, a comprehensive forestry replanting program was implemented, on a 50 year cycle.

CNGT was given a permit over 40,000 acres which, in the late 1960s, was still estimated to contain 500 million super feet of hoop and klinkii pine and 50 million super feet of cedar.[8]

The years 1952–53 proved to be the high point for BGD's post-war dredging operations, with five dredges producing 138,781 fine ounces from 17 million cubic yards of gravel. Thereafter, a rapid decline in gold production occurred as the dredges reached the limits of ground they could work profitably. By mid-1957, Dredge No. 5 was the only dredge still operating.[9] That it continued doing so until June 1965, despite declining grades, was solely due to its ability to handle 12,500 cubic yards of gravel a day, almost twice its design capacity.

1965 also marked the end for Bulolo Gold Dredging, when it was taken over by its parent, Placer Development.[10] Between 1932 and 1965 (less the war years), BGD's dredges had produced 2,318,181 ounces of gold and 1,042,758 ounces of silver,[11]. This was 56% of all gold produced on the Morobe goldfields between 1926 and 1977.

The challenges facing NGG in 1945 were no less significant. Nearly all its dwellings, stores and offices had been destroyed, while plant and machinery at the Golden Ridges mill had been damaged by exposure. Its flumes, part of the water races serving Kulolo and Koranga, had rotted and were unserviceable, while heavy secondary growth and landslides clogged the water races and roads. The viability of NGG's Edie Creek mine had been on a knife edge in 1941. Deterioration of surface plant and underground workings in the intervening period ruled out any possibility of restarting operations there.

NGG's progress in rehabilitating its mining infrastructure was agonisingly slow. In January 1948, in a not-so-faint echo of Blaikie Webster in the 1930s, NGG Chairman, Julius Kruttschnitt, told his Board that the company's program had been

> defeated by a multitude of difficulties, all traceable more or less to the muddling Socialistic policy [of the Australian Labor Government] which has brought about in New Guinea an acute shortage of shipping, supplies and native labour.[12]

As Jim Sinclair noted, this may have been so, but BGD was coping whereas NGG was floundering.[13]

Only after the arrival of a new and highly experienced field manager, John Hohnen, in late 1947 did things begin to improve. The Edie Creek milling plant, with its capacity of about 125 tons a day, was transferred to Golden Ridges in 1951 to treat the ore from Upper Ridges mine. But NGG's salvation, in the short term at least, came with its realisation of the potential of the Golden Peaks deposit discovered near Golden Ridges in 1935. This had not been developed at the time as the ore was considered to have too high a clay content. Between 1953 and 1977, however, more than 1.5 million tonnes of low grade ore produced about 231,748 ounces of gold—which Lowenstein described as *the greatest amount of gold to have been recovered from in-situ mineralisation by any single mining operation on the Morobe Goldfield*.[14]

From 1950, NGG also sought to supplement its mining fortunes with its sawmills, supplying up to 20 pre-cut houses a month to the Administration in Port Moresby. However, its logging areas were much smaller than BGD's and, after the formation of Commonwealth-New Guinea Timbers, the Administration refused to make any more areas available. While its sawmill continued to operate until 1976, it was never able to expand production as much as it wished.

Through the 1960s and 1970s, NGG's fortunes were mixed. A turning point occurred in 1974 when the Mining Inspector closed the Golden Peaks mine, the Namie Creek alluvial workings were obliterated by a flood and the Golden Ridges mill suffered a major breakdown. NGG struggled back to profitability but was eventually taken over by Renison Goldfields Consolidated (RGC) in 1981.

RGC constructed a new plant to treat ore from Upper Ridges, while letting out many of NGG's former leases to tributers. Sinclair notes that 120 tributers were recovering gold worth around 3 million kina a year in the late 1980s.[15] However, the operations did not live up to RGC's expectations and, in 1991, its mining activities finally ceased.

It became evident soon after the war that Bulolo would supplant Wau as the main goldfields centre. NGG's rehabilitation efforts were making little progress and although a few individual miners and companies were working the creeks and rivers, there was little exploration and even less to show for it. By 1948, Wau's European population had reached about 350, and remained around this level until the mid-1950s, after which it declined to around 250.

With its population a quarter of pre-war levels, greatly reduced air traffic and subdued gold mining activity, the buzz that had previously characterised Wau was missing. In May 1953, *Pacific Islands Monthly* described Wau as 'a quiet, small township'. By this time, the focus of many residents had shifted from gold to agriculture. Much of the valley was given over to the production of arabica coffee, while large quantities of commercial vegetables were being shipped out by road and air to Lae and Port Moresby. However, despite the ideal climate for such activities, the emergence of the New Guinea highlands as a major producer of high quality coffee and disruptions to transport led to their gradual contraction.

In contrast, as the dredges and power stations were recommissioned, Bulolo forged ahead. By 1948, it had a European population of around 600, and despite its transformation thereafter from a mining town to one centred on the plywood factory, it remained above 550 through most of the 1960s. After dredge No. 2 had finished chewing up the old pre-war aerodrome, a small township of squatters and former employees formed on and amongst the tailings it had deposited.

In 1957, the Administration began issuing miner's permits to Papua New Guineans. As Sinclair notes, this was the catalyst for the arrival of a large number of squatters from elsewhere in Papua New Guinea. By 1964, there were 2,000 to 3,000 squatters and by 1970 around 5,000.[16]

Existing leases were often worked under tribute. Some of the more skilled miners were quite successful.[17] Their operations co-existed with a much greater number of subsistence miners using primitive equipment. The majority relied—and continue to do so—on recovering minute quantities of gold and low overheads to eke out a living that was at least better than where they had come from.

The growth of large squatter settlements gave rise to considerable tensions with the Biangai and Upper Watut people,[18] who regard the land and the rivers as their own. On several occasions, relations between the locals and squatters from the highlands have become so strained that serious conflict has only been avoided by the forced departure of many squatters from the District.

After independence in 1975, the number of Europeans in the Wau-Bulolo District dwindled steadily. As NGG and then RGC wound down their operations, the Biangai Development Corporation took over many of their buildings, leases and equipment. But a lack of capital, management and business skills impaired its efforts to develop the gold that remained. Nor were the efforts of the Kukukuku Development Corporation established by the Watut people any more successful.

Edie Creek, 2001.

The most productive development was a small mining operation at Edie Creek. In 1990, at the request of RGC, Edie Creek Mining Company Pty Ltd, was formed by Melanesian Resources (51%) to take over its Edie Creek leases. The Kukukuku Development Corporation and Biangai Development Corporation each held 24.5%. Gold production was variable due to the nature of the gold veins being mined. The best annual production achieved was 100 kg.

The departure of RGC in 1991 followed that of many Europeans and resulted in the virtual collapse of the local economy. RGC was the major employer in Wau; it had provided health services for the local community, maintained roads, power, water and sports grounds and supported schools, churches and other community facilities. Being remote from other population centres and now of little economic consequence, Wau attracted little Government funding and its infrastructure — and law and order — steadily deteriorated. The anthropologist Jamon Halvaksz noted that, by 2006, Wau had

fallen into a state of near chaos, with weekly robberies, large settler populations, pervasive alcoholism, marijuana use, and a state of on-going violence that has led the Biangai to refer to [it] as a 'cowboy town'.[19]

The population of Bulolo has grown from 3,000 in the early 1970s to around 17,500 today. The busy township is centred on the activities of PNG Forest Products (PNGFP), the latest incarnation of Commonwealth-New Guinea Timbers. Owned by Singaporean interests (80%) and the PNG Government (20%), it operates the country's largest plywood factory, employing 1,200 workers and producing plywood and sawn timber products from extensive pine plantations. These are used throughout PNG and exported to Australia and New Zealand.

While there are now fewer than 20 expatriates permanently resident in Bulolo, most of whom are employed by PNGFP, there is a growing transient population associated with a major mining development at Hidden Valley — Bulolo being the nearest township and having a hotel and golf club.

All that still exists of the eight dredges are the rusting, skeletal remains of Nos. 2 and 5, a short distance from

No. 5 dredge, 2001.

Bulolo, and No. 6 near Wau[20] — a mute reminder of past glories, though handy adventure playgrounds for local children. A few scraps remain elsewhere. Outside PNGFP's offices, near two large cogwheels, is a dredge bucket, while elsewhere in Bulolo several others have been filled with soil and put to use as steps. While there are pockets of subsistence agriculture in the Bulolo Valley, no effort has been made to reclaim the valley for agricultural or pastoral use, and kunai grass, shrubs and the occasional tree today mask what is essentially a barren, rocky landscape.

Two significant features of the pre-war landscape are notable for their absence: Bulwa and the original power station at the entrance to the valley. Neither was restored after the War and their sites have been reclaimed by kunai grass. The Baiune hydro-electric scheme, now owned by PNGFP, operates in essentially the same way as when it was originally constructed in the 1930s, water races winding their way for many kilometres round (and through) the sides of mountains until they reach the power stations. The scheme stands as a lasting monument to the ingenuity and tenacity of BGD's engineers.

Dredge No. 2.

No. 6 dredge, 2001.

Nationals mining in the Bulolo River, 2001.

In 1929, gold was discovered at Hidden Valley, southeast of Edie Creek.[21] Conditions were miserable, gold recovery negligible and the area was soon abandoned. However, in recent years extensive exploration using the latest technology has resulted in the discovery of a massive resource there. Reserves of 2.8 million ounces of gold have been proven at Hidden Valley and a smaller ore body nearby, Hamata — about 21% more than BGD produced over its lifetime.[22] A joint venture, Morobe Mining Joint Ventures (MMJV), has been formed between the South African company, Harmony Gold Mining, and the Australian company, Newcrest Mining Company, and is developing two open pit operations. Around 255,000 ounces of gold and 4 million ounces of silver are expected to be produced annually over a ten year mine life, though the latter may be extended if further exploration establishes additional reserves. As at 30 June 2009, $A689 million had been expended in bringing the mine into operation.

And so the cycle of death and renewal continues, the scale of today's Hidden Valley operations demonstrating once again that it is not a poor man's field.

Wau's population today is about 12,000, with just a handful of expatriates; its few trade stores and other small shops are sustained largely by subsistence mining activities. But slowly the local economy is turning the corner. In 2006, the Wau Micro Bank was established to provide loans to small ventures; it has been very successful, and branches have since been opened in Lae, Bulolo, Kainantu, Wewak and Madang. There is also growing interest in tourism, with treks along the historical military 'Black Cat' track to Salamaua on the coast and along the World War II Bulldog Track to the southern coast of Papua New Guinea.

However, the valley's temperate climate and striking scenery are still experienced by few visitors. Wau and Bulolo are a long way from the track beaten by most tourists — whether Kokoda or the coastal and island attractions visited by those who prefer to retreat to the comfort of their cruise cabins when the day's sights have been seen. Travelling in this district, though rewarding, is not easy. The Wau-Bulolo road is still prone to landslides; here and elsewhere it is best to avoid the larger pot-holes whose murky contents after rain disguise their uncertain depth. Accommodation can usually be found, though a little local knowledge is necessary to locate it. Personal security is generally less of an issue than in Lae and Port Moresby — the local people are overwhelming friendly.[23]

Reminders of the mining era abound — the scarred landscape, the tailings, the water races, old machinery and the three derelict dredges. Many of the old mining sites are easily located. On the Wau-Bulolo road, a modern bridge crosses Koranga Creek at the place where Shark-Eye Park made his fortune. Further on, the site of Cliffside is evident from the different vegetation, and if there were any doubt, the local village is named Misa But (Mrs Booth). Below Cliffside, Edie Creek empties into the Bulolo, the starting point for Bill Royal and Dick Glasson as they set off up Mt. Kaindi. All along the river, and most of the creeks as well, nationals work their sluice boxes, like miners of old ever hopeful that today will be *the* day.

Wau airstrip still operates — though a few flights a week from Lae and Port Moresby are a far cry from the 50 or so movements a day in the 1930s. Landing and

The last miner's hut, 2001.

Looking up Merri Creek, 2001. Old Day Dawn workings on top right.

taking off on the steep slope is an 'experience'. Equally exhilarating (though not for the faint hearted) is the road to Edie Creek, offering spectacular views back over the valley to the Kuper Range. It broadly follows the same narrow route up Mt. Kaindi, past village women washing their clothes in small mountain streams and patches of bush draped with orchids and other colourful flowers. In some places, previously collapsed sections are still underpinned with logs; in others, the road cambers alarmingly towards the edge.

At Edie Creek, local miners still work the site of Harry Darby's Eldorado lease, though with rather less success. On the hillside above Merri Creek are the remains of the last pre-war house, with ill-fitting corrugated iron walls and chimneys. Nearby is the original Day Dawn mill, so laboriously carried piece by piece up the mule track and bearing the clearly visible date '1930'.

Side by side with these relics are signs of renewal. Historically high gold prices have led Edie Creek Mining and some private investors to form a new company, Niuminco Ltd., to expand existing operations and redevelop NGG's old underground workings as multiple open-pit mines.

From its modest beginnings, Lae has grown to become the second largest city in PNG, with a population variously estimated at between 120,000 and 160,000 and the county's largest and busiest port. There is, however, little evidence of the pre-war township. The aerodrome that grew from Levien's 1927 paddock to become one of the busiest in the world was used for commercial aviation until the mid-1980s when a new and larger one opened at Nadzab, the World War II airfield complex about 45 kilometres out of Lae. The old aerodrome will eventually be redeveloped. This aside, the only visible legacy of the pre-war period are the remains of a glorious avenue of huge raintrees draped with tendrils, planted by the Progress Association around 1937.

Salamaua—the once and future capital of New Guinea—is today a weekend haven for Lae residents, in an exquisitely beautiful and peaceful setting. The

30 kilometre trip takes an hour or two by boat. Behind the narrow coastal plain stretching between Lae and Salamaua, row after row of jagged peaks linked by ridges rise progressively to form a massive, timber-covered mountain range. Clouds usually fringe the top of the highest peaks, their underside a straight line the length of the coastline. Shadows create mottled patterns on the slopes in many shades of green, plumes of smoke rising from the occasional village. A timeless scene.

On Parsee Point and Salamaua isthmus several Japanese anti-aircraft guns point aimlessly at the sky. A dozen or so holiday cottages and houses belonging to Logui village are scattered along either side of the foot track threading its way haphazardly down the isthmus between the coconut palms. Where the Salamaua Hotel once stood, massive *calophyllum* trees have re-established themselves, their low-hanging branches reaching out once more to touch the breaking waves.

At the south-eastern end of the isthmus, 100 yards out to sea, stands a row of rusty metal piles—the remains of the 1930s breakwater built as protection against the encroaching sea. The ground on which the hospital and other Administration buildings once stood has disappeared. At high tide, the sea washes over the isthmus at its narrowest point. It seems inevitable that before long Parsee Point will become an island.

Salamaua, 2003.

Japanese anti-aircraft gun, 2001.

EPILOGUE

Late one evening in July 2003, I was sitting on a small jetty at Salamaua gazing into the empty blackness, the lights of Lae a faint glow on the distant horizon. And I imagined I saw the *Macdhui* standing offshore, its lights shining in the blackness, the ship abuzz with activity, even at this late hour. Behind me, I could hear the raucous clinking and clamour in the Salamaua Hotel bar above the sound of waves breaking on the shore of Bayern Bay. Fortunes were being won and lost, while further along 'the beach' the miners of long ago, alive with expectation, were finishing preparations for their first day on the road …

It was a moment of reflection and some emotion, heightened by the knowledge that, as a young man, my father had sailed into Salamaua as an assistant purser on the *Macdhui*. My grandfather had passed through Salamaua many times. Film footage shows him there as early as 1929, swapping gold and yarns with Harry Darby, while *Pacific Islands Monthly* carried reports of Les and Tom Yeomans showing films of the gold-fields and BGD's operations at the Hotel Salamaua. He was a convivial man, and this was a place he would never have tired of visiting.

My interest in discovering more about my grandfather was always secondary to exploring the bigger picture. I nevertheless hoped I would uncover information that would bring him out of the shadows of history. In this, I've been more successful than I could have dared hope at the outset.

Material on his activities was scattered far and wide. I found personal letters in the National Library between Les and the Chairman of Guinea Airways, Charles Wells, details of his activities as a Director of Guinea Airways in the State Library of South Australia,

Les Waterhouse (centre), with Major Allan Murray Jones (left), General Manager, de Havilland Australia and A.S. McDonald (right), AWA's Chief Engineer.

L.V. Waterhouse (right). The man on the left is believed to be BGD's Chief Engineer, O.B. Hart.

many letters on official files in the National Archives and Australian War Memorial in Canberra. There were also photos he donated to the Mitchell Library in Sydney shortly before his death in 1945, and original lease transfer documents bearing his signature and annotations in an old safe in the Department of Mining in Port Moresby.

Equally unexpected was my discovery of Arthur John, who had been at Bulolo with BGD in the early days, before returning to Sydney in 1934 as my grandfather's personal assistant, a position he held until 1941. In 1999, aged 93, he had published a book dealing largely with his experiences at Bulolo and working for Les. A long and fruitful liaison developed, with Arthur filling in many gaps for me. As this book goes to print, Arthur is 103 years old and still active and alert.

I discovered some film footage taken by Les in the Mitchell Library, donated by Tom Yeoman's son, Peter, after Tom's death. Some detective work led me to Peter, who had several photograph albums. One had belonged to my grandfather, and many of the photos in this book are taken from it.

In 2004, a chance discovery in the National Archives led me to believe that the remainder of Les's films might be in the National Film and Sound Archive in Canberra. While it had no record of them, a search eventually located 13 reels.

In Bulolo, Les's name on a plaque above the entrance records his position as the first Patron of the Bulolo Golf Club—his last physical link with the community he helped establish. Unfortunately, the Waterhouse Cup he donated for golf between the goldfields towns has long since disappeared.

My journey has covered much territory, with many unexpected twists and turns. Slowly, piece by piece, a clearer picture of Les has been revealed—his character, his interests, his business acumen and ethics, and of course the full scope of his role in the development of Bulolo and the goldfields generally.

In November 1939, the Chairman of Guinea Airways, Charles Wells, wrote to Les:

Just a line to congratulate you and your colleagues most heartily upon the information you have published today that your No. 8 dredge went into action on the 7th inst.. This marks the culmination of one of the finest mining and engineering feats in the world's history, and I hope that the efforts of your colleagues and yourself are thoroughly appreciated not only by your shareholders, but by the New Guinea and Australian mining community generally.

I suppose you almost feel that, with the completion of No. 8 dredge, the coming years will be more or less dull routine in the Bulolo Valley. But some day a skilful writer will do you the full justice to which you are entitled, and I can assure you that no one entertains a more genuine admiration for the achievements of Freeman, Banks, Waterhouse and the rest than I do.

It is with this in mind that I dedicate this book to my grandfather's memory.

Michael Waterhouse

ACKNOWLEDGEMENTS

I have been assisted by far too many people in Australia and Papua New Guinea—to be able to acknowledge all by name. There are some, however, without whose support this book, or significant aspects of it, could never have been written and published.

I must firstly express my appreciation for **Ross Garnaut's** unfailing belief in the concept of this book and in my ability to convert it into reality. Also to **Ila Temu**, who co-ordinated financial support for this book's publication within PNG. In this regard, I express my special appreciation to Barrick Gold, Morobe Mining Joint Ventures, Lihir Gold, Bank South Pacific and **Greg Anderson** at the PNG Chamber of Mines and Petroleum.

My thanks also go to **Michael Braund** for his wonderful maps, and his patience with my many small refinements, to **Jim Hoggett** for his many insightful suggestions on the manuscript and to **Suzanne Falkiner** for her editorial suggestions and persuasive encouragement to adopt different perspectives.

Amongst those in PNG to whom I am especially indebted are **Trevor Neale** and **James Saro** (Edie Creek), **Brian Boustridge** and **Gerry Massingham** (Bulolo), **Guyo Saweo** (somewhere on the Bulolo/Upper Watut Divide), **Donna Harvey-Hall** (Wau), **Monica Panga** (Kaisinik), **Jeanette Leahy** (Zenag), **Philip and Cathy Leahy** (Zenag and Salamaua) and **Glen Jacobsen** (Lae and Salamaua). Without the assistance of each and every one, my book—and my experience in researching it—would have been infinitely poorer.

In Australia, many B4s (Europeans who were in New Guinea before 1942) enriched my book with their experiences and by helping me understand and communicate a sense of time and place that has all but disappeared from living memory. Foremost among these, **Arthur John**, was at Bulolo before the first dredge. His recollections and reminiscences have been invaluable. So too those of **Collin Bayliss**, who arrived in Salamaua as a young boy in 1927, returning as a miner after the War. His recollections and knowledge have filled out the story in important respects.

The late **Tom Lega**, who rose from a young dredge hand before the War to dredge master afterwards, had a gift for reducing the complexities of dredging operations into language that could easily be understood by the layman. **Lloyd Hurrell**, a patrol officer before and after the War, was generous with his time and memories concerning the Kukukuku. The late **Peter Yeomans** had a unique connection with the Morobe goldfields, being the first child born there. After his father, the pilot Frank Drayton, lost his life in a plane crash in Wau, his mother married Tom Yeomans. Until his death, Peter was an ever present source of support.

Nor can I overlook the help provided in various ways by several historians, particularly **Jim Sinclair**—who has written many fine books on PNG history—**Hank Nelson** at the ANU, **Jan Roberts** and **Ian Howie-Willis**. Likewise the anthropologists **John Burton**, **Jamon Halvaksz** and **Daniele Moretti**.

Many people helped me with photos, including the former radio operator at Bulolo, the late **Alan Vagg**, **Carl Gunther**—whose father was BGD's doctor before and after the War—**Sue Sneddon** and Doris Booth's niece, **Daphne Landis**. I particularly wish to acknowledge my debt to a writer and a photographer, whose fine work contributed so much. **Jack O'Neill**'s compelling manuscript, *A Prospector's Diary* in the National Library (published after his death as *Up From South*) gleams with evocative descriptions and insights into life on the goldfields and was a source of many quotes.

Harry Downing was an Assistant District Officer with a passion for photography. His remarkable collection of negatives, now held by the Mitchell Library, documents life in New Guinea, and particularly on the goldfields, through much of the 1920s and 30s. The extensive research and writings of **Ian Grabowsky** and **Alan Healy** have also been invaluable.

No work such as this can ever be written without the assistance of many librarians and archivists. Foremost among these were in the Manuscripts section at the National Library, the National Archives in Canberra and Melbourne, the PNG National Archives, the Mitchell Library—and specifically the former Mitchell Librarian, **Elizabeth Ellis**—the Fryer Library, the State Libraries of New South Wales, South Australia and Victoria, and Westpac's Archives.

Michael Waterhouse

GLOSSARY

balus — bird, aeroplane.

banis — fence or enclosure. Also, defensive palisade of bamboo around a village.

betel nut — nut of the Areca palm. Mildly intoxicating when chewed with lime and daka, the bean-like fruit of the daka vine with a peppery taste. The mixture turns red with chewing.

bilum — woven string bag used by women to carry goods and babies; slung over the forehead and down the back.

bokis — box, such as those used by indentured labourers to store their possessions and carry items back to their villages at the end of their indenture.

boi — male employed by Europeans as an indentured labourer or servant.

bull roarer — shaped wooden artefact which, when swung on the end of a long piece of string, generates a loud whirring, sometimes thought to be the voice of a spirit. Used to stir men up prior to a fight.

kanaka — New Guinean who was not an indentured labourer or otherwise employed by Europeans. A villager.

guria — earthquake or tremor.

kaikai — food.

Kaindi — mountain at the back of Wau. Variously pronounced Kai-ende or Kai-endi, but more commonly among Europeans Kain-di.

karuka or karuga — pandanus palm, the trunk of which was often used for fluming and the leaves to thatch villagers' houses.

kaukau — sweet potato.

kiap — government official, most commonly a patrol officer.

kukukuku — (pron. kooka-kooka) known today as the Anga. (See Explanatory Note).

kunai grass — *Imperata arundinacea*. Grows up to ten feet in height. Widely used as thatch for huts.

kunda — strong vine used by village people in lieu of rope, for example in the construction of bridges. Also known by Europeans as 'lawyer vine' or rattan.

laplap — loin cloth.

limbong or limbon — small black *Areca* palm with a hard outer trunk and soft pithy inside which was split down the centre and used for floors and walls in houses, with the outer curve uppermost or inward facing. Also used by individual miners for fluming.

Logui — village near Salamaua. Pronounced Low-gwee or Lau-gwee.

luluai — man appointed by the Administration to keep order in his village, settle disputes, keep tracks free of bush, etc.

make paper — act of signing a contract of indenture.

mal — bark covering used by the kukukuku as protection against the weather and to hide weapons.

meri — New Guinean woman, girl or wife.

matmat — cemetery.

manki — boy.

Motu — language traditionally spoken in and around the Port Moresby area.

pitpit — type of wild sugar cane. Its stems are used for light fences and walls. Also used as a vegetable.

pulpul or purpur — grass skirt, though also sometimes made of leaves and reeds.

sacsac — sago. When used in relation to housing, it may mean the wood of the sago palm or leaves used in thatching.

sarip — long narrow bladed knife made of hoop iron with one edge sharpened and used by labourers to cut grass, e.g. on aerodromes.

singsing — traditional dance used for ceremonial purposes or for pleasure.

tultul — a man appointed by the Administration to advise and assist the luluai. Often having a knowledge of pidgin, he would be used as a messenger and interpreter.

wantok — someone else who speaks the same language and/or comes from the same area.

---

1 Melanesian pidgin terms are drawn largely from F. Mihalic, 1957, and were in general use throughout New Guinea between the wars.

Mining and Other Technical Terms

alluvial — gravel deposited by rivers or streams.

auriferous — gold bearing.

box sluicing — mining where gravel and dirt are washed through a sluice box, in the bottom of which are riffles — strips of cane, wood or metal set an angle to the water flow so as to trap the gold. Lighter material is washed over the riffles and out the end of the box or, in the case of rocks, removed by hand.

claim — small area of ground, usually alluvial, granted to the holder of a Miner's Right to work for gold. Initially (1923) measuring 40 feet by 40 feet, their size was progressively increased. By 1926-27 they could be 30 metres by 60 metres and by 1937 up to 300 metres by 300 metres according to the distance from the nearest gold mine. If outside the limits of a goldfield, an area could be marked out of up to 400 metres by 400 metres.

colours — little flakes or specks of gold. See also 'fly shits'.

dredging and sluicing lease — 21 year lease of up to 240 acres over alluvial ground granted to any person who could work it by dredging or gravitation. It could be pegged in any shape and therefore encompass a creek or river and all the adjacent land worth working. An annual rental was payable to the Administration.

extended claim — claim four times the size of an ordinary alluvial claim. These were later granted where the ground was poor and/or could only be worked with difficulty.

flume — traditionally a wooden section of a water race used to traverse a gully. Miners would split lengths of karuka, a tree of the pandanus family, or improvise using materials to hand, including old 44 gallon drums with their ends removed and either cut in half longitudinally or joined end to end.

fly shits — specs of very fine gold.

gold mining lease — 21 year lease of up to 50 acres permitting the lessee to engage in lode mining.

gravitation sluicing — sluicing where water is brought from a remote source along a flume or other channel and run directly into a sluice box. Contrast with hydraulic sluicing.

ground sluicing — sluicing with water brought from a remote source along a flume or other channel to a terrace where it was used to break down the face. The material dislodged was then passed through a race cut in the ground to trap the gold in stone riffles, while removing extraneous material. The resulting concentrate was then passed through a sluice box in the usual way.

head race — water race above a sluice box or other workings, bringing water to the site.

hydraulic elevator — see jet elevator.

hydraulic sluicing — sluicing using water brought from a higher level by a flume and/or water race, often over a considerable distance, to deliver it to the workings under considerable pressure, where it is then applied using a monitor or nozzle to break down the face of a terrace. The material is then washed through a sluice box.

jet elevator — water jet device through which water passes under high pressure creating suction which raises auriferous material from a sump to a higher level for processing through a sluice box.

lease — see dredging and sluicing lease, and gold mining lease.

lode mining — the excavation and crushing of ore, typically from veins as at Day Dawn, with gold often being leached from the residue using cyanide.

Miner's Right — licence awarded to an aspiring prospector, which gave them the right to look for gold but not to mine it. If they discovered gold, they needed then to peg and apply for a claim or lease.

monitor — large nozzle that is used to apply a jet of water under pressure, so as to to wash and break down overburden and alluvial material to a size that can be passed through a sluice box.

overburden — barren soil, clay and other material overlaying an auriferous (or other geological) deposit.

paddock — area of a claim or lease where mining activities are concentrated. Includes the pond where a dredge operates.

payable gold — the amount of gold that needs to be recovered by a miner to cover his costs, including wages and keep for his labourers, and provide a return sufficient to cover his expenses.

reward claim — awarded to the holder of a Miner's Right who discovered gold at least 15 miles from any claim or lease being worked. It amounted to between five and ten ordinary claims.

reef — narrow vein of quartz (or stringer) containing gold.

retort—device or process used to extract gold from an amalgam with mercury, which was used to separate it from fine sand and other such material.

riffles—strips set in the bottom of sluice boxes to trap gold. They typically comprised interwoven mats of cane or short timber strips placed at right angles to the sides of the box. They created an undercurrent which freed the gold from the sand and mud, trapping it in the gap between the riffles.

sluice box—see box sluicing.

specimen—piece of gold-carrying quartz, usually worn by water and found when sluicing. Also known as a 'slug'.

sponge gold—the gold matrix left behind after the amalgam (with mercury) has been retorted.

tailings—the residue, for the most part rocks, after sluicing or dredging.

tail race—water race below a sluice box or other workings, taking water and other residue away from the workings.

tributer—alluvial miner who works leases held by others and pays the lease owner a percentage of the gold he mines.

wash—alluvial material—stones and gravel.

water race—channel cut in the ground to carry water from a high point so as to increase water pressure used in sluicing operations. A water race was also used at the Upper Baiune Power station to deliver large quantities of water to drive electricity-generating machinery. See also head race and tail race.

WEIGHTS, MEASURES AND CURRENCIES

Weights

1 pennyweight (dwt.)	1/20th of an ounce
1 ounce (oz.)	28.35 grams
1 pound (lb.)	0.4536 kilogram
1 long ton (British)	2,240 pounds
1 short ton (US)	2,000 pounds (or 907.2 kg)

Measures

1 inch	2.54 cms
1 foot	12 inches or 0.3048 metres
1 yard	3 feet or 0.9144 metres
1 chain	66 feet or 20.12 metres
1 mile	1.61 kilometres
m.p.h.	miles per hour

Gold price

pre-31 January 1934	$US20.67
Post-31 January 1934	$US35.00

Currency

1 penny	12 to one shilling
1 shilling	20 to one pound (£1)

Exchange rates (1935)

£A1	$C4.00
$C1.00	5 shillings Australian (= $A0.50)
$US1.00	5 shillings Australian

The value today of any specific amount mentioned in the text can be calculated using the Reserve Bank calculator **http://www.rba.gov.au/calculator/ AnnualPreDecimal.html**

NOTES

CHAPTER 1

1 Marco Polo proclaimed the existence of Lochac, a 'wild region' to the south east of the main Indonesian island of Java, noting that the people there *have a great abundance of gold, so great, indeed, that no-one could believe it without seeing it* … Jack-Hinton, 1964, page 50.

2 Collins, 1867, page 12.

3 Matt Crowe and Arthur Darling were an 'odd couple', Crowe being two metres in height and thin, and Darling not much above 1.5 metres tall, and weighing about 57kg. But their ability and tenacity as prospectors in Papua were legendary.

4 Annual Report for Papua 1906/07, page 79.

5 The name 'Kukukuku' was first used by Europeans in Papua in the early 1900s to describe people who occupied a large area of the mountainous interior.

6 From 1888/89 to 1912/13, Papuan goldfields produced 358,000 ounces of gold, of which 45% came from Woodlark Island, 20% from the Yodda River and 18% from the Gira River. Annual Report for Papua 1912/13, page 36.

7 Gold bearing quartz lodes gradually disintegrate in response to the chemical and mechanical action of air and water. Much of the gold thus liberated finds its way into rivers which may carry it great distances until the slower force of water allows it to settle and form alluvial deposits. This process was well understood and was a catalyst for exploration upstream from such deposits.

8 Sack and Clark, 1979, page 189.

9 Healy 1965, page 112.

10 The story of Arthur Darling draws extensively on Frank Clune's *Somewhere in New Guinea*, 1951, which was based on interviews with Les Joubert, a well known miner.

11 Clune, 1951, page 120.

12 Joe Sloane knew Park well, having been mining in Papua since about 1893. He told Frank Clune in 1943 that he was in no doubt that Darling had told Park the location of the gold at Koranga Creek.

13 Albert Bethune to Frank Clune, 20 March 1953.

14 Auerbach, 1939, 1940.

15 Sack and Clark, 1980, page 110.

16 Cited in Hiery, 1995, page 283.

CHAPTER 2

1 The level of interest among Australians in the Military Administration prompted Les Joubert to write an article for possible prospectors about pre-requisites for successful prospecting and the dangers likely to be encountered. This was published in *The Rabaul Record*, 1 May 1916, pages 6-8.

2 Commonwealth Parliamentary Debates, 29 September 1921, Vol. 97, page 11600.

3 In fact, although Australia was not permitted to benefit from the Mandate, the Australian Government clearly hoped that it would do so. In 1920, Sir Joseph Cook said that if oil were discovered there, *it would be a source of infinite financial gain for Australia*, while in 1922 Prime Minister Hughes referred to New Guinea as *a land fertile and rich in all products … a land of abundance*. Cited in Hiery, 1995, page 107.

4 Lukin, 16 January 1923.

5 The holder of a Miner's Right could apply for a claim measuring 40 feet by 40 feet, but could not work it until the Mining Ordinance was proclaimed to apply to the area in which it was located. The size of a claim was increased later in 1923 to 100 feet by 50 feet and in 1924 to 200 feet by 100 feet.

6 The Ordinance did not distinguish between 'dredging' and 'sluicing' or the circumstances in which miners should apply for a claim rather than a lease. This defect was to cause major problems and ultimately lead to a Royal Commission.

7 Albert Bethune, 20 March 1953.

8 James Twycross, 28 July 1943.

9 Until 1930, Salamaua was spelled 'Salamoa'. For simplicity, the later spelling is used throughout this book.

10 Mason's given names were John Pidcock, but he appears generally to have been known as Harry. Mason kept a diary of which three versions exist, covering overlapping periods, along with a more loquacious document based on the diaries, 'Descriptive Notes on New Guinea Journey 1921–1922'.

11 The Kaiwa and Biangai were the two main tribes travellers from the coast encountered on their way to the Bulolo valley. The Biangai lived on the ridges lining the south-eastern end of the valley, while the Kaiwa were closer to the coast.

12 Mason, Diary, 10 July 1922.

13 At the time of his appointment, Levien was a relieving Deputy District Officer. He was confirmed in the position on 7 April 1923.

14 Vince Slattery to Frank Clune; Alice Innes and Tom Yeomans, Alice Innes papers, Mitchell Library.

15 Jack Nettleton to Frank Clune, 27 April 1949.

16 The Kukukuku lived to the south-west of Koranga Creek and were traditional enemies of the Biangai.

17 There is no record of Clune's correspondence with Ellis in the Clune papers. However, Clune recounted the visit by Ellis in a letter to Nettleton on 12 July 1949.

18 Clune heard this story from George Ellis in 1940. One of the early miners in New Guinea, Fred Smart, informed Clune in 1943 that he had been told this by Park and Nettleton.

19 Clune, 1951, pages 164–165. Ironically, Levien was wounded by an arrow in the chest on this trip. Earning his 'colours' can only have made him feel more secure in his position.

20 Lukin to his mother, 17 February 1923. The extent of cannibalism among villagers living close to the field is discussed in Chapter 15.

21 Levien, in evidence to Edie Creek Royal Commission, April 1927.

22 IAMS, 19 April 1923.

23 Decision by Mining Warden McLean, Weidenbach v. Guinea Gold and D.R. Booth, 11 January 1927.

24 IAMS, 28 June 1923.

25 IAMS, 2 August 1923. This is clearly a reference to Park, whom Levien was using as a cover for his activities.

26 IAMS, 18 October 1923.

27 Harry Mason appears to have left before this, as his diary ends abruptly on 9 February.

28 Bethune, op. cit.

29 i.e. on 21 April 1923.

30 Joe Sloane, May 1943.

31 Wisdom, 1927a (4 February).

CHAPTER 3

1 In other mining jurisdictions, alluvial ground was normally preserved for claims for the holders of Miner's Rights, leases traditionally being granted only where the ground was poor or required large scale equipment to mine profitably. However, the Territory's Mining Ordinance was ambiguous as to the circumstances in which miners should apply for a claim rather than a lease (of up to 240 acres).

2 B.V. Barton, March 1924.

3 Levien, 4 July 1924.

4 Lukin to Secretary for Mines, Rabaul, 1 August 1924.

5 This account of Coldham's work draws primarily on A.M. Healy, 1965 and 1967.

6 Healy 1965, page 116.

7 Charles Wells and Levien had been through Duntroon together during the War, and Wells had obtained Levien's power of attorney when in Melbourne in November 1923.

8 Levien, 1925a.

9 Doris Booth later recounted her experiences in a book, *Mountains, Gold and Cannibals*, on which this brief account draws.

10 Booth, 1929, page 102.

11 Taylour and Morley later reported that Park was said to be recovering an average of 20 ounces per day.

12 A visitor to the goldfields early in 1925 described the process as follows: *Most of the gold is in the wash right at the bottom of the creek. The first thing to be done is to get rid of the water, and this is done by damming the creek and cutting trenches along the banks. The water required for washing purposes is taken from the dam by a half round hollow log called a flume, and is about 12 to 14 feet long. The water comes along the flume and runs through the box. This is cut out of solid trees and is about 18 inches wide and 6 inches deep; the sides are about 1½ inches thick and anything from 5 to 10 feet long. In the bottom of the box are placed strips of half inch cane to make riffles. These are nailed in frames, generally three to a box, to facilitate removal.*
The work is done by boys, who stand in the creek and shovel the dirt, sand and wash into the box. Water coming through the flume washes it away and the gold settles in the riffles and drops to the bottom of the box. A team of 10 boys is required for one box, as it takes 7 for shovelling, one to watch for specimens and two to clear away the tailings which go through the box after being washed. One has to put a lot of dirt through the box to get an ounce of gold. (*The Rabaul Times*, 29 May 1925)

13 Bill Royal, evidence to Edie Creek Royal Commission, 1927, page 1296.

14 Comments made by Bill Royal to Dick Glasson, as recounted to the author by Collin Bayliss, 2001.

15 Clune 1951, pages 199–200.

16 James Hebbard, 1926b (2 June).

CHAPTER 4

1 Clune 1951, page 201.

2 Levien, 1926b.

3 By this time, the size of claims had been increased to 200 feet by 100 feet — still very small by comparison with dredging or sluicing leases of up to 240 acres.

4 Levien, 1926e.

5 Levien, 1926c.

6 Levien, 1926f.

7 Levien, 1926d.

8 Levien, evidence to Edie Creek Royal Commission, 1927b.

9 Clune suggested that Costello was a cousin of Levien's and that he had arrived to help work Park's lease or take it up himself if the Administrator did not consent to its transfer to Levien (1951, page 198). The fact that he had 'form', having been convicted in Melbourne of loitering with intent to commit a felony, was later used by the Administrator to besmirch Levien's reputation.

10 Lukin, 1926.

11 Levien, 1926g.

12 Hebbard, 1926a.

13 Hebbard, 1926d.

14 Hebbard's report, dated 30 June, was not received in Adelaide until 12 August.

15 Oakley, 1926a.

16 Hebbard, 1926c.

17 NGAR 1926–27, page 122.

18 Wisdom, evidence to Edie Creek Royal Commission, 1927c, page 1330.

19 Wisdom, 1926a, 1926b, 1926c.

20 *Argus*, 17 August 1926.

21 Levien, 1926h.

22 *Argus*, 23 August 1926.

23 Ted Bishton, March 2005, page 44.

24 M. Leahy and M. Crain, 1937, page 9.

25 Dickson's actions may have delayed the spread of dysentery and lessened its severity, but in the years that followed dysentery was endemic at Edie Creek, resulting in many deaths.

26 Booth, 1929, page 159.

27 Sir William Glasgow, 1926.

28 Wau was on the lower slopes of Mt. Kaindi in the open valley above the gorge. At this time it was no more than a few huts, but over the next decade it was to become the largest township on the goldfields.

29 NGAR 1926/27, page 123. 42.5% of all labourers had died on on the Lakekamu in 1910. The Administration claimed that the comparable figure in 1926 was 1%. In evidence to the 1927 Royal Commission, Cilento acknowledged that 58 had died since 1925. There were a further 37 deaths from dysentery, mostly in Salamaua, in 1927–28. (NGAR 1927/28, page 98).

30 Gold in situ was typically mixed with a proportion of silver, the amount determining the fineness of gold. At Upper Edie Creek gold was, on average, 551 fine, considerably below that in the upper Bulolo and Black Cat Creek, where it was as fine as 876 and the lower Bulolo valley, where it was typically 660–680 fine. Lowenstein, pages 193, 208. In 1930, this gold was valued at £2/4 shillings (with gold at £4/5 shillings a fine ounce), whereas elsewhere it was as high as £3/15 shillings.

31 Madigan, August 1926. Hydraulic sluicing may take various forms but typically involves the application of water to alluvial gravels under pressure, whereas box sluicing relies on gravitation.

32 Thomas, 1926.

33 Oakley, 1926b.

34 In fact, the Administrator was still dithering over the appointment of a Mining Warden. Five days after Oakley's remarks, Wisdom wrote to the Department that he was *anxiously awaiting the arrival of the Mining Registrar … as there is no-one with any knowledge of Mining Administration available here* (Wisdom, 1926d). Up to this time, the Administration seems to have been content to make do with one of its existing, if inexperienced, staff as Mining Warden (first Lukin and then Oakley), supplemented by a Mining Registrar. Only after the Registrar proved inadequate was an experienced Warden requested from Queensland. He (J.D. McLean) did not arrive until late December 1926.

35 Wisdom, 1926d.

CHAPTER 5

1 Weston, 1978, page 67.

2 Mining Warden's Report, December 1926.

3 Pryke, evidence to Edie Creek Royal Commission, 1927, page 156.

4 Chauncy, 1927, page 160.

5 Initially, mats of rice which weighed 53 pounds were permitted, provided they were unbroken. But some miners abused this latitude, opening them, inserting axe and mattock heads and sewing them up again; and so the limit was fixed rigidly at 50 pounds.

6 O'Neill, page 4.

7 Booth, 1929, page 54.

8 O'Neill, page 5.

9 Booth, 1929. page 69. A.A. Chauncy was also spellbound: *The grandeur of the scenery would almost take one's breath away. Such mighty mountain ranges and gorges I never dreamt existed.*

10 M.G., 1935, page 30.

11 Ibid.

12 J. Murphy, 30 June 1937, 1937a.

13 Bishton, December 2004, pages 47–48.

14 E. Oakley, evidence to Edie Creek Royal Commission, 1927, page 1125.

15 Guinea Gold Minutes, 16 December 1926. In January 1927, the Mining Warden estimated the cost at £1/10 shillings per 50 pounds.

16 Sir William Glasgow, 1926.

17 Native Labour Regulations, 1924. The list of requirements was gradually expanded over time to include specific quantities of trade tobacco, soap and matches, and clothing, the dimensions of sleeping space (7 feet by 3 feet) and beds, which were required to be 9 inches off the floor.

18 Mining Warden's Report, January 1927.

19 In evidence to the Royal Commission, the miner Henry Bond estimated it cost him £60 per month to keep 15 boys, £20 for himself and £20 for medicines and tools. He brought his labourers from New Britain and thus didn't have to pay a recruiter's fee. This suggests that his claim would have been payable if it had produced more than 12.5 ounces a week.

20 M. Leahy and M. Crain 1937, page 36.

21 C. Hendry, evidence to Edie Creek Royal Commission, 1927, pages 582–589.

22 I. Grabowsky, Chapter 2, page 15.

23 F. Pryke, evidence to Edie Creek Royal Commission, 1927, page 156.

24 R.W. Cilento, evidence to Edie Creek Royal Commission, 1927, page 1094.

25 E. Oakley, evidence to Edie Creek Royal Commission, 1927, page 1127.

26 i.e. the number of deaths as a percentage of the average number of indentured labourers. The majority of labourers in the Morobe District worked in mining, either as carriers or labourers.

27 NGAR 1932/33, pages 64–65.

28 NGAR 1932/33, page 64.

CHAPTER 6

1 Edie Creek Royal Commission Report, page 14. The word "excessive" is significant in that it was the reason given by Madigan in March 1926 as the basis for the original objection. Report, page 10. The Commissioner was, in effect, upholding the original objection.

2 ECRC Report, page 6.

3 ECRC Report, page 7. MacGregor was implying that claims rather than leases were normally granted over alluvial ground so that many more miners could be accommodated. However, the Territory's Mining Ordinance was unique in giving the Administrator discretion to grant a dredging or sluicing lease. The suggestion that this discretion may have been hastily inserted was apparently due to the absence of any criteria as to the circumstances in which it might be exercised.

4 ECRC Report, page 16.

5 ECRC Report, page 17.

6 Mining Warden's Report, June 1927.

7 G. Palmer, evidence to Edie Creek Royal Commission, 1927, pages 179–191.

8 O'Neill, page 18.

9 Bishton 2005, page 46.

10 Water pressure increases, the greater the fall from its source. Thus water channelled into pipes and brought from some distance upstream could be applied with great force to the ground through a nozzle or monitor. This enabled barren overburden to be removed more quickly than by pick and shovel, providing faster access to the alluvial gravels. Freeing up labourers meant that the gravels could be shifted more quickly through sluice boxes.

11 Johns, Letter to Inspector, Bank of New South Wales, Brisbane, 23 January 1930.

12 A.A. Innes, December 1935.

13 M. Leahy and M. Crain 1937, page 41.

14 The Mining Ordinance 1928 was eventually amended in 1930 to prohibit the granting *to any holder of a miner's right to enter upon and carry on mining operations on any land comprised in any dredging or sluicing lease* — in effect, the opposite of the November 1926 provision.

15 Levien, 1926i.

16 Levien, 1927a.

17 S.110A of the Mining Ordinance required each lease to be manned by at least one European for each 16 hectares (about 40 acres) or part thereof, though exemptions could be obtained for up to six months if circumstances warranted.

18 In his April 1928 Report, the Mining Warden reported *The Superintendent* [E. Broughton Jensen] *is experimenting with a model aerial dredger for use on the Bulolo River which, owing to the spread and volume of its waters, and the lack of suitable places for diversion, is difficult to work. It involves a specially designed, heavy powerful grab, fitted with suitable teeth, automatically closing, transporting and dumping over grizzles and through sluices.*

19 Wells, 13 February 1928. This letter underlines how the Board's lack of mining experience and knowledge of conditions in New Guinea hampered its effectiveness. Levien had stressed the central importance of labour from the outset. Wells did not visit the country until 1932.

20 Whether Jensen's condemnation of Coldham's water race was motivated by his desire to induce the Board to adopt his dredger is unknown, but his later decision to switch camps from Guinea Gold to NGG so that he could conduct a survey for light rail from Salamaua to the field — another of his dreams — suggests he may have been motivated more by personal considerations than the company's interests.

21 In July, Jensen wrote *The whole of the money spent at Kulolo* [on the long water race] *is bearing results in that we have a kaukau patch 4 miles long by one chain wide with a good level track for carriers running right through it.* (Jensen 1928b) It is doubtful that the Board would have been mollified. In November 1928, Jensen wrote (with unintended irony) to Oluf Moen, who would take over from him, *Our working profits recently have averaged about £500 per month. Our savings due to the use of kaukau instead of air-carried rice have been about £700 per month, so that at a glance it is apparent that the gardens are responsible for our profits.* (Jensen 1928c)

CHAPTER 7

1 At the time Placer acquired its option over the Bulolo leases, it had prospective dredging properties in Colombia and Alaska, but had yet to earn any revenue from mining.

2 Decoto's Report was published in Bulolo Gold Dredging's 1930 Prospectus, pages 15–20.

3 This compares with Levien's 1925 estimate of 23 million cubic yards with a value of 2 shillings a yard.

4 A royalty of 1% had been applied to gold won from dredging or sluicing leases since August 1925 and to claims under Miner's Rights since September 1926. It applied to all gold irrespective of whether a miner was on payable ground. As more than half were not, the increase was not well received. For mines that were marginally profitable, the 5% royalty was also a significant impost. Thus, in 1937–38, Sandy Creek Gold Sluicing estimated that the royalty represented about 10% of total expenditure.

5 Miners' Association to Minister for Home and Territories, 5 March 1928.

6 Wisdom, 1928a.

7 Departmental Minute, 27 April 1928.

8 In 1930, Alice Innes wrote extensive notes on Sheldon's surveying activities, based on a discussion with him. In a letter to Innes, dated 3 September 1944, Sheldon said *Had there been any trace of Administrative honesty there was no time at which the Salamaua-Wau route could not have been achieved — they just sold out in cold blood on all occasions where either honour or intestinal fortitude was in demand.* Innes, 1930.

9 Mining Warden's Report, May 1928.

10 Wisdom, 1928b.

11 Levien, 1929b.

12 Banks, 1929.

13 The events discussed here were related by Mustar to Grabowsky, December 1929.

14 Banks later estimated that the benefit to shareholders of doing this was more than $3 million. Banks, 1937, page 811.

15 Grabowsky, December 1929, pages 106–107.

16 Sinclair, 1983, page 56.

17 Jensen, 1928a.

18 Guinea Gold Minutes, 3 January 1929.

19 Dickinson, December 1928.

20 Grabowsky, March 1929.

21 Guinea Airways Minutes, 2 August 1929.

22 Grabowsky, October 1929, page 10.

23 Sinclair 1983, page 74.

Chapter 8

1 Views expressed on 31 August 1929. Prime Minister's Department 1930a, 18 March.

2 Wisdom, 1930a.

3 Dunstan, 1931, pages 5–6.

4 Ibid.

5 *Bulletin*, 6 June 1928.

6 Urquhart, 13 November 1929.

7 Taylour, 1930.

8 Hyde, 1931.

9 The outline of the commencement of Day Dawn's operations draws primarily on three sources: Morley (1931), the Mining Warden (1931) and Grabowsky (1964).

10 Bank of New South Wales, Salamaua, April 1932.

11 John, 1999, page 81.

12 Arthur Ives, cited in Sinclair, 1998, page 95.

13 O'Neill, page 67.

14 Wisdom, 1921, 1923a.

15 NGGZ No. 333, 15 July 1932. A similar proclamation was made on 30 April 1932 (NGGZ No. 327) declaring land around Wau to be 'waste and vacant'.

16 John, 1999, page 120.

17 Wisdom, 1932.

18 Wells, 1932.

19 Levien's ashes were taken up in a G31 flown by Alan Cross, Guinea Airways' General Manager.

Chapter 9

1 The gold and any silver would combine with the mercury to form an amalgam. This was collected every ten days or so and taken to a retort house where a furnace vaporised the mercury, which passed into a condenser where it solidified as it cooled and was then available for re-use. The furnace also separated the gold and silver. The resulting 'sponge gold' was then smelted and cast into iron moulds. Each bar was no more than 500 ounces. The dredge number and a consecutive number were punched on the face of the bar. It was then sewn in calico and despatched to Australia by registered post.

2 Sinclair, 1983, page 100.

3 Baskett, 1991, page 25.

4 The deep digging dredges, however, covered only a few hundred yards. J.D. Simpson, 1946.

5 Downs, 1999, page 157.

6 A. John, 1999, page 134. Dunkin (1950) dismissively concludes (page 24) that the *agricultural possibilities of the valley flats are meagre and there is therefore no necessity for resoiling*. This was despite BGD running a herd of cattle and growing enough vegetables and fruit to meet the needs of its European and New Guinean workforce. Patrol Officer J.R. Black, who knew the area well, observed that *The enforcement of compulsory resoiling conditions in such rich agricultural areas as the Bulolo Valley seems logical. It seems wrong to permit the destruction for all time of a valuable agricultural asset.* Black, 1936, page 13.

7 From 1939, the Australian Government taxed at 50% that part of the proceeds of gold sales which exceeded £9 per fine ounce. BGD paid $2.2 million in royalties (£A566,00) and $1.3 million (£A343,000) in gold tax up to the cessation of operations in January 1942.

8 Healy, 1967, page 72.

9 The water race was made of 2.5 million super feet of local cedar, which was water and white ant resistant. Sinclair, 1998, page 100.

10 Dunkin, 1950, page 10.

11 Healy, 1967, page 65.

12 BGD accounted for 61% of all royalty payments during this period and 12.3% of all revenue from this source. A full series of import duty figures is unavailable for either BGD or New Guinea. But BGD accounted for 12–16% of all import duties between 1936 and 1940, which collectively accounted for 41% of Administration revenue. Other payments by BGD included survey fees, lease rental fees, company registration fees, stamp duty on mining lease transfers, indenture labour fees and postage—the last being significant, as all BGD's gold was posted by registered mail to Australia. Details of these other costs are unavailable, but a reasonable estimate is that BGD's payments to the Administration over the period represented around 25% of the latter's overall revenue.

13 One noteworthy series of articles, published in 1933 in *The Sydney Mail*, was by Tom Richards, a former Queensland gold miner who had gained fame as the only Rugby Union footballer to play for both the Wallabies and the British Lions, and whose name today is on the Cup awarded to the victor in series between these two sides.

14 Many of the dredge hands were World War I veterans, and their respect for Lord Gowrie doubtless reflected his military record as much as his position as Governor-General. He won the Victoria Cross during the Sudan Campaign in 1899 and during World War I was seriously wounded at Gallipoli. During this war he was awarded the DSO and Bar and mentioned in despatches five times.

15 Banks, 1932, pages 624–625.

16 Mustar, 1934.

17 BGD's sawmill produced 7.6 million super feet of timber over the nine years to April 1940.

18 This excluded gold royalty and amortisation. The eight to nine cents per yard recorded throughout the 1930s would have been even lower but for depreciation of the Canadian dollar in 1934 and 1939.

19 From the beginning, BGD despatched all its gold to Sydney by registered mail, transferring responsibility for security to the Post Office. Gold bars were flown to Lae (and later to Port Moresby) where they were handed over to the Post Office for despatch by ship.

20 At Bulolo these included 13 single men's quarters, each accommodating three men, and six married quarters, staff quarters for four men, residences for the manager, assistant manager and engineer, general office, wireless office, recreation hall, large store, trade store, large warehouse, cleanup and smelting house, a laboratory, machine shop, carpenter's shop, mess hall, refrigerating store and plant, and general hospitals for Europeans and New Guineans. At Bulwa, rougher houses were built for 100 men engaged in dredge construction, as well as a permanent office, store, mess hall, garage, refrigerating plant and machine shop. Mining Warden 1933.

21 McNicoll, 1934, page 108.

22 Lega, 2001.

23 Healy, 1967, pages 86–87.

24 Healy, 1967, pages 89–90.

25 Honeysett, 26 June 1932.

26 Honeysett, 30 June 1932.

27 Sinclair, 1998, page 103.

28 John, 1983, pages 2–3.

29 Healy, 1967, page 85.

30 Healy, 1967, pages 83–84.

31 Very few labourers brought their wives to Bulolo, although they were encouraged to do so by both the Administration and BGD. Those who did were allocated houses in a separate compound—two couples to a house. In 1937, there were only 30 such couples at Bulolo.

32 Thus, for example, BGD's mortality rate in 1935 was 1.8% compared with NGG's 4.3%. Sinclair, 1998, page 104.

Chapter 10

1 Warden's Report, March 1931. In his report for the year to 30 June 1931, the Day Dawn Mine Manager claimed that the landed cost in Salamaua of its 27 ton Babcock and Wilcox boiler was £875. Guinea Airways charged £1,512 to transport it to Wau. It cost a further 3d. per pound to transport it to Edie Creek, a total of £2,016. Similarly, rice that cost £12 per ton in Salamaua cost £70.10.0 per ton by the time it reached the mine. Mining Warden 1931.

2 At the beginning of the 1930s, Great Britain and the USA (and many other countries) were on the gold standard, the pound sterling and dollar being convertible into gold at the rate of £3/17 shillings 10 and a half pence and $20.67 per ounce respectively. The obligation to exchange paper currency for gold effectively prevented governments from pursuing the reflationary policies which would alleviate the effects of the Depression. Finally, in September 1931, faced with the choice of defending the convertibility of sterling for gold or reflating its economy, the British Government abandoned the gold standard. The USA followed in April 1933.

3 Mining Warden's Report, July 1933.

4 The par value of NGG shares was £1 and that of BGD was $5 Canadian, or approximately £A1/5 shillings.

5 *Pacific Islands Monthly*, 22 January 1934; 15 September 1939.

6 *Pacific Islands Monthly*, 23 July 1937.

7 Wells noted in his diary on 4 December 1935 that in negotiations with Guinea Airways' General Manager, Eric Chater, Webster had *made a number of hysterical and bombastic assertions and threats, which Chater coolly countered.*

8 Blaikie Webster, 1936a.

9 See discussion of the Wau-Edie Creek road in Chapter 20, and particularly the observations on the Administration by the Dunstan Report in 1931 on the New Guinea Mining Industry.

10 Webster, 1936c. The substance of Webster's claim was related in a letter to the Minister on 14 February 1936: *The 5% royalty bears very heavily on underground mining and milling operations as compared with dredging or sluicing of alluvials. Put briefly, working under most efficient methods, it will cost at least 30 shillings per ton of ore to cover underground mining and development, stoping, hoisting, crushing and partly milling, at which point the ore from the view of gold recovery is in much the same position as alluvials. One ton of ore is approximately equivalent to 1 cubic yard of alluvial … In addition, mining claims have to bear much higher lease rents than alluvial claims.* (Webster, 1936b).

11 McNicoll, 1936a.

12 Winding engine drivers operated winches used in shafts to raise and lower underground workers and equipment.

13 Webster, 1935a.

14 Cited by Webster, 1935b.

15 Newbury, 1975, pages 32–33. Also NGLC Debates, 26 February 1936.

16 Webster, 1937.

17 The Administrator was strongly opposed to the introduction of legislation for compulsory arbitration in the Territory, as this would make inevitable the development of a system of unions *which could have serious repercussions if the idea was absorbed by the labourers of the Territory.* (McNicoll, 1941).

18 Guinea Gold was not one of the eight as, having disposed of all its leases, it retired from mining activities, content to distribute to its shareholders the dividends received from BGD and NGG.

19 Baskett, 1991, pages 15–16.

20 Baskett, 1991, page 18.

21 Water from races was used to feed hydraulic monitors or elevators operating at pressures of up to 140 pounds per square inch. Monitors (or nozzles) were used to undercut the wash from the face of terraces, while elevators were used to raise alluvial gravels from deep in the river bed. Recovery of gold in each case was by sluicing. (Lowenstein, page 142)

22 The Morobe District accounted for about 97% of total New Guinea gold production in the pre-war period.

23 Dunkin, 1950, page 12.

24 Comprises 67,937 ounces produced by the Edie Creek mill and 144,516 ounces from the Golden Ridges mill. (Lowenstein, page 179) The latter figure includes ore mined at Upper Ridges and transported by aerial ropeway. NGG's various alluvial operations contributed 131,064 ounces (Press reports), of which 53,348 ounces, or more than 40%, reflected the efforts of tributers—both smaller mining companies and individuals.

25 Fisher, 1943, page 2.

26 Ibid.

Chapter 11

1 Levien first contemplated using aviation to fly in dredge machinery in April 1925 in a letter to Charles Wells. (Levien, 1925a) By February 1926, he had firmed up his ideas enough to explore an aerial service with Australian Airways in Melbourne. (Levien 1926d) Within months of Guinea Gold being formed, in May 1926, Levien was exerting pressure for it to become actively involved in aviation.

2 Financial difficulties delayed Parer and McIntosh so that they left England more than a month after Keith and Ross Smith had arrived in Australia. They reached Australia 206 days later, after many calamities—the first single engine plane to achieve this feat.

3 This account of the early days of Guinea Gold's aerial service draws extensively on Ian Grabowsky's draft "History of Civil Aviation" and on Jim Sinclair, who extended Grabowsky's research after the latter's death in 1972. Sinclair, 1983.

4 Mustar, cited in Waterhouse, 1932.

5 Levien had had several clashes with District Officer Skeate towards the end of 1926, who charged him with the murder of a labourer. In March, in his capacity as Magistrate in Salamaua, Skeate committed him for trial in Rabaul. Anecdotal evidence suggests that the Administration wanted Levien out of the way when the Royal Commission visited Salamaua in April–May 1927. The case was promptly dismissed by the Chief Justice in Rabaul, and in the event Levien was the first witness to appear before the Royal Commission.

6 Cited in Grabowsky, January 1927, page 82.

7 ADB, Mustar.

8 Grabowsky, April 1927, pages 91–92.

9 Mustar, 1927, pages 102–103.

10 Ibid.

11 Grabowsky, November 1928, page 243.

12 The average freight rate during 1928 was 1 shilling per pound, or £100 per (short) ton. (Guinea Airways' 21st Annual Report) Passengers are assumed to have been split evenly between inward and outward flights, at £5 and £2/10 shillings respectively.

13 GAL Minutes, 17 May 1929.

14 Grabowsky, March 1928, page 187.

15 Feldt, 1964.

16 Grabowsky, November 1929, page 101.

17 Sinclair, 1983, page 61.

18 Townsend, 1932.

19 Shoppee, 1964.

20 Grabowsky, May 1929, page 34. Up to that time, the absence of an aerodrome or a radio link between Lae and Salamaua sometimes made things difficult. Thus, in April 1929, Alan Cross was forced to summon the doctor to Lae by flying over his house in Salamaua and dropping a note. (Willis, page 33).

Chapter 12

1 Cited by the Controller of Civil Aviation 1933, page 17.

2 Commonwealth Bureau of Census and Statistics. Table compiled by Grabowsky 1968b.

3 Report on the progress of Civil Aviation 1929-1936; Statistical and Technical Review 1937-1938. UK Air Ministry.

4 Grabowsky, January 1934, pages 1–2. The source of Grabowsky's rankings is unknown, but they appear broadly consistent with aircraft movements in New Guinea and with known freight tonnages in New Guinea and elsewhere.

5 Grabowsky, March 1934, page 37.

6 Shortly after they were ordered – on 2 July 1930 – the Administration introduced a 10% *ad valorem* tariff to all mining machinery, aeroplanes and parts, with no exception for equipment ordered before that date but not yet delivered.

7 Hudson, 1979, page 185.

8 See Chapter 9.

9 The cargo compartment was 24 feet long, 77 inches wide and 69 inches high. The hatch was 142 inches long and 60 inches wide, with a concave cover giving an extra 12 inches of headroom over the centre of gravity. Banks, 1932, page 620.

10 Mustar, 1931. By today's standards, the plane was extraordinarily slow. It took off at 65–70 m.p.h., climbed at 75–87 m.p.h and landed at 65 m.p.h. (There was little time for level flight cruising – which was said to be 125 m.p.h.) Grabowsky January 1932, pages 2–3.

11 Grabowsky, April 1931, pages 37–38.

12 *Illustrated London News*, 10 May 1941.

13 During this period *Pat* had two narrow escapes – in July 1934 when the whole centre engine fell off in flight due to metal fatigue, and in October 1934 when the hatch cover blew off and wedged against the tail. In each case, the pilot regained control and landed safely, and within a few days the well equipped and staffed GAL workshop in Lae had *Pat* flying again.

14 By comparison, planes in Australia carried 221 tons of freight during the whole of 1936.

15 Hawkins, 1977.

16 Banks, 1937, page 807.

17 The Chairman, Charles Wells, did not make his first visit to New Guinea until 1932 and, apart from Les Waterhouse and Cecil Levien, only one other Director is known to have visited New Guinea.

18 Grabowsky, July 1930, page 73.

19 ADB, Holden.

20 Grabowsky, March 1933, page 44.

21 GABM, June 1933. Cited by Grabowsky, June 1933, page 117.

22 Cabinet Submission by Minister for Territories, Sir George Pearce, approved 11 December 1935. However bizarre such a decision may appear today, in the 1930s governments were more overtly interventionist. In Australia, as elsewhere, the Government used subsidies to influence the pattern of aviation development. There being no subsidies in New Guinea, a merger was seen as an alternative way of achieving this outcome.

23 Hammond, c.1962.

24 Brogden, 1972, page 179.

25 Grabowsky, January 1934, page 9. The Controller of Civil Aviation was part of the Department of Defence at this time.

26 Grabowsky, February 1934, pages 27–28. Not that any action on a road was forthcoming.

27 This description of the route in from Salamaua draws largely on Affleck, 1964, pages 97–98.

28 This description draws on Affleck, 1964, page 99, and O'Neill, page 202.

29 Affleck, 1964, pages 103–104.

30 Hammond, c.1962.

CHAPTER 13

1 The Kaiwa and the Biangai were not tribes in the sense that each was a cohesive political entity, acting co-operatively in matters such as fighting and garden building, and with a single leader or 'big man'. However, members of each spoke the same language and had the same culture, the Biangai also believing they were all descended from a common ancestor. The word 'tribe' is thus used here in a general sense.

2 Village censuses by patrol officers were often unreliable, depending on whether or not villagers were amenable to being counted. However, the Kaiwa and Biangai had been in contact with Europeans for some time when censuses were conducted in the mid-1920s, so these figures are likely to be fairly accurate.

3 Biangai settlements were located on ridges close to the upper part of the Bulolo valley. To live anywhere but on easily defended ridges in the surrounding hills was to invite attack. The Biangai people today claim that they used to live in the Wau area, and moved as the Kapau expanded into their territory just prior to first contact with Europeans.

4 Burton, 2000a, page 2.

5 Chinnery, 1933b.

6 While there is no known official evidence to support this account, two miners, Roy Struben (1961) and Michael Angelo (1962), who were on the goldfields at the time of Baum's death, each give similar descriptions of Baum's movements during the War. It was also reported in *The Sydney Morning Herald* on 27 May 1931.

7 M. Leahy and M. Crain, 1937, page 39.

8 Anstey, 1927.

9 Chinnery was later appointed Director, Department of District Services and Native Affairs.

10 Chinnery, Evidence to Edie Creek Royal Commission, 1927, page 1221.

11 NGAR 1929–130, page 101.

12 Most police in New Guinea were indigenous, under the control of Europeans. Those working on and near the goldfields had no local ties, having been recruited elsewhere in the Territory.

13 The German nomenclature was adopted, 'luluai' being the word for 'leader' in Tolai, the language of the Rabaul area. (Paramount luluais were appointed in later years with authority over a group of adjacent villages.) A luluai was given a black peaked cap with a broad red band on it. While patrol officers endeavoured to appoint existing leaders as luluais, so as to build on their existing authority, it was often unclear just who these were. In some cases, their distrust of white men led villagers to suggest the appointment of men as luluais who held no position of authority within the village. By the early 1930s, more than 400 luluais had been appointed throughout the Morobe District.

14 In Tolai 'tultul' means the messenger or servant of the chief. He was given a black peaked cap with two narrow red bands.

15 Sheldon, 1930.

16 Appleby, 1927, pages 2–3.

17 Willis, 1976, page 9.

18 McLean, 1927a.

19 Booth, 1929, page 182.

20 McLean, 1927a.

21 There is no evidence to support McLean's vindictive remarks about the tultul or his determination to kill him. It is likely that the tultul's only crime was that, as an Administration appointee, he should have prevented the murders or at least turned the perpetrators over to a patrol officer.

22 Appleby, 1927, page 5.

23 *Daily Guardian*, 1 February 1927.

24 Idriess, 1945, page 155.

25 Park, 1927.

26 Wisdom, 1927b. Wisdom was defending the strong measures taken on a punitive patrol after the murder by villagers of four prospectors at Nakanai, New Britain in October 1926, including the use of a machine gun. The incident gave rise to considerable tension between the Administrator and the Minister for Home and Territories, Sir William Glasgow.

27 There are three known patrols – by District Officer Linehan and Patrol Officer George Ellis in 1921, George Ellis in March 1923 and District Officer Skeate in 1927. No official reports of these patrols are known to exist, but information provided to Frank Clune suggests that the first two patrols resulted in several Kukukuku being shot.

28 The report of this patrol is not known to exist, though Chinnery made handwritten notes from it, recording that it was dated 11 August 1930. Chinnery Papers, 766/5/15.

29 Burton, 2000b, page 11.

30 In the early 1970s it was estimated that there were 20,340 Kapau speakers in the Morobe District, 12,300 Menya speakers and 1,000 Angaatiya, with a further 130 in Manki village. Lloyd 1973.

31 There is no agreed view on the name's derivation, but Kukukuku means cassowary in Motu. The name may have been given to them due to their habit of wearing cassowary femurs across their waist or because they roamed the jungle like cassowaries. Whatever its origin, it is clear is that the name is widely regarded as a derogatory term by many of the people comprising this cultural group. For this reason, the name 'Anga' has been substituted by anthropologists for 'Kukukuku' since the 1960s. However, Burton notes that the Kapau (or Hamtai-speaking) people claim the name comes from 'kouka' or 'boy' or 'son', reduplicated as 'kouka kouka' or 'my son, my son'. Personal correspondence.

32 Chinnery Papers, 766/5/15 and 766/7/1.

33 Hides, 1931.

34 Angelo, 1962.

35 M. Leahy and M. Crain, 1937, page 127.

CHAPTER 14

1 Johns, letter to his parents, 3 May 1931.

2 Flierl, 1931.

3 Radford, 1987, page 63.

4 Or, in the words of the League of Nations Mandate, to promote the material and moral well-being and social progress of the inhabitants.

5 Many of the carriers were from Buang villages from which Baum's carriers had come. The party was also accompanied by the luluai Tol and two Buang tultuls.

6 Feldt, 1951, page 61.

7 Of the six prisoners, one died in Salamaua and five escaped—of whom two were never seen again, two were recaptured in Wau and one was caught by Buang villagers who appear to have tortured him before handing him over. The two who were recaptured were returned to their village early in 1932, and the injured one released in December 1933 after a spell in hospital. Ibid.

8 Both of Penglase's patrol reports refer to the river where Baum was killed as the Kabu. However, the name appears on no maps of the period or subsequently. Black calls it the Yaugwi River, and this name is on a detailed map published in 1935 by the geologist Nason-Jones.

9 The patrol report appears to have been edited to excise all details of what happened when Pitt arrived at the village. This is unusual. Patrol reports are usually quite specific about the nature of any fighting and the number of deaths—as indeed this one is in describing the death of eight New Guineans on 13 November. There was undoubtedly fighting, as no Kukukuku would simply give himself up.

10 N. Penglase, 1932b. The precise location of Wa and Jeki is difficult to determine, as the only map on which they appear is one made by Penglase. They do not appear on the Nason-Jones map, despite this being based on information provided by the three patrols. Whether this reflects their small size or that they were completely destroyed is unknown. However, their approximate location can be determined by comparing Penglase's hand-drawn map and the Nason-Jones map.

11 Hauwernatuwe appears to have been located a couple of miles south-west of Wa and Jeki.

12 Black, 1933. Feldt did not visit the area in 1932. But, as Black only arrived in New Guinea after Penglase and Sansom's patrol, he may not have realised that Feldt's patrol had been in May 1931.

13 Struben, page 186.

14 European names are often corrupted due to language differences and the passage of time, but from the context there is little doubt that Yandoapo was referring to Hellmuth Baum. A Buang man, Banon Lasek, also told the author that, after the death of Baum, *the (Buang) carriers fled*

through the jungle back to Salamaua and reported the matter ... In retaliation a team of kiap and policemen returned to the same area and shot dead many Kapau people. In December 1934, Patrol Officer Murray Edwards wrote to the miner Jack O'Neill that villagers in the area where Baum was killed were very friendly, which prompted O'Neill to observe *Baum's killers must have been well tamed. The patrol which went out there when Baum was killed must have given those kukas a really good hiding.* (O'Neill, page 191).

15 The vague descriptions in many patrol reports of attempts to restore order (or, as Wisdom described it in 1929, "to suppress disorder") in uncontrolled areas reflect limitations imposed on District staff under Australian law, with its focus on individual accountability. In 1929, the Attorney-General's Department advised: *Punitive expeditions may be the only method of bringing unruly tribes to reason and of maintaining order in uncontrolled areas, but these expeditions are against the rule of law inasmuch as they are directed against a tribe or district as a whole without its being possible to distinguish between innocent and guilty individuals.* (Attorney-General's Dept to Prime Minister's Dept, 10 July 1929) Specifically, District staff were not permitted to burn houses or impose collective fines, as proposed by the Administrator. (Memo to Prime Minister, 3 September 1929). These constraints imposed intense pressures on patrol officers. Legally, they could only seek to arrest individual New Guineans they believed were likely to be guilty of murder or theft. But with little or no knowledge of their language and confronted with aggressive group resistance, their chances of success were minimal. While the killing of New Guineans was not condoned, it was tacitly acknowledged that deaths would sometimes occur when patrols tried to arrest individuals and encountered resistance, and so conflicts leading to casualties appear usually to have been reported, though their extent may at times have been understated. While the burning of villages undoubtedly occurred, this was never reported.

16 McCarthy, 1933b. Boko was McCarthy's personal servant on the patrol.

17 McCarthy, 1933a, page 46.

18 In the 1930s the Upper Ramu and Purari areas (part of what is now called the Eastern Highlands) were classified as part of the Morobe District.

19 Chinnery, 1933a.

20 O'Neill, page 83.

21 Peadon, 1933.

22 25 November 1934. O'Neill, page 189.

23 Griffiths, 1933.

24 Cited in Radford, 1987, page 115.

25 Chinnery, 1933a.

26 Black, 1933.

27 E. Taylor, 1933. Sansom's report on his patrols out of the Slate Creek Post (known as Fort Sansom) between July and November 1933 mentions only two deaths. His daily record of events, while mentioning activities regarded as friendly (such as breaking arrows as a sign of peace and being willing to trade) makes only occasional reference to raids on hamlets and no reference at all to any deaths in fighting. W.E. Sansom, 1933.

28 Chinnery, 1933b.

29 The Association was established by individual miners in March 1933. Members who contributed to the cost of sending out prospectors to locate possible new gold-bearing ground were promised a share in any discovery.

30 McCarthy, 1933d, Diary, pages 18–19.

31 Yeomans, 1933.

32 K. Bridge to Frank De Hesselle, 14 March 1934.

33 PMC Minutes, 27th Session, June 1935 (page 19) and 34th Session, June 1938 (page 164).

34 Murcutt (n.d.), pages 5–6.

35 Taylor (1934b) concluded that *it is quite likely that further enquiries will disclose more.* A.I.K. Kituai (1998) claims that in less than seven

days, between 39 and 72 members of the Finintugu community – men, women and children – were killed in reprisal.

36 Sinclair 1984, page 73. While his comments also embraced deaths in connection with Highlands exploration, the same policies applied in the goldfields area, with the same consequences.

37 Angelo, 1962.

38 Sinclair, 1998, page 131.

39 Taylor, 1934a.

CHAPTER 15

1 This chapter deals primarily with the three main Kukukuku groups in the Morobe District – the Kapau, Angaatiya (or Langimar and Manki) and Menya. While miners and patrol officers in and close to the areas they inhabited were few in number, they were the first Europeans encountered by villagers. The Kapau are today known as the Upper Watuts.

2 This framework draws on the elements of cultural first encounters articulated by E.L. Schieffelin 1991, pages 4–6.

3 Blackwood, 1978, page 19.

4 There were no shamans among the Biangai or Kapau, in the sense of a man whose magical powers set him out from others in the community. Guyo Saweo told the author *Our leaders were fight leaders. They looked after everything, including matters to do with spirits. We did not have any special leaders who looked after things such as spirits or gardens.* James Saro independently confirmed that there was no special person responsible for seeing and getting rid of evil spirits. Fight leaders would clean evil spirits away before a fight. However, it is less clear that this was the case among the Menya. Descriptions later in this chapter suggest that shamans were active, as indeed they were in some other Kukukuku groups, such as the Baruya. (c.f. Godelier, 1986).

5 Burton argues that each Upper Watut is born into a named patrilineal descent grouping, or patronymic. However, these do not engage in clan-like activity in the sense of acting together in a co-ordinated way, such as in fighting. Each patronymic is, however, believed to have an 'aptitude'. Thus men of the Titama patronymic are said to have a reputation for second sight and scouting, Apea for looking after the land and Nautiya for cooling disputes. (Burton 2003, pages 207–208).

6 Salisbury, page 114.

7 McCarthy, 1963, pages 103–104.

8 Schieffelin, 1991, page 79.

9 Crittenden noted that, in 1935, when the Hides-O'Malley patrol was approaching Kasebi in Papua, the Nembi people collected bundles of sugar cane and bananas. These not only signified ordinary hospitality but also had ritual importance in ceremonies for the appeasement of spirits and ancestral ghosts. When the patrol arrived, these were presented to Hides, who recorded that they were met by 'friendly men who brought plenty of food'. Crittenden 1991, page 171. While there is no direct evidence that the Kukukuku thought along similar lines, the fact that trading food was not traditionally part of their culture raises the possibility that, particularly in early encounters, offers of food may have been intended to propitiate the spirits that white men were thought to be rather than expressing a simple desire for trade goods. This conclusion is supported by the frequency with which they would attack white men one day and come in to trade food the next.

10 McCarthy 1933c and 1963, page 120.

11 Thus, in his report on a visit to the Upper Markham River in June 1929, Cecil Levien noted that when he met a large number of villagers who were so wildly excited that a clash looked inevitable, he used sign language and presents of salt and trade goods to calm them down. *So what might be considered as hostility by some was passed off as nervousness as far as I was concerned* ... (Levien 1929a). Similarly, Tom Yeomans, on 15 October 1933, while on an excursion from Menyamya testing for gold, encountered a large number of villagers. They were anxious to trade and apparently friendly, but were *afraid and excitable which at times we mistook for hostility.*

12 This was frustrating for patrol officers who would think they had made a good start to bringing an area under control only to find on a subsequent visit that they were back where they started.

13 Downs, 1978, page 230.

14 Hughes, 1977, page 11.

15 Rowley 1966, page 67. Jim Sinclair, who patrolled extensively among the Kukukuku after the war, told the author that there was always the risk of trouble as interpreters did not always translate accurately or were misunderstood, perhaps because of their accent.

16 Crittenden, 1991, pages 185, 189.

17 It didn't seem to occur to McCarthy or Black on their Menyamya patrol in 1933 that gardens which looked extensive may, in fact, have produced barely enough food for the population they supported, and that in these circumstances, payment for food taken was meagre compensation.

18 Mackellar, page 14.

19 Saro thought he had been killed in a miner's camp but was unsure. It would not have helped Baum's position that all his carriers were Buang men, the Buang being traditional enemies of the Kapau.

20 McCarthy, 1933a, page 15.

21 McCarthy, 1933d, page 32-33.

22 M. Leahy and M. Crain, 1937, page 137.

23 McCarthy, 1963, page 102.

24 Milligan, 1937a.

25 Black, 1933.

26 Yeomans, 1933.

27 It should be emphasised that the explanation given here is deductive rather than empirical.

28 This inability to understand guns and tendency to attribute their effectiveness to non-physical causes was evident elsewhere. Schieffelin (1991, page 85) noted that in some cases in Papua when a man was killed by a white man, a witch was divined as being responsible and was killed in revenge. In New Guinea, Europeans were careful never to allow villagers access to weapons and, as their police and carriers came from other areas, there was no 'leakage' of weapons which would have given them the opportunity to learn how guns worked.

29 It was not that fight leaders (or shamans, where they existed) needed to convince warriors that their spells could protect them against bullets, which implies an understanding of bullets as projectiles. It was more a question of convincing them that their magic was stronger than the white man's.

30 Guyo Saweo's account is confirmed by Patrol Officer Lloyd Hurrell's graphic account of cannibalism in his 1951 Menyamya Patrol Report No. 2. The right arm was the one that drew the bowstring and the left leg the one that braced and steadied the bowman.

31 O'Neill, Page 150.

32 O'Neill, page 183.

CHAPTER 16

1 Also exempt were village officials, native police, mission teachers and students, fathers with four or more living children by one wife and men unfit for work or over the apparent age of 40.

2 See, for example, remarks by William Rappard at the PMC's examination of the 1927/28 Report. PMC Minutes, 15th Session, 4 July 1929 (page 61).

3 Wisdom, 1921.

4 Sir Hubert Murray, Papua, 1912. Cited in Chinnery 1936b.

5 Professional recruiters, of whom there were usually between 10 and 15, were only permitted to recruit labourers actually requested by an employer. They could not recruit 'on spec'.

6 O'Neill, page 73.

7 In one case that led to a Government inquiry, intimidation and force were used to secure recruits. In others, potential recruits were told that they would be employed at places other than their true destination: Edie Creek, whose reputation for pneumonia and dysentery made recruiting far more difficult.

8 Throughout the 1930s, five to ten people were convicted annually for illegal recruiting practices.

9 In fact, it is highly likely that most recruits, who had never strayed far from their villages and spoke neither English or Pidgin, were confused and overwhelmed by the unfamiliar surroundings and the occasion, and wouldn't have objected to anything even if they did understand what they were being told. Leaving nothing to chance, however, some recruiters are said to have coached interpreters to give the 'right' answer when a recruit was asked if he was willing to sign the contract. (Mair, page 155)

10 The number fell as low as 15,700 in 1931/32 as copra production was affected by the Depression, climbing gradually thereafter.

11 Curtain, 1980, pages 136–137.

12 Employers paid professional recruiters £10 for a labourer on a three year contract, and it cost between £5 and £10 to repatriate a time-expired labourer.

13 Decoto, 1929, page 18.

14 Mining Warden, 1931 Annual Report.

15 Decker, 1940, page 200.

16 However, competition among employers for labourers with skills and experience, which might have led to an upward drift in wage rates, was prevented by the requirement that labourers re-sign with their previous employer, and not seek out a new one. Decker, page 201.

17 Chinnery, 1937.

18 From the late 1930s, rising Administration concern about village depopulation led to tighter restrictions on re-indenturing and the proportion of labourers re-signing fell—in BGD's case ot 25–30%.

19 NGAR 1921/22, page 52. Privately, Administrator Wisdom argued more bluntly that *to give them more is only to firstly enrich the Asiatic trader, and secondly, increase the native hoards.* Wisdom, 1921, op.cit. The low minimum was said to be justified by the perceived inefficiency of New Guinean labour compared with that in Papua. (Mair, page 143).

20 In 1942, a few skilled indigenous workers were earning £1 or £1/10 shillings per month. By comparison, in 1940, white employees at NGG were earning £1/5 shillings per day. (Mair, 1948, pages 144, 157).

21 This typically took the form of a fixed deposit into a trust fund for the full amount or a guarantee provided by the Yorkshire Insurance Company, which had an office in Salamaua. Numerous defaults by miners led the company to stop providing insurance in the late 1930s, leaving employers with no option but to deposit the total deferred wages and cost of repatriation before signing on labourers.

22 Decker, 1940, page 190. BGD estimated in the early 1930s that its costs were similar. Banks, 1932, page 629.

23 Weston 1975a, page 43.

24 Decker, 1940, page 182. 'Offences against discipline' were set out in Section 109 of the Native Labour Ordinance.

25 The minority report of the 1941 Inquiry into Native Labour reported that *Witnesses in Wau complained that the local jail was regarded as a joke by labourers, and that they nearly always came out fatter than when they went in.* (Page 18).

26 Mair, 1948, page 15.

27 Downs, 1978, page 227.

28 All figures are drawn or derived from New Guinea Annual Reports. Figures were only published intermittently making trends difficult to determine. However, desertion rates on the goldfields appear to have remained high throughout the 1930s.

29 Report of the 1941 Inquiry into Native Labour, page 3. Following growing concern about labour shortages among employers, the Commission was appointed on 31 October 1939 to inquire into all aspects of the native labour system and report on any desirable alterations to it. It was chaired by the Director of District Services and Native Affairs, Robert Melrose. Due to staff shortages, it did not report until mid-1941, though a separate report by two of the Commission's members was issued in 1940 after they had left the Territory for war service.

30 Mining Warden Annual Report, 1931.

31 Taylour and Morley, 1933, page 43.

32 O'Neill, page 246.

33 Mining Warden Annual Report, 1933.

34 This is discussed in greater detail in Chapter 10.

35 The Administration walked a fine line on this issue, claiming that its aim was *to provide such educational facilities as will enable all natives of the Territory an opportunity …… to participate in the economic and social life of their own country* (NGAR 1926–27, page 35), but in practice doing little to encourage technical training or the employment of New Guineans for their skills. The Administration's woeful approach to education generally is discussed in Chapter 23.

36 Inspector of Mines, 1937.

37 Cited by Sir George Pearce in a letter to Senator H. S. Foll, 1 December 1937.

38 Mining Warden Report, July 1935.

39 Decker, 1940, page 197.

40 Kokomo, of Emul village, told Bryant Allen that *If someone was killed, the company* [NGG] *paid a lot of money to his mother and father.* It is unknown whether these were *ex gratia* payments or made under the Employer's Liability Law.

41 The 25% ratio may have been adopted after it was recognised that the number of women in villages was often under-estimated, particularly in newly opened areas, where they would often hide when visited by patrols. (Vial 1938, page 386). In these circumstances, a 5% excess of women over men might significantly understate the disparity. The 25% ratio was itself flawed, as only young fit men left to work as labourers; thus the remaining 75% comprised a disproportionate number of old men. If these were excluded, the proportion of fit young males absent would often be more than one third.

42 In 1935, the adult male absentee rate in 18 villages in the Waria area exceeded 35%. (Proclamation re Recruiting, 1938). In 1937, PO John Murphy found that 61% of able-bodied men in Kaiwa villages (i.e. those between the ages of 14 and 40) were working as indentured labourers. Those able-bodied men remaining in the village represented less than one third of women of child-bearing age. Murphy, 1937b. In evidence to the 1941 Commission, Keith McCarthy suggested that up to one third of *fit* adult males could leave a village without detriment.

43 The pressure on labour supplies induced some recruiters, in 1937, to entice potential recruits to go to villages where recruiting was not prohibited, so they could be recruited there. In consequence, the Ordinance was amended to apply to villagers *born* in the villages concerned.

44 *The indenture system, with its pursuit of deserters and its imprisonment of those who break their contract, is 'really rather like slavery'.* Sir Hubert Murray, 1931, page 9. While he saw no alternative to indentured labour at that time in Papua, Murray's views had evolved from the more philosophical perspective expressed in his book, *Papua,* in 1912.

CHAPTER 17

1 Report of the 1941 Inquiry into Native Labour, page 11. The 'shadow battalion' was a myth. Several years earlier, Patrol Officer Leigh Vial had noted that, when patrols arrived in a village just coming under control, usually more women and girls hid than men and boys, so in newly opened up areas little weight could be placed on total masculinity figures. (Vial, L.G. 1938).

2 NGAR 1937/38, page 143.

3 Curtain, 1980, page 232.

4 Curtain, 1980, page 193.

5 Hogbin 1951, page 188. Busama is a coastal village between Lae and Salamaua.

6 Reed, 1943, Page 224. After 1936, women were permitted to accompany their husbands without having to be indentured themselves. However, few women did so. Reed believed that this largely reflected the wishes of the men, due to the risk of having their wives living among hundreds of men. Villages were also reluctant to see women leave as they were responsible for tending family gardens. So long as they stayed, there was also an incentive for male labourers to return. Although NGG and BGD believed the presence of women was desirable and tried to encourage wives to accompany labourers, most employers baulked at the costs involved.

7 Allen, 1976, page 341. The numbers refer to NGG's shafts at Edie Creek.

8 P. Bengo, 1973, pages 4–5. It appears that Bengo was employed on Dredge No. 6 near Wau. Bengo's reference to shopping in Salamaua is puzzling, but it is possible that BGD occasionally let trusted employees hitch a ride on a plane going to Salamaua to visit the trade stores there.

9 A. Kuluah, 1983, page 6. Kaluah's paper explores how labourers lived and socialised on the goldfields. While he evidently interviewed former labourers, the extent and nature of these interviews are unknown.

10 Downing, 1931.

11 A labourer was not to work more than one eight hour shift in any 24 hour period. After four hours' work, there was to be a rest period of at least half an hour during which he was given a meal of two biscuits and tea or coffee. Labourers were to have a rest period of 24 hours in every seven days. Where more than one shift was worked, a labourer could not be required to work on the same shift for more than six days. NGAR 1931/32, page 105. From 1936, labourers were to be provided with a hot meal no more than two hours before the commencement of any shift and no more than two hours after the completion of any shift. Native Labour Regulations.

12 Reed, 1943, page 223.

13 Nelson, 1976, pages 262–263.

Mipela i no save bung wantaim ol wait skin na sindaun na tok tok wantaim na kai kai wantaim, nogat. Masta bilong mi ino save mekim planti tok gris wantaim mi, nogat. Olsem mi no pilim wait skin i no sindaun klostu long mi na tok tok wantaim mi, nogat. Olsem birua. Ol i bosim Nu Gini bilong wok tasol, i no gat skul i tok long wok. Lainim long han wantaim pait tasol.

We do not sit down with white men and talk and eat together. My master does not joke much with me. Therefore I do not feel that white men are friendly to me and talk to me. They are like enemies. They employ New Guineans for work only. There is no teaching or training for the job. They only teach by pointing and beating.

14 Downing, 1931. The diet scale for labourers employed in heavy labour provided several food groups with some substitutability within and even between groups. A representative prescribed *daily* diet comprised: 1 pound rice or 1½ pound biscuits, ¼ pound dried peas, beans or lentils, ½ pound wholemeal barley, 2/7 of 12 ounces tinned meat, 2 ounces beef dripping, 4/7 ounce sugar, 2/7 ounce salt and tea and 1 teaspoon of marmite. There was some scope for substitution (eg. of kaukau, bananas, yams or taro for rice), but kaukau, tapioca and sago were not to be issued on more than 14 days in every 28.

15 P. Bengo, 1973, page 5. The roll of newspaper was for cigarettes, which goes a long way to explaining why only single copies of three out of more than 40 editions of *The Morobe News* have survived to this day.

16 S. Chinnery, 1998, page 88.

17 NGAR 1937/38, page 25.

18 Hogbin, 1951, page 190.

19 Mission Conference Proceedings, 1927, page 104.

20 Reed, 1943, page 184.

21 Hogbin 1951, page 190.

22 Reed, op. cit., page 226.

23 Reed, op. cit., page 225.

24 The central importance of singsings in New Guinean culture has been well described by Fitz-Patrick and Kimbuna: *The sing sing is a traditional dance, used for ceremonial purposes or purely as an entertainment for the people, and is an extremely important aspect of adult life. The sing sing kiama, for example, is used for ancestor worship, to please the ancestor with the beauty of the decorations, the rhythms and sounds. [Others] are performed purely as a form of entertainment, and sing sing groups from distant tribal areas may be invited to perform if they are well known for their ability. Dancers are usually dressed in elaborate costumes made from leaves, tapa cloth, seeds, shells and exquisite headdresses, which have many feathers arranged in a spectacular display.* (Page 125)

Singsings may occur after a successful period of major confrontation with an enemy tribe, in connection with initiation ceremonies, to placate a displeased ancestor or to please an ancestor so he will refrain from being malevolent and travel peacefully to live in the land of the dead, and to repay friends who helped during the burial. They may also be held during pig festivals or to celebrate successful harvests. They may be sung, with the verses describing gardening activities, mountain streams, rivers, mountains, trees, the moon and the sky. Or, they may act out how animals and birds live and move, and how the sun, moon and water affect their behaviour. Some involve singing and chanting and have no musical accompaniment, while others rely on the beat of kundu drums and not much singing. They may last up to a day and a night. Fitz-Patrick and Kimbuna, pages 126–129

25 Discussion with author, 2001.

26 A.E. Green, 1939. Sio singsings were believed by Administrator McNicoll (1939) to be based on certain initiation rites of villagers of the Sio sub-division of the Morobe District. It is not known how the Sio singsing relates to what Hogbin called the Bagana, *in which each main performer paraded openly with his sleeping partner of the moment. Certain of the movements, which were carried out by separate couples, were unmistakeably imitative of sexual congress.* Hogbin, page 191.

27 McNicoll, 1939.

28 Report of the 1941 Inquiry into Native Labour, page 26.

29 Op. cit., page 43.

30 Bretag, 1941.

31 Weston 1996, page 50.

32 Groves, 1935, page 407.

33 Eekhoff, 1964, page 49.

34 Report of the 1941 Inquiry into Native Labour, Part 2, page 12.

35 NGAR 1921/22, page 52.

36 The anthropologist, R.F. Salisbury, estimated that, among the Siane people of the Eastern Highlands, steel axes cut the time for subsistence work from 80% to 50% of a man's time. Salisbury, page 118. Ian Hogbin concluded that, among the Busama the introduction of superior tools and the cessation of fighting meant that workers who were previously indispensable could be spared. Hogbin 1951, page 199.

37 Hogbin 1970, page 172.

38 Permanent Mandates Commission, Examination of NGAR, 1936/37. PMC Minutes, 34th Session, 20 June 1938 (page 178).

39 Willis, 1973, page 7.

40 Hogbin and Wedgwood, 1943, page 6.

41 Radi, 1971, page 83.

Chapter 18

1 Cited in M. Leahy and M. Crain, 1937, page 41.

2 Innes (n.d.).

3 Johns, letter to his parents, 22 December 1929.

4 D.R. Booth, evidence to Edie Creek Royal Commission, 1927, page 216.

5 Melbourne *Herald*, 3 January 1929.

6 Cited in Nelson, 1982, page 146. A minor modification has been made to the text to incorporate an aspect of the same story related elsewhere by Weston (1978).

7 Johns, letter to his parents, 19 September 1929. By 'GG', Johns means the Governor General.

8 Moore, 1975, page 46.

9 McCarthy, 1963, page 114.

10 Cited in Cole, 1990, page 79.

11 O'Neill, page 201.

12 Bourke, 1963.

13 Grabowsky, November 1927, page 147 and August 1928, page 86;

also B. Sinclair, 1963.

14 Bourke, 1964, page 79.

15 Innes, 1937.

16 Ibid.

17 Underwood, 1968, page 61.

18 A. Goldbrick, *Rabaul Times*, 17 September 1926.

19 Grabowsky, October 1927, page 138.

20 Johns, letters to his parents, 19 September and 26 October 1929.

21 Johns, letter to his parents, 13 September 1931.

22 Groves, 1935, page 473.

23 Johns, letter to his parents, 13 September 1931.

24 Cooke, 1983, page 47.

25 Struben, page 150.

26 Ibid.

27 Eekhoff, 1965, page 49.

28 Mustar, cited in Grabowsky, June 1927, page 114.

29 Weston, cited in Nelson, 1982, page 144.

Chapter 19

1 Struben, 1961, page 161.

2 O'Neill, page 245.

3 Clark, August 1932.

4 Clark, 20 April 1933. Clark was working downstream from Sunshine 'drome, below the junction of the Snake and Watut Rivers.

5 Murcutt, pages 5 and 8,

6 Discussion with author, 2001.

7 Clark, 20 April 1933.

8 O'Neill, page 155.

9 Miners knew this as Japanese River Fever. Dr Carl Gunther at Bulolo identified its cause and, through greater awareness that it was more likely to be contracted in disturbed jungle areas, its incidence among miners was reduced. However, scrub typhus remained a serious problem, and caused several hundred fatalities among allied forces during World War II. An effective drug, chloromycetin, was not discovered until 1948. *Encyclopaedia of Papua New Guinea*, page 785.

10 O'Neill, page 14.

11 Clark, 5 October 1933.

12 O'Neill, pages 242, 246.

13 Idriess, 1945, page 219. In other words, he bet £15 that he would recover.

14 Clark, 17 April 1936.

15 Johns, 28 October 1930.

16 Cooke, 1983, pages 57–58.

17 Alice Innes had trained as a general nurse in the Colonial Hospital, Fiji and had been Matron in the emergency hospital in Auburn, Sydney, during the 1918–19 influenza epidemic.

18 Discussion with author, 2001. Also obituary in *Lae Nius*, May 1979.

19 Alice Bowring had trained as an obstetric nurse. When her husband died in 1913, she was left penniless. She put her son through university in Sydney by nursing, keeping a boarding house, running two cafes and working on the advertising staff of *Smith's Weekly*.

20 Sinclair, 1981, page 32.

21 Bowring, 1943. Alice Bowring's rapport with miners was repaid when she was given a claim and equipment by miners returning to Australia. She turned to mining, later acquiring one of the best known of the early Edie Creek claims, the Queen of Sheba. She remained mining at Edie Creek up to the War, with modest success, returning there in 1946, a captive of the lifestyle.

22 Grabowsky, February 1934, pages 31–32.

23 Clark, 23 July 1935. Cooke (op. cit., page 57) recorded that *Occasionally, when a drinker was too long on a bender and nearing the DT stage, the district officer would put him under the 'dog act' for his own good. A notice was posted up on the court house notice board and copies were sent to the hotel and all stores, prohibiting the sale of intoxicating liquor to the drinker for a period, usually three months.*

24 Bank of New South Wales, Salamaua Branch half-yearly report.

25 Grabowsky, June 1935.

26 Hammond, 1962.

27 Sinclair, 1983, page 160.

28 Hammond, op. cit.

29 Cited in Roberts, page 152.

30 This description draws on Grabowsky, May 1931, Townsend 1933, and Denny 1962.

31 Townsend, 1933, page 433.

32 This description draws on Grabowsky September 1934, O'Neill page 206 and Denny 1962.

33 Hammond, op. cit.

Chapter 20

1 Cited in Roberts, 1996, page 208.

2 *Pacific Islands Monthly*, 20 February 1931.

3 See Chapter 9.

4 *Pacific Islands Monthly*, 15 June 1940.

5 Groves, 1935, page 407.

6 Shackleton, 1937, page 642.

7 Honeysett, Letters, July 1932.

8 D.E. Waterhouse, 1933.

9 Coolgardie safes were small cupboards with wire mesh sides and doors that could be draped with wet hessian to keep the food inside cool. Crosley icy-balls, designed for use in the absence of electricity, were top-opening cabinets with two hollow balls—one inside and one outside the cabinet, linked by an inverted U-shaped pipe. The one inside contained liquid ammonia and the one outside water. The water in the outside ball absorbed ammonia vapour lowering the pressure inside which caused the liquid ammonia to evaporate. This had a cooling effect, lowering the temperature of the ball inside the cabinet to around -7°. Once all the ammonia had evaporated, the icy-ball stopped working. The system was reactivated by heating the outside ball with a small kerosene burner. This expelled the ammonia from the water which, if the inside ball was cool, condensed into the liquid ammonia needed for refrigeration. (Source: http://en.wikipedia.org/wiki/Icy_Ball)

10 Newbury, 1975, page 28. Newbury cites a retail price index drawn up in 1940 for Wau as part of an industrial award.

11 Willis, 1972, page 33.

12 Vagg, 2001.

13 Lae and Salamaua each had a few local roads, but the Administration's equivocation over building a road from the coast through to Wau, which was to have started at Salamaua, meant that no road linking Lae and Salamaua was ever constructed.

14 Dunstan, 1931, pages 25–26.

15 McNicoll, 9 October 1934, page 108.

16 Groves, op. cit., page 408–409.

17 Cited in Grabowsky, April 1933. Alistair was the brother of Ian Grabowsky, the Guinea Airways pilot and later General Manager.

18 Groves, op. cit. page 405.

19 Willis, 1974, page 91.

20 Eight points were awarded for tennis, four each for billiards and snooker and 16 for cricket.

21 Teams of eight competed in four four-ball games and eight single match play games.

22 Cited in Sinclair, 1998, page 103.

23 *Pacific Islands Monthly*, 21 December 1936.

24 Bayliss, 2001.

25 The term 'privileged lifestyle' rarely applied to women married to miners, who often lived a more spartan existence. Mollie Parer, at Black Cat Creek between 1933 and 1937, recalled, *I didn't see a black or white woman for eight months, and the hut had a dirt floor. I was not unhappy. I was with my husband (Bob Parer) and I wanted to be with him. He was gold mining and that was interesting. We'd send the natives in (to Wau) with our letters and they'd come back with all the food and periodicals … No work to do of course; I* *don't know how I filled in the time, but I did.* (C. Bulbeck, 2000, page 53) See Chapter 19 for the experiences of Daphne Murcutt and Jeanette Leahy.

26 Hoile, 1946.

27 Travel details recorded in *The Rabaul Times* indicate that women regularly flew around the goldfields visiting and staying with each other. Jeanette Leahy, living with her husband Mick at Surprise Creek, told the author she would visit Salamaua from time to time for a break.

28 Bank of New South Wales, Salamaua Branch report, September 1941. The Morobe District figures also include missionaries at Finschhafen, where there were more than 100 on the staff—many with wives and children. (Personal communication with Hank Nelson.)

29 Tiger Lil, or Lilian Barclay Millar, arrived in New Guinea in 1923. After the death of her first husband, she married Toby Millar in 1935, remaining married to him until his death post-war. When she died in 1981, aged 78, *Pacific Islands Monthly* recalled that her rhetoric, when aroused, made even brave men quail.

30 Struben, 1961, pages 172–173.

31 Hammond, c.1962.

32 On one occasion, she flattened Eric Weine with a bottle and was said by Roy Struben to posses a hefty punch and use it freely when annoyed. Once when sailing on the Macdhui and not having previously encountered her, Joe Bourke went up to Lil who was standing at the rail and asked 'Do you mind if I smoke?' Turning to him, Lil replied acidly 'Honey, I don't mind if you burst into flames.'

33 Black, 3 October 1936.

34 Roberts, 1996, page 170.

CHAPTER 21

1 Relations in the 1930s between Europeans, New Guineans and Chinese should be viewed in the context of the 'White Australia Policy'. Discrimination against Asians was at its zenith and had wide support in Australia. It was also a time when the colonial attitudes of European powers towards subjugated 'native' peoples whom they were ostensibly trying to civilise were also highly discriminary. This chapter does not seek to justify attitudes that prevailed then or the policies to which they gave rise. It seeks only to provide an insight into race relations as they existed on the goldfields. In broad terms at least, these were representative of race relations elsewhere in New Guinea at the time.

2 Wisdom, 1930c.

3 Wolfers, 1975, page 102.

4 Healy, 1967, page 87.

5 The Native Administration Regulations (s.80) required all natives resident in any town to live in premises provided by their employer or in a reserve set apart for their use.

6 McCarthy, 1963, page 85. McCarthy dismissed 'white man's prestige' as *the ultimate in pleas of the dissatisfied in other parts of New Guinea.*

7 Reed, 1947, page 247. This is also consistent with the attitudes of most of the early experienced miners, such as Shark-Eye Park and Cecil Levien.

8 op. cit., page 189.

9 *Rabaul Times*, 20 May 1938.

10 *Rabaul Times*, 28 July 1939.

11 *Rabaul Times*, 3 February 1939.

12 Kituai, 1998, pages 7–8.

13 Black, 1937.

14 Nelson, page 104.

15 Statistics concerning offences against women published in the New Guinea Annual Reports are irregular but suggest that there were few convictions for rape and even fewer where white women were involved.

16 While details of individual cases are unavailable, the reason for and nature of the offence is likely to have made it virtually impossible for an uneducated New Guinean defendant to prove he was not acting 'with intent'.

17 Citizens Association of New Guinea (broadside), Rabaul, 7 April 1937. (Cited in Reed, 1947, page 250).

18 Reed, 1947, page 251.

19 A Manus labourer, Taiki, previously employed by Koranga Gold Sluicing, appeared before the Coroner in custody as a suspect. The Coroner found that there was not a *prima facie* case against him, and that the murder was by a person or persons unknown. *Rabaul Times*, 8 August 1941.

20 Sherwin, 1941.

21 *Rabaul Times*, 25 July 1941.

22 NGLC Debates, 8 July 1941.

23 In her book on Australian women and children in Papua New Guinea, Jan Roberts concluded that *Australian children growing up in New Guinea in the 1920s and 30s experienced one common thread: the strong bonds which each felt with his or her native so-called servants. New Guinea boys and meris became surrogate parents and friends.* Page 154.

24 Report to Minister by Dept. Home and Territories, 13 October 1923.

25 Wisdom 1923b. Seven years later, Wisdom's views hadn't softened. Writing to the Secretary, Prime Minister's Department, he observed, *The economic situation at present among the Chinese is distinctly bad and many are idle. This is due to the generally depressed condition and to the almost entire stoppage of building and other works. While the causes are to be regretted, I must confess that if the effect is to reduce the numbers of Chinese in the Territory, such a result will be welcome to me. Our policy has always aimed at the reduction of the Chinese to zero if possible and, if not, as low a number as possible. As I have previously stated, this Territory is a paradise for Chinese and they breed rapidly. Even if no more are allowed in they will, at the present rate of increase, swamp the British element in a few years.* Wisdom, 1930d.

26 Many of the 'prohibitions' were not laid down in statute, but relied on compliant bodies such as the Land Board to make the 'right' decision or on a discretionary decision by the Administrator himself.

27 Only one Chinese is known to have been employed by the Administration before the War—Chin Hoi Meen who, in about 1933 when he was 16, worked for the Department of Agriculture as a weather observer and clerk. (ADB, Chin Hoi Meen) A list of members of the New Guinea public service in the *Pacific Islands Yearbook* 1935/36 includes no Chinese names. The Administration did use Chinese as artisans—mechanics, carpenters, plumbers and the like. But these were contractors, not employees.

28 NGLC Debates, 15 January 1935. The non-official member who moved the motion, A.N. McLennan, did, however, refer to *unfair discrimination against the Asiatic*, while another (R.L. Clark) said that *The really Gilbertian idea of applying to a black man's country, with its own peculiar possibilities and problems, this White Australia policy is obvious to everyone.*

29 NGLC Debates, 3 March 1937.

30 Dept. of Immigration and Citizenship Fact Sheet.

31 Letter to Mining Warden, 7 January 1929.

32 McLean, 1929a.

33 Wisdom, 3 August 1921.

34 Weston, page 43.

35 Lae Mission Station Annual Report, 1933, page 4; cited in Willis 1974, pages 124–125.

36 Ibid.

37 *Pacific Islands Monthly*, 15 July 1940.

38 *Rabaul Times*, 1 November 1940.

39 Mining Warden's Report, November 1941.

40 *Rabaul Times*, 1 November 1940.

CHAPTER 22

1 NGAR 1934/35, page 99.

2 Perkins, 1989, page 64.

3 Ian Grabowsky wrote to a friend on 24 July 1936: *Among German nationals there appears a foregone conclusion that the Territory will become German within a very short time … the wife of one of our Australian employees visited the local German mission, and there was astonished to see twenty young Germans wearing a type of uniform, and also on their left arm the swastika.*

(Cited in Sinclair, 1983, page 222). A non-official member, W.E. Grose, expressed concern about Germany's claims in the Legislative Council on several occasions—13 February 1934, 26 February 1936 and 3 March 1937. On the last occasion, he drew comfort from the fact that Senator Pearce, Minister for External Affairs and Minister in charge of Territories had—on 13 March 1936—emphasised *the inviolability and integrity of our Australian territories.*

4 Thus, commenting on a speech on Germany's colonial claims by Adolf Hitler in the Reichstag on 20 February 1938 and another by the Minister for Propaganda, Dr Goebbels on 7 April, Administrator McNicoll said *there is a general presumption that Germany desired to repossess one or two colonies in Africa and has no special interest in the Pacific.* (NGLC Debates, 24 August 1938)

5 Bank of New South Wales, 1939.

6 See discussion in Chapter 10.

7 While there is nothing on the public record to suggest that the Administration equivocated for reasons of military strategy, Japanese aggression in Asia was of increasing concern to Australia, and New Guinea was clearly at risk of invasion. As the early miners found out, the mountain ranges between Wau and the coast were an effective natural barrier against land access. A road, particularly via the Bitoi, would have breached this barrier, and with superior air power to cover troop movements, the Japanese would have had little difficulty reaching Wau. This would have provided a strong base from which to attack Port Moresby by land and air. Had this happened, the Japanese invasion of New Guinea might have had a very different outcome. It is mystifying that the New Guinea Mining Association—many of whose members belonged to the NGVR—should have continued pressing for a road throughout 1941, and even after Pearl Harbor.

8 Given the contempt the Government showed for other aspects of the Mandate (see Chapter 23), this probably had more to do with its reluctance to spend more than it had to in New Guinea than any commitment to the terms of the Mandate.

9 NGLC Debates, 5 September 1939. The authorised strength of NGVR was increased to 23 officers and 482 other ranks in December 1939. Downs, 1999, page 32. At the outbreak of the Pacific War in December 1941, it comprised 12 officers and 284 other ranks. Sinclair, 1998, page 174.

10 Ernie Dover was widely liked as being companionable, courteous and always optimistic, though somehow always just missing out on the 'big one'.

11 His old partner in the leases at the entrance to the lower Bulolo valley, Robbie (G.M.) Robertson, told a story which said much of George's laconic character. *It was at Koranga Creek in the very early days of the field and George was lying on his bunk with a dose of blackwater fever, feeling a bit too close to death. His discomfort was not helped by the persistent attentions of a blow fly, which he vainly attempted to discourage with feebly waiving of his hand, exclaiming finally, 'Go away you bastard. Come back in ten minutes.'* (O'Neill, page 282).

12 Harris (n.d.).

13 Emery, 1990.

14 76 internees were shipped south on the *M.V. Orungal*, 34 from Rabaul and 42 from Salamaua. They included 35 Italian miners, two German miners, a Dutch miner, a Swiss miner, an Italian dredge hand, a German dredge hand and an Italian aircraft mechanic. Some of the Italians were married and had children. Of the total of 76, 13 were naturalised or born in Australia of Italian parents. Department of External Territories, 1940.

15 Weston, 1975c, page 52.

16 M. Murray, 1965, page 28.

17 A 1946 report suggested that the money was eventually put towards Australia's war effort.

18 Edwards was 45 years old and a labour superintendent. In World War 1, he had been in the 1st AIF and then a captain in the British Army. Sinclair, 1998, page 175.

19 Discussion with author, 2001.

20 Niall, n.d.

21 Sinclair, 1998, page 183. The evacuation of Chinese from some centres, late in January 1942, seems to have been the result of actions by individual pilots rather than any organised policy and breached all normal aviation safety standards. The miner Norm Wilde, who had a private pilot's licence, found a Guinea Airways DH 60 Fox Moth abandoned at Port Moresby, filled it with fuel and flew to Salamaua. *In this Moth, which had a normal capacity of pilot and one passenger, I flew 11 Chinese from Salamaua to Port Moresby in one hop. It took me a mile and a half to take off—and then I scraped the tree tops near the 'drome. Pacific Islands Monthly,* March 1942, page 36. Another pilot, Fred Bryce, also flying a Fox Moth, carried nine Chinese women and children in a cabin designed to seat three. *The children could hardly breathe when I shut the door, but there was not a whimper from them.* Sinclair, 1998, page 189.

22 McNicoll, 1942.

23 Sinclair, 1998, page 187.

24 Mills, 1999, page 283.

25 Mingisin, 1978.

26 Godden, 24 January 1942.

27 The Japanese destroyed six planes at Lae, four at Salamaua and three at Bulolo. Apart from the five at Wau, others were in Port Moresby.

28 The Administrator, Sir Walter McNicoll, was evacuated to Wau in a Fox Moth on 23 January, hospitalised overnight and then flown out to Port Moresby.

29 Palili, 1978.

30 Naris Baiko, 2003.

31 Huxley, 2007, page 49.

32 Bengo. 1973. As Ted Knight was BGD's Native Labour Superintendent, it appears that Gotokwa Bengo was working on No. 6 dredge near Wau.

33 O'Loghlen, 1999, page 278. The time between the two bombings is perhaps explained by the fact that the Japanese had turned their attention to Australia, launching a massive carrier-based attack on Darwin on 19 February.

34 This was headquartered in Port Moresby, and encompassed all troops in Papua and New Guinea. In April, as part of a reorganisation, this was retitled New Guinea Force, with Brigadier Morris promoted to Major-General.

35 Papua New Guinea's post-war status as a single administrative and then political entity has its origins in the formation of ANGAU.

36 Godden, 25 January 1942.

37 Cable to HQ 8 MD from NVGR Bulolo, 19 February 1942. Department of the Army, 1942.

38 Waterhouse, 1942b. Several months earlier, Waterhouse claimed that, when he was in New Guinea in June 1941, he had raised with Brigadier Morris and McNicoll the desirability of removing and burying vital parts of the power plants so that they didn't have to be destroyed. Waterhouse, 1942a.

39 Report, 20 July, 1942. Department of External Territories, 1942c.

40 Memo to HQ, New Guinea Force, 4 August 1942. Department of the Army, 1942.

41 Memo from CO, NGVR to CO, Kanga Force, 10 August 1942. Department of the Army, 1942.

42 Huxley, 2007, page 109.

43 McCarthy, 1959, pages 106–107.

CHAPTER 23

1 See, for example, Radi 1971, particularly page 135, Millar 1978, page 306 and O'Faircheallaigh 1989, page 349.

2 In 1940, the enumerated (or counted) population of New Guinea was 669,000. However, as large areas of the mainland still had not been brought under sufficient control to conduct a meaningful census, the actual population would have been significantly greater and the proportion on New Britain and New Ireland therefore well below 20%.

3 Rowley 1958, page 275.

4 Rowley 1966, page 72.

5 At the time, Australia's contribution to Papua's budget was about one third of this amount. Rowley 1958, page 71. By the early 1930s, it had risen to about £50,000 per annum. NGLC Debates, 8 February 1934.

6 League of Nations Mandate, 1921. The Mandate was signed on 17 December 1920.

7 Australia was required to accept imposed prohibitions on the slave trade and forced labour, the supply of intoxicating beverages to natives, the military training of natives (other than for internal police and local defence) and the establishment of military or naval bases or fortifications. It was required also to control the traffic in arms and ammunition and ensure the free movement of missionaries who were nationals of any member state of the League of Nations.

8 Rowley 1958, page 319.

9 E.A. Wisdom was Administrator from May 1921 to June 1933 (though absent on pre-retirement leave for the last 12 months), T. Griffiths from June 1932 to September 1934 (the first 12 months in an acting capacity) and W.R. (later Sir Walter) McNicoll from September 1934 until January 1942.

10 Hudson, 1968, page 303. The Commission comprised four nationals of mandatory powers, five of non-mandatory powers and a representative of the International Labour Office. While not representing their countries in an official capacity, members were highly experienced, usually having had a career in colonial administration, politics or international affairs.

11 PMC Minutes, 6th Session, 1 July 1925 (pages 85–86).

12 PMC Minutes, 34th Session, 20 June 1938 (page 163). William Rappard was born in New York of Swiss parents, completed graduate studies at Harvard University and had been Professor of Economic History and Public Finance at the University of Geneva since 1913.

13 Ainsworth 1924, page 7. Colonel James Ainsworth CMG, CBE, DSO, was formerly Chief Native Commissioner in Kenya. A contemporary internal Home and Territories Dept. paper came to the same conclusion, noting that keeping expenditure within the revenue *is at present impossible if Australia is to effectively discharge its responsibilities under the Mandate.*

14 Op. cit., page 13.

15 Op. cit., page 39.

16 These amounts were additional to £10,000 in 1922–23 for medical services.

17 PMC Minutes, 18th Session, 23 June 1930 (page 49). Lord Lugard had been Military Administrator of Uganda (1890–1892), Governor of Hong Kong (1907–1912) and Governor-General of Nigeria (1914–1919).

18 PMC Minutes, 22nd Session, 8 November 1932 (page 62).

19 The most notable example was the attribution of 65–80% of the cost of District staff to native welfare, despite the greater portion of their time being taken up administering the Native Labour Ordinance. Other dubious examples were £3,531 for the resumption of Expropriation Board properties 'for benefit of natives' (NGAR 1926–27 page 73), £10,397 for the purchase of new schooners and £1,474 for repairs to 'schooners utilised at out-stations' (NGAR 1927–28 page 54). When the PMC queried a similar entry for schooner repairs in the 1931/32 Report, the Australian Representative claimed that *these schooners were necessary for the transport of officials engaged on medical inspections and other work in the interests of natives.*

20 PMC Minutes, 23rd Session, 19 June 1933 (page 26). Count de Penha Garcia was a former Portuguese politician, having been at various times Treasurer and Minister for Foreign Affairs. He was President of the Geographical Society and, in 1931, published a book, *The Portuguese Colonies.*

21 League of Nations 1945, page 23.

22 Ainsworth, op. cit., page 39.

23 Piesse, 1928, page 47. PMC Minutes suggest that the ships (other than one lost at sea) were later sold for £2,950 to the Expropriation Board which was responsible for the sale of expropriated German properties, particularly copra plantations. As the Board's accounts were maintained separately from the Administration's, its finances were beyond the PMC's purview. Nevertheless, Lord Lugard claimed that the Expropriation Fund was £1,500,000 in credit (from the sale of plantations), the PMC Chairman noting that *the Administration appeared to have made a very bad bargain.* PMC Minutes, 13th Session, 13 June 1928 (page 27).

24 These may relate in part to several transactions between 1924–25 and 1926–27 involving 'adjustment of old accounts with the Expropriation Board' and 'Interest on valuation of properties of the Expropriation Board occupied by the Administration', the cumulative effect of which was a cost to the Administration of £9,428. These monies were ultimately payable to the Commonwealth.

25 Thus, in examining the 1926/27 Annual Report in June 1927, three PMC members, including Rappard, attacked the lack of a clear description of the Territory's financial condition. They crystallised their concern formally in the Special Observations: *The figures given in the various financial statements which the mandatory power had forwarded to the Commission did not enable it to form a clear idea of the state of the finances of the Territory …* PMC Minutes, 23 June 1927 (pages 58, 204).

26 NGAR 1927/28, page 52. The sum of £22,917 held in a Trust Fund against this contingency had been transferred to the Administration's revenue account in 1926/27.

27 PMC Minutes, 13th Session, 13 June 1928 (page 25). The 'Special Observation' stated that *The Commission would be glad to learn in what way the financial interests of the mandated territory are represented in the settlement by the mandatory power of the liabilities incurred by the territory to the Australian Department of Defence before and after the inception of civil administration; and also the principles on which the settlement of this question is to be based.* Op. cit., page 229.

28 PMC Minutes, 23rd Session, 19 June 1933 (page 22).

29 The Administration abolished business tax as from 30 June 1925. The 1.5% tax on gross turnover was regarded as inequitable as it often resulted in the taxation of loss-making operations, while a tax on profits was considered impractical. Income tax was abolished at the same time due to high collection costs. A 1% (later 5%) royalty applied on all gold produced — although it was as inequitable as the gross turnover tax. A 10% tariff applied to aeroplane parts, mining machinery and parts and building materials from 2 June 1930 and in the mid-1930s was extended to other machinery.

30 'Observation', PMC Minutes, 31st Session, June 1937 (page 193).

31 PMC Minutes, 15th Session, 3 July 1929 (page 61).

32 Wisdom, 1930a.

33 Feldt, cited in Radford, 1987, page 99.

34 McCarthy, 1963, page 126.

35 However laudable in theory, a free labour system was impractical in the absence of escorted transport between labour-surplus and labour-deficit areas that were geographically distant from each other — as this would involve traversing unfamiliar and potentially hostile territory. After 1933, labourers were permitted to work without contracts for an indefinite period within 25 miles of their villages. With the exception of Lae and Salamaua, this was not an option on the goldfields, as there were few villages close enough. Ironically, a free labour system would also have contributed to the disintegration of village life as, in the absence of fixed-term contracts, labourers couldn't have been forced to return.

36 Remarks by Australia's Accredited Representative, Collins. PMC Minutes, 20th Session, 10 June 1931 (page 22).

37 Stanner 1953, page 13.

38 Op. cit., page 39. Much of the Administration's expenditure appears to have been unproductive. In 1940, J.C. Mullaly, a non-official member of the Legislative Council, expressed concern at the disproportionate expenditure on maintaining the Public Service. *When one considers this young and undeveloped country which has a total revenue of half a million pounds of which approximately £390,000 is spent on salaries and contingencies … then an appropriation of £53,000 for new works – that is development – is* *rather disproportionate, particularly when one realises that a large proportion of that £53,000 … is in connection with staff bungalows, departmental buildings, and things of that sort.* NGLC Debates, 25 September 1940.

39 While deficits were recorded in some years, they were usually small. The cumulative surplus peaked at £61,906 in 1936/37.

40 The Currency Coinage and Tokens Ordinance provided that after the Trust Fund *exceeded £100,000 all further profit made in the making and issuing of Territory coins, and the income from the Fund, will be paid into the revenue of the Territory.* NGLC Debates, 14 January 1935.

41 The extension of control was a slow and difficult process. Villages were often small, belonged to no cohesive entity such as a tribe and spoke different languages even when only a short distance apart. Pressures on District staff often meant that it was a long time before newly contacted areas were visited again by another patrol to consolidate the Administration's influence, undertake censuses and pave the way for recruiters.

42 Activities included
- supervising recruiting activities to discourage abuses and prevent over-recruiting
- undertaking medical examinations before labourers signed contracts and before they returned to their villages
- explaining and supervising the signing of contracts
- collecting bonds from employers to ensure eventual payment of labourers
- pursuing and prosecuting deserters
- inspecting labourers' living conditions: particularly food, housing and health
- inspecting labourers' working conditions: such as hours of work and payment of wages
- overseeing payment of time-expired labourers and ensuring their return to their villages
- overseeing the re-engagement of labourers.

The scale of the challenges District Staff faced can be seen from the fact that in 1939/40 in New Guinea there were around 40,000 indentured labourers, 16,000 new labourers were recruited and 18,000 labourers repatriated. Stanner, page 48.

43 Chinnery, 1933a.

44 Chinnery, 1935b.

45 Taylor, 26 September 1933. This was one of several letters from Taylor to Chinnery over a twelve month period complaining about Griffiths' restrictions on field staff numbers and the effect that these were having on operations.

46 McPherson, 2001, page 210.

47 Cilento 1927. Cilento noted that *The constant resistance of medical officers against the arrogance of Central Administration staff has been (and is) a matter of common comment in the Territory.* In his usual patronising manner, Wisdom observed that Cilento had wanted to override the Administrator's authority and that, while he always put up a plausible case, *an analysis generally shows up the weakness of the man and his case.* Wisdom 1927d.

48 Between 1933 and 1940, more than 1,200 labourers in the Morobe District died from pneumonia or dysentery, an average of 150 a year. New Guinea Annual Reports.

49 *Encyclopaedia of Papua New Guinea*, 1972, page 749.

50 NGAR 1926/27, page 35.

51 PMC Minutes, 36th Session, 19 June 1939 (page 145). Valentine Lug Dannevig was the only female PMC member. She was Norwegian and a social worker with a particular interest in education.

52 Reed, 1943, page 189.

53 In 1939, only 20% of non-indigenous mission staff were from English-speaking countries, with Germans comprising the majority of the remainder and 61% of the total. NGAR 1938/39, page 126.

54 Thus, as late as 1932, the Mining Warden had to refer all applications for manning exemptions to the Secretary for Mines.

55 Two examples: In 1932, the Warden decided to use his spare labour

to cut a graded track for the use of native carriers and mules between Wau and Bulolo. It was two thirds complete when stopped on orders from Rabaul. In 1937, when the District Officer approved a request from Burns Philp for the *Neptuna* to enter at Lae rather than the official port of Salamaua, he was over-ruled by Rabaul.

56 Wisdom, 1930b and 1931.

57 *Sydney Morning Herald*, 18 August 1932.

58 Half yearly report, Salamaua Branch, Bank of New South Wales, 30 September 1932.

59 The 1928/29 Report noted (page 83) that *Aerodromes under the control of the Administration have been established at Lae, Wau* [and] *Salamaua … … In fact, the first two were established by Guinea Gold and the last by New Guinea Goldfields. 'Control' did not include construction or maintenance. The 1933/34 Report noted (page 95) that *The construction of roads for motor transport, from some of the main aerodromes to various mining centres, was completed during the year.* BGD and NGG constructed and maintained all roads outside Wau, other than two-thirds of the road between Wau and Bulolo, which didn't begin until 1934, and the final link between Wau and Edie Creek, which was only completed in 1935.

60 PMC Minutes, 34th Session, 20 June 1938 (page 167). A few months later W.E. Grose, a non-official member of the Territory's Legislative Council, observed *Now it is a matter which is quite within the knowledge of this Council that the Administration has no road policy – we have gone along a line of pottering about in respect of our road development, and certainly as to the nature of the construction of our road system – there is nothing clearly defined … the position still remains that there is no well understood policy in regard to road construction …* (NGLC Debates, 22 September 1938).

61 NGLC Debates, 8 July 1941 Mullaly's recollections were accurate. In 1937, when pressed for details of its policies, the Administration stonewalled: *It is not the practice of governments to make statements of policy in answer to questions in the Legislature.* NGLC Debates, 4 March 1937.

62 Of the three Administrators, only Wisdom is known to have criticised the Government's policies for constraining his activities, but he doesn't appear to have made any effort to secure changes that would have enabled him to administer the Territory more effectively.

63 Sir Joseph Cook: *the policy of the Administration was to educate the native with a view to enabling him to control his own destinies under the supervision of the mandatory.* PMC Minutes, 5th Session, 3 November 1924 (page 131) and the above reference in NGAR 1926/27, page 35.

64 See Chapters 10 and 16. O'Faircheallaigh suggests that the Administration *apparently feared it would act as a precedent and undermine the whole colonial labour system in New Guinea.* (1992, page 914). It is also likely that it wanted to avoid industrial unrest among Europeans whose jobs would be threatened.

65 Black, 1936.

CHAPTER 24

1 *Pacific Islands Monthly*, April 1945.

2 The bridge was opened by Administrator Donald Cleland on 29 January 1955. It was nearly 520 m long, with 17 spans. However, within ten years it had begun to decay and in the early 1970s was replaced with a new bridge, 200 m further upstream, that was 560 m long.

3 Pre-war, employees often worked longer than standard hours, particularly on the dredges, without payment for overtime. This was now no longer possible.

4 In 1946/47, the Government acquired all the shares in Qantas and set out to develop it as Australia's overseas airline. As there was now road transport to Bulolo, BGD showed no interest in acquiring planes to replicate its pre-war aviation activities. Thus, even if Guinea Airways had been licensed, it is unlikely that it would have invested in new planes capable of carrying heavy mining machinery.

5 The BGD representatives who visited Bulolo in 1944 compiled a 280 page list of everything that had been destroyed or removed, as a basis for a claim for war damage compensation. Healy, 1967, page 98. This information also provided the basis for ordering essential equipment enabling rapid progress towards a resumption of operations after the war. BGD was eventually paid compensation totalling £1,312,047/8 shillings and 9 pence. Dunkin 1950, pages 15, 17. War damage compensation payments, whether losses were due to the allies or the Japanese, played an important role in the post-war re-establishment of many businesses. H. Nelson (personal communication).

6 Higher wages were said to have increased the cost of operating dredges (for example, the cost of operating No. 2 rose from 5.9 pence per yard to 7.56 pence, a 28% increase) directly contributing to the closing down of No.s 3 and 6. Healy, page 103.

7 Levien: *I feel certain there is enough cedar on and adjacent to the proposition to pay for* [a] *railway, leaving the mining and pine timber as surplus …* Levien, 1925.

8 *Encyclopaedia of Papua New Guinea*, 1972, page 912.

9 No. 8 ceased operating in March 1953 and No. 2 in April 1955. No. 7 capsized in May 1956 and No. 4 finished in May 1957.

10 Placer Development merged with two other Canadian mining companies in 1987 to form Placer Dome, which was in turn taken over by Barrick Gold in 2006.

11 61.4% of the gold was won pre-war and 38.6% post-war. Lowenstein, page 136.

12 Cited in Sinclair 1998, page 259.

13 Ibid.

14 Lowenstein, 1982, page 65.

15 Sinclair, 1998, page 444.

16 Op. cit., page 338.

17 Lowenstein (page 141) identified two PNG miners who recovered an average of 29 to 34 ounces per month over several years in 1970s. Several others made smaller, though still quite good, returns over extended periods.

18 The Upper Watut people are those formerly known as the Kapau.

19 Halvaksz, 2006, page 347.

20 Nos. 3 and 4 were dismantled and shipped to Chile in the 1950s, No. 1 was used to supply spare parts for the other dredges and Nos. 7 and 8 were cut up and sold for scrap to South Korean interests.

21 See Chapter 8.

22 As at Edie Creek, the Hidden Valley gold is low grade, being mixed with considerable quantities of silver. Silver reserves exceed 40 million ounces.

23 In 2003, the author and his son Paul gave a strongly built young man a lift back towards Bulolo from a bridge across the Upper Watut in the back of our small truck. Only after we had gone some distance did our guide inform us that he was the leader of a local *rascol* gang. At the end, when we let him off, he came round, tapped on the author's window and in perfect English thanked us politely for the lift.

Picture Sources

Photos not attributed in the following list are from the author's collection.

10 ML [L.V.Waterhouse, PXA 1125]. 11 NLA [Map RM 389]. 14-15 ML [ASOPA, FM3/844; Pic Acc 2216; A24]. 19 ML [Harry Downing, NCY2:740. ON54_664]. 20 ML [Small Pictures File, Portraits]. 22 Above WBCA [C.M. Mackay, Album 3]. 22 Below WBCA [1998/0223/179]. 23 ML [Harry Downing, NCY2:246. ON54_21]. 24 ML [Harry Downing, NCY2:237. ON54_14]. 25 Left Daphne Landis. 25 Right ML [AM42]. 26-27 ML [Harry Downing, NCY2:276. ON54_45]. 30 ML [Harry Downing, NCY2:239. ON54_15]. 33 Daphne Landis. 34 Daphne Landis. 36 Author. Also ML [Harry Downing, NCY2:229. ON54_8]. 37 Collin Bayliss. 38 NAA [Series CP660/26, Bundle 1/E834/2; item CP660/25/7]. 44 MUA [J.H.W. Johns, 72/54]. 45 NAA [Series CP660/26, Bundle 1/E834/2; item CP660/25/6]. 47 The Sydney Mail, 28 December 1927. 48 Left Author. Also ML [NCY2:228. ON54_7]. 48 Right Author. Also ML [Harry Downing, NCY2:282. ON54_49]. 49 The Sydney Mail, 28 December 1927. 50 Author. Also ML [Harry Downing, NCY2: 261. ON54_31]. 51 Author. Also ML [Harry Downing, NCY2:243]. 52 Author. Also ML [Harry Downing, NCY2:272. ON54_40]. 53 Author. Also ML [Harry Downing, NCY2:270. ON54_38]. 54 NAA [Series CP660/26, Bundle 1/E834/2; item CP660/25/4]. 57 Author. Also ML [Harry Downing, NCY2:252. ON54_25b]. 58 Collin Bayliss. Also ML [Harry Downing, NCY2:235. ON54_13]. 59 Author. Also ML [Harry Downing, NCY2:265. ON54_34a]. 60 Daphne Landis. 61 NLA [The (Sydney) Sun, 22 September 1926; Wells Papers, MS364, Book 1]. 64 ML [Harry Downing, NCY2:248. ON54_23]. 67 Author. Also ML [Harry Downing, NCY2:259. ON54_30b]. 70 Author. Also ML [Harry Downing, NCY2:340. ON54_90]. 71 Jim Sinclair. 73 Author. Also ML [Harry Downing, NCY2:242. ON54_18]. 74 Daphne Landis. 76 Author. Also ML [Harry Downing, NCY2:249. ON54_24]. 77 ML [Harry Downing, NCY2:278a. ON54_47a]. 78 WBCA [1998/0223/154]. 79 Arthur John. 80 Carl Gunther. 81 WBCA [C.M. Mackay, Album 1]. 82 Above Alan Vagg. 82 Below Collin Bayliss 83 Carl Gunther. 84 Josie Wallenius. 85 Alan Vagg. 86 Alan Vagg. 87 Above WBCA [C.M. Mackay, Album 3]. 87 Below Pat Boys. 89 FL [Wally Doe collection, MS 275; No.37]. 90 Carl Gunther. 91 Pat Boys. 92 ML [L.V.Waterhouse, PXA 1125]. 94 Alan Vagg 95 ML [L.V.Waterhouse, PXA 1125]. 96 Alan Vagg. 99 ML [Harry Downing, NCY2:496. ON54_214]. 100 Australian Museum, Sydney [AMS321 Charles Marshall, 1140m_08]. 104 Australian Museum, Sydney [AMS321 Charles Marshall, 1140m_10]. 105 Pat Boys. 107 NLA [Wells Papers, MS364, Book 1]. 108 NLA [Wells Papers, MS364, Series 5/7]. 109 Noel Butlin Archives, ANU [Burns Philp Papers, N115-509-1]. 110 Dennis Gray. 111 Air and Space/Smithsonian Magazine, August/September 1986. 113 Above Naelo Jenkins. 113 Below Author. Also ML [Harry Downing, NCY2:320. ON54_72]. 115 WBCA [C.M. Mackay, Album 3] Also ML [Harry Downing, NCY2:441. ON54_159a]. 116 WBCA [C.M. Mackay, Album 3] Also ML [Harry Downing, NCY2:469. ON54_182]. 117 Peter Holm. 118 Dennis Gray. 119 Above ML [Harry Downing, NCY2:698. ON54_620]. 119 Below WBCA [C.M. Mackay, Album 3] Also ML [Harry Downing, ON54_158]. 120 Carl Gunther. 124 FL [Wally Doe, MS 275, No.31]. 125 Sue Sneddon. 126 Author. Also ML [Harry Downing, ON54_126]. 127 ML [Harry Downing, NCY2:451. ON54_167]. 129 Ross and Pat Johnson . 130 Author. Also ML [Harry Downing, NCY2:312-314. ON54_66ab]. 131 ML [Harry Downing, NCY2:447. ON54_162]. 134 Sue Sneddon. 135 NLA [Mick Leahy, nla.pic-an20650880-37]. 137 NLA [Harslett collection, nla.pic-vn3792787] Also ML [Harry Downing, NCY2:401. ON54_136]. 141 NLA [J.R. Black Papers, MS 8346/2/20, page 49]. 142 Above Sue Sneddon. 142 Below Sue Sneddon. 143 NLA [J.R. Black Papers, MS 8346/2/20, page 63]. 144 Above Sue Sneddon. 144 Below Sue Sneddon. 145 Sue Sneddon. 146 Author. Also ML [Harry Downing, NCY2:370. ON54_114]. 147 NLA [Harslett collection, nla.pic-vn3792783] Also ML [Harry Downing, NCY2:368. ON54_112]. 156 Author. Also ML [Harry Downing, NCY2:234. ON54_12]. 158 Margaret Ellis (Albert Roberts). 159 C.M. Mackay, WBCA [Album 3]. 162 Australian Museum, Sydney [AMS321 Charles Marshall, 1141m_40]. 163 Australian Museum, Sydney [AMS321 Charles Marshall, 1141m_41]. 164 Alan Vagg. 169 Author. Also ML [Harry Downing, NCY2:232. ON54_11]. 172 Author. Also ML [Harry Downing, ON54_6]. 173 Author. Also ML [Harry Downing, NCY2:729. ON54_653]. 174 Noel Butlin Archives, ANU [Burns Philp Papers, N115-509-3]. 175 Above Author. Also ML [Harry Downing, NCY2:352. ON54_100]. 175 Below Author. Also ML [Harry Downing, NCY2:365. ON54_109]. 176 Above Author. Also ML [Harry Downing, NCY2:357. ON54_103]. 176 Below ML [Harry Downing, NCY2:416. ON54_145]. 177 Above ML [Harry Downing, NCY2:388. ON54_105]. 177 Below Author. Also ML [Harry Downing, NCY2:225. ON54_2]. 178 Jim Birrell. 179 Collin Bayliss. Also ML [Harry Downing, NCY2:700. ON54_621]. 181 WBCA [C.M. Mackay, Album 2] Also ML [Harry Downing, NCY2:526. ON54_243]. 182 NLA [Jack O'Neill collection, nla.pic-vn3791761]. 184 Left Gwen Innes. 184 Right Jim Birrell. 185 Gwen Innes. 187 NLA [Harslett collection, nla.pic-vn3792592]. 189 WBCA [1998/0223/179]. 190 NLA [A.T. Simmons, nla.pic-vn3792729]. 191 Author. Also ML [Harry Downing, NCY2:358. ON54_104]. 193 ML [Mick Leahy, PXA632_vol.1_6y24]. 194 Lee Huxley. 195 Nareda Tait. 196 Nareda Tait. 198 Above Carl Gunther. 198 Below Josie Wallenius. 207 AWM [H. Walter, negative number P01283_010]. 209 AWM [B. Rowe, negative number P02107_004]. 210 ML [L.V. Waterhouse, PXA 1125]. 212 AWM [negative number 099149]. 213 Carl Gunther. 215 Above Left John Longstaff; Brigadier-General Evan Wisdom, 1923, oil on canvas, 71.8 x 64 cm; AWM (ART02999). 215 Above Middle AWM [negative number H15975]. 215 Above Right NLA [Pic-an 10975069-9 or 10975069-6]. 215 Below The Sydney Mail, 7 June 1933. 227 Carl Gunther. 236 Jim Sinclair. Back Cover Paul Waterhouse.

Select Bibliography

Key

AR	*Adelaide Register*
AIMM	Australasian Institute of Mining and Metallurgy
AJPH	*Australian Journal of Politics and History*
AO	*Australian Outlook*
CE&MR	*Chemical Engineering* and *Mining Review*
CPD	Commonwealth Parliamentary Debates
DH&T	Department of Home and Territories
DM	Department of Mining, Port Moresby
DS&NA	District Services and Native Affairs
ECRC	Edie Creek Royal Commission
FL	Fryer Library, University of Queensland
GJ	*The Geographical Journal* (Royal Geographical Society)
GGNL	Guinea Gold No Liability
HSANZ	*Historical Studies. Australia and New Zealand*
IAMS	*Industrial Australian and Mining Standard*
IMM	Institution of Mining and Metallurgy
JMDHS	*Journal of the Morobe District Historical Society*
JPH	*Journal of Pacific History*
MDHS	Morobe District Historical Society
ML	Mitchell Library
MUA	Melbourne University Archives
NAA	National Archives of Australia
NAPNG	National Archives of Papua New Guinea
NGAR	New Guinea Annual Report
NGGZ	*New Guinea Gazette*
NGLC	New Guinea Legislative Council
NGVR	New Guinea Volunteer Rifles
NLA	National Library of Australia
PIM	*Pacific Islands Monthly*
PMB	Pacific Manuscripts Bureau
PMD	Prime Minister's Department
RT	*Rabaul Times*
SLSA	State Library of South Australia
SLV	State Library of Victoria
SM	*Sydney Mail*
SMH	*The Sydney Morning Herald*
UPNG	University of Papua New Guinea
WBCA	Westpac Banking Corporation Archives

Commonwealth Government

Ainsworth, Col. J. (1924) Report on Administrative Arrangements and Matters affecting the Interests of Natives in the Territory of New Guinea, 10 September, Government Printer, Melbourne

Army, Department of the (1942) Report on demolition of Bulolo Gold Dredging Limited plants and equipment in New Guinea, 20 July. NAA Series AWM54, 244/2/35

Attorney-General's Department (1929) Uncontrolled Areas. Memo to Secretary PMD, 10 July 1929. NAA Series A518, BB840/1/3 Part 1

Bureau of Census and Statistics, Transport and Communications Bulletin, Civil Aviation: New Guinea, 1924–41

Controller of Civil Aviation (1930–41) Annual Reports on Civil Aviation in Australia and New Guinea. Melbourne.

Cook, Sir Joseph (1921) CPD, 29 September 1921, Vol. 97, page 11600

Duncan, W.J. (1927a) Administrative arrangements for civil aviation in New Guinea. Memo to Controller of Civil Aviation, 28 March. NAA Series A518, A808/1/3 Part 1

(1927b) Early aviation developments, aerodromes and aircraft. Report to Controller of Civil Aviation, 7 May. NAA Series A518, A808/1/3 Part 1 [Edited version of Duncan's two reports published in *Aircraft*, October–December 1927]

Dunstan, B. (1931) Report of Inquiry of the Mining Industry of the Territory of New Guinea, 24 June. NAA Series A518, Z834/2

External Territories, Department of (1940) Schedule of persons detained in the interests of national security and transferred to Australia in SS Orungal ex Rabaul, 25 July. NAA Series A518, AO16/2/1

(1942a) Defence–Attacks by Japanese on New Guinea. NAA Series A518, item L16/2/3 Part 1

(1942b) Miscellaneous reports by various officers re Japanese attack on New Guinea. NAA Series A518, DD16/2/1

(1942c) Report of Bulolo Gold Dredging Limited plants and equipment in New Guinea, July. NAA Series A518/1, V806/1/3

Fisher N.H. (1943) 'The mineral resources and mining industry of the Mandated Territory of New Guinea' Unpub. Report No. 1943/35, Dept. Supply and Shipping, 27 August. NAA Series A518, AM834/1

Glasgow, Sir William (1926) Press Release on the Morobe Goldfields, 9 October. NAA Series A1/15, 1927/266

Green, A.E., M.P. (1939) Native 'singsings' in vicinity of Wau. Letter to the Minister for External Territories, 6 June. NAA Series A518, BF 840/1/3

(Griffiths, T.) (1938) Report of Committee appointed to investigate new site for the administrative head-quarters of the Territory of New Guinea, 27 April

Home and Territories, Department of (1923) Land and Property: Acquisition of and by Asiatics, Report to Minister, 13 October. NAA Series A518, AA824/1 Part 1

(1924) Financial Experience and Outlook of the Mandated Territory of New Guinea. Internal departmental paper. NAA Series A518, AD 822/1/3 Part 1

(1928) Construction of a road to the goldfields. Minute to Secretary, 27 April. NAA Series A518, AD822/1/3 Part 1

Immigration and Citizenship, Department of (2007) Fact Sheet No. 8. Abolition of the 'White Australia' Policy

Junkers G31 Aircraft used in New Guinea (1931). NAA Series MP113/1, VH-UOU, VH-UOV, VH-URQ and VH-UOW

New Guinea (1914–21 to 1939–40) Territory of — Annual Reports to the Council of the League of Nations

NGVR War Diary (1942)

Papua (1906–1913, 1936–1938) Annual Reports

Pearce, Sir George (1935) Aviation Policy. Cabinet Submission by Minister in Charge of Territories, approved by Cabinet 11 December. NAA Series MP131/1, 192/101/149

(1937) Employment of competent natives in mines. Letter to Senator H.S.Foll, 1 December. NAA Series A518, AV834/2 Part 1

Prime Minister's Department (1923) A Selection of papers printed by the League of Nations relating to the Mandatory system (especially those relating to C Mandates) 1920–1922. Ordered to be printed 25th August

(1929) Powers of District Officers under Uncontrolled Areas Ordinance. Brief to the Prime Minister, 3 September. NAA Series A518, BB840/1/3 Part 1

(1930a) Special Areas, New Guinea Goldfields. Memo to the Prime Minister, 18 March. NAA Series A518, BB834/2

(1930b) Application of S.38A of Mining Ordinance allowing holders of Miner's Rights to enter and work on dredging and sluicing leases. Memo to the Prime Minister, 12 May. NAA Series A518, Y834/2

(1936) Strike at New Guinea Goldfields Limited: Employment of competent natives in mines. File Note, 27 January. NAA Series A518, AV834/2 Part 1

(1937) Size of claims and gold mining leases. Brief to Prime Minister, 19 April. NAA Series A518, W834/2

Royal Commission on the Edie Creek (New Guinea) Leases
1926-27 – Evidence, NAA Series
CP660/25, Bundle 1/volumes 1-4
– Exhibits, NAA Series CP660/26, Bundle 1/E834/2
– Report, 30 August 1927 – NLA Clune Papers, MS 4951 Box
179/504

Australian Administration in New Guinea

Administration (1923-27) Return of gold won from the Morobe Gold
Field, 1-10-23 to 21-4-27. ECRC Exhibit 55. NAA Series CP660/26,
Bundle 1/E834/2
(1926) List of dredging and sluicing leases 'ceased and determined'.
NAA Series A518, N834/2
(1926-27, 1929) Gold Declarations, Edie and Merri Creeks, 23
November 1926 to 25 July 1927, 4 January to 31 December 1929.
DM
(1927-28) Gold Declarations, Edie and Merri Creeks, 1 August to 28
December 1927, 14 January to 22 December 1928. NAA G219, 4
(1927-28) Gold Declarations, Salamaua, February to March 1927,
August to December 1928. NAA Series G220, 1 and 3
Appleby, S.J. (1927) Report on the Native Disturbances, Biololo
(Rabaul) area, 21 June. NAA Series A1/15, 1927/728
Black, J.R. (1936) Patrol Report No. B.29/35-36. The Waria, Biaru and
Bulolo River systems, 16 February. NLA Black Papers, MS 8346
Series 2/5
(1937) Alleged lack of discipline among native labourers. Memo to
the District Officer, Salamaua, 20 May. NLA Black Papers, MS 8346
Series 2/5
Bretag, A.J. (1941) Speech in the Legislative Council on native
behaviour, 8 July.
Bridge, K.W.T. (1934) Monthly Intelligence Report for Otibanda Post
(March), 4 April. NAA Series A7034, 50
Chinnery, E.W.P. (1927) Evidence to ECRC, 27 May. NAA Series
CP660/25, Bundle 1/volume 4
(1930) Notes from Patrol Report by Alan Roberts to Upper Watut,
11 August. NLA Chinnery Papers MS 766 Box 11 Series 5/14
(1933a) 'Uncontrolled Watut Watershed'. Memo to Acting
Administrator, 10 January. NLA Chinnery Papers, MS 766 Box 12
Series 6/4
(1933b) 'Natives Lakekamu, Tauri and Watut Watersheds'. Memo
to Acting Administrator, 7 February. NLA Chinnery Papers MS 766
Box 12 Series 6/4
(1935a) 'Field Staff'. Memo to Administrator, 8 January NLA
Chinnery Papers MS 766 Box 12 Series 6/5
(1935b) Memo to Administrator (on Field Staff), 31 January NLA
Chinnery Papers MS 766 Box 12 Series 6/5
(1936a) Supplementary Notes on the 1934-35 Annual Report for the
Information of Accredited Representatives. NLA Chinnery Papers
MS766 Box 12 Series 6/3
(1936b) 'Methods of Recruiting, Control and Repatriation of Native
Labour in New Guinea'. International Pacific Health Conference,
Melbourne, 15-22 December. NLA Chinnery Papers MS 766, Box 36
Series 16/2
(1937) Additional Notes on 1935-36 Annual Report for the
information of Accredited Representatives. NLA Chinnery Papers
MS 766, Box 12 Series 6/2
Cilento, R. (1927) Letter of resignation to the Administrator, 21 May
1927 NAA Series A452, 1959/5894
Commission to Inquire into the matter of Native Labour in the
Territory (1941) Majority Report. NAA Series A11740, 16
(1941) Minority Report by H.C.Hosking and D.S.Hore-Lacy. Part II.
NAA Series A518, BG 840/1/3
Downing, H. (1931) Goldfields desertions and possible causes. Memo
from ADO to District Officer, Salamaua, 18 June. NAPNG S.20/3
Edwards, M.S. (1934) Patrols undertaken from Otibanda Post during
December 1933, 2 January. NLA Chinnery Papers MS 766, Box 14
Series 7/4

Feldt, E.A. (1931) Patrol Report No. B.17 of 1931/32 Across the Upper
Watut Divide to investigate the murder of Helmuth Baum. 29 May
NLA Chinnery Papers MS 766, Box 14 Series 7/2
(1932) Report of Air Reconnaissance, 18 January. NLA Chinnery
Papers MS 766, Box 14 Series 7/2
(1936) Compensation for Accidents to Natives. Memo by Mining
Warden to District Officer Salamaua, 8 October. NAA Series G215,
S.20/1
Griffiths, T. (1933) Boot Allowance. Memo to Heads of Departments
and District Officers, 6 June. NLA Black Papers MS 8346 Box 1
Folder 4
(1934) Restrictions on Chinese. Letter to Bureau of Overseas Chinese
Affairs, Rabaul. 10 September. NAA Series A518, AA824/1
Hurrell, L. (1951) Patrol Report No. 2/1950-51. Menyamya Patrol to the
Headwaters of the Tauri and Banir Rivers, 19 March. NAA Series
A7034, 139
Hyde, A. (1931) Goldfields: Black Cat. Memo from Mining Registrar to
Mining Warden, 8 August, NAPNG item S.9/3
Inspector of Mines (1932-1941) Monthly and Annual Reports NAA
Series A518, AM834/2 Parts 1-2
Legislative Council (1934-1941) Debates
Lukin, J.H. (1924) Cost to a miner of working on the field. Letter to
Secretary for Mines, Rabaul, 1 August. ECRC, Exhibit 81. NAA
Series CP660/26, Bundle 1/E834/2
(1926) Applications for dredging and sluicing leases on Edie Creek
by W.G. Royal, A.A. Royal, A.F. Chisholm and R.M. Glasson. Memo
to Administrator, 10 May. NAA Series A1/15, 1927/266
McCarthy, J.K. (1932) Investigation of the Leahy Bros. Incident: Tauri
River, August. NAA Series A7034, 31
(1933a) Patrol Report No. 19/32-33 Salamaua to Upper Reaches of
the Langimar River, 12 March to 26 April. NLA McCarthy Papers
MS 5581, Box 14
(1933d) Patrol Report No. 15/33-34. Otibanda Police Post to the
Tauri River, 7 August to 1 December. NLA Chinnery Papers MS 766,
Box 14 Series 7/4
McLean, J.D. (1927a) Expedition against the natives of Rabaul village
and Kaisinik. Letter to the Acting Administrator, 21 January. NAA
Series A1/15, 1927/728
(1927b) Reply to allegations by Rev. J. Flierl regarding punitive
expedition against Kaisinik, 13 June. NAA Series A1/15, 1927/728
(1929a) Admissions Asiatics to Goldfields. Memo to the President,
Bulolo Goldfields Progress Association, 15 January. DM
(1929b) New Find at Hidden Valley. Memo to Secretary for Mines,
Rabaul, 30 October. NAPNG S.9/2
(1930) Discovery of Payable Gold by Mr. E. Rowlands on Ramu
River. Memo to Acting Secretary for Mines, Rabaul, 12 November.
NAA Series A518/1, F834/2
McNicoll, W. (1934) Report of a Tour of Inspection to the Morobe
District, 2-19 October 1934. Report to the Council of the League of
Nations, 1934-35. Appendix B
(1936a) Strike – Employee New Guinea Goldfields Ltd. Memo to
Secretary PMD, 10 January. NAA Series A518, AV834/2 Part 1
(1936b) Taxation in New Guinea. Memo to Secretary PMD, 28 April.
NAA Series A518, AN822/1/3
(1939) Native 'sing-sings' in the vicinity of Wau. Memo to Secretary
PMD, 17 July. NAA Series A518, BF 840/1/3
(1940) Despatch to Australia of persons detained in the interests of
National Security. Memo to GOC, Eastern Command, 23 July. NAA
Series A518, AB16/2/1 Part 2
(1941) Dispute between the management of New Guinea Goldfields
and miners employed by that company. Memo to Secretary PMD, 6
May. NAA Series A518, AV834/2 Part 2
Milligan, J.S. (1937a) Report of attacks on patrol party and on Kobakini
Base Camp by natives of Towedo and Hogeneiwa. Report, 22
November. NAA Series A518, E841/1
(1937b) Report of patrols from Kobakini Base camp during
September, October and November, 17 December. NAA Series

A7034, 185

Mining Warden (1927–1941) Monthly Reports. NAA Series A518, AA834/2 Parts 1-6

(1931, 1933, 1936–40) Annual reports. NAA Series A518, AA834/2 Parts 1-6

Mission Conference Proceedings (1927) Report of Mission Conference, Rabaul, 20 June to 11 July 1927. NAA Series A518, A838/1 Part 1 Attachment

Murphy, J.J. (1937a) Diary of Patrol to the Buangs, June–July. FL MS99/7

(1937b) Effect of Taxation on the Natives in the Kaiwa Area, 20 August. FL MS99/15/6

Oakley, E.W. (1926a) Precis of report on patrol to Bulolo Goldfield April, May 1926. Memo to Government Secretary, Rabaul, 2 June. NAA Series A1/15, 1927/266

(1926b) Disturbance among miners. Memo to Deputy Administrator Cardew, 21 September. NAA Series CP660, Bundle1/E834/2, Exhibit 116

(1927) Evidence to ECRC, 19 May. NAA Series CP660/25, Bundle 1/volume 3

Penglase, N. (1932a) Patrol to the Papuan border south of the Watut Divide. Patrol Report No. 9 of 1931/32, 11 January 1932 NLA Chinnery Papers, MS 766 Box 14 series 7/2

(1932b) Special Patrol to the Kabu River for the purpose of arresting the murderers of Helmuth Baum and eight native carriers, 14 April. NLA Chinnery Papers, MS 766 Box 14 series 7/2

(1942) Air Raid on Salamaua, 21 January. NLA McNicoll Papers MS 2101, folder 21

Phillips, F.B. (1928) Report of Commission of Inquiry into native labour matters, Morobe District. NAA Series A518/1, AD840/1/3

Sansom, W.E. (1933) Patrol Report [B.13/1933–1934] — Watutabinga/ Gumi area to bring it under Government influence, 12 November. NLA Chinnery Papers, MS 766 Box 14 Series 7/3

Searl, H.F. (1939) Report on the improvement of harbour facilities at Salamaua, 21 September. NAA Series A518, X808/1

Taylor, E. (1933) (Comment on) Patrol Report B.13/1933–1934 — Watutabinga/Gumi area, Upper Watut. Memo to Director DS&NA, Rabaul, 27 November. NLA Chinnery Papers, MS 766 Box 14 Series 7/3

(1934a) (Comment on) Patrol Report 15/33–34 — Tauri River. Memo to Director DS&NA, Salamaua, 20 January. NLA Black Papers MS 8346, Series 2/4

(1934b) Murder of Bernard L. McGrath on the Karmontina River, by natives of Finintugu and Ikanofe villages. Memo to Director DS&NA, Rabaul, 17 March. NAA Series A518/1, L841/1/Part 2

Taylour, H. (1930) Inspection of Black Cat Creek and Bitoi River Alluvial Gold Workings. Memo to Warden, 25 November. NAPNG S.9/3

(1933) Unemployed Europeans — Morobe District. Memo from Warden to Government Secretary, Rabaul, 15 June. NAPNG S.9/1

Thornton, L. (1932) Report on Ports and Harbour Facilities for the Goldfields and Markham valley 'areas of the Morobe District, 2 September. NAA Series A518, X808/1

Townsend, G.W.L. (1932) Air Navigation (Investigation of Accidents) Regs. Memo to Controller of Civil Aviation, 1 November. NAA Series MP113/1, VH-UIW

(1933a) Inquest into deaths of William Naylor, Emil Clarius, Angatoi, Bimsik and Luandi, 19, 24 January. NAA Series A518, L841/1/Part 1

(1933b) Report of special patrol — Murder of W. Naylor and E. Clarius, 21 January. NAA Series A518, L841/1/Part 1

Weidenbach v. Guinea Gold and D.R.Booth, Decision by J.D.McLean, Mining Warden, 11 January 1927 and associated depositions, DM

Wisdom, E.A. (1921) Policy on the 'Native Question'. Memo to Secretary PMD, 3 August. NAA Series A518, F840/1/3 Part 1

(1923a) Waste or vacant land. Memo to Secretary DH&T, 19 August. NAA Series A518, P840/1/3

(1923b) Discrimination against Asiatics. Report to Minister for H&T, 13 October. NAA Series A518, AA824/1/Part 1

(1924) Uncontrolled Areas Ordinance. Memo to Secretary, DH&T, 17 December. NAA Series A518, A846/1/44

(1926a) Not a poor man's field. Cable to DH&T, 4 August. ECRC Exhibit 144. NAA Series CP660/26, Bundle 1/E834/2

(1926b) Not a poor man's field. Cable to DH&T, 6 August. ECRC Exhibit 145. NAA Series CP660/26, Bundle 1/E834/2

(1926c) Not a poor man's field. Letter to J.G. McLaren, Secretary DH&T, 10 August. NAA Series A1/15, 1927/266

(1926d) Developments on the field. Memorandum to Secretary DH&T, 16 October. NAA Series A1/15, 1927/266

(1927a) Response to questions by Minister. Memo to DH&T, 4 February. NAA Series A1/15, 1927/266

(1927b) Policy on punitive measures following attacks by natives. Memorandum to Minister for H&T, 22 February. NAA Series A518, L840/1/3 Part 1

(1927c) Evidence to ECRC, 31 May. NAA Series CP660/25, Bundle 1/volume 4

(1927d) Resignation of Dr. R. Cilento. Letter to Secretary, DH&T, 15 June. NAA Series A452, 1959/5894

(1928a) Road to the goldfields. Cabled memo to Minister for H&T, 14 March. NAA Series A518, G834/2

(1930a) Need for field to be developed by large companies. Memo to Secretary PMD, 24 April. NAA Series A518, V834/2

(1930b) Value of gold to the Territory. Memo to Government Secretary, Rabaul, 8 August. NAA Series A518, S834/2

(1930c) Administrator's views cited in Departmental Memo to Prime Minister, 15 May. NAA Series A518, V834/2

(1930d) Discrimination against Asiatics. Memo to Secretary PMD, 5 December. NAA Series A518, AA824/1/Part 1

(1931) Agricultural and pastoral possibilities. Memo to Secretary PMD, 6 May. NAA Series A518, AA834/2 Part 2

(1932) Address on launching BGD Dredge No. 1, 21 March, Typescript of speech, Wells Papers, NLA MS 364/5/7

Woodman, H.E. (1933) Discovery of Payable Gold, Upper Purari River. Report to District Officer, Madang by Assistant Mining Warden, 15 February. NAA Series A518/1, F834/2

Selected legislation, ordinances, regulations and proclamations

New Guinea Act 1920–1935
Gold Buyers Ordinance 1931–1938
Land Ordinance
Mining Ordinance 1928–1940 and Regulations
Mining and Works Regulation Ordinance 1935–41 and Regulations
Native Administration Regulations 1924
Native Labour Ordinance 1935–1939 and Regulations
Native Taxes Ordinance 1921–1938
Salamaua to Wau Road Loan Ordinance 1938
Uncontrolled Areas Ordinance 1925–1938

Proclamations:
— Waste and vacant land at Bulolo (1932) NGGZ July, No. 333
— Recruiting (1938) NAA Series A518, Item AG 840/1/3

Published books, monographs, papers and reports

Affleck, A.H. (1964) *The Wandering Years*, Melbourne
Anon. (1939) 'Jungle Gold. The Story of Guinea Airways', in *Guinea Airways: Air Routes in Australia, New Guinea and Papua*, Intava Products
Australian Dictionary of Biography online:
    Feldt, E.A. (J.C.H. Gill)
    Griffiths, T. (W. Perry)
    Chin, Hoi Meen (P.H. Cahill)
    Holden, L.H. (C. Bridge
    Levien, C.J. (A.M. Healy)
    McNicoll, W.R. Sir (R. McNicoll)

Mustar, E.A. (D. Langmore)

Parer, R.J.P. (K. Isaacs)

Stewart, F.S. (J. Sinclair)

Waterhouse, L.V. (M.H. Waterhouse)

Wisdom, E.A. (R. McNicoll)

Beaglehole, J.C. (1966) *The Exploration of the Pacific*, London

Baskett, G. (1991) *Islands and Mountains*, Lawson

Blackwood, B. (1978) The *Kukukuku of the Upper Watut* (ed. C.R. Hallpike), Oxford

Booth, D. (1929) *Mountains, Gold and Cannibals*, Sydney

M.J. Bourke and others ed. (1993) *Our Time but not Our Place. Voices of Expatriate Women in Papua New Guinea*, Melbourne

Bulbeck, C. (2000) Australian *Women in Papua New Guinea*, Cambridge

Bulolo Gold Dredging (1930) Prospectus

Bulolo Gold Dredging (1931–1942) Annual Reports

Burton, J. (1996) 'C'est qui, le patron? Kinship and the Rentier Leader in the Upper Watut'. Working Paper No. 1, Resource Management in Asia-Pacific, Canberra

Chinnery, S. (1998) *Malaguna Road*, Canberra

Clune, F. (1951) *Somewhere in New Guinea*, Sydney

Cole, T. (1990) *The Last Paradise*, Sydney

Cooke, J. (1983) *Working in Papua New Guinea 1931–1946*, Upper Mt Gravatt

Crittenden, R. (1991) 'Across the Nembi Plateau', in Schieffelin, E.L. and Crittenden, R. 1991

Decker, J.A. (1940) *Labour Problems in the Pacific Mandates*, London

Decoto, L.A. (1929) *Report on the Bulolo River Dredging Leases, New Guinea – Mandated Territory*, 22 August (BGD Prospectus, 15–20)

Doe, W. (1997) *Wandering Wally*, Bathurst

Downs, I. (1978) 'Kiap, Planter and Politician: a Self-portrait', in Griffin, J. (ed.) *Papua New Guinea Portraits – The Expatriate Experience*, Canberra

(1986) *The Last Mountain. A Life in Papua New Guinea*, St. Lucia

(1999) *The New Guinea Volunteer Rifles NGVR 1939–1943. A History*, Broadbeach Waters

Dunkin, H.H. (1950) *Operations of Bulolo Gold Dredging Ltd.* (Originally published as articles in CE&MR February to May 1950), Melbourne

Eggleston, F.W. (ed.) (1928) *The Australian Mandate for New Guinea*, Melbourne

Firth, S. (1982) *New Guinea under the Germans*, Melbourne

Fitz-Patrick, D.G. and Kimbuna, J. (1983) *Bundi. The Culture of a Papua New Guinea People*, Nerang

Gash, N. and Whittaker, J. (1975) *A Pictorial History of New Guinea*, Milton

Godelier, M. (1986) *The Making of Great Men. Male Domination and Power among the New Guinea Baruya*, Cambridge

Godwin, J. (1968) *Battling Parer*, Adelaide

Green, T. (1999) *Central Bank Gold Reserves. An Historical Perspective Since 1845*. World Gold Council, New York

Guinea Airways Ltd (1928–1941) Annual Reports (1942) Diary

Hahl, A. (1980) *Governor in New Guinea*. Translated and edited by P.G. Sack and D. Clark. Canberra

Healy, A.M. (1967) *Bulolo. A History of the Development of the Bulolo Region, New Guinea*. New Guinea Research Bulletin No. 15, Canberra

Hiery, H.J. (1995) *The Neglected War. The German South Pacific and the Influence of World War 1*, Honolulu

Hogbin, H.I. (1951) *Transformation Scene. The Changing Culture of a New Guinea Village*. London

(1970) Social Change, Melbourne

and Wedgwood, C. (1943) *Development and Welfare in the Western Pacific*, Australian Institute of International Affairs, Sydney

Hooley, B.A. and McElhanon (1970) 'Languages of the Morobe District – New Guinea', in Wurm, S.A. and Laycock, D.C. (eds.) *Pacific Linguistic Studies in Honour of Arthur Capell*, PacificLinguistics Series C No. 13, Canberra

Hore-Lacy, I. (ed.) (1981) *Broken Hill to Mount Isa. The Mining Odyssey of W.H. Corbould*, Melbourne

Horton, T.W. (1929) *Report on the Bulolo Dredging Area (Southern and Central Leases)*, 24 December (BGD, 21–22)

Hudson, K. (1979) *Diamonds in the Sky: A Social History of Air Travel*, London

Hudson, W.J. (1971) *Australia and Papua New Guinea*, Sydney

Hughes, I. (1977) *New Guinea Stone Age Trade. The Geography and Ecology of Traffic in the Interior*, Canberra

Huxley, J. (2007) *New Guinea Experience. Gold, War and Peace 1940–1965*, Loftus

Idriess, I. (1945) *Gold Dust and Ashes*, 18th edn., Sydney.

Jack-Hinton, C. (1964) 'Marco Polo in South-East Asia', in C.Jack-Hinton, C. (ed.) *Papers on Early South-East Asian History*, Singapore

John, A.W. (1999) *Fortune Favoured Me*, Cheltenham

Kituai, A.I.K. (1998) *My Gun, My Brother. The World of the Papua New Guinea Colonial Police 1920-1960*. Pacific Island Monograph Series 15, Honolulu

Kuluah, A. (1983) 'Wokim Gold Long Morobe, 1922–1942' Paper to Conference on Small Scale Mining in PNG, University of Technology, Lae, 5–7 June

League of Nations (1921) *Mandate for German Possessions in the Pacific Ocean Situated South of the Equator other than German Samoa and Nauru*, London

(1923–24 to 1937–38) Permanent Mandates Commission Minutes relating to the Examination of Reports for New Guinea

(1945) The *Mandates System: Origin – Principles – Application*, Geneva

Leahy, M and Crain, M. (1937) *The Land that Time Forgot*, London

Lowenstein, P.L. (1982) *Economic Geology of the Morobe Goldfield, Geological Survey of Papua New Guinea*, Memoir 9, Hong Kong

McCarthy, D. (1959) 'South-West Pacific Area – First Year: Kokoda to Wau', in *Australia in the War of 1939–1945*, Series One – Army. Vol. 5

McCarthy, J.K. (1963) *Patrol into Yesterday. My New Guinea Years*, Melbourne

McNicoll, R.R. (1969) 'Sir Walter McNicoll as Administrator of the Mandated Territory', in *The History of Melanesia*, papers of the Second Waigani Seminar, 30 May–5 June 1968. Port Moresby, Canberra

McPherson, N.M. (2001) 'Wanted: Young Man, Must Like Adventure. Ian McCallum Mack, Patrol Officer', in McPherson, N.M. (ed.) *In Colonial New Guinea: Anthropological Perspectives*, Pittsburgh

Mair, L.P. (1948) *Australia in New Guinea*, London

Mihalic, F. (1957) *Grammar and Dictionary of Neo-Melanesian Pidgin*, Illinois

Millar, T.B. (1978) *Australia in Peace and War. External Relations 1788–1977*, Canberra

Mills, Buster H. (1999) *Recollections*, in Downs 1999

Moore, J.H. (1975) *The Young Errol Flynn: Before Hollywood*, Sydney

Murray, Sir Hubert (1931) *The Scientific Method as Applied to Native Labour Problems in Papua*, Port Moresby

Murray, M. (1965) *Escape: A Thousand Miles to Freedom*, Adelaide

Nason-Jones, J. (1935) *Map of Part of the Morobe District, New Guinea Mandated Territory and of the Gulf and Central Divisions, Papua*, Sydney

Nelson, H. (1976) *Black, White and Gold. Goldmining in Papua New Guinea 1878–1930*, Canberra

(1982) *Taim Bilong Masta. The Australian Involvement with Papua New Guinea*, Sydney

New Guinea Goldfields Limited (1930–1942) Annual Reports

O'Faircheallaigh, C. (1989) 'Colonial Administration, Mineral Revenue and Economic Development: New Guinea 1926-40', in Latukefu, S. (ed.) (1989) *Papua New Guinea: A Century of Colonial Impact 1884–1984*, Port Moresby

(1992) 'Mining, Development and the Colonial State: New Guinea 1926-40'. Paper to International Mining History Congress, Bochum, FRG September 1989, in Tenfelde, K. (ed.) *Towards a Social History of Mining in the 19th and 20th Centuries*, Munich

O'Loghlen, C.M. (1999) *Recollections*, in Downs 1999 *Pacific Islands Year Book 1935–36, 1942, 1950*. Sydney Parer, M. (1993) 'A Joyous Arrival, a Sad Departure', in M.J. Bourke, 1993 Piesse, E.L. (1928) 'Financial

Relations of the Territory of New Guinea with the Commonwealth', in Eggleston, F.W. (ed.) 1928

Placer Development Ltd. (1928–1941) Annual Reports

Radford, R. (1987) *Highlanders and Foreigners in the Upper Ramu. The Kainantu Area 1919–1942*, Melbourne

Radi, H. (1971) 'New Guinea under Mandate 1921–41', in Hudson, W.J. 1971

Reed, S.W. (1943) *The Making of Modern New Guinea*, Phildelphia

Roberts, J. (1996) *Voices from a Lost World*, Sydney

Rowley, C.D. (1958) *The Australians in German New Guinea 1914–1921*, Melbourne
(1966) *The New Guinea Villager. The Impact of Colonial Rule on Primitive Society and Economy*, London

Ryan, P. (ed.) *Encyclopaedia of Papua New Guinea*, Melbourne

Sack, P. and Clark, D. (1979) *German New Guinea. The Annual Reports*, Canberra

Sack, P. and Clark, D. (1980) *German New Guinea. The Draft Annual Report for 1913–14*, Canberra

Salisbury, R.F. (1962) *From Stone to Steel*, Melbourne

Schieffelin, E.L. (1991) 'The Great Papuan Plateau', in Schieffelin, E.L. and Crittenden, R.
and R. Crittenden (eds.) *Like People You See in a Dream. First Contact in Six Papuan Societies*, Stanford

Sharp, A. (1960) *The Discovery of the Pacific Islands*, Oxford

Sinclair, J.P. (1981) *Kiap. Australia's Patrol Officers in Papua New Guinea*, Sydney
(1983) *Wings of Gold. How the Aeroplane Developed New Guinea*, Bathurst
(1984) *Uniting a Nation. The Postal and Telecommunication Services of Papua New Guinea*, Melbourne
(1986) *Balus. The Aeroplane in Papua New Guinea*, Bathurst
(1998) *Golden Gateway*, Bathurst
(2001) *Mastamak. The Land Surveyors of Papua New Guinea*, Hindmarsh

Souter, G. (1963) *New Guinea. The Last Unknown*, Sydney

Stanner, W.H. (1953) *The South Seas in Transition*, Sydney (1982 reprint)

Struben, R. (1961) *Coral and Colour of Gold*, London

Townsend, G.W.L. (1968) *District Officer*, Sydney

UK Air Ministry, Directorate of Civil Aviation (1929–1936) *Report on the Progress of Civil Aviation*
(1937–1938) *Civil Aviation. Statistical and Technical* Review

Vacuum Oil Company (c.1933) *Guinea Gold*, Sydney

Van der Veur, P.W. (1966) *Search for New Guinea's Boundaries: From Torres Strait to the Pacific*, Canberra

Whittaker, J.L. and others, (1975) *Documents and Readings in New Guinea History: Prehistory to 1889*, Milton

Willis, I. (1974) *Lae. Village and City*, Melbourne

Wolfers, E.P. (1975) *Race Relations and Colonial Rule in Papua New Guinea*, Sydney

Wu, D.Y.H. (1982) *The Chinese in Papua New Guinea: 1880–1980*, Hong Kong

Newspapers and Journals

Anon. (1922-24) Reports on gold mining possibilities in Morobe District. *IAMS* 30 November, 14 December 1922, 11 January, 18 January, 1 February, 19 April, 3 May, 28 June, 2 August, 18 October 1923, 17 April, 24 April 1924
(1926a) 'Gold in New Guinea/Field remote and dangerous' *The Argus* 17 August
(1926b) 'New Guinea Goldfield. Richness of Edie Creek' *The Argus* 23 August
(1926c) 'Mining Notes: New Guinea's Hinterland. The gold discoveries'. Detailed interview with C.J. Levien, *AR* 27 August
(1928a) 'The Bulolo Goldfield, New Guinea', *CE&MR* 20:153–156, 6 February
(1928b) Report on the New Guinea Goldfields *The Bulletin* 6 June
(1933a) 'Transporting Gold Dredges by Aeroplane. The Bulolo Enterprise in New Guinea' *CE&MR* 25:185–187, 6 March
(1933b) 'New Guinea Airways Progress: System unequalled throughout the World' *Aircraft* 12:3, 16–17, 53. December
(1941–1942, 1946) Morobe Spitfire, *Pacific Islands Monthly* January, March, April, June 1941, January 1942, April 1946

Auerbach, E. (1939) Letter to Editor *Pacific Islands Monthly* 15 September
(1940) Letter to Editor *Pacific Islands Monthly* 15 July

Banks, C.A. (1932) 'Air-Transportation of Gold Dredges in New Guinea' *Transactions, IMM* 41: 616–638
(1937) 'Air transportation and operation of gold dredges in New Guinea' *Transactions, IMM* 46:803–811

Bengo, P. (1973) 'My Father on the Goldfields and at the Outbreak of the Second World War' *Oral History* No. 3, History Department, UPNG, May

Birrell, E. (1973) 'Early New Guinea through a woman's eyes' *JMDHS* 1:2, August

Bishton, E. (2004-2005) The Diaries of Edward (Ted) Bishton *Una Voce* December, March

Blackwood, B. (1939) 'Life on the Upper Watut, New Guinea' *GJ* 94:1, 11–28, July

Bourke, J.M. (1964) 'Keep in a cool place and stow away from boilers' *Pacific Islands Monthly* June 1964

Braithwaite, J.B. (1938) 'Gold Mining in New Guinea' *CE&MR* 15 February

Burton, J. (2003) 'Fratricide and inequality: things fall apart in eastern New Guinea' *Archaeology in Oceania* 38:203–216, October

Chapman to Mount Hagen' *GJ* 84:5, 398–412, November

Chauncy, A.A. (1927) 'Two Years in New Guinea'. Paper read to the Institution of Surveyors, New South Wales, 21 December 1926 *The Surveyor* February, 36:4, 160–171

Chinnery, E.W.P. (1934) 'The central ranges of the Mandated Territory of New Guinea from Mount

Coldham, J.C. (1928) 'A Reconnaissance map of the Bulolo Goldfields, Territory of New Guinea' *Proceedings, AIMM* 71, September

Collins, A.K. (1867) Lecture on the Riches of New Guinea, Masonic Hall, Sydney, April 13th, Sydney (Newspaper cutting in ML)

Curtain, R. (1978) 'Labour Migration from the Sepik' *Oral History* 6:9 Institute of Papua New Guinea Studies

Dickinson, A. (1933) 'New Guinea' *The Mining Magazine* 48:5, 265–277, May

Feldt, E. (1951) 'Kukukuku Patrol' *Pacific Islands Monthly* April
(1960) 'When Bill Cameron was Salamaua' *Pacific Islands Monthly* August
(1961) 'Errol Flynn at Salamaua' *Quadrant* 3, 1961

Fink, R.A. and Grosart, I. (1963) 'Race Relations in Papua and New Guinea' *Australian School of Pacific Administration Staff Seminar No. 3.*

Fisher, N.H. (1938) 'Alluvial mining in New Guinea' *Walkabout* 1 May
(1940) 'Gold occurrences in New Guinea' *CE&MR* 11 March

Flierl, J. (1931) News from Lutheran Mission, New Guinea *Lutheran Herald* 29 June

Goldbrick, A. (anon.) (1926a) 'Some Salamaua sketches' *RT* 17 September
(1926b) 'A Pioneer of Salamaua: Burleigh Gorman' *RT* 22 October
(1926c) 'Morobe Goldfields: How to get there' *RT* 29 October

Groves, W.C. (1935) 'The Lure of New Guinea Gold' *Life* 15 May. 405–409, 472–474

Halvaksz, J. (2006) 'Cannibalistic Imaginaries: Mining the Natural and Social Body in Papua New Guinea' *The Contemporary Pacific* 18:2, 335–359

Hawkins, R. (1977) 'Three zeros—and Bertie hangs up his goggles' *Paradise* (Air Niugini) No. 3, January

Healy, A.M. (1965) 'Ophir to Bulolo: The history of the gold search in New Guinea' *HSANZ* 12:45, 103–118 (October)

Hilder, B. (1967) 'Return to Paradise.' Profile of 'Tiger Lil' *Pacific Islands Monthly* June

Hoile, I. (1946) 'The Land of Eternal Spring' *The Bell-Bird* (Gosford High School Magazine)

Holzknecht, P. (1973) 'Presenting Bertie Heath—Aviator' *JMDHS* 1:2, August

Hudson, W.J. (1965) 'Australia's Experience as a Mandatory Power' *AO* 19:1 April, 35–46
(1968) 'New Guinea Mandate: The View from Geneva' *AO* 22:3 December, 302–316

Hughes, S. (1935) 'Vale Burleigh Gorman. Death of well-known pioneer of Salamaua, N.G.' *Pacific Islands Monthly* 21 March

IMEB (1940) 'That was Seven Years Ago' *Pacific Islands Monthly* 15 June

Innes, A.A. (n.d.) 'Gateway to Adventure—and Romance'. Typescript for broadcast, ML MS1408 Item 1/1
(1929) 'Dream Women and Real Women of Salamaua' *The Sun* 27 January
(1937) 'The Thirteen Sleepers of Salamaua' *Smith's Weekly* 18 September
(1944) 'Wild Way to Wau' *Pacific Islands Monthly* October

John, A. (1937) 'From village to compound' *CE&MR* 8 July

Johnson, H. (1935) Letter to a friend about settling in at Edie Creek, May. *Una Voce* December 1997, 30
(1942) Letter concerning the December 1941 evacuation from Edie Creek, January. *Una Voce* December 1999, 20

Joubert, A.L. (1916) 'Gold in New Guinea' *The Rabaul Record* 1 May

Kelly, C. (1959-1961) 'Geographical Knowledge and Speculation in Regard to Spanish Pacific Voyages' *HSANZ* Volume 9, 12–18

Lawrie, C. (1937) 'A Colony in the Air' *Walkabout* 1 August

Levien, C.J.(1926h) Report of interview *SM* 28 August
(1926i) Report to GGNL Board, 16 November *AR* 10 December
(1927a) Report to GGNL Board, 8 December *AR* 15 January

Lloyd, R.G. (1973) 'The Angan Language Family', The linguistic situation in the Gulf District and adjacent areas, Papua New Guinea. K. Franklin, (Ed.) *Pacific Linguistic Series C. No. 26*, Canberra

M.G. (1935) 'The Old Track In' *Pacific Islands Monthly* 20 November
(1936) 'Salamaua. Memories of the 'Rush' Days of New Guinea' *Pacific Islands Monthly* 24 January

Millar, T. (1945) 'War-torn Lae and Abandoned Salamaua' *Pacific Islands Monthly* April

Mingisin (1978) Interview, in Curtain 1978

M.K.V. (1938) 'New Capital of New Guinea. Salamaua' (Unidentified newspaper), 25 July. NAA Series A518/1, AK800/1/3 Part 1

Moretti, D. (2006) 'The gender of the gold: an ethnographic and historical account of women's involvement in artisanal and small-scale mining at Mount Kaindi, Papua New Guinea' *Oceania* 76 (2): 133–149

Morley, I.W. (1931) 'The Daydawn Mine, New Guinea' *CE&MR* 23:7–8, 5 October

Mustar, E.A. (1927) 'The World's Worst Aerodrome' *Aircraft* 30 June
(1931) 'Commercial Aviation in New Guinea' *Flying* September

Newbury, C. (1975) 'Colour Bar and Labour Conflict on the New Guinea Goldfields 1935–41' *AJPH* 21:3, 25–38, December

Palili (1978) Interview in Curtain 1978

Perkins, J. (1989) ' "Sharing the White Man's Burden". Nazi Colonial Revisionism and Australia's New Guinea Mandate' *JPH* 24:1, April

Placer Development (1930) 'Bulolo Gold Dredging. Important Announcement by Placer' *Oil and Gold*, January

Richards, T. (1933a) 'New Guinea: Land of gold, stone age customs and daring flying men' *SM* 17 May
(1933b) 'New Guinea: The Romance of Gold-Hunting No.II' *SM* 24 May
(1933c) 'New Guinea Goldfields No.III' *SM* 31 May
(1933d) 'New Guinea Goldfields No.IV' *SM* 7 June

Robson, R.W. (1934) 'Adventuring with death and Deckert' *Pacific Islands Monthly* 17 October
(1938) 'The Romance of Bulolo, and some of the men who have transformed New Guinea' *Pacific Islands Monthly* 15 December
(1958) 'How they climbed into Edie Creek' *Pacific Islands Monthly* March

Shackleton, W.S. (1937) 'Aviation in New Guinea' *The Aeroplane* 26 May, 52:1357, 642–646

Sherwin, V.H. (1941) 'Striking Funeral Oration' *Morobe News* 28 June

Shlomowitz, R. (1988) 'Mortality and Indentured Labour in Papua (1885–1941) and New Guinea (1920–1941)' *JPH* 23:1, April

Sinclair, J.P. (1961) 'Patrolling in the Territory of Papua and New Guinea' *Australian Territories* 1:4, June

Special Correspondent (1936) 'Progress on the New Guinea Goldfields' *Pacific Islands Monthly* 19 March

Stone, R. (2006) 'Hitler Down Under' *NLA News* October, 10–13

Taylour, H. and Morley, I.W. (1933) 'The Development of Gold Mining in Morobe, New Guinea' *Proceedings, AIMM* 89, March

Townsend, G.W.L. (1933) 'The Administration of the Mandated Territory of New Guinea' *The Geographical Journal* 82:5, November

Tudor, J. (1946) 'Wau Road', *Pacific Islands Monthly* December

Underwood, A.C. (1968) 'Memories of the goldfields' *Pacific Islands Monthly* August

Urquhart, L. (1929) Speech to subscribers of the Mining Trust *Financial Times* 13 November NAA Series A518, AA834/2 Part 1

Vial, L.G. (1938) 'Some Statistical Aspects of the Population in the Morobe District, New Guinea' *Oceania* 8:4 June

Waterhouse, D.E. (1933) 'Women travel by Air to Social Engagements on New Guinea Goldfields' *Adelaide News* 16 February

Waterhouse, L.V. (1932) 'Air Transportation in New Guinea' *The Australasian Engineer* Vol 32, 7 December

Webster, Blaikie J.P. (1936c) Address to 6th Annual General Meeting of New Guinea Goldfields, 28 February 1936. *Pacific Islands Monthly* 19 March 1936
(1937) Address to 7th Annual General Meeting of New Guinea Goldfields, 11 February 1937. *Pacific Islands Monthly* 24 February 1937

Weetman, C. (1938) 'Everybody Flies' *Walkabout* 1 December

West, F.J. (1958) 'Indigenous Labour in Papua-New Guinea' *International Labour Review* 77:2, 89–112 February

Weston, B. (1975a) 'Recruiting in the Markham Valley' *JMDHS* 2:3, March
(1975b) 'Pre-War Shipping, Huon Gulf, New Guinea—Part One' *JMDHS* 3:1, July
(1975c) 'Pre-War Shipping, Huon Gulf, New Guinea—Part Two' *JMDHS* 3:2, December
(1978) 'Stirring Days in the New Guinea goldfields—or gold dust in the sky' *Pacific Islands Monthly* August
(1987) 'Roaring days at Edie Creek' *Pacific Islands Monthly* October
(1988) 'New Guinea goes to air' *Pacifi0c Islands Monthly* July
(1993) 'When Salamaua boomed' *Pacific Islands Monthly* March. Reprinted in S. Inder (ed.) Tales of Papua New Guinea, Sydney 2001
(1996) 'Mi laik Mek Pepa (I would like to make a Contract)' *Una Voce* June. Reprinted in S. Inder (ed.) Tales of Papua New Guinea, Sydney 2001

Willis, I (1973) 'Village and Town: The changes produced in villages around Lae by expatriate settlement' Address to *MDHS* 1 August.
(1976) 'A New Guinea Outrage: The Killings at Kaisinik, 1926-7' Address to *MDHS* May

Winchester, C. (ed.) (1936) 'New Guinea Gold. How mining has been rapidly developed in inaccessible country by air transport' in *Wonders of World Aviation* 1:10, London

Wisdom, E.A. (1928b) Comments on goldfields road *The Argus* 21 November

Wright, M. (1968) 'When Eric Feldt was boss of New Guinea's wild and rugged Morobe' *Pacific Islands Monthly* May

Unpublished papers, articles, statements, letters, diaries and ephemera

Allen, B.J. (1976) Information Flow and Innovation Diffusion in the East Sepik District, PNG. Ph.D Thesis, ANU

Angelo, M. (1962) Letter to Grabowsky, 29 April NAA Series B1968/0 Book B, Item 27

Anstey, F. (1927) Letter to Prime Minister Bruce, 8 June. NAA Series A1781, A236

Bank of New South Wales (1929-41) Half yearly reports, Salamaua Branch, WBCA
(1934-41) Half yearly reports, Wau Branch, WBCA

Banks, C.A. (1929) Letter to Administrator, 9 October. Grabowsky (c.1968; October 1929, pages 2-3)

Barton, B.V. (1923) Preliminary Report. Kaili Gold Options N.L., Bulolo River, New Guinea 9 December. DM
(1924) Final Report on Kaili Gold Options N.L., Bulolo River, New Guinea, 31 March. DM

Bethune, A. (1953) Letter to Clune, 20 March, NLA Clune Papers, MS 4951 Box 179/499

Black, J.R. (1933) Diary, NLA Black Papers, MS 8346, Box 3, Series 2/20
(1936) Diary, NLA Black papers, MS 8346, Box 5, Series 2/31

Bond, H. (1927) Evidence to ECRC 26 April. NAA Series CP660/25, Bundle 1/vol 1

Booth, D. (1927) Evidence to ECRC 28 April. NAA Series CP660/25, Bundle 1/vol 1

Bourke, J.M. (1963) Letter to Grabowsky, 11 February. Series B1968/0. Book C, Item 28

Bowring, A. (1943) Letter to Alice Innes, 14 July ML MS1408 Item 1

Bulolo Gold Dredging (1940) Data supplied to Frank Clune concerning BGD's activities. NLA Clune Papers, MS 4951 Box 176/481

Bulolo Goldfields Progress Association (1929) Letter to Mining Warden, Edie Creek, 7 January. DM

Burton, J. (1995a) 'Hidden Valley: Some historical matters to start with' Hidden Valley Project, Working Paper No. 1, April
(1995b) 'Condemned forever to fight Social mapping at Hidden Valley, Morobe Province, PNG' Hidden Valley Project, Working Paper No. 2, July
(1996) 'Settlement Formation and leadership in the Upper Watut', Hidden Valley Project,Working Paper No. 4, April
(1998) 'Land ownership in the Upper Watut valley: Issues and outcomes' Hidden Valley/Hamata Project, Working paper No. 11, February
(2000a) 'Settlement history of the southwestern Biangai and catalogue of national museum site codes' Hidden Valley Working Paper No. 12, August
(2000b) 'First Contacts between outsiders and the Watut and Biangai people of the Wau and Bulolo area' Draft Hidden Valley Working Paper No. 13, October

Cardew, H.C. (1927) Evidence to ECRC 26 May. NAA Series CP660/25, Bundle 1/vol 4

Cilento, R.W. (1927) Evidence to ECRC 7 and 19 May. NAA Series CP660/25, Bundle 1/vol 3

Clark, G. (1931-1937), Letters. With O'Neill, J. — A Prospector's Diary NLA MS 3901

Clune, F. (1940) Letter to Wells, 27 May NLA Clune Papers, MS 4951 Box 177/490
(1949) Letter to Jack Nettleton, 12 July NLA Clune Papers, MS 4951 Box 175/470
(n.d.) Clune Papers NLA MS 4951

Collopy, J.A. (1930) Report to Controller of Civil Aviation following tour of inspection of aircraft, aerodromes, ground engineers and general aviation activities in the Territory of New Guinea, 7 July. Grabowsky (c. 1968, July 1930, pages 79-83)

Curtain, R. (1980) Dual Dependence and Sepik Labour Migration, Ph.D Thesis, ANU

Denny, O. (1962) Letters to Grabowsky, 7 December. NAA Series B1970, 20.

Dickinson, A. (1928) Letter to the Administrator, 5 December. Grabowsky, (c. 1968, December 1928, pages 246-249)

Eekhoff, H.G. (1964) Personal reminiscences, unpublished ms

Emery, R. (1990) NGVR and ANGAU. Oral history transcript, Australian War Memorial, 13 March

Feldt, E.A. (1964) Letter to Grabowsky, 16 April, NAA Series B1968, Book D

Fetchko, P.J. (1972) Anga material culture. MA Thesis, George Washington University

Flierl, J. Rev. (1927) 'The Tragedy of the Piololo (Bulolo) People' Submission to the Administration regarding Warden McLean's punitive expedition, 10 May. NAA Series A1/15, 1927/728

Godden, F. (1942) Diary. NLA Clune Papers, MS 4951, Box 175/477

Grabowsky, A.K. (n.d.) personal experiences on the Wau-Edie Creek Road, in Grabowsky, I. (1968) April 1933

Grabowsky, I. (c.1968) History of Civil Aviation in New Guinea to July 1935. Unpublished ms prepared for Department of Civil Aviation NLA MS 7560. Also NAA Series B1967
(n.d.) Inward correspondence. NAA Series B1968.
(n.d.) Outward correspondence. NAA Series B1969.
(n.d.) Reference notes. NAA Series B1970.
(n.d.) Reference material. NAA Series B1970.

Guinea Airways Limited Minute Book, SLSA BRG 8/1/vol 1

Guinea Gold N.L. Minute Book, SLSA BRG 65/1/1/1

Hammond, H.T. (c.1962) Letter to Grabowsky. NAA Series B1970, Item 20.

Harris, H.L. (n.d.) Bankers in the Bush. Australian Manuscripts Collection, SLV unpublished ms

Hebbard, J. (1926a) Letter to A.E.H. Evans, Secretary GGNL, 29 May. GGNL Minute Book, SLSA
(1926b) Letter to A.E.H. Evans, Secretary GGNL, 2 June, GGNL Minute Book, SLSA
(1926c) Letter to A.E.H. Evans, Secretary GGNL, 21 June. GGNL Minute Book, SLSA
(1926d) Letter to C.V.T. Wells, Chairman GGNL, 30 June. GGNL Minute Book, SLSA

Hendry C. (1927) Evidence to ECRC 7 May. NAA Series CP660/25, Bundle 1/vol 2

Hides, J. (1931) Patrol to Tauri and Tiveri River headwaters, including notes on the people of the Kiapou, 15 February to16 April. NAA Series A7043, 3

Honeysett, K. (1932) Letters. (Copies provided to author by Josie Wallenius)

Innes, A. (1956) Papers. ML, MS 1408
(1977) Oral history, NLA Oral DeB 965-967

Jensen, E.B. (1928a) Letter to A.E.H. Evans, Secretary GGNL, 11 May. SLSA BRG 65/5
(1928b) Letter to A.E.H. Evans, Secretary GGNL, 30 July. SLSA BRG 65/5
(1928c) Notes for Oluf Moen, 23 November. SLSA BRG 65/5

John, A. (1983) Bulolo Revisited (unpublished article)

Johns, J.H.W. (1929-32) Correspondence. MUA

Leahy, M.J. (1931) Extracts from Diary, Langimar Trip. NLA Chinnery Papers MS 766 Box 14 Series 7/6

Leggatt, E.W. (1935) Diary (of a miner), 5 January to 30 September. ML MS 1672

Levien, C.J. (1923) Miner's Right, ML DL/93/591
(1924) Letter to Mining Warden, 4 July. ECRC Exhibit 88. NAA Series CP660/26, Bundle 1/E834/2
(1925a) Letter to Wells, 6 April. Exhibit A1, Transcript of Hearing in the High Court of Australia, A.E.H. Evans v. Deputy Commissioner of Taxation for South Australia, May 1934. NLA Clune Papers, MS 4951 Box 177/490
(1925b) Letter to Wells, 5 July. Exhibit A3, Transcript of Hearing in the High Court of Australia, A.E.H. Evans v. Deputy Commissioner of Taxation for South Australia, May 1934. NLA Clune Papers, MS 4951 Box 177/490
(1926a) Letter to Mining Warden, 19 February. ECRC Exhibit 82. NAA Series CP660/26, Bundle 1/E834/2
(1926b) Radiogram to Wells, 22 February. NLA Wells Papers MS 364/4/5
(1926c) Letter to Wells, 24 February. NLA Clune Papers, MS 4951 Box 152/336
(1926d) Letter to Manager, Australian Airways, 24 February. NLA Clune Papers, MS 4951 Box 152/336
(1926e) Letter to Mining Warden, 27 February. ECRC Exhibit 83. NAA

Series CP660/2, Bundle 1/E834/2

(1926f) Letter to Wells, 7 April. Extracts from private letters. Transcript of Hearing in the High Court of Australia, A.E.H. Evans v. Deputy Commissioner of Taxation for South Australia, May 1934. NLA Clune Papers, MS 4951 Box 177/490

(1926g) Letter to Wells, 18 May. Extracts from private letters. Transcript of Hearing in the High Court of Australia, A.E.H. Evans v. Deputy Commissioner of Taxation for South Australia, May 1934. NLA Clune Papers, MS 4951 Box 177/490

(1926j) Radiogram, 16 December. GGNL Minute Book, SLSA

(1927b) Evidence to ECRC, 26 April. NAA Series CP660/25, Bundle 1/vol 1

(1929a) Letter to Secretary GGNL. 9 June, NLA Wells Papers MS 364/4/1(2)

(1929b) Letter to Wells, 12 December. NLA Wells Papers MS 364/4/1(23)

Lukin, J.H. (1923) Letters to his mother, 16 January and 17 February. NLA Clune Papers, MS 4951 Box 153/340

McCarthy, J.K. (1933b) Letter to Laurie McCarthy, 8 May 1933. NLA McCarthy Papers MS 5581 Box 3/15

(1933c) Letter to mother from Menyamya base camp, 4 September. NLA McCarthy papers MS 5581 Box 14/41

(1933e) Letter to Laurie McCarthy, 26 September 1933. NLA McCarthy Papers MS 5581 Box 14/41

(1933f) Letter to mother from Otibanda Police Post, 6 November. NLA McCarthy Papers MS 5581 Box 3/15

Mackellar, M.L. (1972) Violence among the Kukukuku, UPNG, unpub. thesis

McKenzie, H.J. (n.d.) Personal Recollections (copy provided to author by Jim Sinclair)

McNicoll, Sir W. (1942) Letter to Ron McNicoll, 26 February. NLA McNicoll Papers MS 2101, Box 3/25.

Madigan, P.E. (1926) Letter to the Administrator, 5 August. NAA Series CP660/26, Bundle1/E834/2, Exhibit 62

Mason, J.P.D. (1922-1923) Papers, ML MS 74

Meehan, J.W. (1996) C.J.Levien, The pre-Morobe Goldfields days. unpublished ms

Miner's Association (1928) Failure to construct road from coast. Cable to Minister for H&T, 5 March. NAA Series A518, G834/2

Murcutt, D. (n.d.) Reminiscences, unpublished ms (copy provided to author by Jan Roberts)

Mustar, E. (1934) Letter to Controller of Civil Aviation, 29 January. NAA Series MP113/1, VH-URQ

Neill, R. (1930) Chairman, Prospecting Committee, Morobe District Miners' Association. Letter to Prime Minister on financial support for prospecting, 12 May. NAA Series A518, S834/2

Nettleton, J. (1949) Letters to Clune, 27 April and 12 July. NLA Clune Papers MS 4951 Box 175/470

Niall, H. (n.d.) The war comes to Morobe. NLA MS 5264 unpublished ms.

O'Neill, J. (n.d.) A Prospector 's Diary. New Guinea 1931-1937 NLA MS 3901 (also PMB 625) (Published as Up from South, ed. J. Sinclair)

Palmer, G. (1927) Evidence to ECRC 28 April. NAA Series CP660/25, Bundle 1/vol 1

Park, W. (1927) The Kaisinik killings. Letter to Minister for H&T, 3 February. NAA Series A1/15, 27/2571

Peadon, J.L. (1933) Annual Report of John L. Peadon, Upper Ramu, in Mining Warden's Annual Report 30 June 1933.

Pryke, F. (1927) Evidence to ECRC 27 April. NAA Series CP660/25, Bundle 1/vol 1

Royal, W.G. (1927) Evidence to ECRC 30 May. NAA Series CP660/25, Bundle 1/vol 4

Sheldon, E.J. (1930) Notes from discussion with Alice Innes, Innes Papers ML MS 1408, item 2

(1944) Letter to Alice Innes, 3 September, Innes Papers ML MS 1408, item 2

Shoppee, L. (1964) Letter to Grabowsky, 8 December. NAA Series B1969, 29

Simpson, J.D. (1946) Evidence in High Court case No. 17 of 1945, New South Wales Registry, between Bulolo Gold Dredging Ltd and the Commonwealth of Australia, 30 April.

Sinclair, B. (1963) Letter to Grabowsky, 23 July. NAA Series B1968/0 Book C, 29

Slattery, V. (n.d.) Notes of discussion with Clune, NLA Clune Papers MS 4951, Box 152/336

Sloane, J. (1943) Correspondence with Clune, NLA Clune Papers MS 4951, Box 176/484

Smart, F. (1943) Notes of discussion with Clune, NLA Clune Papers MS 4951, Box 179/499

Thomas, E.J. (1926) President, Morobe District Miners' Association. Motions passed by miners. Letter to Warden, 20 September. ECRC Exhibits 18 and 114. NAA Series CP660/26, Bundle 1/E834/2

Twycross, J.K. (1943) Letter to Clune, 28 July. NLA Clune Papers MS 4951 Box 175/470

Waterhouse, L.V. (1934) 'Air Transportation and Gold Dredging in New Guinea', unpublished lecture

(1942a) Destruction of BGD's power plants. Extract from letter, 21 April. NAA Series A518/1, L16/2/3 Part 1

(1942b) Scorched earth activities. Letter to Senator James Fraser, Minister for External Territories and Minister assisting the Minister for the Army, 4 June. NAA Series MP 508/1, 82/713/229

Webster, B.J.P. (1935a) Transcript of meeting between Blaikie Webster and the Administrator, Salamaua, 15 November. NAA Series A518, AV834/2 Part 1

(1935b) Complaints about Administration's treatment of NGG. Letter to the Administrator, 4 December. NAA Series A518, AV834/2 Part 1

(1936a) New Guinea Air Services. Letter to Sir George Pearce, Minister in Charge of Territories, 20 January. NAA Series MP 131/1, 192/101/381

(1936b) Taxation in New Guinea. Letter to Sir George Pearce, Minister in Charge of Territories, 14 February. NAA Series A518, AN822/1/3

Wells, C.V.T. (1928) Letter to Cecil Levien (when all seemed lost), 13 February

(1932) Diary, 1932, 1935. NLA Wells Papers MS 364/7/3

(1928) Papers, NLA MS 364

Willis, I. (1972) 'The expatriate community and the growth of a town at Lae 1921-42' unpublished ms

Yeomans, T. (1933) Diary, Dixson Library z/B1109 (Reel CY2127)

Interviews — Notes on discussions

Baiko, Naris (2003) (Logui village) Salamaua, July

Bayliss, C. (2001) Toowoomba, June

Bowman, F. (2001) Melbourne, September

Goad, J. (2001) Brisbane, June

Hendry, B. (2004) Sydney, June

Hurrell, A.L. (2001) Tweed Heads, June

Isaiah, R. (2003) (Upper Watut/Kapau) Jamaini village, July

John, A. (2001) Melbourne, September

Lasek, B. (2001) (Buang) Bulolo, March

Leahy, J. (2001) Zenag, March

Lega, T. (2001) Brisbane, June

Meawat, D. (2003) (Upper Watut/Kapau/Nauti) Wau, July

John, A. (2001) Melbourne, September

Nadawiko, M. (Upper Watut/Kapau) Edie Creek, June

Naguol, K. (2001) (Sepik), Wau, March

Omas (2001) (Sepik) Wau, June

Panga, M. (2001) (Biangai) Kaisinik village, March

Saro, J. (2001) (Upper Watut/Kapau) Edie Creek, June

Saweo, G. (2003) (Upper Watut/Kapau/Nauti) Bulolo-Watut Divide, July

Sinclair, J.P. (2001) Alexandra Headland, June

Vagg, A. (2001) Melbourne, September

Yandoapo, B. (2003) (Upper Watut/Kapau/Titama), near Jamaini village, July

Index

flies second W34 from Melbourne 110–111; advocate for Junker G31 68, 110, 116

N

Nakanai expedition 133, 247
Namie Creek 28, 29, 30, 32, 34, 40, 78, 127, 229
Nason-Jones, J. (geologist) 248
Native Administration Regulations 200, 201, 253
Native Labour Ordinance and Regulations 55, 156, 221, 244, 250, 251, 255
Naylor, Bill (prospector) 138, 140, 149–150, 151, 182
Neal, Norman (miner) 58, 173, 215
Nelson, Hank (author) 162, 202, 253, 257
Nembi people 149, 249
Nepa (settlement) 16, 28
Nettleton, Jack (miner) 23–26, 28, 29
Newcrest Mining Limited 233
New Guinea, origin of name 12; partition between European powers 12; Rabaul, capital 12, 189, 217; transfer of capital to mainland 205
New Guinea Act 1920 18, 217, 218
New Guinea Goldfields Ltd (NGG) 72, 77, 91, 98, 102, 103, 104, 114, 122, 123, 157, 161, 172, 177, 179, 185, 191, 193–194, 196, 204, 207, 223, 224, 251; options over leases and claims 72, 73, 74, 75, 99, 128; preparation for mining 73–74, 178, 180; manning exemptions 75, 77; testing of leases 75, 77–78, 98, 99, 100, 111; poor decision-making 72, 99–100, 101, 104; relations with Administration 77, 101–102; relations with Guinea Airways 72, 101, 112, 120, 121; labourers' living and working conditions 161–164, 200, 250; alluvial mining 75, 77, 78, 98, 99, 103, 104, 229, 246; profitability, erosion of capital and share price 78, 99, 100–101, 103, 104, 246; comparison with BGD's performance 98, 100, 102, 104, 246; post-war activity 227, 228–229
New Guinea Mining Association 197, 206, 254
New Guinea Volunteer Rifles (NGVR) 206, 207, 208, 211, 212, 213, 214, 254
Niall, Horrie 208–209
Niuminco Limited 234
'Not a poor man's field' 41–42, 43, 55, 59, 233
Nurton, A. (patrol officer) 140

O

Oakley, Edward (acting Mining Warden) 41, 44, 45, 53, 55, 130, 243
O'Dea, Tom (pilot) 198
Oldörp, Rudolph (prospector) 14–15
O'Kane, Harry (miner) 76, 185
O'Loghlen, Coleman (resident) 212
Omas 164
O'Neill, Jack (miner) 48–49, 57, 81–82, 140, 152, 154, 157, 162, 172, 182, 183, 184, 201, 238, 248, 254
Otibanda – see also Surprise Creek 133, 137, 138, 139, 141, 143, 144, 150, 152, 188
Owanga village 139, 149, 150

P

Pacific Aerial Transport (PAT) 121
Palili (labourer) 211
Panga, Monica (villager) 132, 151

Papua 6, 12, 13, 18, 19, 101, 106, 133, 135, 141, 144, 148, 153, 155, 159, 205, 211, 212, 217, 226, 249, 250, 254, 255; Australian prospectors 13, 14, 15, 16, 17, 19, 20, 28, 30, 32, 36, 48, 91, 206, 242; border crossings into German New Guinea 13, 15, 16, 17, 20; Kukukuku 127, 133, 135, 242
Parer, Bernie (miner) 184
Parer, Kevin (pilot) 121, 209–210, 211
Parer, Mollie (miner's wife) 252–253
Parer, Ray (pilot) 8, 61, 106, 109, 116, 121, 122, 124, 246; financial difficulties 108, 112; near misses 114; relations with miners 111, 112
Park, Shark-Eye (William, miner) 8, 16, 20, 28, 33, 47, 190, 206, 233; background and character 19–20, 170; Koranga Creek pre-1923 17, 20, 23, 24, 242; teams up with Nettleton 23–25, 28, 29; relationship with Levien 25, 26, 28, 29, 30, 39; Koranga Creek operations 24, 27, 28, 33, 243; defends Biangai 132–133
Patrols, objectives 25, 128–129, 136, 138, 139, 140, 141, 144, 220, 221, 222; use of force 133, 136–138, 141, 144, 145, 247, 248–249; A. Roberts (1930) 133; E. Feldt and W.E. Sansom (1931) 136, 138; N. Penglase and M. Pitt (1931) 136–137, 248; N. Penglase and W.E. Sansom (1932) 137, 138; G.W. Townsend and N. Penglase (1933) 138; K. McCarthy (1933) 139; W.E. Sansom and W.H. Bird (1933) 141; K. McCarthy and J. Black (1933) 141–143, 182; J. Black (1936) 224
Peadon, John (miner) 140
Pearce, Sir George (Minister in charge of Territories) 247, 254
Penglase, Nick (assistant district officer) 136–137, 138, 248
Permanent Mandates Commission (PMC) 101, 140, 216, 218–219, 223–224, Australian Government's policy objectives 218; financial support for Territory 218–219; state of Territory's finances 255; financial transfers to Australian Government 219, 255; economic exploitation of Territory 153, 220; native administration and welfare 219, 220, 221, 224, 255; indentured labour system 220; expenditure on education 222; expenditure on roads 223; representation on Legislative Council 224; night work by labourers 161
Pilhofer, Rev. Georg 21, 168
Pitt, Mark (patrol officer) 136–137, 138
Placer Development Limited 64, 65–66, 68–70, 78–80, 91, 92, 98, 155, 228, 244, 257; option over Guinea Gold leases 64, 65; southern leases 65–66, 79, 88, 89, 91; northern leases 65, 66, 88; road transport concerns 65, 67–69; air transport decision 69–70
PNG Forest Products (PNGFP) 230, 231
Police, New Guinean 43, 128, 130, 131–132, 136, 137, 138, 139, 141, 142, 143, 150, 165, 167, 247, 249
Polo, Marco 12, 242
Poole and Steel Ltd, ship builders 81
Population 32, 34, 41, 42, 43, 56, 58, 74, 94, 154, 173–174, 179, 180, 183, 189–190, 197, 199, 200, 207, 229, 230, 233, 234
Port Moresby 12, 13, 16, 28, 72, 114, 121,

122, 195, 208, 211, 213, 229, 233, 245, 254
Poverty Creek 103
Power, hydro-electric 32, 40, 60, 79, 88, 91, 92, 93, 100, 116, 228, 229, 254; power station at the gorge 80, 81, 83, 85, 89, 91, 118, 194, 213; Lower Baiune 89, 91, 93, 227, 231; Upper Baiune 91–92, 93, 95, 119, 190, 213, 227, 231, 241; Preston, Jim (prospector) 17, 20
Priebe, Ossie (crane operator) 118
Purari (area) 140, 144, 145, 182, 248
Pursehouse, Lloyd (patrol officer) 209
Pryke, Frank (miner) 13–14, 48, 54
Pryke, Jim (prospector) 13

Q

Qantas 27, 256

R

Rabaul 123, 193, 216, 217, 222; attack by Australians (1914) 18; attack by Japanese (1942); strike (1929); volcanic eruptions 205
Radford, Robin (author) 136
Radi, Heather (author) 168
Radio – see communication
Ramu; goldfield 140, 144, 145, 150, 182, 186; Valley 139, 186; River 13, 68; Upper 140, 144, 150, 182
Rappard, William (PMC member) 218, 219, 255
Recruiters 21, 32, 33, 47, 53, 94, 144, 154, 157, 160, 174, 178, 244, 249, 250, 256
Reed, S.W. (sociologist) 161, 162, 165, 166, 201, 202, 222, 250–251
Renison Goldfields Consolidated Ltd (RGC) 229, 230
Retez, Inigo Ortiz de (ship's captain) 12
Returned Sailors and Soldiers' Imperial League of Australia (RSSILA) 195
Richards, Tom (journalist) 245
Roads and tracks, BGD powerhouse to Bulolo, Bulwa and Baiune 88, 95, 193; Wau to Edie Creek 74, 76–77, 101, 190, 193–194, 234, 256; Salamaua to the goldfields (1920s) 29, 32, 46, 62, 63, 65, 66–69, 71, 72; Salamaua to the goldfields (1930s) 101, 103–104, 122, 123, 205, 206, 252, 254; Wau to Bulolo 85, 91, 121, 193, 194, 233, 256; Labu to Bulolo (post-war) 226, 228
Roberts, Alan (patrol officer) 133
Roberts, Jan (author) 199, 253
Robertson, G.M. (miner) 254
Ross, Les (pilot) 209
Rowley, Charles (author) 149, 216, 217, 255
Royal, Albert 34
Royal, Bill (miner) 32, 34, 36, 38–39, 42, 44, 49, 56, 190, 233

S

Salamaua 9, 21, 23, 24, 28, 34, 43, 44, 47, 48, 49, 51, 56, 59, 70, 76, 80, 108, 111, 122, 132, 134, 136, 139, 140, 150, 153, 165, 166, 167, 171–172, 185, 195, 196, 197, 199, 205, 207, 226; description 21–23, 174–178, 189, 191, 234–235; importance for miners 32, 33, 41, 42, 46, 47, 53–54, 56, 58, 130, 131, 175, 185, 253; administrative centre 42, 178, 191, 223; shops and services 41, 121, 161, 172, 174, 178, 179, 192, 204, 250; aerodrome 22, 71, 72, 74, 99, 114, 115, 122, 123, 179, 223, 256; boat day 159, 162, 174,